The Sage Dictionary of Criminology

REFERENCE

The Sage Dictionary of Sociology

Steve Bruce and Steven Yearley

SAGE Publications
London ● Thousand Oaks ● New Delhi

SAGE Publications Ltd
1 Oliver's Yard
55 City Road
London EC1Y 1SP

SAGE Publications Inc.
2455 Teller Road
Thousand Oaks, California 91320

SAGE Publications India Pvt Ltd
B-42, Panchsheel Enclave
Post Box 4109
New Delhi 110 017

British Library Cataloguing in Publication data

A catalogue record for this book is available
from the British Library

ISBN 0 7619 7481 4
    0 7619 7482 2

Library of Congress Control Number Available

Typeset by C&M Digitals (P) Ltd, Chennai, India
Printed on paper from sustainable resources
Printed in Great Britain by the Cromwell Press Ltd, Trowbridge, Wiltshire

Contents

Preface

We would like to welcome readers to our new dictionary. It has been written with a number of aims in mind. First, we have tried to ensure that nothing said in any entry is more obscure than the term it is supposed to explain. It is always frustrating to look something up only to find that the definition is less understandable than the original concept. Second, and not always easy, we have tried to ensure that we really understand what we are saying; newcomers to the discipline may find it reassuring that we are sometimes perplexed by the work of our colleagues. Third, we have aimed for consistency of comment. Most comparable reference works are written by large teams and what is said in one entry often jars with what is said in another. All of our entries are joint productions which, while they do their best to explain fairly their subjects, often express our preferences. Fortunately neither of us is terribly doctrinaire.

A common weakness of technical reference works is that while they address ignorance of the matter in hand, they assume too much general knowledge. We have tried to take nothing for granted; in particular we have made a point of briefly explaining the origins of ordinary language terms. Although our prose is always correct, it is never pompous or overly formal and we have even allowed humour to intrude.

Last, we have tried to keep entries relatively brief. We have not listed all the works of the authors mentioned or gone into lengthy biographical details. In an age of Internet search engines, such information is readily available. This dictionary offers readers an accessible and lucid starting point for their enquiries and we hope people will find it a pleasure to use.

We would like to take this chance to thank our colleagues. Steve Bruce is very grateful to David Voas and Tony Glendinning for help with the statistics entries. Steve Yearley is similarly appreciative of the help of Andy Tudor with the entry on Anthony Giddens and grateful to Phil Stanworth who persistently excused the borrowing of his books without permission.

A

ABSOLUTE POVERTY Also known as subsistence poverty, this is an idea of **poverty** derived from the minimum requirements for subsistence: what a person must have to live and to make a living.

ABSOLUTE RATES OF MOBILITY We can describe social mobility in absolute or relative terms. The absolute rate of mobility is the proportion of people in a particular social **class** who move up or down in the socio-economic hierarchy. Relative social mobility is the proportion of one social class that moves up or down compared with the proportion of another class that moves. The distinction is important because the two measures can give a very different impression of the degree of social mobility.

ABSOLUTISM This denotes a political regime in which the ruler (usually a monarch) is not constrained in the exercise of power either by custom or by rule of law, and which has an effective centralised administration so that the ruler's will can be turned into action. The idea plays an important part in models of political evolution. Max **Weber** saw the absolutist state as a progressive stage between feudalism and modern capitalism: it created a bureaucratic administration, gradually gained a monopoly of the legitimate use of force, and used that force to impose law and order and hence

predictability. While this fits the history of western Europe, in eastern Europe and other parts of the world absolutism retarded rather than encouraged progress.

ABSTRACTED EMPIRICISM C. Wright **Mills** in *The Sociological Imagination* (1959) derided social scientists who allowed the primary task of understanding to be subverted by technical issues of data collection and analysis. Mills thought his colleagues misled by a desire to imitate the natural sciences. Excessive concern with the internal validity of statistical techniques and the assumption that if it could not be quantified, it was not evidence, meant that what passed for sociology was actually closer to alchemy: elegant but pointless. Worse, because the survey data favoured by empiricists related to individuals (e.g. their attitudes or their demographic characteristics), the importance of social structure was under-estimated. Mills's critique is a useful caution against losing sight of the purpose of research, but its blanket application as an argument against quantitative research is improper. Empirically-minded historical sociologists (such as Charles Tilly) and students of social mobility (such as John **Goldthorpe**) have ably demonstrated that it is possible to combine statistical and technical sophistication in data collection and analysis with insightful theory and a due appreciation of the role of social forces.

ACCOMMODATION   When used to describe relations between discrete populations (defined, for example, by ethnicity or religion) the term suggests groups finding ways of co-existing without losing their defining characteristics. It is often contrasted with acculturation: the process in which a minority is absorbed into the majority and entirely loses its distinctiveness. Assimilation falls somewhere between the two. Robert **Park** described assimilation as achieving a degree of cultural solidarity sufficient at least to sustain a national existence. Only extreme **nativists** took this to mean the complete eradication of cultural distinctions. With wide-scale migration (e.g. of Muslims to western Europe), the extent to which the modern state can or should require religio-ethnic minorities to accommodate has become an important political issue.

ACCOUNTS   The descriptions and justifications that people (or 'actors') give of their actions. Sociologists differ in the extent to which they regard actors' accounts as central to the sociological enterprise. Those who think sociology should explain meaningful social action insist that such accounts are essential to understanding the motives and reasoning that make action meaningful. Scholars (such as structuralist Marxists), who regard external social forces as the primary causes of conduct, pay little attention to actors' accounts because they cannot suppose that people are fully or even dimly aware of what causes them to act in one way rather than another.

   For those who are interested in accounts there is always a problem of knowing to what extent accounts can be taken as reliable guides to the past (especially those given in some circumstance where the account is intended to persuade: courtroom testimony, religious testimonies, chat-show confessions). The point is not so much that people lie (though they do); it is that the needs of the present often cause us to re-interpret the past. Validity is further challenged by our habit of retrospective re-valuation. We cannot help but see our past from our present. As our lives change, so does the way we recollect, view, interpret and account for our past.

   Ethnomethodology argues the intriguing case that accounts should be the primary focus of sociological study, not for what they can tell us about people's motives, but for what they tell us about the social relations involved in representing our motives to each other and what they reveal about the mechanics of 'account giving'.

See **vocabularies of motive**.

ACCULTURATION   See **accommodation**.

ACEPHALOUS   From the Greek meaning 'without a head', this term is used to describe a political system with no single overarching authority: the traditional African lineage political system, where authority is exercised at the level of the **clan** or the lineage segment, is an example.

ACHIEVED STATUS   See **status**, ascribed.

ACHIEVEMENT   This is the successful accomplishment or performance of some socially defined task. Talcott **Parsons** regarded it as a defining characteristic of modern societies that people were recruited or selected for particular social roles by achievement (acquiring specific credentials or qualifications, for example) rather than by **ascription**. Acquiring credentials does play a much greater part in attaining social positions in modern than in traditional societies: for example, civil service, church, army and police officials are now trained and tested for promotion; they do not inherit or buy their offices. But it remains the case that inherited and ascribed characteristics such as race and gender continue to play a major part in people's **life-chances** and their social **stratification**.

ACTION   Any unit or sequence of individual social activity that is purposeful and involves deliberation is action. The implied contrast is with **behaviour**. This useful pairing allows us to range conduct on a scale according to the amount of conscious deliberation, thought or choice involved. At the behaviour end we would place conduct which is in some sense driven by forces beyond our knowledge and control. Such forces can be internal (e.g. a biological reflex or an instinct) or external (e.g. as when we uncritically or even unknowingly accept the preferences of our social class). At the action end we would place conduct based on fully-conscious decision-making. Social science disciplines and schools within them are often defined by their general preference to see human conduct as action or behaviour. Psychologists and biologists (especially geneticists) tend to see behaviour where sociologists see action. Within sociology, Weberian and symbolic interactionists tend to see action where structuralists (especially Marxists) see behaviour.

See **agency and structure, Blumer, Giddens, Luhmann, Parsons**.

ACTION RESEARCH   This is a type of research in which the researcher not only studies some social phenomenon but assists in changing it, often in an experimental manner. Examples could include assessments of new criminal-justice proposals according to which perpetrators of crime are obliged to meet their victims and to listen to victims' accounts of the effects of the crimes. Such approaches reflect the fact that much social research is commissioned by groups and agencies which wish to understand some problem so as to solve it. Although the phrase is associated with the 1960s, the idea that researchers have a moral obligation to assist their subjects has an enduring appeal to those who study groups which they believe to be relatively disadvantaged. If imposed on all sociological work, such an injunction would create obvious problems for the discipline; we would only be able to study people of whom we approved.

See **ethics of research, value-freedom**.

ACTION THEORY   A key question in sociology concerns the primary focus of the enterprise: do we study social action or social structure? Max **Weber** and those influenced by him, see sociology as the explanation of social action (hence action theory) and understanding actors' meanings, purposes, beliefs and values as the essential first step in that work.

Weber distinguished four main types of action: traditional or customary (because our people have always done it like this); affective (because it is emotionally satisfying); value-oriented (because it is the right thing to do); and instrumental (because it is the most effective way to achieve a certain end).

Implicit in action theory is the assumption that people are by and large rational; that they act for what count for them as good reasons. However, as Weber's four types show, this rationality is not confined to the very narrow notion of 'maximising benefits' that economists use; in Weber's view it may be perfectly rational to follow a custom (such as marrying one's third cousin) even when personal advantage might be maximised by marrying a stranger.

The contrast between action theory and various forms of **structuralist** sociology is often exaggerated. Action theorists have generally paid considerable attention to the social structures that shape individual action and are in turn shaped by it. Structuralists generally identify social structures by, and illustrate them with, examples of individual action.

ACTION FRAME OF REFERENCE Talcott **Parsons** elaborated a complex theory that begins with a systematic analysis of action in which people choose between competing ends and means in circumstances that limit those choices socially and physically. The main social limits are norms and values. From these foundational concepts, Parsons generates a complex model of the **social system** in which, critics argue, the choosing individual gradually disappears and the social system with its norms and values becomes the primary determinant of behaviour.

ACTOR-NETWORK THEORY This approach, associated primarily with French social scientists Michel Callon and Bruno Latour, examines how innovations, usually in knowledge or technology, become established in society. They argue for a 'sociology of translation', the central claim of which is that innovations succeed because other actors' interests are translated into the new enterprise. Latour argues, for example, that Pasteur's famous work on disease prevention succeeded because Pasteur translated the interests of vets, farmers and livestock into his research programme: pasteurisation came to appear to be in the interests of them all. Latour and Callon stress that innovations typically work because their proponents are skilled at building alliances (actor-networks) between many heterogeneous agents; such alliances can include human actors (such as vets) and non-human ones (such as bacteria or sheep).

Critics have focused on two issues. First there is the problem of identifying the 'interests' of non-human actors. Second, they worry about the circularity of the argument that conflicts over innovation are won by the stronger alliance. The problem is that the strength of an alliance is finally demonstrated by the fact that it won the controversy. The supposed strength explains the victory but the only evidence of the strength is the victory itself.

ADAPTATION This denotes the way in which social systems of any kind (the family, an organisation such as a school, the nation-state) respond to their environment. In **structural-functionalism**, adaptation is one of the four functional pre-requisites that all social systems must satisfy if they are to survive.

AD HOC HYPOTHESIS This signifies a subsidiary proposition added to a theory to save it from **refutation**. In the philosophy of science developed by Karl **Popper** the reliance on ad hoc hypotheses to plug holes is the defining mark of bogus science and he cites **Marxism** and Freudianism as two intellectual systems preserved from **falsification** only by ad hocery.

AD-HOCING This term is employed by ethnomethodologists to characterise reasoning and description in everyday interaction. Since the words used in everyday speech are not subject to rigorous definition there can be no set criteria for establishing what other people mean or are talking about. If you are trying to describe someone whom you met at a party there is no single correct description of them. Instead your description is taken as adequate when other people claim to recognise the description. In the same way, all descriptions are taken to be ad hoc; their adequacy can only be adjudged in practical terms.

ADJACENCY PAIR This term was introduced by proponents of **conversation analysis** to refer to turns at talk that occur in patterned pairs, such as questions and answers, or greetings and returned greetings, or invitations and acceptances/declinings. The point is not that questions are usually followed by answers but that questions make answers normatively expected. The failure to supply an answer can thus be heard as the second speaker's responsibility. Failure to supply an answer may be viewed as being evasive or slippery. To fail to return a greeting can be to snub someone. Conversation analysts suggest that it is from these normative minutiae that the orderliness of everyday interaction is built.

ADOLESCENCE This denotes the emotional and behavioural states supposedly associated with becoming an adult, the period in the life-cycle between childhood and adulthood and, more specifically, the period when the physical changes associated with biological puberty occur but the person's sexual maturity is not yet socially recognised. Although most sociologists accept that biological changes do affect character, so that some of the emotional turbulence now commonly expected of adolescents can be explained by biology, we also recognise that there is a large element of social construction in adolescence: the prosperity of modern societies has allowed the expansion of the indeterminate period between childhood and adulthood and the creation of distinctive **youth cultures**.

ADORNO, THEODOR (1903–69) A leading member of the **Frankfurt School**, Adorno fled Germany in 1934 for the USA. His work, often expressed in deliberately obscure language, ranged widely but he is best known for his criticisms of popular culture (which he saw as an industrial product designed to manipulate the masses) and for his contribution to *The Authoritarian Personality* (1994), a seminal influence on the study of right-wing extremism. He was highly disdainful of a vision of sociology as a primarily or exclusively empirical enterprise because it would lack the critical edge which, as a Marxist, he regarded as the main point of social theory.

ADVANCED CAPITALISM In Marxist theory the final stage of the evolution of capitalism is characterised by concentration of ownership and increasing intervention in the economy by the state as it tries to manage increasingly common and virulent economic crises. This phase supposedly culminates in the final crisis and the transition to socialism. Contrary to Marxist expectations, of course, capitalism has shown itself remarkably robust and thus remains in its advanced stage. Late capitalism is not itself static and sociologists continue to disagree over how best to characterise present-day capitalist society.

See **globalisation, risk society, end-of-history**.

AETIOLOGY See **etiology**.

AFFECT This denotes the emotional or feeling element (as distinct from the purely cognitive element) of mental experience. What I am doing when I learn my father has died is cognitive; what I am doing when I feel saddened by that knowledge is affective.

AFFECTIVE DISORDERS Disorders of the emotions such as anxiety and depression, as distinct from cognitive disorders, form one of the major groupings of types of mental illness.

AFFECTIVE INDIVIDUALISM Social historians such as Lawrence Stone believe that there was a radical change in the nature of the family in 18th-century England (which then spread globally). Previously, families had been deeply embedded in extended kinship networks and wider communities and the family was not the primary focus for the emotional attachments of its members. Sex was as much a matter of creating new personnel as a source of pleasure. Marriage itself was instrumental in that economic and political advantage often played a greater part than emotional ties in the choice of partners. With industrialisation the family shrank in size and in social roles. The modern domesticated nuclear family is characterised by close emotional ties, domestic privacy and the careful rearing of children for expressive rather than instrumental reasons. Affective individualism captures the essence of wider changes: 'affective' because emotional attachment displaces more mundane and practical considerations and 'individualism' because the modern family is constructed around the bond of personal attraction between free-acting individuals.

As always with such grand attempts to encapsulate the essence of a major change, the notion can be criticised for exaggerating the extent of change and too closely associating it with particular causes. However, affective individualism does accurately capture a real difference between families of the modern western world and those either of feudal Europe or many parts of the non-industrialised world.

AFFECTIVE INVOLVEMENT; AFFECTIVE NEUTRALITY   See **pattern variables**.

AFFIRMATIVE ACTION   See **positive discrimination**.

AFFLUENT SOCIETY   John K. **Galbraith**'s *The Affluent Society* (1958) drew attention to a tension in the USA: it was indeed affluent but the private prosperity of the majority was accompanied by a good deal of public squalor and there was a significant minority who had not only been left behind economically but also in effect dis-enfranchised. Arguably the two problems remain with us and have been extended globally: individual affluence comes at the expense of public services and also creates major environmental costs. Moreover, in many economies where the average standard of living has increased markedly, the poorest, though they may also have prospered, have fallen far enough

behind the average to be in various ways excluded from **civil society**.

See **citizen**.

AFFLUENT WORKER   This term was popularised by the titles of three volumes from a seminal 1960s British project led by John **Goldthorpe** and David Lockwood. The study of affluent manual workers in the British car industry was intended to test the **embourgeoisment** (or 'becoming middle class') thesis. Marxist theories suppose the working class is defined by its lack of ownership of the means of production (and hence lack of power). The embourgeoisment alternative is that attitudes and behaviour are influenced more by wealth than by ownership and control; as workers become better paid they will become more like the middle classes. The Affluent Worker studies came to importantly different conclusions. These workers had become more like the middle class in some respects (e.g. buying their own houses and favouring domestic over community leisure activities) but they continued to vote for the Labour party and remained active in trade unions. In these activities, rational self-interest was more important than traditional community loyalties; 'instrumental collectivism' had replaced class solidarity.

See **orientations to work**.

AGE SETS   These are broad age bands that define the social status, roles and patterns of behaviour appropriate for those who belong to them. Graduation from one age set to another is often marked by rituals or **rites of passage**. In many simple societies, age sets are a crucial element of the social structure, but even in industrial societies age remains an important variable for the allocation of legal rights and responsibilities.

AGEING   The chronological process of growing older obviously has a biological basis: the human physique and its associated capacities change over time in a manner that is regular, even if the timing of changes varies from person to person. Sociological interest in ageing concentrates on the social expectations that we have of the elderly. At its simplest, there is a clear contrast between the way that many traditional societies regard their oldest members (as repositories of wisdom and experience) and the relatively low status that modern societies offer the elderly.

AGEISM   The success of campaigns to outlaw racism and sexism inspired the creation of this term to describe discrimination based on negative stereotypes about the elderly and their capacities.

AGENTS OF SOCIAL CONTROL   This term is used mainly in **critical sociology** to describe a variety of agencies that contribute to ensuring that members of society conform. In addition to such obvious ones as the police, courts and prisons, the term would also embrace social workers, teachers, clergymen and others whose controlling influence is not so immediate but is nonetheless taken to be significant.

AGENCY AND STRUCTURE   A major fault line in sociology concerns the relative freedom of individuals. Beyond such obvious constraints as the rule of the law and the power of the police, courts and prisons, there are more abstract social forces and structures, and sociologists differ in the relative weight they assign such structures in determining individual thought and action. Agency denotes individual capacity for free thought and action; structure denotes the constraints on individuals that result from the fact that repeated patterns of action, legitimated by ideologies, form the environment that shapes us (e.g. as we are socialised into a particular set of beliefs, values and attitudes in childhood) and limits our actions (by, for example, allocating the resources necessary for certain actions in an uneven manner). Clearly there are elements of social structure that materially affect our lives; the opportunities open to women are not the same as those open to men and the difference is a product not just of biological differences but of the social significance that societies give to those biological differences. Very few sociologists would deny the importance of both agency and structure but they differ systematically in their views of the proper focus for sociology; and precisely the extent to which, and the manner in which, individual action is determined by social forces. That is, there is a division about what sociologists should study and there is a separate division about how we expect to explain that which we study.

Structural-functionalists and Marxists believe that that proper subject of sociology is not the individual but the social structure and the relationships between elements of that structure. In this view, individuals are of interest only as the carriers of properties of the structure. Emile **Durkheim** studied **suicide** not because he was interested in the motives of those who kill themselves but because he believed certain types of suicide and the rates at which they occur are characteristics of a certain type of society. At the other end, Weberian sociology, **phenomenology** and **symbolic interactionism** take social action as the proper focus for sociology study.

Analytically separate from the question of what sociology should study is the issue of where we expect to find the effective cause of whatever interests us.

See **structuration**.

AID   This encompasses a variety of resources (such as food, technical expertise, military hardware, medicines and capital) that are given to less developed countries by the developed world. Social scientists differ markedly in their assessment of the effects of aid. **Modernisation** theory supposes that such aid is usually helpful to development; **dependency theory** sees it as a novel form of colonial oppression that maintains, rather then reduces, the advantage of the industrial capitalist West by, for example, opening up markets for western exports or by supporting governments which are the West's political allies. In the last quarter of the 20th century the issue of aid became inseparable from that of international debt since many developing countries became impoverished as a result of colossal, ill-advised loans taken out in the 1970s.

See **debt crisis**.

ALIENATION   The term is very widely used to convey a sense of improper loss or detachment. Originally used in the active form, 'to alienate' meant to remove something from someone; 'alienation' was thus a particular form of theft or confiscation. This was superseded by the passive form so that 'to be alienated' no longer meant to have been stolen and came to mean instead 'to have had something stolen from you' and shifted from property to human relations. Alienation was the state of not having proper human relations.

The word was popularised by Karl **Marx** (1970) in his *Economic and Philosophical Manuscripts of 1844* as a description for the estrangement of people from their true human nature. People are essentially creative. They re-shape the material world into objects and in so doing put some of themselves into the things they make: the products of their labour. In pre-capitalist society, the making of objects for one's own use or for fair exchange was properly human. In capitalist society, because the workers do not own the means of production but have to sell their labour, they are allegedly 'alienated' in four senses:

(a) from the product of their work because they have no control over the fate of the goods they produce; (b) from the act of production itself because work is no longer a creative act but is merely a commodity that is bought and sold; (c) from their 'species being' because work under capitalism lacks what should be its distinctly human quality; and (d) from each other because what should be social relations of exchange are replaced by the market relationships of buying and selling.

For Marx and Marxists the above is the scientific analysis of social realities. Alienation is not a fancy name for unhappiness; workers under capitalism are alienated whether they appreciate it or not.

Although Marxists present their analysis of labour under capitalism as a scientific theory, it rests on an untestable (and many would argue, unusual) assertion about what humans are really like: desirous of expressing themselves through work. Were we to start by asserting that people are essentially comfort-seeking and that what they really need is a pleasant, safe and secure life, then there would be no reason to suppose that capitalism was any more alienating than other economic systems; all could be judged by the extent to which they deliver benefits. The whole approach is open to the even-more damning criticism that by starting with a utopian view of the purpose of human production and exchange, it misses the fact that the working lives of most serfs and peasants in precapitalist societies were generally less pleasant than those of workers under industrial capitalism which, however alienated they might be, were markedly more prosperous.

Since Marx's time, the term has been broadened to include almost any sort of undesired separation and it is often psychologised so that it denotes personal unhappiness at some state of affairs, not the state of affairs itself. In some usages it comes close to Emile **Durkheim**'s notion of **anomie**; in others to Max **Weber**'s account of responses to the large-scale impersonal rational bureaucracies of the modern world.

In the 1960s the term returned again to the sociology of work in Robert Blauner's (1964) *Alienation and Freedom*. He identified various forms of alienation that resulted from different types of modern work; each linked to the degree of personal control (or, as in the title 'freedom') inherent in different ways of working. In a developmental model, he argued that as production moved from craft work, through the use of machines, to the factory assembly-line, the degree of personal control went down and that of alienation rose. However, he concluded that in the final stage – that of automated continuous-flow production – the control of the labour process returned to the worker as the job became more complex and hence more satisfying.

See **de-skilling**.

ALTERITY   This synonym for 'otherness' is popular in **postmodernist** writing. Learning to distinguish between the self and other is an essential part of child development and a vital tool for ordering our perceptions of the world. It may be taken further to construct whole classes of people as 'other' and hence not fully human, and then to project on to that class qualities we fear and reject in ourselves. Once we assign qualities to people by including them in such categories we have prejudice and **stereotyping**.

See **othering**.

ALTHUSSER, LOUIS (1918–90)   A French structuralist Marxist, Althusser became famous in the late 1960s for his attempt to re-assert a scientific form of Marxism against the rather woolly and humanistic forms it had taken. He particularly rejected the centrality of the notion of **alienation** and the importance of Karl **Marx**'s early works in favour of *Das Kapital*, which, somewhat implausibly, he claimed to be science (and as important

science) as the work of Galileo or Charles Darwin. In his later years he became sceptical of this claim and, indeed, seems to have recanted most of his views. Now barely read, Althusser was extremely popular in the 1970s. His standing fell with that of the French Communist party (of which he was the leading intellectual). He was always psychologically unstable and in 1980 he murdered his wife. He passed his remaining decade in various secure psychiatric institutions.

His re-reading of the mature works of Marx generated a number of phrases (**ideological state apparatuses, repressive state apparatuses, interpellation, over-determination**) which were very popular for a short time. In some ways he softened Marxism: he allowed that the superstructure (in particular ideology and politics) shaped the context for the economic base; he treated ideology as a collection of real social relations rather than as an illusion; and, for someone who was essentially a structuralist, he gave individuals unusual prominence as the agents of social relations. For all that, he has left little trace on non-Marxist social science, mostly because he undertook little empirical social research.

ALTRUISM   Generally altruism is a concern for others rather than for oneself. Altruistic behaviour is often contrasted with egoistic or selfish behaviour (for example in Emile **Durkheim**'s theory of **suicide**).

ALTRUISTIC SUICIDE   See **suicide**.

AMBIVALENCE   This signifies the presence in one person at the same time of two competing or conflicting emotions or attitudes. It is a particularly important idea for Sigmund **Freud** who reported the closeness of love and hate.

AMPLIFICATION OF DEVIANCE   See **deviancy amplification**.

ANALYSIS OF VARIANCE (ANOVA)   This is a statistical procedure used to test differences between the distribution around the means (see **measures of central tendency**) of some characteristic within and between various groups. For example, we might wish to know how social class affects life expectancy. We would collect information about age at death and social class, divide the sample into, say, five social classes, and then see how the degree of variation within any of the social classes compares with the difference between the five classes. If the variation within each class is markedly less than the variation between them, then we would conclude that social class is strongly associated with (and in this case therefore in all likelihood a major determinant of) life expectancy.

ANALYTIC INDUCTION   This denotes a method of analysis common to forms of qualitative sociology. The analyst formulates a hypothesis on the basis of known cases and then progressively modifies it to accommodate 'decisive negative cases': observations that do not fit the starting hypothesis. As with any method of induction, the quality of the conclusions depends on the willingness of the analyst to continue to seek out contrary or anomalous cases. The procedure must also be used sensitively since endless modification of the original hypothesis can lead to a descent into blandness, with successive modifications taking the form of **ad hoc hypotheses**.

Ordinary people regularly practise a form of lay sociology. What should make the explanations offered by professional sociologists more compelling is that, while lay people will often be satisfied once they find an explanation that fits the very limited number of cases that have come to their attention (all sociologists are bearded because the two sociologists I know have beards), the professional will exhaustively seek out further cases. Analytical induction need not depend, however, on the professionalism of any one analyst because the competitive nature of the profession should ensure that critics will challenge any hypothesis by seeking out further cases that do not fit.

See **grounded theory**.

ANIMISM   Most generally, animism is the belief that natural objects and phenomena (such as trees, stones and winds) have souls. In 19th-century evolutionary theories of religion, it was treated as the simplest form of religious belief system, common to peoples at the most primitive level of social evolution. Such evolutionary models were thoroughly partisan in that they placed the religion of those people who promoted them (western European liberal Christians) at the peak of evolution. Nowadays, students of religion tend to be more concerned with the social functions than with the detailed content of religious belief systems and the tendency is to suppose that all religions serve similar purposes.

ANNALES SCHOOL   An important group of French social historians was associated with the journal *Annales d'histoire économique et sociale* (later titled *Annales. Economies, sociétés, civilisations* and then *Annales. Histoire. Science Sociales*) founded by Lucien Febvre and Marc **Bloch** in 1929. The school opposed the conventional approach to history as the chronology of major political events and stressed instead the importance of social history, social structure and long-term historical trends. The school has made major contributions to classical debates in sociology (such as the explanation of the transition from feudalism to capitalism). The work of Fernand Braudel has been particularly influential for modern social science through Immanuel Wallerstein's **world-systems theory**.

ANOMIE   From the Greek 'a-nomos' or 'without rules', this is a social condition of breakdown and confusion associated with either the absence of group rules or serious conflict over them. The first major use in sociology is associated with Emile **Durkheim**'s *Division of Labour in Society* (1893) and *Suicide* (1897).

For all that Durkheim insisted that sociology should study societies and not individuals, his use of anomie in *Suicide* was an important contribution to our understanding of **human nature**. He pointed out that the behaviour of most animals is very largely instinctive. Their biology determines and sets limits on their needs; when a pig has satisfied its appetite it stops consuming. It also arranges their co-ordination; bees instinctively obey the signals contained in the secretions of their fellow bees. Humans lack such instinctive constraints. Accordingly, however much they have or acquire, they can always wish for more. The person who finally gains the much-desired car can soon wish for a better one or for two cars. Hence we are potentially always threatened by constant yearning and unhappiness at not attaining our constantly inflated ambitions. Society performs for humans the task that instinct performs for other animals. Culture establishes the expectations into which we are socialised. In a stable society people internalise social rules or norms about appropriate desires and aspirations that roughly fit their circumstances. To put it crudely, as people can never be made content by giving them what they want (because they will always want more), they are instead made content by being persuaded that what they have is what they deserve. This balance of culturally-produced aspirations and circumstances, can be disrupted by sudden social, political or economic change. We might expect suicide rates to go up in times of economic depression: poverty makes people unhappy. But Durkheim argues that they also rise in times of economic boom. When people find that their circumstances allow them to exceed the aspirations to which they have been socialised, they lose that cultural strait-jacket of norms and find themselves psychologically adrift. They suffer a condition of anomie.

The evidence Durkheim used in *Suicide* would now be regarded with some considerable scepticism, but his account of anomic suicide is intuitively plausible and important for understanding the way in which society may shape the individual. Radicals sometimes chide Durkheim for the conservative implications of anomie: if personal stability rests on stable norms, then order itself becomes virtuous, almost irrespective of the specific contours of that order.

Robert K. **Merton** fitted Durkheim's notion into a general theory of deviance. In the classic essay 'Social Structure and Anomie', Merton (1938) argued that, while the primary effect of social structures and cultures is to encourage conformity, the disjuncture between the two spheres may inadvertently create encourage deviance. The culture of the USA encourages all Americans to desire (and believe they deserve) the same goals: upward mobility and wealth. It also establishes norms regulating how those goals should be pursued: with hard work and educational attainment. But the social structure clearly distributes the means to achieve those goals unevenly. Hard work and striving at school would earn the typical black citizen far less than the typical white citizen. That opportunities are very far from equally distributed will lead many people to feel relatively deprived and hence justified in abandoning their commitment to striving only by the legitimate means. That they feel cheated causes people to give up faith in the rules (hence anomie).

Merton imaginatively expands this observation about the social structural encouragement to crime into a typology of deviant behaviour. The conformists have access to the approved goals and the legitimate means. Innovators remain positive about goals but negative about legitimate means: thieves for example want the same things as everyone else but follow unacceptable routes to achieving them. Retreatists reject both the goals and the means: serious drug-takers and alcoholics would be examples. Ritualists have given up on the goals but remain strongly committed to the legitimate means: an example is the bureaucrat who regards rule-following as the end in itself. Merton's final category consists of rebels; people who reject some elements of both the goals and the means and substitute goals and means of their own.

Not surprising for something so ambitious, Merton's essay has been widely criticised. Placing such emphasis on the social structure leaves white-collar innovation unexplained; why should people who have full access to the legitimate means for getting on still cheat? More generally, it assumes that, prior to disappointment at being cheated by the social structure creating anomie, the default position was conformity. Nonetheless it is still profoundly influential, particularly on studies of subcultures and delinquency.

APARTHEID   An Afrikaans term for separation (as in 'apart'), this denotes the policy to segregate people by race pursued by the South African government between 1948–94. The policy involved an elaborate classification of race, rules to discourage the integration of races (especially inter-marriage) and a discriminatory allocation of rights. Race discrimination is a common feature of many societies and until the 1960s many US states had a variety of race laws but the South African example is one of the few where a state attempted to maintain an all-encompassing structure of racial discrimination.

See **civil rights movement** (US).

ASCETICISM   All the major world religions have wings inspired by the notion that physical pleasures and comfort should be denied in order to purify or improve the soul. The distinction between other-worldly asceticism (in a monastery or convent, for example) and this-worldly asceticism (adopting an attitude of monastic discipline while still living and working in the normal world) is central to Max **Weber**'s explanation of the rise of capitalism.

See **Protestant Ethic thesis**.

ASCRIBED STATUS   See **status**.

ASCRIPTION   In general usage, to ascribe is to give, impute or attribute certain features to some object, person, event or act without justification. In the absence of good evidence, to assert 'all politicians are corrupt' is to ascribe a characteristic to a class of people. The implied contrast is with discovery. Instead of finding out what politicians are really like, the observer has given them a certain quality. This sense of something given or undeserved is carried over into the modern social science pairing of ascription with achievement. High social position may be ascribed or achieved. In feudal society rank is usually inherited; in modern societies it is often achieved by individual effort and merit.

ASIATIC MODE OF PRODUCTION   This notion was originally proposed by Karl **Marx** and Friedrich **Engels** to explain the relative backwardness of oriental societies such as China and Egypt and developed by Karl Wittfogel, a member of the **Frankfurt School**, in his *Oriental Despotism* (1957): Asiatic economies were supposed characterised by an absence of private property, state control over public works (in particular irrigation systems; hence the related description 'hydraulic societies'), a self-sufficient village economy, an absence of autonomous cities and simplicity of production methods.

Without private property there could be no class struggle between the landowners and peasants; hence stagnation. While class struggle occurs naturally in the West it arises in the East only because colonialism brings capitalist exploitation.

Detailed research has failed to support the idea that a range of Asian societies had a common economic structure; the belief that they had owed more to western ignorance and stereotyping than to accurate comparative study. The idea fits awkwardly with Marxist thinking because it describes a quarter of the world as an exception to what Marxists otherwise claim is a universal model of progressive evolution through class conflict. Equally suspect, it makes colonialism a good thing and makes Asians at least partly responsible for their own backwardness.

The notion has now been largely abandoned. The consensus among left-wing scholars is that the backwardness of the East has very little to do with any intrinsic properties of those societies and is largely to be explained by western exploitation.

See **dependency theory, orientalism**.

ASSIMILATION   See accommodation.

ATTITUDE   Given the difficulty in knowing in detail the actions of people in society, sociologists have often had to content themselves with investigating people's attitudes. A great deal of sociology has been concerned with studying changes in attitudes and with mapping the way that attitudes vary with gender, class, education and so on. However, this whole endeavour assumes that attitudes denote a relatively stable system of beliefs concerning some object, that result in an evaluation of that object. Thus when we talk of an 'attitude to abortion' we suppose that people know what abortion is, that they approve or disapprove, and that they are not

whimsical. In any particular instance, all three assumptions may be contested. By inserting questions about made-up issues into an otherwise normal battery of questions, survey researchers have demonstrated that people will not only claim to know about a fictitious item of proposed legislation but will also declare themselves strongly in favour or against it. However, there is plenty of survey evidence that people do have relatively stable attitudes towards many aspects of their worlds and that these attitudes vary with shared characteristics such as education and social class.

ATTITUDE SCALE   Although more important in psychology, where it is common to look for personality characteristics that are relatively free of context (such as dogmatism or authoritarianism), attitude scales are used in many fields of social research. Questions are designed to assess not just whether someone is pro- or anti-something but how strongly they feel in either direction. Sophisticated statistical methods are now used to assess the extent to which responses to attitude scales form single clusters.

See **scale**.

AUTARCHY   The meaning would be clearer if it were 'auto-archy' because it signifies 'self' rule in the sense of absolute sovereignty or despotism: a type of regime in which the ruler is not constrained by any 'other'.

AUTHORITARIAN PERSONALITY   In 1950, Else Frenkel-Brunswick, Daniel J. Levinson, Theodor **Adorno** and R. Nevitt Sandford published *The Authoritarian Personality*, which popularised the idea that certain people, by virtue of their upbringing, acquired a character that predisposed them to accepting anti-democratic political beliefs. Rigid discipline and conditional affection created a personality that found comfort in submission to authority while directing aggression towards outsiders, usually racial minorities. The notion was initially extremely influential because it seemed to explain the anti-Semitism and **fascism** of the previous two decades and because it accepted the popular assumption that how one was raised as a child was profoundly important. It fell out of favour with sociologists and political scientists because, although intuitively plausible, there was little evidence for the existence of a distinctly authoritarian personality type. The evidence that a distinct personality made people receptive to political ideas fitted equally well even if one reversed the causal connection; it was equally possible that being socialised into an authoritarian political culture shaped people's personalities.

See **open and closed mind**.

AUTHORITY   If people obey a command because they fear the consequences of refusing, they are responding to power. If they obey because they believe they should, they are responding to authority. Authority is that subtype of power that is accepted as legitimate. Max **Weber** distinguished three different types of authority. Traditional authority involves an appeal to custom and ancient practice. Legal-rational authority involves obedience to formal rules, which have been established by proper procedure: civil servants who distribute passports according to the regulations of a bureaucratic organisation can invoke this sort of authority for their actions with charismatic authority, the charismatic leader is obeyed because followers believe he or she possesses an extraordinary character (usually derived from a special relationship with the divine) that trumps existing rules or prevalent customs. An exemplar is the Christ figure in the New Testament who presents his radically innovative teachings in the form 'It is written … but I say to you …'

and justifies his rejection of the tradition only with the claim to be the Son of God.

Very loosely we can understand much about the differences between pre-modern and modern societies by noting that traditional authority is prevalent in the former and legal-rational authority (especially as embodied in bureaucratic organisations) dominates the latter. Charismatic authority may periodically appear in all sorts of societies but it is less common in modern societies.

AUTOMATION   A simple way of understanding the evolution of work is to see it as the gradual replacement of animal power by inanimate power and control. Prehistoric people used only their own strength. Early modern people used their own strength and that of domesticated animals, augmented by such simple machines as the inclined plane and the block and tackle. Modern buildings are erected by people operating machines powered by fossil fuels. Automation marks that stage of technological advance in which work is performed primarily by machines that are only remotely controlled by people. Truly automatic processes are closed systems, which require no human intervention once the machines that perform the work have been designed and assembled. The invention of the silicon chip computer has greatly enhanced our capacity to automate not just the manufacture of goods but also the processing of people.

Sociologists are interested in the effect that automation has on the workers directly involved and on society more generally. In his classic *Alienation and Freedom* (1964), Robert Blauner argued that automation would return to workers much of the job satisfaction that earlier stages of mechanisation had removed. A counter argument is that automation makes work less intrinsically satisfying by reducing the levels of skill and discretion needed to perform tasks (see **de-skilling**). For example, developing photographic images used to be a highly skilled craft; now it can be done by a machine that needs very little skill to operate. Harry **Braverman** argued that while the disappearance of unskilled manual work and the corresponding growth in the number of white-collar workers might superficially seem progressive, the change was actually the reverse: while-collar workers were becoming proleterianised.

The effects of automation are difficult to assess conclusively because we need to balance the effects of changes to particular jobs with an acknowledgement that new jobs are created. The job of developing photographs may have been de-skilled but this has only been possible because new and highly skilled jobs have been created in the design of the machines that have taken over the craft. That is, a high technology economy, while making routine what were previously complex tasks, creates new work in the design and maintenance of the technology.

AUTOPOIESIS   This ungainly neologism has been borrowed from biology and systems theory, where it refers to the idea that systems may be self-producing. The orderliness of biological cells, for example, is primarily generated by the operation of the cells themselves, not by external factors. Certain computer programs can also be written so as to create self-organising environments. Recently, sociologists have adopted this language as a way of trying to capture how it is that societies generate their own orderliness. At present, this seems to be merely the latest in a long line of borrowings from the life sciences and most uses of the term, including those by Niklas **Luhmann**, seem to be metaphorical rather than literal.

AVERAGE   See **measures of central tendency**.

B

BACK STAGE OR REGION In Erving Goffman's **dramaturgy**, the back stage is contrasted with the front stage; it is the space in which people can relax and drop their **role** performance. In the example of a restaurant, the kitchen is the back stage area in which waiters can joke, mock customers and toy with the food. When they come through the door into the restaurant's front stage, they are supposed to slip effortlessly into the controlled performance of the attentive waiter.

BAKHTIN, MIKHAIL (1895–1975) A Russian writer concerned with literature and language, Bakhtin's life was inextricably caught up with the history of the Soviet Union. Like many unorthodox intellectuals he was arrested in the late 1920s and was forced into internal exile. Later, one of his books was destroyed at the publisher's premises during the attempted Nazi invasion of the USSR; the book never appeared because, though he had kept notes, he famously used up a large share of them as make-shift cigarette paper during the war. Bakhtin was a pioneer in the socio-linguistic analysis of fiction, particularly novels. He was also fascinated by the phenomenon of carnival, specifically in carnivals dating from the European Middle Ages during which grotesque and improper behaviour was encouraged and social hierarchies were disrupted. For Bakhtin, carnival indicated the widespread potential for subverting established world-views and

the status quo. It is this aspect of his work that has most appealed to contemporary cultural commentators.

BARTHES, ROLAND (1915–80) Barthes was a key figure in the development of **semiotics**, the study of signs, where he adapted the linguistic arguments of Ferdinand de **Saussure** to apply to the analysis of culture and cultural symbols. Saussure had emphasised that words are arbitrary indicators of meaning: there is nothing about the word 'snail' that fits it to describe snails. Another word would do just as well. Barthes argued that cultural symbols are often just as arbitrary: thus, a deerstalker and cape have come to stand for the garb of a detective. From this point it is a short step to suggest that the study of culture is fundamentally about reading cultural signs. Barthes often distinguished between what something denotes (what it literally stands for or represents) and what it connotes (what it implies or suggests). Cultural goods are often valued for what they connote as much as what they denote. Thus, a 'designer' handbag often functions no better as a handbag than would other makes, but is valued for what it connotes.

BASE AND SUPERSTRUCTURE Karl **Marx** used the terms to express the relationship between the economy (the base) and other features of society (the superstructure): the nature of the economy and its level of productivity is held to determine such other things as the political structure, the legal system, the nature of the state and so on. Marx recognised that the real world is not that simple and that actual relationships may often run in the other direction (for example, the ability of a state to maintain law-and-order will have a major effect on economic development) but it is a defining characteristic of Marxist thought that, in the big picture, the influence of the base on the superstructure is greater than the latter's effect on the former.

BASIC HUMAN NEEDS Lay people and professional social scientists talk often of basic human needs but it is not easy to find agreement about just what they are once we move beyond the purely biological needs of food and shelter. If we starve or freeze to death we are no longer human. But what else is foundational? The list is commonly extended to take in what are thought to be necessary preconditions for full participation in social life. This raises the question of exactly which needs are given by our human constitutions and which are a result of socialisation into a particular culture. For example, some sociologists of religion argue that almost all societies have religions because the human condition creates a need for gods; others counter that religions socialise people into feeling the needs that religions can satisfy. As is clear in his discussion of alienation, Karl **Marx** supposes that the opportunity to express oneself through creative work is a basic human need.

BATAILLE, GEORGES (1897–1962) French philosopher Bataille lived a dual life. By day he was a respectable librarian at the Bibliothèque Nationale and philosopher; by night he was a sadist and alcoholic who wrote pornography. He is mentioned in social theory because Roland **Barthes**, Jacques **Derrida**, and Michel **Foucault** have all claimed him as a prophet of **postmodernity**. In the 1920s he was involved in surrealism, in the late 1930s in anti-fascist politics, and after the Second World War he founded and edited *Critique*, a major influence on Foucault and Jean **Baudrillard**.

BAUDRILLARD, JEAN (1929–) Although he is often classed with **Lyotard** and **Derrida** as a postmodernist, French sociologist Jean Baudrillard is better described as a disappointed Marxist who, like the members of the **Frankfurt School**, turned his attention to popular culture and the media in an attempt to explain the failure of the working class to play its revolutionary role. He is best known for the argument that modern societies are so saturated by the mass media that reality loses its meaning. People are no longer participants in their own lives but observers of what the media has turned into 'spectacles'. An example is pornography, which ought to represent unconstrained sexual excess but has been turned by the media into nothing; a symptom of the dreary and relentless commodification of everyday life. Baudrillard can therefore be seen as proposing a peculiarly radical form of **semiotics**; in our 'age of simulacra' there are only signs and representations. All prospect of access to real things has disappeared. This situation he terms hyperreality. With his own flair for publicity, Baudrillard famously claimed that the 1991 Gulf War did not happen apart from its appearance on television. That said, it is clear that the war actually took place, but its meaning and the details of what happened are inseparable from the televised coverage.

BAUMAN, ZYGMUNT (1925–) His career began in his native Poland at the University of Warsaw in the 1950s but when he became disillusioned with **Marxism** he was encouraged to emigrate to Israel. He then moved to

Leeds in northern England. He first came to prominence with *Modernity and the Holocaust* (1989) in which he argued that the Holocaust was a particularly modern phenomenon to be explained by modern technology, by modern bureaucratic methods for handling large numbers of people, and by the lack of responsibility that Bauman regarded as a consequence of modernisation. He later became associated with various aspects of **postmodernism**.

BECK, ULRICH (1944–) Ulrich Beck's work became widely known to an international audience in the early 1990s when his book *Risk Society: Towards a New Modernity* (1986) was first published in English translation. Though the book is wide-ranging and often surprisingly impassioned in its arguments, most readers agree that he makes two novel claims. First, he proposes that contemporary societies differ from their predecessors because of the central importance of the handling of risk. Of course, early modern societies – in the 16th and 17th centuries for example – faced many threats. Bad weather might ruin harvests, disease might strike uncontrollably. Such risks were beyond human control. Subsequently, industrialisation and the growth of medical and technical knowledge allowed people to exercise more control over their environments. Weather forecasting diminished the threats to harvests. There was less risk and people were optimistic that further risks would come under control. Insurance and compensation schemes allowed people to be indemnified against risk to a large extent. However, by the final quarter of the 20th century risk had re-emerged. This time the risks were typically of human creation. Societies are threatened by the possibility of catastrophic nuclear power station failures or by climate changes caused by emissions into the atmosphere, and, unlike the case of typical industrial risks, it is hard to see how one could meaningfully

insure against such hazards. The handling and regulation of such risks becomes so consequential that it changes the character of contemporary societies. Society is no longer primarily a class society, it is a risk society.

Beck's second claim is that, in risk societies, there are widespread difficulties with the generation of authoritative knowledge. On the face of it, this claim is similar to that of **postmodernism**. However Beck argues that the problem confronting knowledge is really one of 'reflexive modernisation'. In other words, in the face of the new risks, medical, scientific and technical knowledge is subjected to closer and closer scrutiny. Faced with this relentless self-examination, expert knowledge becomes less certain and often more divided. Some experts speak in favour of nuclear power, others against. The authority of technical knowledge goes into decline.

Beck's work has become increasingly widely acknowledged largely because – unlike many sociological theorists – his ideas appear to have been borne out in readily understandable ways. Following the publication of his book there were major risk problems surrounding 'mad cow disease' and the planting of genetically modified crops. Beck's observations seemed to be bang on target.

BECKER, HOWARD S. (1928–) Although he made important contributions to the study of professional socialisation with *Boys in White: Student Culture in the Medical World* (1961) and to sociology of music with his studies of jazz musicians (he was an accomplished jazz pianist), Becker is best known for his pioneering work on **labelling theory** and his insistence that **value-freedom** was an obstacle to sociology's mission to give a voice to the underdog.

BEHAVIOUR Although commonly used as a synonym for action or conduct, behaviour is usefully contrasted with action so that it refers to the automatic or reflex (such as jumping when stung) while action denotes intention, purpose and conscious thought. While there is little difficulty in distinguishing extreme cases of both, much social conduct falls into an ambiguous middle ground in that it is so much a product of effective socialisation that the actor would require a considerable effort of will to act otherwise.

BEHAVIOURISM　　Strictly speaking a school within psychology rather than sociology, behaviourism was an attempt to set up a programme to study behaviour scientifically. Behaviourists argued that scientific analysis depends on verifiable observations. But, since consciousness, meanings and motivations are private, they cannot be observed. A scientific approach to human conduct must therefore depend on analysing connections between observable inputs – stimuli – and observable outputs – responses. The programme never took off as a way of studying human conduct since these 'scientific' interpretations of human behaviour seemed much poorer than actors' own accounts or the accounts of novelists. However, the behaviourists' insistence on studying observable and verifiable aspects of human conduct has been echoed across the social sciences (especially **ethnomethodology**).

BEHAVIOUR MODIFICATION　　This denotes a variety of techniques for the deliberate reshaping of human behaviour based on structured learning. One such is systematic desensitisation: the treatment of phobias by gradually introducing the sufferer to the feared object in a controlled setting. Another is the token economy favoured by some mental hospitals, schools and other institutions: individuals are awarded tokens when they perform some desired action (such as getting dressed or tidying up) and accumulated tokens are exchanged for rewards such as

special meals or a day out. A third form of behaviour modification is aversion therapy, which works by negative reinforcement. An example is the implanting a chemical in the stomachs of alcoholics which causes vomiting when alcohol is drunk.

BELIEF SYSTEM　　This denotes any complex of interrelated propositions. The 'system' implies a degree of coherence and the presence of some integrating general principles. Christianity is an example of a belief system. Max **Weber** used Weltanschauung or **worldview** in the same way. Although there is no consensus about finer points of usage, worldview suggests something broader, less propositional and more taken for granted than belief system.

BELL, DANIEL (1919–)　　This American sociologist and essayist is best known for his argument in the *End of Ideology* (1960) that antagonistic class ideologies had declined in industrial societies. *The Coming of Post-Industrial Society* (1973) was an attempt to depict the sort of society that had displaced the class-ridden societies which sociology had tried to comprehend. Also influential was *The Cultural Contradictions of Capitalism* (1976), which argued that the individualistic hedonistic culture, typical of advanced capitalist societies, was a threat to the rationality required by the economic system.

BENJAMIN, WALTER (1892–1940) Benjamin was a German essayist and literary critic allied to left-wing groups. During the 1920s he became acquainted with members of the **Frankfurt School** and, like them, was interested in the role of popular culture. For many years he was best known for an essay on 'The work of art in the age of mechanical reproduction' (1992), which analysed what would happen to ideas of elite cultural value and originality when artworks could be reproduced without the intervention of artists or skilled performers. As the Nazis rose to power, he left Germany for France. He later tried to flee France also but committed suicide in 1940 in the Spanish Pyrenees when his escape failed. Benjamin's reputation rose at the end of the 20th century when *The Arcades Project* (1999) was published in full. This ambitious work was an attempt to record an alternative narrative of reality that 'issued forth from unconscious collective memory'. Benjamin collected thousands of snippets of observation from shopping arcades in Paris, Berlin, Naples and Moscow: he noted street fashions, postures, advertising texts and images. He has come to be celebrated as a pioneer in studies of cultures of consumption.

BENTHAM, JEREMY (1748–1832) The English political philosopher, jurist and social reformer is best known to contemporary sociology for the use Michel **Foucault** makes of his prison reform schemes. It is unfortunate that Foucault's presentation of Bentham's design for the panopticon (a shape of prison that would allow constant surveillance of prisoners by guards) has led current students to regard him as a reactionary oppressor. In the context of the state of British prisons at the time, Bentham was a progressive radical (something recognised by his being made a citizen of France by the revolutionaries in 1792) who, among other good works, founded University College, London. He was a leading **utilitarian** and was responsible for the dictum that the proper object of all government was 'the greatest happiness of the greatest number'.

BERGER, PETER LUDWIG (1929–) Co-written with Thomas Luckmann, Berger's *The Social Construction of Reality* (1967) was extremely influential in making widely known in the English-speaking world the phenomenological approach to sociology pioneered by Alfred **Schutz**. He also wrote extensively on the sociology of religion (especially on **secularization** and **charisma**). Because he took the view that, in the context of liberal democratic societies, competing religious perspectives must undermine the authority and plausibility of religion, he was initially a strong advocate of the secularisation paradigm but in later work he argued that privatised relativistic religion could survive.

With his wife Birgitte Berger, he wrote *War over the Family* (1983): an attempt to steer a middle-way between the growing body of feminist criticism of the family and functionalist defences of the institution.

He also made important contributions to the sociology of development. His *Pyramids of Sacrifice* (1974) was a critique of both capitalist and communist approaches to the Third World but he later became convinced that capitalism offered the best opportunity for economic and social advance. He thus set himself against the popular **dependency** and **world-systems theories**. As a director of research programmes he was influential in reviving the Weberian sociological concern with the cultural conditions for economic development.

BERNSTEIN, BASIL (1924–2000) See **elaborated and restricted codes**.

BHASKAR, ROY (1944–) See **critical realism**.

BIAS In general usage this denotes the pre-supposition or preference that distorts our observations or conclusions. The term is also used by statisticians to refer to the difference between the hypothetical 'real' distribution of some characteristic in a population and the extent of it in a particular sample; the difference is referred to as a 'sampling bias'. For example, if we know from the census that the population of a particular town is 52 per cent female and find that in our postal survey only 45 per cent of respondents are female, we may multiply the scores given to the answers from women respondents to compensate for that bias and give a proportionate weighting to female responses.

BIRTH RATE   The birth rate for a society or population is normally the number of live births per 1000 people of all ages in one year.

BLACK   Brief terms used to describe groups of people are always contentious, as are the implied groupings of people so described. Even terms that are not intended to be insulting may come to be seen as such and require replacing by terms that have not yet acquired derogatory connotations. Over the 20th century 'Negro' gave way to 'coloured' and then to 'black'; the favoured term of 1960s US activists. By the end of the century 'black' was in turn giving way to 'Afro-American' and 'people of African origin'. Asians often object to the use of 'black' or 'non-white' because it treats as homogenous such various peoples as Africans, West Indians, Pakistanis and Indians. On the other hand, some insist that a simple black/white dichotomy is useful because it reflects the reality of racial discrimination in many societies.

Sociologists need to be alive to their choice of terms for ethnic groups both to avoid offence and to tap the worldviews of those who interest us. Surveys that use terms that do not correspond to respondents' categories and experience will not generate useful data. In qualitative research and small-scale surveys we can adopt the terms used by those we study. In large surveys (such as national censuses) researchers normally pilot a tentative classification in order to find the best combination of brevity and effectiveness.

BLACK-COATED WORKER   The term was coined by English sociologist David Lockwood to describe routine clerical and office workers in the days when a dark suit was required office wear. It was superseded by 'white-collar worker' as suit cloth became more varied in colour, more women entered the labour market, and offices became commonly heated to a temperature where suit jackets were removed on arrival.

BLACK ECONOMY   See **informal economy**.

BLAU, PETER (1918–2002)   One of the pioneers of detailed studies of **bureaucracy**, Blau extended Max Weber's work with an interest in the 'informality' that social interaction adds to formal organisations and with attention to the dynamic aspects of organisations. He was also important in developing **exchange theory** (with its central place for rewards and penalties in shaping social interaction) to explain both the stability of social structures and social change. He was unusual among exchange theorists for his stress on the constraints that social structures, though created by them, impose on actors.

BLOCH, MARC (1886–1944)   A French medieval historian and co-founder of the **Annales School** of historical research, Bloch is best known to sociology for his *Feudal Society* (1961): a magisterial study of feudal society as a whole that greatly informed our understanding of the differences between feudal and capitalist societies.

BLUE-COLLAR WORKER   Usually part of a contrast pair with 'white-collar worker', this is the preferred US term for an industrial manual worker and often carries the implication of union membership.

BLUMER, HERBERT (1900–87) Blumer published relatively little. The collection of essays *Symbolic Interactionism: Perspective and Method* (1969) is almost his entire corpus. But he exerted an enormous influence on US sociology from his position at the University of Chicago. He was very young, when on his mentor's sudden death, he was invited to take over George Herbert **Mead**'s lectures on social psychology. He gradually moved Mead's thought in an overtly sociological direction and coined the term **symbolic interactionism** to describe the end result.

Over a long career he made distinctive contributions to the study of race relations and collective behaviour but he is probably best known for his methodological critiques of positivism. In the classic Chicago tradition of preferring detailed ethnography to statistical analysis of survey data, he was particularly critical of what he saw as an inappropriate borrowing of the idea of the **variable** from the natural sciences. However, he also accepted the limitations of qualitative research. In an important commentary on W.I. **Thomas** and Florian Znaniecki's *The Polish Peasant in Europe and America* he conceded that the **life-history** data method of that study could not generate data that would provide a decisive test of the interpretations which the analysts made of the data.

BODY, SOCIOLOGY OF In the 1980s a number of sociologists promoted an interest in the embodied nature of the human being as a counter to the over-intellectualised tradition of sociology which tended to concentrate on the self as a mind with ideas, reasons and motives. Talcott **Parsons**, for example discusses the expressive, ritual and affective aspects of **socialisation** but gives pride of place to values and to a social system based on information. Obviously we inhabit bodies and that corporeal existence produces an interest in sex, in food and in emotions; we take pleasure in the co-presence of other bodies.

An acknowledgement of the body has been important in a variety of fields beyond those (such as the sociology of health) that are directly concerned with the body. Much religion, for example, is concerned with the management and discipline of the body. In the field of sociology of deviance too, it has been noted by **Foucault** and others how much punishment has focused on regulation of the offender's body. Our understanding of forms of social interaction such as conversation are improved by noting the role of physical gestures: 'looking someone in the eye' or tilting the head to show that you are ready to receive communication.

To date, much writing on the body has not gone beyond programmatic assertion and there has been some difficulty (in discussions of **gender**, for example) in reconciling the claim that the body is a vital part of the human person with the sociological axiom that social action is produced by culture interpretations of physical realities rather than directly by the realities themselves.

See **emotions, sociology of**.

BODY LANGUAGE The term 'body language' has quickly passed into everyday use and has no strict technical usage in sociology. Generally, it refers to the idea that our bodies are expressive and that people give off signals that may or may not be in line with what they are consciously trying to communicate. There are many lay-person's guides to body language that claim to be able to teach you how to recognise when someone is sexually attracted to you or lying, or both. Recently, **conversation analysis** has turned more of its attention to the co-ordination of talk and gesture, though to date, findings have been relatively limited.

BOURDIEU, PIERRE (1930–2002) Probably the leading French sociologist of his day, Bourdieu contributed both to substantive and methodological debates. Though, like many others, he wrestled with problems of **agency and structure**, his most influential work concerned the sociological significance of culture and **cultural capital**. He investigated in considerable detail the ways in which cultural attainments confer enduring socio-economic advantage and he highlighted the role of taste in entrenching and perpetuating social divisions. His empirical studies, for example in his book *Distinction* (1984), often focused on the meaning and maintenance of high-brow/low-brow distinctions within various cultural fields. According to Bourdieu, acquired patterns of taste, accomplishment and ways of behaving make up one's **habitus**.

BOURGEOISIE   This French term is used by Marxists to denote the capitalist class: those who monopolise the ownership of the capital. Note that in this sense capital is not confined to ready money but means more generally the resources required for production. In more general usage the term is a synonym for middle class.

See **petite bourgeoisie**.

BOWLING ALONE   See **social capital**.

BRAINWASHING   See **conversion**.

BRAVERMAN, HARRY (1920–76)   Although never a full-time academic, Braverman had a huge influence on the sociology of work. His *Labor and Monopoly Capital* (1974), which he described as an attempt to update Karl **Marx**'s *Capital*, sold over 120,000 copies. His argument that the **de-skilling** of modern work was the result of a deliberate attempt by capitalists to weaken organised labour was a product of 14 years as a factory metal

worker and then a long career in Trotskyite politics.

BRICOLAGE   This French term denotes the process of transforming the meaning of symbols and objects through novel uses and unexpected arrangements of normally unrelated things. The term was introduced to social science by Claude **Levi-Strauss**'s *The Savage Mind* (1967) to describe the practice of creating objects out of whatever came to hand where the structure and outcome were more important than the constituent elements. It later become common in cultural studies to refer to the way in which members of particular social groups create a novel style out of mundane items. An example is the 1980s punk use of safety pins and plastic bin liners in a novel dress style.

BUREAUCRACY   In general use this denotes a particular form of administration but it was given a more specific meaning by Max **Weber**. Weber's **ideal-type** of bureaucracy was constituted by the following: a high degree of specialisation and a clearly defined division of labour so that for every task there is clearly just one office responsible; a hierarchical structure of authority with unambiguous lines of control but with that control clearly limited; a formal body of rules to govern the business; a clear separation between the resources of the organisation and the private property of its officers; effective record-keeping; long-term employment; and promotion on the basis of merit or seniority. For Weber, the modern bureaucracy had the advantages of efficiency, predictability and equity.

Subsequent work has added a number of important observations. Robert K. **Merton** noted a potential inefficiency in bureaucracy. When officials are too deeply socialised into the culture of bureaucracy, rule-following can itself become the primary purpose and officials may so lose sight of the goals of the enterprise as inadvertently to subvert them.

Detailed studies of actual bureaucracies drew attention to the fact that bureaucrats could often be creative with the rules and the structure of the organisation. William H. Whyte's (1956) seminal study *Organization Man* amply demonstrated that the formal lines of command could often be by-passed by officials cultivating personal contacts outside the work place, that individual interests and personality could make a considerable difference to how the roles associated with offices were actually performed, and that for all the apparent formality, individuals remained creative. Studies of bureaucracy in relatively poor countries have shown that no number of rules prevents corruption. In effect, officials can threaten clients with a ritualistic attitude to the task (your passport application will take its proper place in an infinitely long queue) or you offer a bribe for the official to expedite your case.

The third major development came from the work of scholars influenced by Harold **Garfinkel**'s **ethnomethodology**. In Weber's view and in the view of those who added qualifications about informality within formal organisations, the rationality or formality of formal organisation was intrinsic: that is, it lay in the nature of the organisation itself. Building on Garfinkel's (1967) seminal 'Good organisational reasons for "bad" clinic records' essay, a number of scholars argued that rationality was actually a property, not of the organisation itself, but of the way that people in the organisation defended or accounted for their actions. David Sudnow's (1965) classic essay 'Normal crimes' makes the point with a study of plea-bargaining in the California court system. In order to keep the justice system working, offenders had to be persuaded to accept a plea-bargain: to avoid trial, the offender would plead guilty to a lesser offence than the one the police thought had been committed. What determined the choice of substitute charge was not the belief that the new offence had been committed but the fact that it carried a sentence sufficiently shorter than that which the offender would get for the original charge, to make the bargain attractive but not so much shorter that the defender and judge would think an injustice had been done. For example, the standard substitute for certain kinds of sex offence was 'loitering around a school yard' even if, as was usually the case, the offence took place nowhere near a school. Because public defenders and public prosecutors shared a common stock of practical knowledge, they were readily able to produce the required outcomes, by using 'rules of thumb', even though achieving the desired end required disregarding the penal codes. In effect, decisions were made and then the rules of the organisation were used to create the appearance of formal rule-following.

As automation has removed many of the more routine aspects of work, many business leaders have argued that the inefficiencies of the large-scale bureaucracy outweigh its advantages and there has been a move to smaller organisations with flatter structures that allow workers greater autonomy to be creative. However in public administration and government, the Weberian bureaucracy remains the preferred model mainly because its insistence on rule-following and formality is seen as a necessary protection against discrimination and prejudice.

BUTLER, JUDITH (1956–) Her (1990) *Gender Trouble* is a significant influence on feminist sociology and on thinking about sexuality. It argues that feminism has made a major mistake in arguing that 'women' form a group with common characteristics and interests and in viewing **patriarchy** in ways which assumed that masculine and feminine cultures would inevitably be built on male and female bodies. For Butler, gender is not a fixed attribute but an achievement. It is a performance; what you do at particular times, rather than who you are. The cultural configurations of gender with which we are familiar can be disrupted by subversive action; by creating gender trouble through the proliferation of genders and the transgression of received gender conventions.

Butler is a professor of comparative literature and rhetoric. Her work is famously opaque, so much so that in 1998 she came first in a bad-writing contest run by the journal *Philosophy and Literature*. Furthermore, she does not approach her studies as a social scientist and, stimulating though her ideas may be, they are not supported by any systematic evidence. Like a lot of what passes for theory in cultural studies, her work is largely conjecture and flamboyant calls to action.

C

CADRE   Generally the term denotes a small permanent core of soldiers or officials that can be expanded as necessary. Specifically it was used to denote elite groups within ruling communist parties.

CALVINISM   As a result of the Reformation in the 16th century, the western Christian Church divided in two. The part which continued to accept the authority of the Pope of Rome we now call the Roman Catholic Church; the rest is Protestantism, which is itself divided into a number of significantly different streams with an enormous variety of churches, sect and denominations within each. Calvinism is the ascetic strand of Protestant thought based on the teachings of the French reformer John Calvin (1509–64). That this version of Christianity became influential in Holland, Britain and the American colonies (the heart of the development of the modern economic system) explains why Max **Weber** suspected the relationship he elaborated in his writing on the **Protestant Ethic thesis**.

CAPITAL   In its general sense, capital is any asset, financial or otherwise, that is itself a source of income or can be used to produce income. For example, manufacturing equipment would be a part of an industrialist's capital. In mainstream economic theory, capital is one of the four means of production, along with land, labour and raw materials.

CAPITALISM   The term denotes that economic system in which goods are produced for profit (rather than one's own immediate use) and sold (rather than bartered) in a free market (rather than one in which the government regulates prices and the right to sell). Capitalism is further distinguished from previous economic systems such as **feudalism** in that there is an at-least-hypothetically-free market in labour, which is bought and sold like any other commodity. Workers in capitalism are free to sell their labour to the highest bidder rather than being themselves the property of a feudal lord or slave master. In a capitalist economy the means of production are privately owned and are typically concentrated in the hands of a small capitalist class.

Marxists believe that conflict is an essential feature of capitalist economies because the capitalists exploit the workers by paying their employees less than the value they produce. Marxists also hold that capitalism is essentially unstable. Karl **Marx** mistakenly believed that, owing to competition between manufacturers, capitalists would have to steadily increase the extent to which they exploited their workers and that eventually the workers would revolt. The 'contradictions of capitalism' would eventually lead to its overthrow and replacement by **socialism**, an economic system in which the means of production would be communally owned.

In fact no capitalist economy has ever been entirely free of government intervention. In times of crisis, such as the rationing associated with wartime shortages, the state has assumed control of whole sections of the market and even in peace-time the governments of most western states have regulated parts of the economy through, for example, selective taxation and the provision of unemployment benefit. At the other extreme to Marxist commentators, some right-wing reformers argue that many socio-economic problems arise because contemporary societies are not capitalistic enough.

CAPITALISM, TRANSFORMATIONS OF   Karl **Marx**'s predictions for the future transformation of capitalism proved entirely wrong. Where some form of socialist economy was established (as in Russia in 1917, and subsequently in the USSR's post-Second World War/empire, and in China after 1949) it was in marginally capitalist economies that lacked most of the features of the Marxist model and the shift resulted from forced political change, not from the internal contradictions of the economy. The mature capitalist economies that Marx studied proved remarkably robust. Far from being 'immiserated' (i.e. made more miserable) their working classes prospered and it was the socialist economies of communist eastern Europe that were undermined because of their failure to satisfy the economic aspirations of their people.

The main changes in capitalism have been the diffusion of capital, the division between ownership and control, and the globalisation of capital. The creation of the joint-stock company and the evolution of financial markets have given a large proportion of the population a small capital stake. Insurance companies, banks, pension funds and building societies (in the USA, savings and loan companies) invest savers' funds in the stock market and spread ownership. Increasingly those who own large amounts of capital no longer, as their grandparents did, invest it in the family enterprise but spread it thinly around a large number of enterprises. Whether these changing patterns of ownership make much difference to the behaviour of capital is unclear. Individual capitalists may have lost some ownership to institutional share-holders but, provided enterprises remain profitable, institutional owners tend not to interfere in the running of enterprises. That is, the ownership of capital may have been enormously broadened but control of it has not been.

The second major change is the **managerial revolution**: most commercial and productive enterprises are no longer run by the people who own them but by professional managers, hired for their expertise in management. Again this change may be less significant than it seems for sociologists' continued identification of a capitalist class because the most senior managers are normally rewarded in part with shares in the enterprises they manage. Thus their interests turn out to be rather similar to those of the owners.

The third change is the globalisation of capital. Over the first half of the 20th century, firms became larger as local companies were bought up or merged into national companies; in the second half of the century many national companies became international. The ending of national restrictions on the movement of capital and the creation of international markets in goods and services have allowed the growth of companies that now have a turnover greater than the gross domestic product of many small countries. This has given large companies an unprecedented freedom from government regulation in that they are able to switch operations from country to country in search of the most favourable operating environment. Capitalism is no longer simply a national-level phenomenon and national transformations of capitalism seem no longer on the cards.

This final change potentially has enormous consequences for sociology in that it challenges the importance of the state as well as the sociological assumption that societies are national societies.

See **globalisation**.

CARGO CULT   In the modern colonial era, Melanesia saw the periodic outbursts of a variety of **millenarian** movements which combined elements of indigenous and western beliefs into a view that religious rituals would persuade the gods to deliver to the natives the 'cargo' that the white man had stolen. The cargo cults would often promote ritualistic imitations of western behaviour (e.g. clearing ground for airstrips and making imitation radios). Worse, many added the belief that placing oneself entirely at the mercy of the gods (by, for example, burning houses and destroying cattle and grain stores) would hasten the delivery of the cargo. As local people came to understand western technology better, such cults became less common.

CARNIVAL   Carnivals are major annual festivities commonly occurring in Catholic countries in the week before Lent. Surpluses saved up during the year are extravagantly consumed before the period of 40 weekdays of fasting, commencing on Ash Wednesday, during which Christians prepare themselves for the Easter celebrations of Christ having risen from the dead. Common features of such events are playful symbolic reversals of social roles and a temporary relaxation of sexual mores.

See **Bakhtin**.

CARTESIAN   Cartesianism refers to the system of thought associated with the French philosopher and mathematician René **Descartes** (1596–1650). Of most relevance to social science is his pioneering work on the 'mind/body' problem. Descartes saw that there was a problem in understanding human action of the following sort: we can comprehend how a person moves a hand by contracting muscles in the arm, but we cannot understand in the same way how the wish to move the hand leads the arm-muscles to contract. One process seems wholly mechanical while the other crosses from the mind to the body. Descartes was fascinated by this mind/body interaction and speculated about where in the body this interaction might take place.

It is clear that Descartes's understanding of this process must be wrong; our consciousness must somehow arise from our body rather than sitting in some parallel dimension giving it orders. All the same, four hundred years on, we are still not much further advanced in our understanding than he was. Descartes's account also corresponds well with commonsense western experience of the mind and body. For many everyday purposes, we feel ourselves to be ghosts in the machines of our bodies. Given sociology's concerns with people's motives and intentions, sociology recurrently throws up the mind/body problem anew.

CASTE   As a system of social stratification, caste differs from class in its rigidity and in the basis of legitimation. Membership of castes is ascribed rather than achieved and social contact between castes is heavily constrained and ritualised. The exemplar is India. Although Hindu castes are described as occupational groupings, the basis is religious. Castes are held to differ in degrees of ritual purity. The highest castes are the priestly Brahmins (the 'twice-born') and the Kashatriyas: originally the warrior caste but now including major landowners. Next comes the Vaishyas (or business people) and the Sudras (or workers). Finally, and outside this structure, are the Harijans (or untouchables), also known as Dalits, who perform the most menial and degrading jobs and who are considered ritually impure. Within each of these broad divisions are innumerable smaller jati (or species or breeds) made up of specific regional or occupational groups.

Caste does not allow for individual social mobility; it is fixed because it is congenital.

Personal achievement will not change caste position and each jati is careful to prevent lower castes marrying in. The only possibility of this-worldly mobility is for an entire jati to improve its status relative to another by becoming more 'sanscriticised': that is, aping more closely the mores of the Brahmin caste. Hence the only method for achieving change within the system, reinforces rather than weakens it.

The system is kept in place by temporal power (like the medieval guilds, the jati can control entry and monitor its members) and by spiritual power. The ideological basis of control is formed by the Hindu notions of reincarnation and karma. The soul does not die with the body but is re-born. Precisely how you will be re-born depends on the balance of good or bad karma (or merit) you have accumulated. The major source of good karma is the correct performance of the rituals and social obligations associated with your caste. The pious conforming Hindu can hope for a better life next time around.

In principle, all post-independence governments of India have been opposed to caste but it has proved resilient.

CASTELLS, MANUEL (1942–)   See **information society**.

CATHARSIS   The idea originated with the ancient Greek philosopher Aristotle, who believed that watching a tragedy performed purged the spectator of powerful emotions. It has since come to mean any release of strong emotion. It has a particular meaning in media and cultural studies where it describes the counter-argument against those who fear imitation. The imitation argument is that watching scenes of sex or violence stimulates the viewer to imitate what is portrayed. The catharsis case is that watching scenes of violence provides the viewer with a vicarious alternative and thus purges the desire to engage in what is depicted. The difficulties of measuring the effects of mass media products are such that this debate is no nearer a clear resolution than it was 30 years ago.

CAUSATION, CAUSAL RELATIONSHIP   When two events occur in the same time and place, one just before the other, and the second seems highly unlikely to have occurred without the first, then we suppose there is a causal relationship between the two: dropping the lighted match on the petrol caused it to explode. When we see the same relationship repeated endlessly we may even derive a 'law'. Not only are we sure there is a causal relationship between heating a metal bar and it expanding, we can observe a regular relationship, for each type of metal, between the amount of heat and the amount of expansion.

Philosophers like to agonise about causation but most of us have no difficulty at all with the idea. What causes some anxiety for sociologists are (a) the particular nature of purposive action and (b) the use of 'functions' as causes.

Clearly, to the extent that humans have freedom, we cannot treat the causes of social action in exactly the same way as the heating of metals. I may say I have taken to my bed 'because' I have a cold but as it is possible for me to struggle off to the office sniffling, the cold is not causing me to have a day off; rather the cold is, in my circumstances (such as not much liking my job), a good reason for taking the day off. We can apply the same re-construction to some large-scale social phenomena such as voting for the Nazi party in 1930s Germany. When we list the causes of the rise of Nazism (resentment at the enfeeblement of Germany after the First World War and economic depression, for example) we are not claiming that these things forced Germans to vote for Hitler; we are using 'caused' as an abbreviation for 'in this particular set of circumstances and for these people, provided good reasons for'. This leaves unresolved the tricky question of whether there are universal standards of 'good reasons for' acting or whether good reasons are to some degree idiosyncratic or culturally variable. Sociologists are still divided over this matter.

The second problem concerns social functions. Sociologists are often concerned with the consequences or effects of some piece of social action or some institution. For example, we may argue that organised religion serves the important social function of creating a sense of social cohesion. There are problems borrowing the method of functionalist biology, in which organs are analysed in terms of their functions for the body as a whole, and these are discussed under **functionalism**. It is tempting to slide from saying that organised religion has the consequence of creating cohesion to suggesting that societies have organised religion because they require or wish social cohesion. In the case of the conscious individual there is no difficulty treating a consequence (something that comes after the act) as a cause (which must come before it) because we can bridge the time gap by asserting that the actor desired the consequence and acted as she did to bring it about: she wanted to make new friends so she joined a badminton club. But it is not equally appropriate to reason in this way for societies as a whole since, unlike the badminton enthusiast, societies do not have coherent wishes; this is the problem with any talk of **latent functions**.

CENSUS   This term is usually used to denote a government-sponsored universal and compulsory survey of all the individuals in the state. Censuses are extremely useful for social researchers precisely because they include everyone and because people have to answer. The information thus gathered is vastly more extensive than that which can be derived from any social survey. It also

provides us with benchmarks against which we can judge the representativeness of survey samples on certain criteria such as age, gender, religion or occupation. Nonetheless, there may be problems with compliance as people may resent the obligation to respond to the census and may therefore give false or misleading information.

CENTRAL TENDENCY   See **measures of central tendency**.

CENTRE AND PERIPHERY   These terms are used by sociologists in a conceptual rather than geographical sense; London, Paris, Washington, Stockholm, Helsinki and Moscow are all at the edges or corners of the countries of which they are the capitals but they are nonetheless the centres of their societies. The contrast pair is commonly used to draw attention to the unevenness of economic development and modernisation. The centre is more urbanised, more densely populated, wealthier, more commercialised, more diverse in its culture and more liberal in most matters than the periphery. In the first instance this is simply a matter of uneven development but there is often a reactive element. People in the periphery may exaggerate some of their differences from the centre in order to reinterpret what could be counted as a deprivation, as a virtue. If the centre becomes more secular, the peripheries may add an element of intent to their greater religiosity and take pride in this element of their supposed backwardness. For most of the 20th century, people in the highlands of Scotland, Sicily and the Carolinas contrasted themselves approvingly with the evils of the cosmopolitan world.

The contrast pair has also been used in international contexts. In his **world-systems theory**, Immanuel Wallerstein argues that from the 16th century onwards a capitalist world system began to develop with France,

Holland and England as its core. They became wealthier by exploiting other countries, which supplied raw materials and cheap (or, in the case of slavery, free) labour. Later Wallerstein added the intermediate category of semi-periphery to describe countries such as those of Latin America and South Korea that had attained a degree of industrialisation and hence were less dominated by the core.

CHAOS In everyday use, chaos means a disorderly mess. But the word has a technical meaning within the natural sciences. Some equations are chaotic in the special sense that, though they may look straightforward, they do not result in any predictable trend. Anyone who has lain in a bath and tried to guess when the next drip will fall from the tap has experienced this phenomenon. Water seeping from the tap adds to the droplet but it's impossible to guess exactly when it will splash down. In what seems like a paradox, some things in nature appear to follow a rule but are nonetheless unpredictable. The weather is believed to have this property. No matter how much you knew about today's weather, the weather in two weeks would still remain unpredictable. The weather may be deterministic, in that it is governed by equations to do with heat from the sun, evaporation of the oceans and so on, but it is chaotically deterministic.

To say that something is chaotic in this special sense does not just mean that it is too complex to predict in practice (like the ball on a roulette wheel) but that there are inherent limits to its predictability. Social scientists have been interested in chaos for various reasons: in part because some social phenomena (currency markets, for example) may themselves be chaotic in this technical sense but also because chaos speaks of limits to scientific prediction. The idea has thus proven attractive to advocates of **postmodernism** and to others worried about **determinism**.

CHARISMA; CHARISMATIC AUTHORITY In general usage, charisma is now simply the property of being attractive and telegenic; Presidents Kennedy, Reagan and Clinton were repeatedly described as charismatic. The claim would have been more compelling if they had been ugly and inarticulate and still became so popular because Max **Weber** borrowed the term for a 'gift of grace' from the Christian tradition to signify extraordinary (and often divine) powers claimed by or for an individual. Narrow sociological usage of charisma is almost exactly the opposite of popular usage in that what most clearly fits the Weberian notion, is drawing intensely loyal support when the leader who claims charismatic authority utterly lacks conventional sources of power and influence.

See **authority, routinisation of charisma**.

CHICAGO SCHOOL The University of Chicago housed one of the USA's first sociology departments (founded 1892) and its pioneering school of urban sociologists. What at the time seemed like its major achievement – the ecological model of the city as a series of concentric circles – is little attended to these days, but the department's commitment to detailed interpretative studies, what would now be called **ethnography**, left an enduring mark on the profession. Louis Wirth's (1928) *The Ghetto*, Henry W. Zorbaugh's (1929) *The Gold Coast and the Slum*, and Paul G. Cressey's (1932) *The Taxi Dance Hall: A Sociological Study in Commercialized Recreation and City life* are examples of classic Chicago work.

CHI SQUARE (χ^2) See **significance, tests of**.

CHODOROW, NANCY (1944–) In *The Reproduction of Mothering*, Chodorow (1978) examined the ways in which mothering reproduces gender identity. Using Freudian psychoanalytical ideas she argues that young girls remain 'mother-identified' even after the Oedipus complex symbolically separates the male child from his mother. For Chodorow the acceptance of the domestic ideal is the foundation of women's oppression. Although popular with feminists, her work, like that of **Butler**, **Irigaray** and **Kristeva** builds complex interpretative and inferential developments on a small and rather unsystematic evidential base.

CHOMSKY, NOAM (1928–) Widely accepted as the most renowned contemporary theorist of linguistics, Chomsky has claimed that the wide range of grammatical structures evident in language (the syntax of various languages) is underlain by common 'deep structures'. In *Syntactic Structures* he (1957) showed how a common deep linguistic structure (**deep structure**), combined with a straightforward set of transformation rules, could generate a very wide range of apparently dissimilar surface structures. In subsequent work he sought to apply a similar 'transformational' approach to semantics (meaning) and phonology (pronunciation). The significance of this claim for social science more generally is that his theory proposes that humans are in some sense innately highly prepared for language, and if they are hard-wired for language, then humans cannot be wholly the product of learning from their environment as other social scientist have often supposed. His view about this innate ability provides a striking challenge to popular conceptions of human nature.

Chomsky is also widely known for his strident critiques of western and particularly US foreign policy and militarism. He is always careful to claim that his political views and linguistic theory are wholly separate enterprises; indeed there is very little that is conventionally left-leaning about his linguistic theories. His political writings, though sharply observed, often appear tendentious.

CHURCH See **religious organisations**.

CICOUREL, AARON (1928–) Long associated with **Garfinkel**, **ethnomethodology** and **conversation analysis**, Cicourel (1964) first became widely known in sociology because of his book *Method and Measurement in Sociology*. This work was ethnomethodological in the sense that it concentrated on the practices through which sociologists derived, recorded and in a sense created the phenomena in which they were interested. However, unlike strictly ethnomethodological studies which do not seek to engage with the worlds they document, this study assumed that sociologists would have an interest in his ethnomethodological critique and even reform their procedures in response. Subsequently, Cicourel turned to more substantive sociological analysis particularly in medical and educational sociology.

CIRCULATION OF ELITES This phrase, about all that is left of the legacy of Vilfredo Pareto (a theorist Talcott **Parsons** thought central to sociology), captures perfectly his rejection of the progressive views of thinkers such as Karl **Marx** and Herbert **Spencer**. Pareto first coined the term 'elites' to avoid talking of a ruling class (with all that implied about the economic base of political power) and argued that, rather than there being an innate tendency for societies to develop in a liberal and democratic direction, two types of elites regularly replaced each other. The types were defined by psychological characteristics: lions were conservative; wolves were innovative but untrustworthy.

CITIZEN Initially the term was used by the Greeks to denote members of that small elite within a city-state that had political rights and it was contrasted with a 'subject': someone who had a master. Until the rise of the

nation-state, citizenship was either entirely absent or restricted to a very few. The modern nation-state represented an important break with earlier formations in that its legitimacy was based on its ability to embody the will and aspirations of an entire people who were in some sense all equal participants in a horizontal fellowship. This egalitarian rhetoric was eventually given substance in the expansion of the franchise until, by the early part of the 20th century, most industrial democracies gave the vote to all their members.

T.H. **Marshall** expanded the idea of citizenship by defining it as the status of a person who is a full member of a community and arguing that it had three components. First, there were civil rights (such as the right to freedom of expression, access to information, freedom of association and equality before the law); second, political rights (expressed mainly as the right to choose the government); and third there were social and economic rights: Marshall regarded the right to social welfare as an important safeguard against sections of the population being enfranchised in theory but in effect excluded from society by poverty.

Marshall tended to assume that the three components are acquired in the order set out above. However, feminist authors have noted that women's acquisition of citizenship entitlements has not necessarily followed that of men with, for example, voting rights often preceding full equality before the law.

Since the collapse of communism in the late 1980s there was been renewed interest in the notion of citizenship. With socialism no longer seeming a viable alternative to capitalism and the old rhetoric of state intervention unpopular, critics of capitalism have turned again to the ideas of **civil society** and citizenship.

CITY   A city is distinguished from towns and villages by it greater size, by the range of institutions its houses, and by the wealth of activities possible within its boundaries. The first cities naturally appeared in fertile areas where the surrounding countryside was sufficiently productive to liberate part of the population from agricultural work and to support a range of specialist trades. In England, the importance of the national Christian church was such that a city was marked by the presence of a cathedral. The defining characteristic of a cathedral was not its size (though they were very large) but its role as the administrative headquarters of a bishop and hence as a centre for public administration.

CIVIL INATTENTION   In *Behaviour in Public Places* Erving **Goffman** (1963a) noted a variety of tacit rules that maintain civility between strangers in public. Civil inattention denotes the ways in which we show others that we are aware of their presence without causing offence by intrusively attending to them. Like many of Goffman's ideas, it was obvious once he described it. What made Goffman such an influential figure was that he was the first sociologist to pay systematic attention to the small details of interaction ritual that sustain social life. In many western societies, civil mattention is a particularly important accomplishment for women to develop if they are to avoid the intrusive attention of heterosexual males.

CIVIL RELIGION   This denotes a set of beliefs, rites and symbols that indicate and celebrate the individual's relationship to the civil society, nation and state, and claim divine support for the nation's history and destiny. The term originated with Jean-Jacques Rousseau's distinction between the religion of man, which was a private matter between the individual and God, and the religion of the citizen, which was a public matter of the individual's relationship with the society and government. A civil religion binds all members to society, instructs them in their duties and, if necessary, mobilises them to war in support of the state.

Much influenced by the **functionalism** of Talcott **Parsons**, Robert Bellah argued that there was a US civil religion, distinct from the Christianity to which most Americans belonged. Key texts are the Declaration of Independence (with its claims for divine approval) and President Lincoln's Gettysburg Address. The 'feast days' of this civil religion are Thanksgiving, Veterans' Day and Memorial Day. The rituals are saluting the flag and singing 'God Bless America'.

The idea has been vigorously criticised. It may well be that certain manifestations of US patriotism perform the same social functions as institutional religion (creating a sense of cohesion, for example) but that does not mean it is a religion: a fever and an electric blanket both make me feel hot but they are not the same thing. The frequent references to God in US civil pronouncements may reflect either the habits of the age or the politician's desire to enlist as many allies as possible. We know that many patriotic rituals are performed without the deep involvement we would expect from a religion, and where we do find strong entanglement of religious faith and patriotism, it is because those people are religious in the conventional sense and believe that God is on their side. There is no need to claim a distinct civil religion and little clear evidence for one.

Less contentiously the term is used to describe religions that actually deify the state or its rulers: Confucianism in pre-Communist China and state Shinto in Japan are examples. It is also used to describe one aspect of conventional religion: acting as a guarantor of national identity and a promoter of national interests. For example, the Catholic Church has long played an important social role as guarantor of Polish national identity in the face of repeated conquest and oppression by more powerful neighbours on all sides: Lutheran Swedes, Lutheran Germans and Russians (who were first Orthodox Christians and then atheistic communists). As the only institution that was not taken over or severely compromised by Soviet communists, the Catholic Church performed a vital function of cultural defence. So long as it did so it was supported by many Poles who were not strongly committed to its religious teachings and ritual practices; hence its depiction as a civil religion.

CIVIL RIGHTS   Sometimes used as a synonym for human rights, civil rights may have a slightly narrower meaning. Both notions imply that all of us should be treated equally, irrespective of such characteristics as wealth, colour, religion or gender. Civil rights suggests more: particularly both the protection of the law and protection from the state. In the USA the Bill of Rights makes human rights, civil rights. In the UK, where, until the incorporation of the European Convention on Human Rights in 1998, there was no written protection of such rights, it is more common to talk of civil liberties.

Although the language of civil rights is often used by campaigners to suggest that they have a case that no decent person could refuse, what should count as the basic human or civil rights is itself a matter of political argument. The obvious difficulty is that any extensive list will contain irreconcilable items. For example, if a religion supports the view that women should be subordinate to men, then women's rights and religious liberty will clash.

CIVIL RIGHTS MOVEMENT (US)   In theory the subordinate status of blacks in the USA ended with the victory of the Union states in the Civil War of 1861–65. Blacks were left formally free but in reality still enslaved. In the south they were denied the vote and the protection of the law, were segregated and given only the most rudimentary public services. Slavery was replaced by 'Jim Crow'.

The Jim Crow laws were named after a character in a pre-Civil War minstrel show. Thomas Dartmouth Rice, a white actor, became famous for 'blacking up', mimicking black vaudeville artists and performing a comic song-and-dance routine in which he repeatedly sang: 'Weel about and turn about and do jis so/Eb'ry time I weel about I jump Jim Crow'. Jim Crow laws were designed to achieve, in the new urban setting, the degree of segregation and subservience that informal pressures and patterns of interaction had previously maintained in the rural south. In Alabama, white nurses could not be asked to nurse black men; buses, toilets and restaurants were segregated; inter-racial pool and billiards games were prohibited; mixed race marriages were void. Georgia segregated public parks, restaurants, burial grounds, barber shops and psychiatric hospitals and required that segregated baseball grounds be two blocks apart. Mississippi not only banned inter-racial marriage but also made it an offence to print, publish or circulate arguments in favour of such mixing. Furthermore, in all the southern states complex laws were used to make it difficult (if not downright impossible) for blacks to register to vote.

The civil rights movement may be dated from the 1955 Montgomery boycott of buses. The next nine years saw considerable conflict as southern blacks, led by trusted clergymen and aided by white liberals from the north, staged a variety of usually non-violent protests. Racist whites attacked the protestors and American public opinion was scandalised by the white violence, by the failure of the white authorities to control it and by open connivance in the flouting of the law. President Lyndon B. Johnson used his considerable political capital to force through Congress the sweeping Civil Rights Act of 1964 (which outlawed segregation of public facilities) and the Voting Rights Act 1965 (which used the power of the federal government to effectively enfranchise blacks). These and other legislative actions did not end racial conflict or immediately redress black grievances but they removed the major injustices that had been the focus of the civil rights movement.

CIVIL SOCIETY   The term was first popularized by Adam **Ferguson** and his colleagues in the **Scottish Enlightenment** of the late 18th century in contrasting the democratic institutions of the West with the despotisms of the East. Later it came to mean the inter-locking array of non-governmental institutions that fills the space between the family and the state: churches, trade unions, voluntary associations such as the Freemasons and the Buffaloes, and sporting clubs are examples. A large and active civil society is held to be essential for a pleasant and effective society in that it brings individuals together outside of their family bonds in non-commercial relationships and acts as a counter to the power of the state. The defining feature of **totalitarian** states (such as those of communist eastern Europe) is that they destroy civil society, by either banning those forms of it they do not control or taking control of them.

CIVILISATIONS, CLASH OF   This phrase was popularised by US political scientist Samuel Huntington's use of it for a 1993 article which was later expanded into a book. The civilisations in question are the West (Protestant and Catholic Christian), Islamic, Hindu, Orthodox Slav, Confucian, Japanese, Latin American and 'possibly' African. He argues that the main divisions of the post-Cold War world will be around culture rather than ideology or national identity. Although nation-states will remain the principal international actors, they will, like family members rallying round, form alliances based on shared culture. Second, he anticipates that resentment at western cultural penetration and political domination will cause the other civilisations to oppose the West, which will be weakened by relative economic and demographic decline. Accordingly, he proposes that western societies should strengthen commitment to their core civilisational values, stop interfering with other civilisations, and concentrate on maintaining a stable balance of power between the core states of rival civilisations.

Huntington has been much criticised by those who on principle reject the idea that religion is important in international relations, for exaggerating the internal cohesion of his civilisations (see **orientalism**). He has been accused of being an ideologue for the West, though his willingness to treat other cultures as civilizations with virtues suggests otherwise. He has been faulted for over-looking research which suggests that all cultures, as they become richer, tend to change in similar directions. It is claimed that he exaggerates the inherent conflict between civilisational values: are Islamic values really that different to Christian ones? His concern over the relative financial decline of the West, reasonable in the early 1990s when the Asian economies were booming, a decade later seemed like a poor prediction. The thesis is also not supported by studies of current wars; most still concern national rivalries between neighbours (irrespective of sharing a civilisation) and secessionist struggles.

Ironically, Huntington might become right for the wrong reasons. The 2003 Iraq war and other US foreign policy initiatives have had the effect of greatly increasing anti-American sentiment in the Muslim world.

CIVILISING PROCESS   See **Elias**.

CLAN   A clan is a unilineal kin group (i.e. descent is traced back to one parent, not both) claiming descent from a common ancestor, and is often represented by a totem. Clans can be either matrilineal (that is recruiting the children of female members) or, more commonly, patrilineal (recruiting the children of male members) and are often internally divided into lineages.

CLASS   All societies have some form of stratification. The simplest societies allocate duties and rights on the basis of age and gender. Hindu India divides people by **caste**. Feudal societies divide people by **estate** or station. Modern industrial societies are divided by class. A variety of ways of describing class all have in common attention to the economy and the organisation of production. For Karl **Marx** and Marxists, the crucial divide is between those who own the means of production (the capitalist class) and those who have to live by selling their labour (the proletariat or working class). Although there are important fractions within these classes, this basic division is the key to understanding much else about societies based on capitalist economies.

Max **Weber** builds his class scheme around the twin pillars of property ownership and market situation. He recognised major differences within the mass of the population who did not own capital. Professionals who possess highly valued and scarce skills are able to demand greater rewards and greater control over their working lives then the unskilled who, precisely because they are readily replaceable, have a relatively weak position in the market place.

In the 1970s, when it was clear that western class structures were not falling into the shape Marx expected, a number of neo-Marxists attempted to resolve the anomaly of the professional middle class. Nicos **Poulantzas** followed Louis **Althusser** in arguing that the mode of production (and hence class) could not be defined simply by economic considerations; definition needed also to incorporate political considerations (supervisors versus non-supervisors) and ideological ones (mental versus manual labour). Erik Olin Wright distinguished ownership and control of the means of production. Although both scholars saw themselves as updating the Marxist theory of class, their conclusions seem remarkably similar to the position where Weber started.

In practice, much social research is based on neither Marx nor Weber. The Marxist model has the advantage of being based on a clear theory but it is of little value for research because the capitalist class narrowly defined is extremely small compared to those who do not own the means of production and is rarely available for study. The Weberian model is more useful for research in that it generates a larger number of similar-sized classes but, until the 1970s when John **Goldthorpe** and his colleagues developed a class model on Weberian principles that was adopted internationally, almost all research on class used the rather ad hoc divisions that had been created by government officials in the early 20th century. The British Registrar-General's classification of occupations was a creative mix of attention to wealth and typical pay levels, some notions of autonomy and discretion, and an estimate of social worth, so that routine non-manual workers were ranked higher than skilled manual workers: a reflection of the general preference for clean over dirty work. On the grounds that they required lengthy periods of education and were widely respected, clergymen and teachers were ranked higher than their salaries would merit.

Unease about the detailed rankings of occupations in most schemes, lack of detailed information about people's jobs and pay, the relatively small numbers of people in even large-scale and expensive surveys, and the importance of other variables (such as age, gender and religion) encourage social researchers to simplify class classifications and in much social research the effects of class are explored with just two class categories: manual and non-manual.

Arguments about how we should define class and the complex technical problems in collecting and analysing information might suggest that the notion is pointless. It is not. Over the second half of the 20th century a vast body of social research pointed repeatedly to the enduring importance of social class in determining life-chances, social attitudes, patterns of consumption and political preferences.

At the end of the 20th century it became fashionable to argue that class was no longer of great social importance. Technological evolution was removing swathes of manual work and eroding the differences between blue-collar and white-collar work. Greater prosperity and cheaper goods meant that the gross differences between classes in appearance and material possessions had gone. Almost all households in the USA and UK have cars, televisions, central heating, a wide range of clothing and the like. In the 1930s, members of the working class were readily distinguishable from the middle classes: they smelt and were shabbily dressed. With the exception of small segments at the top and bottom, most American or British people are now superficially similar. Technological evolution has also reduced the centrality of work in the sense of how much time it takes up. In the 1950s it was common for people to work 10 hours each weekday and at least half of Saturday. The typical working week is now only half of that. In Europe at least, most jobs now provide a month or more of paid holidays in addition to the large number of public holidays. Hence people now spend far less time at work and with work colleagues and more time with family and friends. All of these changes add up to good reason for supposing that how we earn our living is less significant now than it was in 1950 and that the key to social identity lies not in production but in consumption.

This is an exaggerated picture. The lives of white-collar and blue-collar workers may be superficially similar and there has been a noticeable decline in deference, but it is still the case that social realities (such as health, income, longevity, values) remain influenced by class. And even the core of the consumerist idea is suspect; increasing prosperity has allowed the bulk of the population to enjoy a larger number of the same consumer goods but rich people have their own 'top end' of consumption that is denied to others and the tastes of university-educated professional workers still differ markedly from those of manual workers.

See **class consciousness, occupational scales, proletarianisation**.

CLASS CONFLICT   It is an essential part of Marxist thought that the social classes identified by the ownership (or otherwise) of capital be in conflict. Classes have irreconcilable collective interests and the war between them is the engine for social evolution. Modern capitalism has actually been characterised by an almost complete absence of class conflict. Groups of workers have pressed for greater rewards and better conditions but such contests have often involved workers competing against each other and have not challenged the fundamental nature of capitalism nor the fact of a class system. In the 20th century the major threats to capitalist societies came not from class but ethnic and national conflict: for example, the two world wars and the Spanish Civil war.

CLASS CONSCIOUSNESS, CLASS-FOR-ITSELF; CLASS-IN-ITSELF   With any form of classification system there is a question of whether those we classify see themselves in the same way as we see them. All the **class** schemes discussed allocate people by objective characteristics; people either own or do not own the means of production, have similar positions in the labour market, and their jobs offer a certain level of freedom and discretion, irrespective of what they think about those characteristics. There are occasions when sociologists are interested in the consequences of class that are not mediated by some form of awareness. For example, there is a strong association between class and the incidence of certain illnesses. However, much sociological interest in class supposes that the

members of a class share common beliefs and values and act in concert; people have a subjective or personal appreciation of their class position and some sense of group identity: objective class position should be matched by class consciousness. Karl **Marx** distinguished between class-in-itself (the objective reality) and class-for-itself (the awareness of this and the development of an appropriate political response). When the objective and subjective do not match we may either doubt the value of our classification system or find particular explanations of why people are blind to their common position.

The failure of the working class to act in concert is usually described by Marxists as **false consciousness** and explained by the ideological work of the capitalist class promoting various forms of divide and rule. For example, a chauvinist upper class may stimulate racial and ethnic rivalries so that white workers think of themselves as superior to black workers.

A less contentious explanation of the absence of class consciousness is that changes in the **class structure** (see below) mean that throughout the 20th century there has been too much movement through classes for people to associate strongly with them. Classes have been more like hotels than stable communities; people have been passing through.

A third explanation is that Marx was simply wrong about the importance of social class as he defined it.

CLASS, STATUS AND PARTY   Max **Weber** regarded this trinity as providing a fairly comprehensive description of the major divisions in modern society. Class (or market situation) was the objective condition of place in the economy, defined by wealth and earning opportunities produced by possessing scarce skills. Because it described similarities of circumstance, class might form the basis for occasional collective action but there was no implication of a necessary class consciousness.

Status referred to actual groupings of people defined by specific positive or negative social estimations of honour who have a sense of common identity (visible in attempts to protect their privileges, in common customs and in excluding marriage patterns): Ivy league college-educated professionals would be an example of a status grouping within a class structure. A Hindu jati would be a status grouping in a **caste** structure. Political parties may be based on class or status or some other identity such as regional minority. In essence, Weber was countering the simple Marxist model of class by drawing attention to the diversity of sources of division.

CLASS STRUCTURE, CHANGE IN   Since the late 19th century there have been major changes in the class structure of modern economies because the nature of work has changed. The shrinking of agriculture (and other forms of primary production such as fishing, mining and logging) has continued as technological developments have allowed fewer people to do more. Large numbers left the land and moved into manufacturing. In the 1950s the white-collar middle class began to grow relative to the manual working class and by the end of the 20th century white-collar had outstripped blue-collar work. Precisely how the class structure of advanced societies has changed will depend on how we define, measure and divide class. For example, the model devised by US Marxist Erik Olin Wright produces a much larger working class than does that used by John H. **Goldthorpe** and European colleagues. Nonetheless, when either model is applied to historical and contemporary data the general patterns of change remain the same.

CLERGY   Originally a term identifying an official of the Christian Church and now applied widely to professional leaders in any religious tradition, it shares a common root with 'clerk': a reminder of the Middle Ages when literacy was largely a preserve of the church.

CLIENTALISM, CLIENT–PATRON RELATIONSHIP
See **patron-client relations**.

CLOSED MIND   See **open and closed mind**.

CLUSTER SAMPLING   This is an alternative to random sampling in selecting respondents to represent a general population for study purposes. A random sample for a postal survey could be constructed by using some formula such as picking every 1000th address from a zip or postal code list. The cluster alternative is to start with some organising principle (such as dividing post codes by the social class of the area) and then selecting one wealthy area, one middling area and one poor area, and picking a set number of respondents from each. Cluster sampling is often used because it is cheap and quick; if you plan to conduct face-to-face interviews you want your respondents to be in close groups rather than spread around the country. But it will produce a distorted image of the general population if the initial principle of clustering is mistaken. For example, a survey of political attitudes may produce unrepresentative results if, unknown to the survey analysts, an area chosen to produce wealthy people has become popular with staff of the local university (who are likely to be unusually cosmopolitan and liberal).

COERCION   This denotes the use of force (or the threat of force) to achieve a particular purpose.

See **power**.

COGNITION   Mental life can be described as having two components: thinking or knowing, and feeling. Cognition, the first component, is concerned with perception, language, memory and problem solving.

See **affect**.

COGNITIVE DISSONANCE   Dissonance (contrasted with consonance and resonance) was originally a musical term denoting a clash of sounds or an unpleasant combination of notes. In the 1950s Leon Festinger used the term in a study of behaviour that was inconsistent with knowledge (or cognition). Why, when we know that smoking is very bad for us, do we continue to do it? Festinger supposed that we all have some deep need for consistency and that we will attempt to harmonise our beliefs and behaviour, either by changing the behaviour or selectively re-shaping what we know (every smoker has an uncle who smoked heavily and lived to 80). Looked at closely, Festinger's work does not actually explain anything but the term became extremely popular.

COHABITATION   A pompous term for 'living together' used to describe people who, in the view of the speaker, should be married, this is slipping out of use simply because the relationship it describes is now so common in the West as to be unremarkable. Infinitely preferable to 'cohabitee' is the Scots 'bidie-in' (from 'bide' meaning to stay).

COHORT, COHORT ANALYSIS   Originally a term for a unit of the Roman army (10 of which made up a legion), this is now used to describe any group of people with the same time-specific experiences: for example being born, entering university or joining the police force in a particular year. The cohort is important because its experience represents one of three possible explanations of change. Suppose we find in a large survey that the band of people aged 60 and above are much

more likely than the younger age bands to attend church. This could be explained by an ageing effect: as we get older and nearer our deaths we become more mindful of our souls. It could be explained by an historical change that came after this age band formed its habits: the removal of a prohibition on secular forms of leisure on a Sunday may have permanently made church-going relatively unattractive. Or, and this is the cohort effect, this band may have had some common experience which made it unusually church-going. Distinguishing these is important. If it is the first, church membership will remain stable; if it is the second it will decline; if it is the third, it may well bounce back.

It is often difficult to untangle ageing, historical and cohort effects in survey data but the fact that they are different should restrain us from jumping too quickly to conclusions from observed social trends.

COLLECTIVE ACTION, COLLECTIVE BEHAVIOUR Although preferring one over the other sometimes reflects underlying assumptions about the nature of the matter in hand, more often these terms are used interchangeably to describe social phenomena that range from the crowd, as the least enduring and structured, to the professionally-led social movement – the most organised and enduring expression of collective action. The term implies the following: the collective action/behaviour has some specific and finite goal; that goal involves remedying or redressing some wrong; and ordinary people are active. Rioting in protest against high food prices; campaigning to end racial segregation; mobilising sentiment against the transporting of live animals are all examples.

See **social movement**.

COLLECTIVE CONSCIENCE   This is the English translation of the term popularised by Emile **Durkheim** (1912) in his *Elementary Forms of the Religious Life* to refer to the shared beliefs and moral attitudes that give cohesion to a society. The collective conscience is particularly important in simple societies based on **mechanical solidarity**. In complex modern societies a common conscience is less important as an integrating principle because the advanced division of labour creates inter-dependency irrespective of a collective conscience.

COLLECTIVISATION This denotes the amalgamation of small peasant holdings into large agricultural units under state direction and was a feature of Stalin's agricultural policy in the Soviet Union in the 1930s.

COLLECTIVISM Specifically this refers to a political doctrine that advocates communal or state ownership of the means of production and distribution or a political system based on such a doctrine.

COLONIALISM Most generally this is the political rule of one nation, country or society by another, usually some way off. But it now more commonly refers to the domination of large parts of the world by white Christian European states in the 19th and 20th centuries. States differed considerably in they ways they colonised. The British often tried to expropriate the wealth of their colonies without disrupting native society and culture; for example, until the middle of the 19th century there was considerable resistance to allowing Christian missionaries to evangelise in the colonies. The preferred model of exploitation was to rule indirectly through local potentates. The French empire took the very different form of imposing French culture and ruling directly through French officials, with the colonies being given a place in the Paris government.

COMMAND ECONOMY As the name suggests, this is a structure of production and distribution in which decisions about what to produce result not from market forces but from central government direction. The economies of the 20th century communist states were largely command. Although they permitted individual initiative in small-scale enterprises, major enterprises such as mining, heavy industry and transport were run by government agencies which decided how many tractors should be made, of what quality and at what price they should be sold. Over the longer term, command economies are generally inefficient because workers have little direct stake in the success of the enterprise, consumer preferences have little impact on the economy and the goals of managers easily shift from running their enterprises efficiently to flattering their political masters.

It should be noted that in times of crisis (during major wars, for example) the governments of the most free-market oriented economies have been willing to take command of vital interests.

COMMODIFICATION The term may denote a distinguishing feature of market (normally capitalist) economies; rather than producing goods and services to satisfy their own needs, people produced 'commodities' to be sold in a market. Especially when used by Marxists, the term is pejorative and rests on the romantic notion that struggling to produce enough to meet one's own immediate needs is somehow more noble (even if less efficient) than producing for a market.

Arlie Russell **Hochschild** has drawn attention to the ways in which emotions are now marketed as commodities. Dating clubs, commercial child-minding services, party planners; such emotional-work services test the boundaries we place between what may reasonably be bought and sold and what should involve personal commitments beyond commerce. That we have such boundaries is clear from usage: the 'commodification of steel manufacture' is not condemnatory; 'the commodification of sex' is. All the same, as the service sector grows in free market economies more and more areas of life are likely to become commodified.

Still, the use of 'commodification' which implies or asserts that modern relationships have become dominated by the cash nexus is usually mistaken. Even in advanced capitalist societies, non-commodified work is an important part of the social world. Almost half of most people's time is taken up with non-monetarised (i.e. not directly paid) work: domestic labour is a very large part of that. A 2000 survey showed that 45 per cent of Americans over 18 spent five or more hours a week in unpaid voluntary and charity work outside the home. It remains common for people to engage in unpaid reciprocity: one person helps a friend move house; that friend helps another repair a car and so on. And even when money changes hands it is often the case that the money has only a tangential relationship to the activity and that making a profit is not the primary purpose of the exchange. For example, a housewife regularly provides hot meals for a confused elderly female neighbour; a relative of the woman insists on giving the helper a large sum of money as a Christmas present. Or someone with easy access to horse manure gives a trailer load to a neighbour who grows roses and the rose-grower insists on paying for the delivery. This sort of loose reciprocity, although it involves money, is closer to gift-giving than to commodified exchange and it remains extremely common, even in advanced industrial capitalist societies.

COMMON-SENSE KNOWLEDGE   At one level, sociologists are interested in common-sense knowledge because this is the knowledge that people use to make judgements and navigate their way around the world. **Goffman** is a leading analyst of commonsense

understood in this way. However some sociologists, notably **ethnomethodologists** and **social phenomenologists**, are more interested in the character of common-sense knowledge, particularly in contrast to what they assume scientific knowledge is like. For example, though the words used in everyday speech are not subject to rigorous definition and there are no set criteria for establishing what other people mean or are talking about, people manage well enough with this seemingly unsystematic body of knowledge. From this observation, ethnomethodologists and phenomenologists have gone on to argue that sociology follows a false path when it tries to ape the sciences and should content itself with the more everyday credentials of common-sense knowledge. Such arguments typically rest on an exaggerated sense of the 'scientificness' of communication within science and overlook the way that commonsense is refined in various institutions such as the law. The divide to which they wish to draw attention does not actually exist in the form they suppose.

See **ad-hocing**.

COMMUNAL VIOLENCE   The downside of **community** is that the strength of social bonds within it is often matched by ill-feeling to those outside the community. 'Communal violence' is often used to denote widespread murderous attacks by one group (usually defined by religion and ethnicity) on its neighbours, where what is at stake are not national boundaries but the relative power and prestige of groups within the state.

COMMUNE   This generally denotes a self-selecting group of people living and working together, sharing some or all of their possessions, and assisting each other with domestic tasks and child-rearing. Unlike extended families or small villages, most communes have a specific purpose. Most have been religious in origin, united in the belief that their communal way is divinely ordained and that they are creating heaven on earth. Those that have survived more than one generation have paid attention to the two great threats: members being seduced by the outside world and falling out among themselves. Successful communes have managed to isolate themselves and have developed mechanisms for defusing potential conflict. The Hutterites, for example, farm using traditional methods which prevent them becoming too prosperous and when they grow beyond a size where face-to-face relations can be maintained, they buy new land and start another commune.

Most communes have been short-lived. Many were created in the expectation that a messiah would soon come and end this world and did not survive the disappointment of their **millenarian** dreams. Some died out because they failed to attend to the basic requirements for self-reproduction. For example, the Shakers, a 19th century US communitarian sect, prohibited all sexual activity; as they failed to maintain a supply of adult recruits, the commune literally died out, leaving only a simple style of furniture design as their legacy.

In the second half of the 20th century, communes in Western Europe and North America were also formed on secular bases. Usually in urban areas and sometimes in the context of 'squats', which repossessed abandoned buildings, these faced the same threats to survival as the earlier religious communes and were uniformly short-lived.

If spelt with a capital letter, the term refers to the revolutionary government established in Paris in 1870–71.

COMMUNICATION   While definitions differ according to the theoretical frame of reference, they all include the following five fundamental elements: an initiator, a recipient, a mode of communication, a message and an effect.

Humans differ from other animals in the vast capacity for communication that language gives. One of the aspects of communication that particularly interests sociologists is the way that modern technologies allow time and space to be transcended. Writing, printing, and such technological forms of communication as the radio, television, telegraph, fax, mobile phone and e-mail all allow easy storage of communicated information and almost instant communication across great distances. The consequences of modern communication are paradoxical. On the one hand, effective communication allows effective control and there is much concern about the enhanced powers of the modern state to monitor its citizens through such things as the recording of credit card payments and closed-circuit television monitoring of shopping precincts. On the other hand, the Internet and the mobile phone have been extremely effective in allowing individuals to subvert government attempts at censorship and information control. A good example was the 2003 failure of the Chinese government to restrict news of an outbreak of Sudden Acute Respiratory Syndrome (or SARS).

See **time-space distanciation**.

COMMUNISM   This term generally denotes the practical aspect of **Marxism**: the belief that human societies can be organised in a thoroughly egalitarian way by having the means of production commonly owned and thus removing the basis for class conflict. Without class, there would be no need for a state to protect the interests of the ruling class and it would wither away.

Marx and Engels (1967) used the term in the title of *The Communist Manifesto* (published in 1848) but for most of the 19th century radical parties that adopted some or all of the Marxist programme called themselves **socialist**. It was not until 1918, after the successful Russian revolution, that the Russian Social-Democratic Labour party changed its name to the Communist Party of the Soviet Union.

COMMUNITY   Although often used in the geographical sense as a synonym for neighbourhood, the term does have a quite precise meaning in sociology, derived from Ferdinand Tönnies' (1887) *Gemeinschaft und Gesellschaft* (or *Community and Society*). The community of the pre-industrial rural society had the following characteristics. A small group of people interacted with each other over many years and many separate spheres of life: work, leisure, church, family. Relationships were many-sided, intimate and enduring, and created networks of reciprocal obligation that survived from one generation to the next. The stability and close contacts allowed considerable social cohesion.

In the urban industrial society very large numbers of people interact with each other over very narrow and specific tasks and only briefly before moving on. Many relationships are based on contract. I employ the plumber to fix my shower and pay him the agreed sum. I need never see him again; he will not call me when he needs help and I am not obliged to marry his daughter. The pre-industrial village dweller dealt with the same 20 people all his or her life; the typical city dweller deals with 200 people every day, most of them only fleetingly. One simple way of capturing the point is to think of compulsion. The modern city dweller can choose a plumber from a hundred listed in a trade directory, can choose his religion from the hundreds of churches and chapels within easy travelling distance, and can choose which of his many neighbours he wishes to befriend. The feudal villager was given his social world.

As is the case with much of early sociology, there is a great deal of nostalgia and romanticism built into this paired contrast but it contains an essential truth. Whether one sees it as freedom from intrusive and sometimes oppressive relationships or as the loss of something important to psychic stability, the modern city allows a degree of anonymity that was almost impossible in small-scale pre-industrial societies. This is not to say that community is unknown in the city; especially where major social divisions constrain interaction (e.g. in an ethnic minority neighbourhood) then one may have an unusual degree of stability and hence intimacy in relationships. But the difference in degree of compulsion remains.

For this reason, many current uses of the term community seem quite inappropriate. Groups of people who share common interests, beliefs and values and who may interact only in some mediated way (through the Internet, for example) are described as communities when the term 'voluntary association' is more appropriate. The crucial point is the absence of some sense of necessity or compulsion; however active people are in a steam engine restoration society or white witch network, they can easily withdraw without any great disruption to other parts of their lives.

See **intentional community**.

COMMUNITY STUDIES   The defining characteristic of the community study is not its research methods (which usually involves **ethnography** but may also include attitude surveys and the collection of detailed descriptive statistics) but its attempt to get to grips with all the socially salient features of a particular small locality. An early American classic, which shows what is involved if one takes seriously the ambition to comprehend a community rather than an activity or institution, is W. Lloyd Warner's (1940) *Yankee City* research which is reported in four long books. Though considerably shorter, Norman Dennis et al.'s (1956) *Coal is Our Life: an analysis of a Yorkshire mining community*, is a good British example. It is implicit confirmation of the view of Ferdinand Tönnies that **community** was being displaced that the sort of community studies common in the 1950s are now rare. Longer travel-to-work distances and greater mobility mean that place and proximity less define social relationships than they once did. Detailed ethnographies are now more likely to concern disparate individuals drawn together for a specific purpose, than a town or village.

COMPETENCE　　This word has come to have three meanings that sociologists may come across. First, **Chomsksy** introduced a distinction between competence and performance to indicate the way that speakers of a language who master the (in his view in-built) rules may nonetheless produce utterances that are ungrammatical. The utterances are the performance whereas the set of rules that have been mastered are the competence. Other social scientists have adopted this terminology as a way of talking about the difference between what people may know or be able to do and what they do on any particular occasion. People with fully developed social skills may still make a gaffe without that necessarily indicating a lack of competence.

Ethnomethodologists and others who study small-scale interaction have alerted social scientists to a range of skills that are so widespread as to be almost invisible: the skill of recognising irony, of thanking appropriately and so on. Under special circumstances – for example, when dealing with machines programmed to respond to human talk – these ubiquitous skills may become problematic. Thus one way of interpreting the claims of **ethnomethodology** is to see it as asserting that people are far more competent than they are routinely acknowledged to be by social scientists who often take these everyday skills for granted.

Finally, in an ugly usage, those who are concerned with developing people's social and occupational skills – for example, in training service staff – have begun to speak of particular skills as 'competences', with competence or competency as the singular form of the word.

COMTE, AUGUSTE (1798–1857)　　Rarely read now, Comte performed the signal service to the discipline of coining the term 'sociology' which first appeared in his 1838 *Cours de Philosophie Positive*. For Comte, sociology was an empirical observation-based comparative science which would dominate the highest stage of human evolution. He believed that thought developed through the stages of the theological, the metaphysical and the positive. Societies evolved from the primitive through the intermediary to the scientific. Comte saw the increasing division of labour making societies more complex, specialised and internally differentiated. Like Emile **Durkheim** later, he saw modernisation as paradoxical; increased division of labour made people more dependent on each other and thus increased social solidarity but it also created class divisions and a gulf between the public and private worlds.

Comte divided sociology into two: social dynamics and social statics. The first was concerned with principles of evolution; the second, which anticipated **functionalism**, was concerned with the function of specific social institutions (such as family, private property and the state) in maintaining social order. Although we can find elements of Comte's work that are obvious precursors to modern sociology, the overall project seems thoroughly alien because it was intended as a utopian blueprint. The positive era would be characterised by reliable knowledge, rational government and a new religion centred on humanity, not god. The positive society would be governed by bankers and industrialists, guided by sociologists!

CONCEPT　　A concept is an idea. Sociologists are concerned about concepts – the concept of the family or of power and so on – because various writers may use the same term but mean different things by it. Given that sociologists are in the business of trying to make systematic interpretations of society it is important that their good work is not undermined by hiding competing concepts behind the same term. Conceptual analysis – an analysis of precisely how the word 'class' is used, for example – can thus be a key component of sociology.

CONCOMITANT VARIATION   This is a rather clumsy way of denoting an empirical (that is, actual rather than logical) relationship between two variables where the magnitude of one goes up or down in proportion with the magnitude of the other. The effect of heating a metal strip is a concomitant variation in length and heat. Constant concomitance is what we have if the relationship holds for all values of heat. If we persistently find that (a) as people grow richer (b) they more frequently vote for a right-wing party, we have concomitant variation and can begin to consider that (a) might cause (b). The sad fact for the social sciences is that, compared with the natural sciences, we very rarely find relationships of constant concomitance.

CONDITIONED REFLEX   See **conditioning**.

CONDITIONING   Conditioning is an important aspect of work within the **behaviourist** school. Behaviourists were interested in studying human conduct as scientifically as possible and believed that their approach must depend on analysing connections between observable inputs (or stimuli) and observable outputs (or responses). Conditioning is a form of learning that can be observed in this scientific way. If a bell rings before food appears for a dog, in time the dog will come to salivate just when the bell rings, even in the absence of food; this is a conditioned reflex since previously the dog would not have salivated at the whim of a bell-ringer. Some behaviourists hoped to be able to understand aspects of human culture in terms of the conditioning of

infants and children; this programme did not get very far.

CONFESSIONAL TECHNOLOGIES   This translation of a term coined by Michel **Foucault**, as with so much of his work, misleads as much as it informs. He does not mean 'technologies' at all; he means social practices (a combination of ideas and activities) which encourage people to see themselves as requiring or benefiting from the assistance of psychiatrists, therapists, social workers and the like in becoming 'normal'. 'Confessional' is clear in that it borrows the Catholic Church notion that the burden of sin can be removed by admitting it to a professional who has the power to prescribe rituals for its discharge. But 'technologies' seems to have been chosen to remind us of Foucault's claim that such methods of policing the self are peculiarly modern.

CONFIDENCE INTERVAL   Sociologists often use a sample to try to understand the characteristics of a population as a whole. For example, if we wish to know how common car-theft is in the whole of France, we could ask a sample of French people for their experience of car theft. But the conclusion drawn from a sample is unlikely to be exactly the same as it would be were we able to ask the whole population. The confidence interval is a way of using the sample result to express a range of estimated values for the population as a whole. We might, for example, be able to say that we have a 90 per cent confidence that the annual risk of car-theft is 8 plus or minus 2 per cent. That is, our sample was sufficiently large and well selected that we think there is only a 1 in 10 chance that the overall population's rate of car-theft is more than 2 percentage points different from that detected in our sample.

CONFLICT THEORY   Any theoretical perspective (such as **Marxism** or **feminism**) informed by the idea that society is dominated by a conflict of interest between those who have access to wealth, power and status and the rest, may be described as a conflict theory. From its standpoint, there are two implied contrasts. Other approaches (Parsonian **structural-functionalism**, for example) may be criticised for assuming too much consensus or (as with **symbolic interactionism**) for ignoring power differentials.

CONJUGAL ROLES 'Conjugal' simply means 'of marriage' and the term refers to the reciprocal roles of marriage partners.

CONSANGUINITY Literally meaning 'of the same blood', the term is used in anthropology and in many legal systems to refer to a blood kinship tie. It is contrasted with 'affinal', so that my bond with my son is consanguineous while my bond with my wife is affinal. In some societies, degrees of consanguinity are important for deciding the order of inheritance or for regulating choice of marriage partners. Because they share more of 'the same blood', siblings are closer than cousins.

CONSCIOUSNESS Consciousness is a puzzle for scientists and philosophers since they are unclear how brains and minds are able to be conscious of themselves. Nonetheless, consciousness is a given for sociologists since it is clear that people are, generally speaking, conscious of themselves. As Erving **Goffman** has so clearly documented, in our everyday lives we monitor our social selves, consciously thinking about not only whatever task or purpose we have in mind but also how other people view us. When I cannot find my car in the supermarket car park I may make a show of being lost and befuddled, not for my own benefit, but to indicate to other shoppers that I am not prowling around, looking out for cars to break into. I am conscious of myself but also conscious of how other people may view me. Consciousness in this sense is part of the fabric of **inter-subjectivity** that binds people into a common, taken-for-granted world.

CONSCRIPTION Generally meaning being signed up for something against your will (or in the US drafted), this more particularly denotes being required by the state to undertake military service. Most modern states maintain small professional armies and reserve the right to conscript sections of the general population as required.

CONSENSUS; CONSENSUS THEORY Denoting the existence within a group of fundamental agreement about basic beliefs and values, consensus is important in sociology because beliefs about its extent identify a major fault line. Some sociologists (e.g. Talcott **Parsons**) believe that shared values are vital to maintaining social order; others suppose that common interests or coercion play a larger part in explaining the persistence of social systems.

See **conflict theory, structural-functionalism**.

CONSERVATISM The meaning of this is entirely situational in that, as a political doctrine, it means defending the institutions, values and habits of the existing order. As a set of political attitudes it means the opposite of 'radical'; it is a general disposition to support the status quo. As the world changes so too do the things that conservatism wishes to defend.

CONSPICUOUS CONSUMPTION In his *The Theory of the Leisure Class*, Thorstein Veblen (1899) argued that a defining characteristic of the leisure class was that its members purchased goods and services not for their obvious utility but for show: to demonstrate that they could afford such things.

See **positional goods**.

CONSTRUCT　　Construct is often a fancy word for an idea or concept. For example, some psychologists maintain that people build and maintain a relatively stable image of themselves; this is known as a 'personal construct'. Generally, therefore, a construct is a special kind of idea: one that is durable and has been deliberately cultivated.

CONSTRUCTIONISM　　See **social construction of reality**.

CONSUMER CULTURE　　This rather vague term refers to the idea that since the 1970s wealthy capitalist societies have become much more focused on **consumption** than production. Consumer culture refers both to the interest that citizens have in the consumption aspects of their life – their interest in fine dining, fashion, home improvement and so on – and to the industries that have developed to cater to this taste. Television programmes that show you how to dress or to do a 'house makeover' are part of consumer culture, as are decorating magazines and the supplements in newspapers devoted to lifestyle enhancement.

CONSUMPTION　　Denoting the process in which goods and services are used, consumption has been given markedly less attention than production by sociologists, for the good reason that since, in most societies to date, people's time and energy has been largely taken up with work, their place in the production process has greatly influenced much else about them, and few have had enough discretionary income for consumption to rise much above the bare necessities. Arguably

the increasing affluence of modern societies and the shrinking of the presence of work in our lives means that consumption should be studied as an important social phenomenon in its own right.

See **consumer culture**.

CONTAGION EFFECT　　See **copycat effect**.

CONTENT ANALYSIS　　At its simplest, content analysis is the reduction of freely occurring text (e.g. a speech or a newspaper article) to a summary that can be analysed statistically. One may try to capture the essence of a text by counting certain words. For example, we could analyse the respective place of religion in US and British politics by comparing the frequency of references to God in speeches to the respective legislatures. The problem, of course, is that the meaning of words is rarely simple and the meaning of a text is rarely apparent from its words taken in isolation. Summarising a text in statistical form may give a spurious appearance of objectivity to what is always an artful and creative process of interpretation. The digitisation of text and the speed of the modern computer allows the application of extremely sophisticated analytical frames to texts but they do not remove the filter of interpretation. One response is to have texts coded by a number of operators and checked for consistency. This would still not give us the 'correct' reading of a text or the intention of the speaker or writer but it does give us a consensus version.

Although content analysis as such is not at fault, it is often associated with an evidential weakness at the heart of much cultural analysis. Researchers may suppose that some text means the same to the audience as it does to them. They may also assume that the text has the consequences for the audience that they guess the producers of the text intended.

CONTEST AND SPONSORED MOBILITY This contrast pair was used by R.H. Turner and L.M Killian (1960) to draw attention to different ways in which education could serve as a channel for social mobility. The distinction can be clearly seen in a comparison of the British state schooling system of the 1950s and that of the 1990s. In the 1950s children were tested at the age of 11. A small number went to high quality schools where they were educated for university and financially and socially supported as they gained the qualifications for entry into elite positions. The 'comprehensive' school system that largely replaced the two-tier model in the 1970s offered contest mobility: a much larger number of children were encouraged to compete for access to universities and hence to the professions. Experts may argue over exactly how fair a contest is presented by any education system but the distinction is a useful one.

The pair were also used to contrast the UK and US patterns of social mobility. As part of a general contrast of the supposed old class-ridden Europe and the new classless USA, social mobility rates in the US were assumed to be much higher than in the UK and to involve more open competition. In the UK the ruling class selected a small proportion of the working class and 'sponsored' its mobility. While there was some truth to the contrast, detailed empirical research from the 1970s onwards suggested that the differences were exaggerated.

CONTINGENCY TABLE See **cross-tabulation**.

CONTINGENT This means liable but not certain to happen. It can be used to stress unpredictability (as in 'the contingencies of war') but in social science it more often signifies a real causal relationship rather than a connection by definition. It is certain to be the case that the next triangle I find will have three sides because that is ensured by the definition of triangle, not

by the regularity of the world. Whether I enjoy the next film I see is a contingency. The word is also used as a synonym for 'caused by': as in 'my pleasure in the watching this film is contingent on there being no smoking in the cinema'.

CONTRADICTORY CLASS LOCATION The phrase was coined by US Marxist Erik Olin Wright in his attempt to remedy the defects of Karl **Marx**'s class model and to identify which occupational groups might form alliances with the working class in revolutionary struggle. In the absence of a complete polarisation of class around ownership of capital, a variety of class locations are characterised by 'contradictions'. For example, managers, like the workers they manage, are exploited by capitalists but, like capitalists, they exercise control over others. We are tempted to say that Wright and others could have saved themselves a great deal of remedial work by simply admitting Marx was wrong but Wright's explorations of the complexities of class have stimulated a great deal of useful debate and comparative research.

CONTROL GROUP Knowing how effective some change is requires that we have a base line against which to make comparisons. In experiments to test new drug therapies, for example, cases are allocated randomly to the experimental group that will receive the treatment and the control group that will be given a placebo. The former can thus be compared with the latter to identify the effects of the therapy. In the 'double-blind' method neither the researchers nor the patients know which cases are in which group. Such experiments are not possible in sociology but we can sometimes create something like a control group by careful selection of cases to compare.

CONTROL THEORY Traditionally most explanations of crime have supposed that being law-abiding is the human default position and that criminality needs explaining. Travis Hirschi's 1970s control theory of crime starts at the other end. It supposes that the potential for crime is widespread and that no special motives need be invoked to explain it. Most crime is opportunistic and what mostly deters people are their attachments to law-abiding parents and peers, their rational assessment of the risks and costs of being caught, their involvement in others things (put simply, if you are very busy with the swimming club you have less opportunity to become delinquent) and their beliefs (which for some will prevent delinquency). As we get older we acquire good reasons not to commit crimes (such as spouses and children; commitment to a career; status in our social circles and the like) that acts as controls on our actions. Putting it this way identifies those groups that do not have much at stake: the young and the poor.

In the 1990s, Hirschi amended his theory to give much greater weight to the role of parenting, effective early socialisation, conscience and self-control.

CONTROLLING FOR Sociologists very rarely have the opportunity to construct experiments. Normally we work with 'naturally occurring' research materials. We cannot study one human characteristic in isolation from others and hence it is always possible that what we take to be a case of A causing B may actually be a matter of C causing both A and B. In a survey of church-going we discover that people who describe themselves as Catholics are more likely to go to church than those who describe themselves as Protestants. We might waste a lot of time constructing an explanation for the greater loyalty of Catholics before we notice that through some accident of sampling our Catholics are markedly older than our Protestants. We suspect that age has a strong effect on church-going so we 'control' for age by dividing our sample into age bands and

comparing Catholics and Protestants within each age group. We may well discover that the initial correlation disappears.

Without the ability to create experimental controls, sociological attempts to create clear and uncontaminated comparisons rest on selecting the cases to be compared so that they are alike in as much as possible except for the variables whose relationship we wish to explore.

CONVERGENCE THESIS See **industrial society**.

CONVERSATION ANALYSIS Conversation analysis (or CA as it is often known) grew out of **ethnomethodology** but is now in many respects rather distant from ethnomethodological concerns. In their pioneering ethnomethodological studies Harold **Garfinkel** and Harvey **Sacks** were concerned to show how the orderliness of society is actively produced by the actions of participants. Conversations became one arena for displaying this orderliness. For example, in a regular conversation no-one is in charge of the distribution of turns at talking. But most conversations are remarkably orderly, with little overlap and a series of 'turns' for each speaker. Somehow the orderliness of conversation is spontaneously produced by the speakers themselves.

Telephone conversations early on became important to CA. In part this was because in a phone conversation all the speakers have to go on is the preceding talk (and whatever assumptions and background knowledge the speakers bring to their interaction); there are no non-verbal cues. But it was also because phone calls could be recorded and then the analyst would have virtually the same access to the interaction as the participants themselves. In fact, as the tapes could be replayed over and over again, the analyst had something of an advantage over the conversationalists.

From these unfocused beginnings CA has developed into a major branch of sociology.

It has achieved at least three important things. First, CA has uncovered a lot of the ways in which ordinary talk is structured, for example through looking at how conversations are terminated, how topics are chosen or avoided, and how special turns at talk known as **adjacency pairs** (such as greetings) operate. This work has even been influential outside sociology, for example in linguistics and psychology. Second, CA has been able to throw light on institutional talk by comparing specialised forms of talk – courtroom interrogation, pilots' conversations with air-traffic control, calls to emergency services – with everyday talk. Many jobs are done mainly through talk – even being a family doctor is mostly talk – so CA has contributed significantly to the sociology of work. Third, CA has introduced innovations in the standard of evidence available to sociologists. Not only do conversation analysts work on recorded materials that can be thoroughly checked by other social scientists, they have also developed methodological tools to check the validity of their analyses. For example, if they claim that a greeting makes a return greeting normatively appropriate in normal conversation, they can study this both by looking for examples of returned greetings and by looking for occasions when greetings are not returned. If on such occasions the co-conversationalist treats the absence of a greeting as 'trouble' then the conversation analyst has some form of independent warrant for her claims. For this reason, conversation analysts often see their generalisations as more robust and better tested than those of other qualitative sociologists, and they quite commonly see CA as a highly scientific form of study.

CONVERSION This denotes a radical change of beliefs, usually accompanied by a corresponding change in attitudes, action and personality. Explaining conversion is a major concern of students of religion. Competing explanations can be grouped according to the cause of change. In the early 1960s it was common to suppose that people who abruptly changed beliefs had been 'brainwashed'; skilled manipulators could, by depriving people of sleep and food, scaring them literally witless and seducing them with the prospect of approval and reward, reduce people to a state of credulity and persuade them to accept ideas they would normally find implausible. This was thought to have been done effectively by Chinese prison guards to Americans captured during the Korean war. A careful reading of Robert Lifton's (1961) *Thought Reform and the Psychology of Totalism* or Edward Schein's (1961) *Coercive Persuasion* reveals that no such claims are made for brainwashing but the idea became popular in the 1970s when large numbers of middle-class young people (whom, it is implied, should have known better) briefly joined exotic **new religious movements**. The clearest evidence that movements such as the Moonies did not have the power to brainwash is that the vast majority of people whom the Moonies tried to recruit did not convert and almost all members left within a few months.

Sociologists have preferred one of two approaches that correspond to the classic divide over **agency and structure**. Some take a rather passive view of the convert and explain conversion by pointing to antecedent problems (such as **anomie**), structural constraints such as the strength of family and friendship ties, and ties to advocates of the new worldview. Others stress agency or free will and see conversion as an accomplishment. It is not something that happens to a person but something a seeker achieves.

An important general observation from the study of conversion is that ideological change may actually come late in the social process. Many 'converts' begin by playing the role of a believer with a degree of **role-distance** and only if they find the role satisfying do they gradually come to internalise the new beliefs.

Conversion has been an important site for developing ideas about the relationship between **accounts** and actions. Rather than naively taking what believers say about their conversions as raw material for explaining them, we are aware that conversion testimonies are themselves a stylised and scripted performance, designed for a purpose other than merely explaining the past; like courtroom testimonies, they are intended to have an effect on the hearer.

COOLEY, CHARLES HORTON (1864–1929)

For modern purposes, the most important part of Cooley's work was his attempt to abolish the dualisms of society/individual and body/mind. He believed that the self and society could only be defined in relation to each other: society inevitably shaped the individual; individuals constituted society. His idea of the **looking-glass self** was taken up by George Herbert **Mead** in his general theory of the self.

COPYCAT EFFECT

Also known as the contagion or imitation effect, this is the supposed power of the mass media to create a rash of imitative behaviour. If a popular TV soap shows someone committing suicide by piping exhaust fumes into her car, then suicides by that method go up in the weeks afterwards. Outside the artificial setting of an experiment, such effects are notoriously hard to prove. A practical difficulty is that much of the evidence comes from people who, in being forced to **account** for some deviant or criminal act, blame it on prior example. We are then unsure if we have a genuine example of imitation or someone opportunistically trying to evade responsibility.

CORPORATE CRIME

The phrase conveys the point, often neglected in criminology, that organisations can, in two senses, commit crimes. They can break the law (as when senior officials of a corporation instruct staff to construct fraudulent accounts). They can also inflict harm of a scale and nature which, were it done by an individual, would be regarded as a crime. For example, a corporation may cause serious damage to the health of its workers. Organisational crime should be distinguished from **white-collar crime** (which often involves crimes against employers; embezzlement is an example) and from organised crime.

CORPORATION

From 'corporal' meaning 'belonging to the body', this denotes a group of people legally structured so as to act and be treated as if it were a single person. Normally a corporation would elect its own officers. Local governments, large businesses, a professional association; all of these may be corporations.

CORPORATISM

When confronted with the increasing democratisation of politics at the end of the 19th century, the Catholic Church promoted an alternative to mass politics, which it saw as encouraging class conflict. Its preferred model was the world of the medieval guilds: groups with a common interest (businessmen, tradesmen, workers, farmers and the like) would each form a corporation and the leaders elected from each body would negotiate a division of political power. Corporatism was popular with some right-wing European politicians in the first half of the 20th century and informed some of the more benign authoritarian regimes established in such states as Lithuania and Latvia in the 1930s.

Latterly the term has come to be used to refer to one way in which modern states can be organised. In, for example, Germany (and previously in West Germany) business leaders, leading government politicians and trades union leaders met in regular forums to discuss policy initiatives, to settle major pay claims, negotiate reform of welfare entitlements and so on. In the USA and post-1980 Britain, by contrast, relations between the executive and unions were more oppositional. For many years it appeared that the corporatist model worked better in delivering economic prosperity and extensive social welfare provision, though the ability of corporatist states to cope with international economic competition from low-wage countries and with the growing costs of the welfare state has recently come to appear questionable.

CORRELATION　　This denotes a regular relationship between two variables. If our survey data shows that the people with the highest A also have the highest B, then we have a positive correlation between A and B. If they also had the lowest C, then we would say there is a negative correlation between A and C. Identifying correlations in data sets is, however, only the start of analysis. A correlation of itself does not tell us if A causes B, B causes A or if both A and B are caused by some third unknown variable.

There are a variety of statistical measures of correlation, each more or less suitable to different sorts of data (see **measurement, levels of**) with differing patterns of distribution. For example Pearson's *r* is commonly used to describe the correlation between two variables that have been measured on interval or ratio scales where the values follow a normal or bell-shaped distribution. When it is not possible to assign actual values to variables but only to place them in a rank order and when the distribution is not bell-shaped, Spearman's rank correlation coefficient is more appropriate. The only thing the amateur needs to know is that data must be described with an appropriate statistic.

COUNTER-CULTURE　　In the 1960s this term was popularly used to describe people who 'dropped out' of the social, economic and cultural mainstream to live alternative lifestyles. Common themes of the counter-culture included sexual freedom, recreational drug use, criticism of conventional family life or conventional occupations as sterile and oppressive, and criticism of industrial capitalism and western rationality. The counter-culture never posed a threat to the mainstream. Very few people dropped out entirely; for most being a hippie was a weekend and holiday pursuit. However, it was successful in promoting those cultural and social innovations that were compatible with a modern industrial economy. Sex outside marriage, recreational drug use, rock music, diversity in dress styles, an interest in eastern religion; all are incorporated in the mainstream.

COVERT RESEARCH　　Some styles of research are invariably public; people cannot complete a survey questionnaire without being aware of it (though we can do subtle things with question placement). But it is possible to study people without their knowledge. We could study a new religion by pretending to be a believer or watch and overhear diners by working as a waiter. As Laud Humphreys did in (1970) *Tearoom Trade: Impersonal Sex in Public Places* we could pretend to interview people for one research purpose while actually collecting some of that information for a quite different purpose.

There are very good reasons for covert research. As was found with the **Hawthorne effect**, knowing that they are being studied may change the behaviour of the people we wish to study. Respondents may choose to mislead us. If the purpose of participant observation is to learn what life feels like for a member of some sect, declaring that intention may well compromise the research because, even if other members are happy with being studied, they are unlikely to treat the researching participant in the same way as they would treat ordinary members.

Finally, being undercover may well be the only way to study groups engaged in deviant or criminal behaviour that are powerful enough to control access. In brief, covert research may be the only way to acquire certain information and experiences.

COVERT RESEARCH, ETHICS OF   Led by the example of medical research, where it is now standard to require that those studied give their informed consent, some sociologists argue that covert or hidden research is always unethical and that social researchers should identify themselves as such. While this may seem a reasonable requirement, for the reasons given in the previous entry, it would close off important parts of the world.

Rather too much can be made of the ethical problems of covert research. After all, unlike medical research, most social research is not doing anything to people. If it remains truly covert and identities are so well disguised on publication that those who have been studied never become aware of it, it is difficult to see what harm is done to our subjects. Second, covert researchers often act out fully the roles they have adopted as they conduct their research. That they reflect more professionally and rigorously on their experiences and observations than do the people they work alongside does not of itself make them that different from their subjects. In the research reported in his classic *Organization Man*, William H. Whyte (1956) worked for a number of corporations and did a perfectly good job. That he also kept notes on what he did and observed and drew inferences from them caused no disruption to the firms for which he worked. We may scruple that he sometimes led people on (for example promising to assist a female secretary in her amorous pursuit of a friend in return for some indiscretion over personnel files) but this could be defended on the grounds that had he not been a researcher, he might well have done the same thing for less good reasons.

One sensible way of settling the ethical dilemma is to consider if the activity or group in question is public or private. If a new religion claims that we are all doomed if we fail to follow its revelations and aims to recruit from the general public, it seems reasonable for the covert researcher to join it and study it because the new religion has placed itself in the public domain. Given the general requirement to respect privacy, spying on people who have not put themselves in the public domain seems harder to defend.

See **ethics of research**.

CRIME   Crime is that particular subset of deviance or failure to conform to rules where the rules in question are legal codes. This definition could be operationalised in a thoroughly pragmatic way by treating as crime only that which the appropriate legal authorities have determined is criminal, but many sociologists would regard that as unduly restrictive and wish to include acts which in some sense or other should have been regarded as crimes. This then introduces the complexity that the actor, the agent of social control, and the observer may differ in their judgement either of general principles (should pollution be treated as a crime?) or of specific instances (would this act have been treated as a crime had it come before a different judge or jury?).

CRIMINOLOGY   Less an 'ology' than a substantive area of interest explored from a variety of disciplinary perspectives, criminology has undergone an important expansion in its scope since the 1970s. Initially criminologists took a rather narrow view of their field, taking for granted the laws, the infraction of which constituted crimes, and concentrating on trying to explain why some people broke the law. More recently, criminologists have also studied the creation of law and its differential enforcement and punishment. For example, feminist criminologists have pointed to the patriarchal nature of attitudes to domestic violence. Until the last quarter of the 20th century the legal systems of many western countries regarded the violence inflicted by men on their spouses as a private matter. As an example of differential enforcement we may note that in the USA blacks are often given more severe sentences than whites for apparently similar offences.

Explanations of crime have followed the contours of well-established general models for explaining other sorts of conduct. Cesare **Lombroso** believed that criminality was genetically transmitted and that criminals could be recognised by head and face shape. Each sociological perspective has its preferred approach to crime. Some functionalists have stressed the role of poor parenting and faulty socialisation in preventing the inculcation of law-abidingness. Others have followed Emile **Durkheim** in suggesting that, although too much would be harmfully disruptive, some crime is useful in giving upright citizens regular opportunities to display their shared commitment to decency. Rather against the **structural-functionalist** tendency to stress the integration of institutions, Robert K. Merton pointed out that crime could be a reasonable response to failures of the social structure evenly to provide legitimate means to achieve the cultural goals which American society offered evenly to all citizens. In his view certain types of crime were not so much alien intrusions as by-products of features of the social structure itself. The main contribution of **symbolic interactionism** is focused not so much on initial criminal acts as on the unintended consequences of societal reaction to criminality. The point, now accepted by most social control agencies, is that to respond to the crimes of the young by excluding perpetrators from conventional roles and forcing them into the company of professional criminals, may well encourage further crime by reducing opportunities for non-criminal careers and allowing young people to be socialised into criminal values.

Marxists have developed a **critical criminology** that stresses the class basis of the definition and punishment of crime. Feminists have raised important questions about the role of women as perpetrators and as victims of crime and have drawn attention to the previously neglected topic of the influence of gender on the social definition of crime.

For the good reason that this is what scares most people, criminology has traditionally been concerned with crimes of violence, theft, robbery and burglary. One of the most useful contributions of sociology (since Edwin Sutherland coined the term 'white-collar crime' in 1939 through to the work of Richard Quinney) had been to draw our attention to the very large amount of middle-class crime that stretches from small-scale office fiddling to the major scandal of the 2002 collapse of the Enron energy corporation. It is clear that while certain kinds of crime may be more common among the working class and the poor than among the middle class, criminality itself is not confined to any particular class, gender, race or status group. Criminologists have also tried out new methods for the study or crime, including victim studies – which focus on people's experiences of crime rather than on officially recorded infractions – and longitudinal studies that follow **cohorts** of people to map when in their life-course they are most deviant and liable to be charged with criminality.

CRITICAL CRIMINOLOGY　Also known as radical criminology, this 1970s development from the sociology of deviance argued that much crime was a reasonable reaction of exploited and dispossessed people to the inequities of capitalist society. In the US Richard Quinney was a leading exponent of this view; in the UK, Ian Taylor, Paul Walton and Jock Young's (1975) *The New Criminology* was a pioneering text.

The critical criminologists were reasonably accused of romanticising crime and of finding revolutionary intent in action that was actually far more exploitative and damaging to the working class than anything done by capitalists. Young later came to appreciate this and coined the term **left realism** for a view of working-class crime that much more honestly recognised that it really did have victims and that most victims were poorer and weaker than those who victimised them.

CRITICAL REALISM   Developed mostly in Britain in the 1970s and 1980s, critical realism is a school of Marxist thought anchored in philosophical analysis. Authors such as Roy Bhaskar used philosophical arguments about **realism** to suggest that success in the natural sciences comes about when scientists identify the real causes that underlie regularities in the natural world. From here it is a short step to the idea that good sociology too must identify the underlying casual powers. Critical realists thus derived a 'template' for what social scientific explanations should look like and then proceeded to argue that a version of Marxism was the form of sociology best suited to identifying the causal powers driving social change.

CRITICAL SOCIOLOGY   This is an umbrella term used to designate sociological work which sees itself as critical of the economic, social and political organisation of contemporary societies. Most critical sociologists are approximately Marxist in their orientation though many feminists would be happy to be so described also. Beyond this basic outlook critical sociologists need not have much in common and lack the specific philosophical basis for their critique that is to be found in **critical theory**.

Given that a certain degree of scepticism is a pre-requisite for nearly all sociology, since we are often in the business of testing the lay explanations that people offer for their actions and of trying to expose the hidden causes and consequences of social action and social arrangements, self-proclaimed critical sociologists often distinguish themselves by having an overt political agenda. All too often they are conspicuously uncritical about their own political preferences.

CRITICAL THEORY   Though the term 'critical' is a label that has sometimes been used to designate any sociological theory that is critical of the status quo (**critical sociology**), critical theory has a more technical meaning. Critical theorists claim that their sociological work is both a description of contemporary society and a critique of it. To many mainstream (particularly North American) sociologists this appears to confuse a description of facts with a judgement about values, and thus to violate the ideal of **value neutrality** in scientific thought. However, critical theorists argue that we are able to apply rational analysis to matters of value as well as to those of fact. Indeed the sociologist fails to fulfil their ethical role if they apply critical thinking only to facts and not to values.

In particular, the very same rational tools that we apply in analysing society are said to contain an approach to thinking about values as well. The social theorists of the **Frankfurt School** maintained that we can apply the same rational approach to thinking about justice, exploitation and fairness as we apply to analysing society empirically. Jürgen **Habermas** took this further by finding (or claiming to find) the value criteria within the very language of analysis. According to Habermas, academic inquiry, and more generally the search for truth, presupposes an 'ideal speech situation' (or ISS) of unfettered speech; within this ISS we can find ethical values already presupposed by the way we conduct our analysis. In this way, critical theorists claim to study society empirically but also to be able to conduct a political and cultural critique of society and social institutions at the same time. For most critical theorists, this is to fulfil a key task that Karl **Marx** set himself: to produce an authoritative description of society which was simultaneously a critique of that society's limitations. All critical theory thus challenges the fact/value distinction and claims that the systematic analysis of society predisposes us towards certain values and away from others (such as arbitrary authority). Contemporary mainstream political theorists such as Charles Taylor have a lot of sympathy with this line of reasoning even if they don't call themselves critical theorists.

CROSS-TABULATION This describes the simplest way of looking for a connection between two or more variables: we look across a table. In what is called a contingency table, the following table gives some fictional data for the social class of fathers and sons; the columns of the table describe the father's class and for each column the row cell shows what percentage of sons have that class. If all sons had the same class as their fathers the numbers in the diagonal running from top left to bottom right would be 100 and the other cells would be empty. The size of the numbers in cells on either side of the diagonal gives us a rough idea of how far the actual inheritance of class varies from that.

	Father's Class		
	Class 1	Class 2	Class 3
Son's Class (%)			
Class 1	60	20	10
Class 2	20	60	10
Class 3	20	20	80
Total	100	100	100

Making inferences from the spread of data in a contingency table obviously gets more complex the greater the number of variables we wish to consider and how finely divided each of them is, which is why we input data into programmes such as **SPSS** and use computer-generated statistics to ask the sorts of questions of the data which, in the simple model given here, we can pick out by eye.

CULT   See **religious organisations**.

CULTURAL   CAPITAL Pierre **Bourdieu** introduced this concept to draw attention to the importance for social mobility and social differentiation of assets other than wealth and political power. He argued that middle-class parents were able to pass on to their children (hence the capital metaphor) the great asset of understanding and exemplifying the middle-class culture that informed the education system.

Analysts of cultural capital present it as an asset in three ways. Most obviously, speaking in the same way and possessing the same stock of cultural knowledge as teachers is likely to make middle-class children better thought of. That their homes and schools share the same cultural background also makes middle-class children feel more comfortable and confident in the school system. But there is a more subtle effect: simply because they are more familiar, middle-class children are often credited with greater intelligence and skill than objective measures would suggest they possess. Or to present the same point from the other side, without necessarily intending to, teachers often under-estimate the competence of working-class children by taking the lack of surface cultural competence as a sign of underlying inadequacy.

Plausible though these ideas are, Bourdieu's claims are not well supported by large-scale empirical research on social mobility. If cultural capital is very important we should have seen the link between social class of origin and educational attainment strengthen considerably over time; in international studies this appears not to be the case.

CULTURAL DEPRIVATION THEORY   In the 1950s and 1960s it was common for the failure of the children of the working class and of some ethnic minorities in the USA and the UK to perform as well as white middle-class children to be explained by their cultural deprivation: the failure of the home and the neighbourhood to provide appropriate (primarily linguistic) skills and suitable encouragement. The idea remains popular with right-wing politicians and educationalists but has fallen out of favour with sociologists, who are generally reluctant to endorse the value judgement implicit in describing as inadequacy what may just be cultural difference. Pierre **Bourdieu**'s cultural capital serves the same purpose of explaining educational failure by the gulf between some home cultures and the culture of the school without supposing that the latter is the standard against which home backgrounds should be measured.

CULTURAL DOPES   Theoretical approaches such as **structural-functionalism** and **Marxism** have been criticised for viewing people as little more than passive carriers of features of the social structure, shaped by social forces beyond their control and often beyond even their knowledge. The phrase 'cultural dopes' was coined by Harold **Garfinkel** as a way of focusing attention on the error at the heart of structuralist theories.

CULTURAL IMPERIALISM   This is the imposition of American or western values upon non-western societies, largely through the export of mass media products. US-based trans-national media and communications now dominate so much of the world that

scholars talk seriously of a threat to weaker nation-states. It is certainly true that US media products dominate the market but it does not automatically follow that they are persuasive. The popularity of Islamic fundamentalist attacks on the USA shows that many people can take US culture as an enemy to be opposed rather than as a friend to be imitated. Even when there is a positive correlation between western media penetration and social change (for example, an increase in individual assertiveness) this need not mean that the first caused the second. At least some of what are called western values (e.g. a desire for greater personal freedom) are quite likely to become more popular as increasing prosperity allows their expression, and increasing prosperity permits greater consumption of electronic media products. Some of what is taken to be cultural imperialism may be internally-driven change.

CULTURAL PLURALISM   Like its close relative 'multiculturalism', this term both describes and promotes. As description it refers to a situation of a plurality of cultures (with the implication that they are co-existing tolerantly): that of New York where a large number of religious, ethnic and linguistic groups live side-by-side is an example. The term is also used to describe a deliberate policy of encouraging awareness and acceptance of alternative cultures.

CULTURE   The culture of a society is the totality of its shared beliefs, norms, values, rituals, language, history, knowledge and social character. Although very broad in scope, the term usually has the clear sense of excluding the economy, the polity and those elements of the social structure least requiring constant re-affirmation. It implies those things that are conscious, that are kept in being only because we choose to maintain them. Although many elements of our culture confront us as external things apparently outside our control (e.g. we are born into a language which we more or less automatically adopt) there is a sense in which we can change our culture much more easily than the economy or the polity.

The term also implies a contrast in the other direction: inward. That which is entirely a matter of biology is not culture. Culture is a human creation into which we are socialised and which we can, with some effort, modify.

In common usage the term refers to the more sophisticated expressions of human creativity – opera, ballet, orchestral music – and preceding adjectives can identify alternatives such as **mass culture**, low culture and **popular culture**.

CULTURE OF POVERTY　The phrase was originally used by Oscar Lewis in the early 1960s to express the idea that poverty created its own distinctive culture which inhibited the development of attitudes and practices that would allow people to rise above it. Fatalism was one such restraint. Lewis was challenged by scholars who stressed the structural causes of poverty (especially in the developing world) and by others who questioned the accuracy of his ethnography, arguing that far from being fatalistic, shanty town dwellers often worked together to make the best of their difficult circumstances.

The argument about the relative weight in causing poverty of culture and social structure periodically returns in new guises. In the 1980s there was concern about the existence of a self-reproducing 'underclass' whose members lacked any great familiarity with paid work and were dependent on either crime or welfare. In the late 1990s, the argument was made cross-cultural when, as an alternative to the view that the enduring poverty of the Third World was a result of western imperialism, scholars began to explore the possibility that differences in economic development might be at least partly caused by internal features of societies.

See **underclass**.

CUSTOMS　Denoting the established norms and patterns of behaviour of a particular society, the term often implies patterns of behaviour that are very old (and somewhat redundant) and characteristic of a particular society: Appalachian customs, rural Japanese customs.

D

DARK FIGURE OF CRIME   Before a possibly criminal event appears in official government crime statistics it must be observed, reported to, and taken seriously by, the police and recorded as a crime. Each of those represents a considerable hurdle. In many cities, police forces are too stretched to do anything about minor thefts and robberies; hence there is little incentive to report such crimes. Victims of some serious crimes (rape or fraud, for example) may be reluctant to report them because they fear any investigation, prosecution or publicity could be almost as damaging as the original crime. Police forces and government agencies have been known to manipulate crime statistics for public effect. The dark figure of crime is an estimate of the gap between the official statistics and the real crime rate calculated from surveys that ask people about their experiences as victims of crime.

DARWINISM, SOCIAL   Named after the English naturalist Charles Darwin (1809–92), Darwinism is the theory of evolution (or systematic change and adaptation) by means of natural selection. Those members of a species best suited to their environment survive and reproduce; those least suited die. Over very long time periods this produces new species. We now think of social evolution as an extension of biology but the idea of evolution was popular in a wide variety of intellectual fields in the mid-19th century and the phrase 'the survival of the fittest' was coined, not by Darwin but by Herbert **Spencer**, one of the founders of sociology, to explain the historical development of societies. One of the best known forms of social Darwinism is eugenics. Popular in Britain and the USA at the end of the 19th century, eugenics argued that the same deliberate selection that stockmen had for centuries applied to sheep and cattle, should be applied to people so that the best should be encouraged to breed and the weak, the criminal, and the stupid should be discouraged (or prevented) from breeding. Although periodically revived by racists who argued that certain peoples were superior to others (the Nazis in Germany in the 1930s, for example) eugenics fell from favour because it proved difficult to separate which human characteristics were genetic and which were a product of nurture and environment; few people would accept the ethics of preventing certain groups from producing; and no effective programme could be designed.

Social Darwinism was abandoned by modern social science because it became obvious that there was no scientific basis for ranking certain individuals, classes or races as innately superior to others and that the entire way of thinking was self-serving; invariably the proponents put themselves and people like themselves at the top of the evolutionary trees they constructed.

See **evolution**.

DATA   The plural of datum (the Latin for 'given'), data are facts or observations: the bits of information from which inferences are drawn. Although qualitative social scientists would regard their observations as every bit as factual as the statistics produced by quantitative research instruments such as surveys and tests, the term often implies facts that can be quantified and analysed statistically; hence data banks, data bases and the like. Strictly speaking 'data' should be treated as a plural; hence 'the data show that' rather than 'the data shows that' but it is increasingly treated as a singular noun.

DAVIS-MOORE DEBATE   See **stratification**.

DEATH RATE   The crude death rate is the number of deaths per 1000 living members of a population per year. The standardised death rate is the number of deaths for any given cohort or age group per year. Crude death rates are generally not very informative since a country or region may have a low crude death rate either because it is a healthy place to live or because there just happen to be a lot of young people in the population, young people being less likely to die in the short term than the elderly. The standardised rate is more commonly used because it allows comparisons to be made. The main use for crude death rates is as one half of the equation (with crude birth rates) that describes population growth or decline.

DE BEAUVOIR, SIMONE (1908–86)   A Parisian philosopher and novelist, de Beauvoir is best known in the social sciences for her two-volume *The Second Sex* (1949). In this work she argued against the idea that there was something essentially feminine about women although she also stressed the ways in which women's experience is biologically different from men's. To capture the nature of women's subordination she adopted the existentialist terminology of 'the other'. In mainstream Western culture women are defined as 'the other' in contrast to men. Ideas about what women are like have been developed by men as part of men's self-understanding: where men are rational, women are emotional and so on. Women are thus the second sex because their identity has been devised by men in the course of men's development of their own male identities. They are what men are not.

DEBORD, GUY (1931–94)   A leading figure and chief theorist of the **Situationist** movement, Debord argued that capitalism had commodified all relationships and spread alienation in the public and private spheres. People are distracted from this loss by the false allure of the 'spectacle': new needs and possibilities manufactured and maintained by advanced capitalism and purveyed by the mass media. Debord was strongly influenced by surrealism and much of his work displays a lively and caustic humour. It is said, for example, that his earliest book was bound with sandpaper covers so that it would destroy the books next to it on the shelves. His themes are picked up in the work of Jean **Baudrillard**, particularly in relation to the latter's ideas about **simulacra**.

DEBT CRISIS   In the post-colonial period, developing countries faced one key problem. It was hard for them to get enough capital to develop their industrial base and the supporting infrastructure. If they invited foreign firms to bring their own capital in, those firms tended to keep the money and know-how to themselves. But the international funding bodies were not keen to lend money to governments or private companies to set up steel mills, power stations and harbours, let alone schools and hospitals. All this changed in the 1970s when windfall profits from high oil prices meant that petroleum-exporting countries squirreled away vast amounts of money in western banks which then had to find ways of using the funds to make a profit themselves. They focused a lot of their lending on developing countries, particularly ones seen as ripe for 'take off' such as Brazil and the Philippines.

These loans raced ahead but the lending policies were too lax. In some cases corruption worsened the situation. Within a few years many of the countries were unable to meet the repayments on the loans. In the early 1980s Mexico became the first country to threaten to default on its debts. In Latin America many countries found that their debt repayment obligations took up 50 per cent or more of their foreign earnings. This had an enormous impact on these countries in two ways. First, it meant that they seemed to stop developing economically. While the developed world got richer each year, they seemed only to get more indebted. Second, the IMF (International Monetary Fund) assumed the role of financial policeman offering countries help with their loans in return for economic reforms: for example, the cutting of government spending, the ending of food subsidies and the sale of nationalised assets. This seemed like a new form of imperial government.

Lower inflation through the 1990s meant that many countries gradually saw their debts decrease as a proportion of their exports but by the end of the millennium there were still many 'heavily indebted poor countries' (as the IMF calls them). Plans to write off their debts were put forward but are still stalled in wrangles between richer countries.

DEBT PEONAGE   *Peon* is the Spanish term for serf; the lowest status of agricultural worker. Until the 20th century it was common for landowners in agrarian societies to ensure they had a steady supply of labour by placing the workers in their debt and then requiring work to discharge it. In some

systems the period of bondage was short; a migrant to the American colonies might be 'bonded' to the man who paid his passage for two years. In some places the obligation is never discharged and it might accurately be described as disguised slavery. Debt peonage was common in Mexico and other parts of Latin America and is still found in many Third World countries.

See **hacienda**.

DE-CENTRED SELF   The **self** has always been a difficult notion for sociologists. For most purposes, sociologists can just work with commonsensical versions of the self. But there are acknowledged tensions between our experience of the self as autonomous (I decide what I will do, what job I would like to try to get and so on) and the realisation that the self is conditioned by its surroundings. Explicit sociological reflection on this topic dates back at least to George Herbert **Mead**. More recently several authors have returned to the theme of the self with **postmodern** and post-Freudian writers focusing on the supposed emptiness of the postmodern self. **Derrida** has also been stimulated by the conceptual complexities of our idea of the self, complexities which he sees as ideally suited for **deconstruction**. The de-centred self has come to be the favoured term among these writers though they use the term in slightly differing ways.

DECONSTRUCTION   Deconstruction was introduced as a technical term by Jacques **Derrida** to refer to a form of textual, philosophical analysis that was concerned with uncovering strains and contradictions within texts and arguments. The term was more loosely used in the study of literature to refer to an approach which rejected a conventional concentration on the author and the obvious meanings of a text in favour of searching for hidden meanings and assumptions. These could be found by recognising the genre to which a text belonged, by discovering inconsistencies or absences in the text and by examining peripheral aspects such as footnotes and digressions. The idea was taken into social science by scholars who argued that society could be treated as a text and 'deconstructed'. While deconstructing a text can generate novel insights, the method has the obvious weakness that there is rarely any warrant for treating one reading of any text as superior to any other; the conclusions seem subjective and arbitrary. Some scholars willingly embrace the resulting **relativism** as part of a general rejection of the possibility of social science; others simply assume that their reading is the correct one.

DE-DIFFERENTIATION   Any process in which complex and variegated arrangements are replaced by simpler more uniform ones could be described as reversing **differentiation** but de-differentiation is particularly associated with postmodernism. Modern societies differ from pre-industrial ones in the extent to which social roles and social institutions are divided (or differentiated). For example, Max **Weber**'s model of **bureaucracy** requires an absolute separation between the property of the office and the property of the official. Postmodernists argue either (or both) that modern societies have always been less rationally differentiated than social scientists have supposed and that, since the 1970s, there has been a clear shift away from the neat divisions of modernity so that life has become more chaotic, ambiguous and incoherent. Like many postmodern claims this is more popular among media commentators, who are impressed that some of their friends work from home (and hence blur the family/work and public/private divides), than it is with social scientists.

DEEP STRUCTURE AND SURFACE STRUCTURE   These terms are associated with the linguistic theories of Noam **Chomsky**. All languages have a structure, for example their grammar (called syntax by linguists). But Chomsky argued that, despite their apparent syntactic diversity, human languages must have a common structure at a deeper level. This deep structure plus various 'transformational rules' give rise to the wide range of surface structures. Part of the evidence for the common deep structure is the fact that human infants normally acquire languages so quickly at a specific stage in their development; they can even learn several languages at the same time. They must, he reasons, be predisposed to the acquisition of the deep structure and the transformational rules.

The terminology of the deep and surface structure has entered the language of the social sciences more generally, though outside linguistics it is not typically used to imply that there is any in-built predisposition to acquire the deep structure.

DEFERENTIAL WORKER   To defer is to give way to the wishes of others out of respect (rather than out of fear). Stable hierarchical societies depend on a culture of deference in which subordinate people accept the right of their masters to rule. The term 'deferential worker' was coined in Britain in the 1950s to describe the blue-collar or manual worker who voted for the Conservatives on the grounds that his superiors better deserved to run the country than his fellow workers. In late 1970s work on English agricultural workers, Howard Newby argued that deference often did not involve any sense of inferiority but was simply an acceptance of power relations: it was less an attitude than conformity to a social role.

DEFERRED GRATIFICATION   The phrase describes any circumstance where people make sacrifices now in the expectation of greater rewards in the future. It is commonly used in comparisons of economic decisions and in descriptions of middle-class attitudes to the value of education. The child who could leave school to take a poorly paid job but who stays in full-time education in order to get a better paid job later is engaging in 'deferred gratification'.

DEFINITION OF THE SITUATION The American sociologist W.I. **Thomas** (one of the founders of **symbolic interactionism**) coined the aphorism: 'if men define situations as real, they are real in their consequences'. His point was that if we wish to understand action, what matters is the subjective reality of the actor, not the objective reality. If I run from my house shouting 'Fire!' the reason is not that the house is on fire; it is that I believe it to be on fire. That I am wrong may be interesting in other respects but it does not change the explanation. The notion is important in reminding us that the immediate cause of social action lies in the consciousness of the actor. It does not mean, as some critics would have it, that if people wish something to be the case then it is so. That I believe the USA to be a classless society will explain why I act one way rather than another; that social class is actually still an important social force in the USA will explain why the long-term consequences of my actions are not what I expected.

DEGRADATION CEREMONY Harold **Garfinkel** used this phrase to refer to the communicative work that transforms a person's status and identity to something less honourable and prestigious. In his work on **total institutions**, Erving **Goffman** used the phrase 'mortification of the self' to refer to procedures (such as replacing personal clothes with a uniform, shaving heads, and removing personal possessions) designed to undermine the new inmate's old self in preparation for the creation of a new persona.

DEGRADATION-OF-WORK THESIS See **de-skilling**.

DE-INDUSTRIALISATION In most western industrial societies, the proportion of total output that comes from making things and the proportion of the working population engaged in manufacturing, have declined since the 1960s. This is partly because of a growth in service industries (and more recently what is called the 'knowledge economy') and partly because of our success in creating labour-saving devices that make manufacturing less labour intensive. Since the 1970s there has been a growth in the international division of labour, with multinational companies relocating manufacturing that does require considerable human effort to developing countries with lower labour costs and less rigorous regulatory regimes. The fact of de-industrialisation has stimulated important arguments about the continued value of models of social class that were based on 19th-century economies. It also means that to talk of Europe, Japan and North America as the 'industrial societies' is increasingly misleading since, though the manufacture of airliners and luxury cars is still concentrated in these countries, the industrial activities of ship-building, iron smelting and so on are concentrated elsewhere, for example in China and India.

See **class structure**.

DELEUZE, GILLES (1925–95) After a career as a relatively conventional historian of philosophy at the Sorbonne and in Lyon, Deleuze was among the first prominent academics to respond at a conceptual level to the impact of the student and workers' uprising of May 1968. He moved to the University of Vincennes, Paris in 1969 and took the lead in trying to tie together work in philosophy, politics, psychoanalysis and literature. His most renowned work (the two volumes loosely focused on capitalism and schizophrenia entitled *Anti-Oedipus* (1984) and *A Thousand Plateaus* (1988)) were co-written in the years after the 1960s with Félix Guattari (1930–92), a political activist and **Lacanian** psychoanalyst. Expelled from the French Communist Party in 1956, Guattari had become very active as a Trotskyite and was later pivotal in the formation of the 1960s ultra-left in France. Their works can be seen as reflections on the continuation of capitalism and the apparent willingness of capitalism's victims to acquiesce in its perpetuation. They regard capitalism as a destructive force that undermines all existing affiliations, groups and communities. None the less, this chaotic force has a joyful kind of energy – hence the schiz-ophrenia of life under capitalism. Their works, notably their writings about the **rhizome** (a metaphor deployed to press for the virtues of non-hierarchical networks), are best approached as experimental reflections on the uneasy experience of living with capitalism. Their publications have been influential in lit-erary studies and, despite neither author being a sociologist and them not conducting socio-logical investigations in any conventional sense, on sociology.

DELINQUENCY   Literally meaning misdeed or neglect of duty, the term is sometimes used simply as a synonym for crime or deviance, but it better refers to a particular kind of rule-breaking that falls somewhere between the deviant and the seriously criminal; where the rules are minor laws or significant social norms. It is often qualified as *juvenile* delin-quency in recognition of the fact that a great deal of minor crime is committed by teenage and young men, many of whom give it up when they acquire adult responsibilities. Many early studies of juvenile delinquency, especially those associated with the **Chicago School** explained it by reference to the organisation of urban gangs, delinquent subcultures and

the limits on the legitimate opportunities for working-class men. Critical criminologists have sometimes romanticised delinquency by presenting it as a form of resistance to oppres-sive dominant values.

See **anomie, criminology, deviance amplification, labelling theory, subculture**.

DELINQUENT DRIFT   David Matza's (1964) *Delinquency and Drift* was a counter to 1950s theories which supposed that there were spe-cific causes of delinquent motives and actions which bore down on certain types of people. Matza saw the delinquent as much more a choosing actor but also suggested the choices involved in becoming a delinquent were small ones; drift rather than conversion. Crucial to that drift was learning a variety of ways of justifying actions (or **neutralisation techniques**) so that people could commit delinquent acts while still thinking of them-selves as decent. In the same way as Robert K. Merton's **anomie** model can be criticised for assuming that people start honest and require to be shocked out of their law-abidingness, Matza's model may be unnecessary where people are raised in a subculture which entirely rejects the dominant values. Nonetheless, Matza's work is useful because it draws atten-tion to the situational nature of much delin-quency and to the gradual development of delinquent careers and because it recognises that delinquents and criminals do not gener-ally view themselves as unprincipled, immoral or unethical.

DELINQUENT SUBCULTURE   The term describes a group (typically of youths) which shares norms and values at odds with those of the rest of society. In the 1930s, the **Chicago School**'s combination of interaction-ist theory and interest in local community studies encouraged researchers to study the development of criminal and anti-social attitudes and behaviour in high crime areas of the inner city. Now widely accepted, the main themes of that research were then radical: that delinquency was explained by features of groups (rather than by individual pathology) and that becoming delinquent was a social process pretty much like becoming anything else. The subculture was seen as a solution to the low status, poverty and lack of opportunity of young people (especially young men) in the inner city.

DEMOCRACY   At its simplest, democracy is rule (the Greek 'cracy') by the 'demos' or the people. In very small political units, it is possible for everyone to have a say in decisions; in larger units, the people must choose representatives to rule in their interests and on their behalf. In modern parliamentary democracies the representatives generally form parties which offer competing agendas to the electorate for approval.

The reality of democracy is more complex. The nature and limit of the demos needs to be established. Many polities that have been described as democratic, excluded whole classes of people; for example, women, slaves, people born elsewhere, and those with little or no property. Arguably the USA was not a democracy until the 1960s because until the Voting Rights Act of 1965 and associated legislative changes, blacks in much of the old Confederacy were effectively disenfranchised. The democratic credentials of many eastern European polities in the communist era were flimsy: they had elections but as only candidates approved by the ruling party were allowed to stand we may suspect those elections were not an effective vehicle for conveying the will of the people – and what the people were allowed to will was determined by the communist party. Similarly the parliamentary democracy established in Iran after the Islamic Revolution of 1979 is constrained by Islam, as interpreted by an oligarchy of Islamic jurists who vet candidates and laws. No

political culture can be free of presuppositions. The will of the people is always constrained by dominant assumptions about what is good and true and valued, but we can distinguish polities by the extent to which they are formally constrained by some ideology that trumps what any particular generation of the demos wishes.

A variety of circumstances seem essential for democracy. Effective choice requires that people have appropriate knowledge and have opportunities for the exchange of ideas; hence the importance of a free press. Some external constraint on the actions of elected governments (an independent judiciary or a constitutional guarantee of rights, for example) is also required to ensure that, once elected, a government does not abuse its position.

DEMOGRAPHIC TRANSITION   This signifies a particular combination of population changes associated with the shift from agrarian to industrial society. Agrarian societies typically have high birth and death rates; that infant mortality is high and adults die young is balanced by largely unrestricted fertility. In the early phase of industrialisation, death rates fell but birth rates remained high and population grew rapidly. Finally, birth rates fell to restore the balance. What is not clear is whether this pattern will be repeated in countries modernising at the start of the 21st century. Rates of population growth have been faster in many **Third World** countries than they were in Europe when it experienced industrialisation and their economies have not grown fast enough to keep pace and to provide the security and improved living standards that are associated with reduced family size.

DEMOGRAPHY   From the Greek for people (demos) and writing (graphein), this is the study of population characteristics such as fertility, mortality and migration.

DEMONISATION   See **moral panic**.

DENOMINATION   See **religious organisations**.

DEPENDENCY THEORY   In opposition to those who believed that the underdevelopment of the **Third World** was largely a result of intrinsic characteristics of those countries, the Marxist Andre Gunnar Frank argued that the economic problems of the undeveloped and developing worlds were a direct result of exploitation by the West. The West grew by enslaving other peoples, expropriating their raw materials and making them a market for its finished goods. With the end of open imperialism, the domination of the West became more subtle: the economies of the Third World were distorted by being encouraged to produce, not for their own needs, but to serve the needs of the West. Small countries that were given over to one or two export crops (such as bananas or tea) have expensively to import everything else and are vulnerable to fluctuations in western tastes. This subservient form of development he termed **underdevelopment**; the word came to be used a verb so that Britain could be said to have underdeveloped India, or Portugal Mozambique.

Though Frank's basic point is unarguable, by the 1990s social scientists were again interested in the intrinsic characteristics of developing societies because however valuable the idea of dependency is as a general description of the relationship between First and Third Worlds, it did not allow us to understand in full the diversity of experience in the developing world. Some states have prospered; others have faltered. There is a renewed interest in the sort of comparative economic sociology, pioneered by Max **Weber**, that examines the role of culture and social organisation in hindering or encouraging economic development.

DEPENDENT VARIABLE   See **independent and dependent variables**.

DEPRIVATION   Most narrowly, deprivation is the act of taking something away or the state of having been thus deprived. It was also for a long time used for the state of not having the survival basics of food and shelter. It is a mark of the West's increasing prosperity that we now use it for the condition of not having something we would reasonable expect a person to have.

See also **relative deprivation**.

DEPRIVATION, MATERNAL   See **maternal deprivation**.

DERRIDA, JACQUES (1930–2004)
Derrida was born in Algeria and moved to Paris to study in the 1950s. He devised the idea of **deconstruction** as an approach to philosophical, and other, texts. Most philosophical systems to date had depended on trying to demonstrate how various phenomena sprang from an underlying principle; philosophers argued among themselves about what this principle was: some were materialists, others idealists and so on. Derrida switched attention away from the principle itself to the way in which the principle is identified and expounded. He proposed that there is always a tension and instability in the way in which philosophical systems are built up and presented in philosophical texts. Accordingly, his ambition for philosophy was not to do what had always been done, not to replace one philosophical system with another, but to explore the inerasable tensions and instabilities within philosophical writing. This programme is what he called deconstruction. It differed from critique in that it did not seek to substitute one school of thought with another but to work on the resources available within existing texts.

This approach can also be applied to other forms of text, including professional texts by social theorists and the texts of various sorts produced in everyday life. And it is for the analysis of literary texts that Derrida's work has been most widely adopted. For example, in North America Derrida is more generally admired by literary scholars than by philosophers. The difficulty of his writing has been both a discouragement and, to others, a lure – on the assumption that wisdom must lie behind the difficulty. This mix of popularity and inaccessibility is reflected in the availability of Derrida-style work on Winnie-the-Pooh and other humorous themes. Derrida himself is fond of puns and humour, so such work seems entirely fitting.

See **de-centred self, deconstruction**.

DESACRALIZATION   This term was used by Bryan Wilson to refer to one element of the process of **secularisation**. An important part of the general loss of power, popularity and persuasiveness of religion in the West is the replacement of sacred and supernatural assumptions by this-worldly and rational ways of thinking. That we regard having fits as a symptom of a medical problem rather than as evidence of an unusual spiritual state is an example.

DESCARTES,   RENÉ   (1596–1650) Descartes was a celebrated philosopher, mathematician and natural philosopher (a scientist before the term existed). For today's sociologist, Descartes's main importance arises from his contribution to the famous 'mind/body problem'. He saw that there was a problem in understanding human action of the following sort: we can comprehend how a person moves their hand by contracting muscles in their arm, but we cannot understand in the same way how the wish to move the hand leads the arm-muscles to contract. One process seems wholly mechanical while the other seems to cross from the mind to the body. Descartes was fascinated by this mindbody interaction

and speculated about where in the body this interaction might take place and what form the interaction might take.

Noam **Chomsky** has invoked the name of Descartes when arguing that humans are predisposed to language acquisition through some special compatibility between our brains and the **deep structures** of language. Chomsky (1966) entitled his book on this topic *Cartesian Linguistics*.

DESCENT GROUP   A descent group is any social unit that is identified by a common ancestor, real or imagined. Though central to the organisations of the small traditional societies studied by anthropologists, such groups feature little in modern industrial societies.

DE-SCHOOLING   This is one of the silliest social science ideas of a credulous decade: the radical 1960s. Ivan Illich and others argued that schools were coercive institutions that socialised children into the competitive and de-humanising ideology of modern capitalism, prepared them to accept their allotted place in a life of drudgery and stunted their creativity. A wide variety of alternatives to a nation-wide state-supported education system were promoted; none caught on. In retrospect it is remarkable that those who were attracted to the idea of 'de-schooling society' failed to see how very un-radical their idea was. Under any regime the children of middle- and upper-class parents would continue to inherit their family advantages, but for the children of immigrant and lower-class families formal schooling was one of the few avenues for upward social mobility.

DESCRIPTIVE STATISTICS   See **inferential statistics**.

DE-SKILLING   In the classic *Labor and Monopoly Capital*, Harry **Braverman** (1974) argues that capitalist employers use technological developments to reduce the skills required for production so that workers become more readily replaceable and hence less powerful, wage levels are lowered, unemployment and insecure work is increased, and workers become increasingly alienated. Although it is possible to describe the changes in any one occupation in such terms, national studies of occupational structures as a whole have not supported Braverman's Marxist prognosis. While some skilled jobs have disappeared, new equally skilled jobs have been created; unemployment levels have fluctuated rather than moved consistently upwards; and average wage levels have gone up, not down.

See **proletarianisation**.

DESPOTISM   See **absolutism**.

DETERMINISM   Almost always used as criticism, this denotes a range of theories that have in common the belief that people have little conscious choice in their actions and are shaped by forces beyond their knowledge or control. The later works of Karl **Marx** could be described as economic determinism; those of Talcott **Parsons** as expressing structural determinism. While very few social scientists would subscribe to a rigid version, most sociological explanations involve a degree of determinism in that we frequently identify causes of social action that actors will not have fully appreciated.

DETERRENCE   Literally meaning 'putting off' or 'discouraging', deterrence is commonly used in criminology and in political sociology to refer to constraining the rational actor by increasing the penalty for the unwanted action. So the threat of being caught and punished, as well as the scale of the punishment, should deter the criminal. In an International Relations example, one state may seek to deter its enemies by increasing its defence spending or mobilising its forces on a contested border.

DEVELOPED WORLD   Many labels in the social sciences are changed periodically both because the phenomena so described change and because labels gradually acquire derogatory connotations. First, Second and Third Worlds are used to describe, respectively, the first group of industrialised nations (those of western Europe North America, Japan and Australasia); the communist bloc of eastern Europe; and Asia and Africa. With the collapse of communism, the admission of a number of former communist states to the European Union, and the rise of a number of Asian economies (Hong Kong, the Philippines, South Korea and parts of Malaysia), this three-fold classification now seems rather dated.

DEVELOPMENT, UNEVEN   See **uneven development**.

DEVIANCE   Often used as part of a pair with 'crime', deviance is the breaking of social rules that are not part of a legal code. For example, religious dissent, homosexuality and mental illness have all in their time and place been regarded as forms of deviance.

Much of the sociology of deviance, especially from the 1960s, was concerned less with explaining the original acts of deviants than with the societal reaction of deviance. Howard S. Becker's **labelling theory** and Erving **Goffman**'s work on **stigma** focussed attention on the responses of others to the deviant.

Deviance was held to be caused by society in two senses. In the first place, an act or characteristic is only deviant because the social group has created the rules which define what is acceptable and what is deviant. Beyond the statistical sense, what makes homosexuality 'abnormal' is a set of norms that accept only heterosexuality.

Another society could decide otherwise; in that sense deviance was always situational. The second sense of the social causation of deviance concerns the practical application of rules. Actions, characteristics and people have to be judged by some agency or person to be deviant. While this shift of attention from the attributes of the deviant to the social process of attributing deviance, generated a large amount of insightful research into labelling processes and their consequence in **deviance amplification**, some work degenerated into a sentimental romanticising of deviants and some mistakenly claimed too much for labelling (as when sociologists unhelpfully overlooked the neuro-physiological bases of some types of mental illness).

While deviance is generally seen as a problem to be solved, Emile **Durkheim** drew attention to the positive social functions of deviance. In *The Rules of Sociological Method* he (1895) wrote: 'crime is normal because a society exempt from it is utterly impossible'. One important function of deviance is to innovate. Behaviour which is now regarded as radical and dangerous may be next decade's orthodoxy or, to put it another way, a society of total conformity would be lifeless. True as this may be, it does not explain why innovative behaviour should be regarded as deviant in anything but the statistical sense. Innovation would presumably be as virtuous even if it was not initially stigmatised and repressed. Although Durkheim does not himself make the connection, his second positive function of deviance could have been presented as an answer: opportunities to stigmatise and demonise deviance are useful for building social solidarity. The need to unite periodically against a common threat is so great, Durkheim believes, that in a community of saints, where no-one committed any major sins, infractions of petty rules would be elevated to major sins in order to provide occasions for demonisation and reinforcement of the collective conscience.

DEVIANCE DISAVOWAL   It is an important qualification of the **labelling** perspective that not all those labelled as deviant accept that judgement. In a variety of ways people may distance themselves from the label, arguing either that it is inappropriate or that it does not reflect the 'real me'. Alcohol and drugs are frequently used to explain why, though the actor admits the **primary deviation**, the usual corresponding judgements of the self should be suspended: 'When I'm sober I wouldn't hurt a flea. It's the drink, not me!'.

See **neutralisation**.

DEVIANCY AMPLIFICATION   The term was first coined by Leslie. T. Wilkins in the slightly different form of 'deviation' amplification. It quickly came to stand for a variety of ways in which the responses of such official agents as the police, courts and psychiatrists to some initial act of deviance may encourage the novice deviant to become more rather than less deviant. For example, far from deterring him, punishing a young person for a minor crime may encourage further crime by alienating the person from conventional society, reducing the chances of finding a legitimate occupation and forcing him into the company of more experienced criminals. When the person re-offends, the official agents and bystanders say 'Look, we were right! This person always was a criminal' and are confirmed in their judgements. The criminal is further excluded and more fully acquires the identity of criminal, and so on.

Although the idea clearly has a great deal of intuitive appeal, it can reasonably be criticised for a lack of specificity. Those who have used it to explain increasing deviance have rarely been able to explain why such amplification spirals operate in some cases but not others and why many of those labelled as deviant abandon deviance.

See **deviation, primary and secondary, labelling theory, moral panics**.

DEVIATION, PRIMARY AND SECONDARY
Edwin Lemert's (1951) *Social Pathology* introduced the distinction between primary deviation (by which he meant the initial offending behaviour) and secondary deviation (the symbolic re-organisation of the self and social roles that may follow from the societal reaction to the primary deviation).

DEWEY, JOHN (1859–1951) The eminent US philosopher is known for two contributions to the social sciences. He was an early pioneer for progressive child-centred education; witness his *Democracy and Education* (1916). He was also a pragmatist who rejected essentialist philosophies in favour of a view that saw objects defined by the uses to which people put them. Like Charles Horton **Cooley**, he rejected such dualisms as mind–body, man–nature and fact–value. Knowledge was always socially situated.

DIALECTICAL MATERIALISM As an approach in the social sciences, materialism gives little or no place to ideas or culture in the explanation of social action and social institutions, and insists that what really matters is the economy and the world of production. The dialectic is an idea popularized by Georg **Hegel** who believed that history progressed through a series of clashes between an idea (the thesis) and its opposition (the antithesis) to a new idea (the synthesis). Karl Marx replaced ideas in Hegel's model by material forces. In its philosophical form the idea of dialectical materialism remained thoroughly obscure (though communist states claimed it as ideological justification) but it provided Marx with a coherent historical sociology. In historical materialism (presented clearly in Marx and Friedrich **Engel**'s (1967) *Communist Manifesto*) the past can be conveniently summarised as follows: for every system of production there is an appropriate social organisation of class and property. While economic forces continually develop and become more productive, the class and property structure remains unchanged. This increases the tension between economic forces and social relations until it is resolved (the synthesis) in a radically new form of economy with new class and property relations.

Like all such simple models that try to encompass the history of the world in a few terms, historical materialism is illuminating if taken generally and nonsense if taken seriously.

DIASPORA From the Greek for 'through' and 'scatter', the term denotes a people that has been dispersed. The Jews, who spread out into smaller communities around the world after being expelled from Palestine in the 4th century BC, formed the classic diaspora, but with migration becoming more common in the 20th century, a number of religio-ethnic groups now form diasporas. As well as being interesting in their own right for their capacity to maintain some sense of group solidarity despite being widely dispersed, such diasporas are also significant for the part they may play in the politics of their homelands. Because they see their own prestige within their adoptive countries rising with the prestige of their homelands, diasporic groups may be more aggressively nationalistic than the majority in the homeland. For example, the Hindu nationalist Bharatiya Janata party, which came to power in India in the 1990s, received considerable financial and moral support from Indians in Europe and North America.

DICHOTOMY Any variable which has only two mutually exclusive conditions is dichotomous. As the number of cases which fall outside the two categories of male and female is trivial, we can regard sex as a dichotomy.

DIFFERENTIAL ASSOCIATION In opposition to biological models of criminal behaviour, Edwin H. Sutherland (1934) in his

Principles of Criminology argued that crime was learnt by people in primary groups whose members were criminally inclined. People became criminal by being socialised so that the weight of views favourable to crime exceeded those that encouraged them to be law-abiding. The idea was subsequently developed by Donald R. Cressey with whom Sutherland collaborated on *Principles*. The term is a little misleading in that it is not the degree of 'associating' with law-abiding or criminal people as such that is thought to explain crime; rather it is the balance of attitudes (supportive and dismissive) to the law that is the proximate cause. That one acquires a particular set of attitudes is in turn explained by one's associations.

Differential association was important in promoting the idea that, although becoming a criminal was in one sense unusual (in that what one learnt was to reject very basic social norms), it was in many respects like learning to become a doctor and should be explained with the standard sociological repertoire of ideas about socialisation, peer groups, actions and rewards.

It may seem obvious but it is worth noting that differential association offers a more persuasive explanation of the crimes of habitual or career criminals than of such crimes as murder and other forms of personal violence, which tend to be isolated acts.

DIFFERENTIAL OPPORTUNITY STRUCTURE
Richard A. Cloward and Lloyd B. Ohlin's (1960) *Delinquency and Opportunity* was a creative attempt to improve Robert K. Merton's theory of **anomie** by adding to it Edwin H. Sutherland and Donald Cressey's work on delinquent subcultures and **differential association**. Merton regarded a certain form of deviance (which he called innovation) as a response of those who were fully socialised into a desire for material success to the fact that they were denied access to the legitimate means for achieving it. Hence they

turned to illegitimate means. This rather took for granted that illegitimate means for getting on were freely available. Cloward and Ohlin coined the phrase 'differential opportunity structure' to draw attention to the fact that opportunities to become delinquent were also unevenly distributed.

DIFFERENTIATION   Most simply this is the process of 'becoming more different'. More particularly, it is the term used to describe a fundamental feature of modernisation: the fragmentation of social spheres, roles and institutions into ever more specialised parts. For example, in most of pre-industrial Britain, the family had economic, educational and reproductive functions. With industrialisation, most work moved out of the home into shops, factories, and commercial farms and an ever-larger proportion of the population was schooled in educational institutions. In most European countries the Christian Church of the Middle Ages was not solely a religious institution; it also provided the bureaucracy for government, schooled children, ran the universities, provided rudimentary social welfare and health care, exercised a considerable policing role, and was a major landowner. In the 18th and 19th centuries the churches lost most of their non-core functions. Where they were retained (in schooling, for example) they were increasing subject to secular, not religious standards and control.

Differentiation denotes not just a finer division of labour of activities, but also a separation of values. In place of the unified life-world of the simple pre-industrial society, modern societies are made up of a variety of spheres which may be informed by notably different values. In the home and at leisure we are allowed to be expressive; pursuing the relationships we wish for their own value. At work we are expected to be rational, instrumental, efficient and universal. We may marry whom we wish but our hiring and firing policies should be rational and universalistic.

See **de-differentiation**.

DIFFUSION   The term denotes the spread of cultural attributes from one culture to another. Diffusion has long been an alternative to evolutionary theory as an explanation of the origins of cultural variation. Robert Lowie believed that cultures were patchworks of borrowed characteristics, in which the superior traits spread furthest from the centre of diffusion, so that the most widespread characteristics must be the oldest. One diffusion interest was to identify the origins of human culture. For early anthropologists, Egypt was a favoured candidate for status of cradle of civilisation. Modern anthropology has largely given up this pursuit and now supposes cultures to have developed largely independently of each other.

DIFFUSION OF INNOVATION   Innovation research can be traced to the French sociologist Gabriel Tarde (1962), otherwise best known because his highly individualist model of human behaviour was used by Emile **Durkheim** to exemplify what Durkheim's stress on the social was supposed to replace. His 1903 *Laws of Imitation* proposed that the take-up of some new idea or practice followed the pattern of an italic 'S': slow spread initially followed by a rapid rise as most people took up the innovation and then a flattening out as the stragglers finally caught on. In the 1940s agricultural sociologists studying the take-up of a new type of seed corn in Iowa revived interest in the S-curve and sociologists at the Bureau of Applied Social Research, Columbia University (including such leading scholars as Elihu Katz, Robert K. **Merton**, Paul **Lazarsfeld** and James Coleman) studied personal influence and innovation in a variety of settings such as medical prescribing

of a new drug, the use of radio appeals to sell war bonds and election campaigns.

One point of this tradition was to identify characteristics of people who were more or less slow to innovate. For example, the farmers who first planted the new type of corn were the wealthiest and the most cosmopolitan. The slowest innovators were the poorest farmers and the most socially isolated. Another was to stress the role of social relationships. Against the school of thought (exemplified by Theodor **Adorno**) that saw the modern world as a **mass society** in which individuals denied proper human relationships would be vulnerable to recruitment for extremist political causes, the diffusion of innovation tradition identified the importance of social networks in spreading new ideas. Although mass communication was important in spreading 'awareness' of an innovation, 'adoption' was heavily influenced by personal influence – and it wasn't always the same groups of people that were influential; the relevant social influences could be topic-specific: for example, in matters of fashion women were likely to look to younger female friends for a lead.

Diffusion of innovation has periodically re-gained popularity in mass media research, in explanations of religious **conversion** and in the **social movements** literature more generally. It is also popular in management studies.

See **two-step flow of mass communication**.

DILTHEY, WILHELM (1833–1911)   Although a philosopher, Dilthey is widely regarded as one of the founders of the interpretative or hermeneutic tradition in the social sciences. The details are of little interest now but his attempts to create a philosophical basis for the human sciences were important in German academic arguments about the social and natural sciences or **Geisteswissenschaften and Naturwissenschaften**.

DIONYSIAN   Dionysus was the Greek god of wine; the Roman equivalent is Bacchus. The term Dionysian is associated with Friedrich **Nietzsche** who argued that the moral philosopher should not be cool, rational and detached, but passionate and engaged in a Dionysian manner. Sociologists use the term either in relation to Nietzsche's work or in describing contemporary cultural practices that celebrate excess and lack of control, such as binge-drinking on nights out.

DISCOURSE   When sociologists talk about discourse they will, generally speaking, be alluding to one of two things. They may first of all be talking about a socio-linguistic phenomenon; work of this sort is usually referred to as **discourse analysis**. The second possibility is that they are talking about a much more pervasive phenomenon whose analysis is usually associated with Michel **Foucault**.

In his historical analyses (which he often called 'archaeologies'), Foucault sought to identify characteristic ways of describing and understanding the world. For example, 19th-century theories and religious and medical practices relating to sexual behaviour interpreted sexual desire, masturbation, prostitution and pornography within a broadly unified framework. This framework is the 19th-century discourse of sexuality. Contemporary 'liberated' understandings of sex are also a discourse. By calling it a discourse, Foucault draws attention to the extent to which actors within the historical framework have the experience of simply describing how the world is. They are unable to recognise that the framework itself could be utterly transformed. People are subject to the discourse.

In this work, Foucault's analysis differs from Marxist ideas about a dominant ideology since he is interested not in the ways in which people come to believe that the present situation is natural and legitimate but in the fact that a form of sexuality (or ethics or government), different from the present, is simply unthinkable.

DISCOURSE ANALYSIS   This refers to the empirical analysis of discourses and has some similarities with **conversation analysis** and the study of rhetoric. Discourse analysts draw attention to the ways in which people express themselves through standardised and often institutionalised ways of talking and writing. For example, passengers on British trains are no longer 'passengers' but 'customers' while shoppers in US superstores are known as 'guests'. When speakers use these terms they convey information and interpretations which are carried by the discourse as much as by the things they deliberately say. Discourse analysts usually attribute a good deal of explanatory significance to these discourses, for example the discourses that teachers employ to describe children or that surgeons use to describe patients. Accordingly, discourse analysis (DA) is the systematic study of these discourses, usually accompanied by the assumption that the influence of the discourse itself is greater than the speakers themselves can see.

There are various informal schools of DA, some using formal socio-linguistic terms, other being more descriptive and informal. Unlike conversation analysts, analysts of discourse usually have difficulty in corroborating their interpretations from their subjects' talk, precisely because discourse analysis assumes that the discourse is more influential and pervasive than speakers recognise.

DISCRIMINATION   Taken literally, discrimination is merely the ability to tell one thing from another; to discriminate is to make choices or to have preferences. In casual modern use and in public policy it is always an abbreviation for 'improper discrimination'. In appointing a postal worker it would be proper to reject a man who couldn't read; that clearly relates to the matter in hand. It would be improper to reject a woman, a man with red hair, or every third candidate.

Considering differences between the three examples will clarify usage. The third does not entirely fit discrimination because the reason for rejection is impersonal; everyone has an equal chance of being rejected in this method. Nor does the second; this time because the reason is idiosyncratically personal. Very few people have anything against red-haired men; it would not in other settings be a disadvantage. The first is the typical case because it involves a group characteristic (gender) which the applicant cannot help and which is irrelevant to the job.

DISCRIMINATION, POSITIVE   See **positive discrimination**.

DISCURSIVE FORMATION   See **discourse**.

DISEMBEDDING AND RE-EMBEDDING MECHANISMS   According to Anthony **Giddens** these twin mechanisms are important characteristics of the modern world. Abstract systems (for example, symbolic tokens such as money) spread social relations far and wide across time and space: we can now hire financial services from a call centre in India and order made-to-measure suits from Hong Kong via the Internet. In so doing, traditional social bonds with neighbours are weakened. This disembedding makes us feel insecure so we try to re-embed through new forms of relationship (e.g. e-mail friendships) and community (Internet sites) and new forms of politics (e.g. promoting the rights of a lifestyle group).

See **risk, reflexive modernity**.

DISNEYFICATION   Like **McDonaldisation**, this involves using a successful commercial enterprise to stand as a metaphor for wider social change. It has two meanings; one relating to the early Disney cartoons and the other to the Disneyland theme parks. In the

first and older sense, it denotes altering a cultural product such as a fairy-tale to make it more pleasant, bland, colourful and unthreatening (and, sometimes, to make it more American). In the second it denotes 'theming' an area of life, de-differentiating consumption (in the sense of combining such separate activities as eating, taking exercise, and purchasing entertainment), extensive collateral merchandising (the film comes with the tee-shirt, the book, the DVD, the toys, the school lunch bag and so on), and the creation of emotional labour (as in hiring people to ensure that customers not only consume the product but have the appropriate emotional response to it).

Implied in both sense of Disneyfication is global reach. As with McDonalds, Disney has become a highly successful global brand, recognised in most parts of the world. As with McDonaldisation we can both recognise the usefulness of the idea and suspect a degree of exaggeration. Although Disney cultural products (and local imitations) are widely popular, they have not extinguished local mass media products. One critic illustrated the global reach claim by saying that the *Ramayana* (a great epic poem that is a central sacred text in Hinduism) would be Disneyfied. Far from it: a thoroughly gory and extremely lengthy version of the *Ramayana* was shown widely on Indian television in the late 1990s and is held by some commentators to have played a major part in arousing Hindu nationalist violence: hardly the consequences supposedly associated with US cultural imperialism.

DISSONANCE   See **cognitive dissonance**.

DISTRIBUTION, STATISTICAL OR FREQUENCY   In statistics, the spread of any set of values for a variable (e.g. where the variable is height, and the values are different numbers of centimetres) is its distribution. There are various common patterns of distribution of social phenomena but the best known is the 'normal' or bell-shaped curve (or, if you want to be pompous about it, unimodal symmetrical) distribution. A surprisingly large number of things do match the bell curve quite closely. It is important to notice when data do not have a normal distribution because the assumption of one underpins many common statistical tests.

DIVINATION　　Divination is the art either of telling the future or of diagnosing the hidden cause of some calamity, usually by consulting some sort of oracle.

DIVISION OF LABOUR　　The phrase denotes both the division of a workforce so that people specialise in particular tasks and the deliberate separation of complex tasks into their component parts for increased efficiency. In *The Wealth of Nations*, Adam Smith (1776b) described the specialisation made possible by grouping workers together in factories as the defining characteristic of industrialisation. Following Auguste **Comte**, Emile **Durkheim** argued that the division of labour in the first sense contributed to the cohesion of modern societies by making us increasingly interdependent. Karl **Marx** regarded the division of labour as one of the causes (with **private** property) of alienation and imagined that it would be abolished under socialism. In later works he back-tracked and admitted that a 'realm of necessity' in which work was specialised, would continue.

DOMESTIC DIVISION OF LABOUR　　The phrase was used by feminists to draw attention to the significance of what is the oldest and most common division of labour: the division of work by gender with women performing unpaid work in the household and in childcare. Feminists influenced by Marxism sometimes use the term 'reproductive labour', after a distinction made by Friedrich **Engels**

between productive or value-creating work and the labour required to keep workers alive and fit to work and hence to replenish the labour force. Most usages equate domestic work with housework but some broaden it to include the emotional work of caring for others. Despite disagreements about exactly how to define and measure domestic labour it is clear that it forms an important base of inequality between the sexes and is a major hidden subsidy to the conventional productive economy.

DOMESTIC VIOLENCE　　The term was popularised by feminists in the 1970s to refer to male violence (psychological as well as physical) against women in the home and to press the policy case that such violence should not be viewed as a private matter but as a subspecies of violence against the person that should be policed as aggressively as similar violence between strangers. Typically the police and courts have been reluctant to act against domestic violence, in part because of the sexist attitudes commonplace in these male-dominated agencies but also because of the considerable difficulty in building a successful prosecution where the evidence often boils down to one person's word against that of another. Political campaigns and the increasing presence of women in law-enforcement agencies have changed the climate in most western societies so that family violence is no longer accepted but the evidential problems remain.

DOMINANT IDEOLOGY THESIS　　Ideology suggests something more than a body of ideas; it implies distortion and dishonesty for a particular purpose. The well-known quotation from Karl **Marx** and Friedrich **Engels** – 'The ideas of the ruling class are in every epoch the ruling ideas' – neatly expresses the proposition that elites rule, not just by the threat of violence, but also by persuading their subjects that their rule is legitimate.

They do this most effectively by promoting a general worldview in which their dominance appears earned, natural or inevitable. Marxists argue among themselves about how much store Marx actually set by dominant ideologies as a device for incorporating subordinating classes. Historians argue about just how effective attempts to indoctrinate the masses were. The intention of the author of the popular Victorian hymn 'All Things Bright and Beautiful' is clear from the sentiment expressed in 'The rich man in his castle/ The poor man at his gate/God made them high and lowly/And ordered their estate' but we may doubt the success of the enterprise. We know that the Christian Church in the Middle Ages tried very hard to educate, indoctrinate and control its people; we also know that the people often distorted the official doctrine, retained pre-Christian superstitions, and developed their own unorthodox versions of what was intended as a dominant ideology. That radical and revolutionary ideas do emerge shows how often the ruling class fails. The collapse of the USSR in the 1980s offers an interesting counter to the dominant ideology thesis. For 60 years the Communist party had almost absolute control over every state and social institution – far more power than any feudal monarch – and it utterly failed to convert its citizens to Marxism-Leninism.

On the other hand, it is clear that whole peoples do share some common ideas and assumptions about the world. However diverse in their details, almost everyone in Christendom in the Middle Ages accepted that the world had been created by a God who exercised moral judgements and that the Church had the power to mediate those judgements. The phrase 'pervasive worldview' might be a suitable way of describing near-universal agreement over some basic big ideas.

DRAMATURGY Previous sociologists had borrowed from the theatre the idea of role as a way of suggesting that individual action is shaped and actors are co-ordinated by social conventions, but Erving **Goffman** took the metaphor of social life as drama much further. For example, he uses the contrast between frontstage and backstage areas very effectively to analyse the way our behaviour changes when we go 'on'. He extended the **symbolic interactionist** interest in the self as a social creation by treating the self as performance. To be a saint, being saintly was not enough; you had to act out saintliness.

DRIVE Possibly a better translation of Sigmund **Freud**'s *Trieb* than 'instinct', the term suggests basic biological or psychological urges, as in 'the sex drive'. The idea plays little part in current mainstream social science because increasing knowledge about the enormous variety of behaviour found around the world makes it hard to claim plausibly that we have any drives. We may talk loosely of the will to survive and the sex drive but people kill themselves and celibacy is not that rare.

DUAL LABOUR MARKET Some social scientists divide the world of paid work into two. The primary labour market consists of well-paid, secure and long-term employment (with, for non-manual workers, a career). The secondary market provides low-wage, insecure and unstable employment. This division is used in Marxist and in feminist theories of work (as in the claim that women are largely confined to the secondary market). The simplicity of the distinction is misleading; three or four labour markets would be more accurate and many people shift between them at different stages in their lives. But it does convey the important point that jobs differ importantly in characteristics other than pay.

DUALISM Generally any view that either things or ways of viewing things can be divided into two discrete blocks could be described as dualism. An example is the unfortunately common practice of using two very different ways of explaining social action: we treat our own actions as rational while supposing those of others to be irrational. This is 'explanatory dualism'.

DURKHEIM, EMILE (1858–1917) Despite dying from a stroke at the young age of 59, Durkheim produced a number of major studies that rightly establish him, with Karl **Marx** and Max **Weber**, as one of the three founders of modern sociology. Like the others, he produced pioneering studies of substantive sociological topics (mostly concerned with the novel characteristics of modern industrial societies) and contributed to debates about the appropriate methods for sociological study.

In his doctoral thesis, published as *The Division of Labour in Society* (1893), Durkheim presented his contrast between the bases of social cohesion in pre-modern and modern societies. Rather confusingly (because it suggest the machines characteristic of the industrial society), he used the term 'mechanical' solidarity to describe the basis of social solidarity in primitive societies where individuals and institutions were little differentiated and people hung together by their common adherence to a shared body of values and symbols. Put simply, the society stayed together because its component people were very similar in having been socialised into a single culture. Modern industrial societies are too large and complex to cohere by similarity; increased specialisation of work and the differentiation of institutions encourage diversity and individualism. These would in turn threaten social cohesion were it not that at the same time they create greater inter-dependency. The modern society is sustained by 'organic' solidarity. Like the human body, the whole only survives because of the workings of the separate organs but equally each organ can only

survive if the whole lives. However, a potential problem remained since the decline of a collective conscience raised the threat of **anomie**. His idea that people required some sort of externally-imposed cultural straitjacket in order to find satisfaction (because without it greater wealth would simply stimulate an expansion of the desires) explains why, for a long time, Durkheim was dismissed as a right-wing ideologue. Always interested in public policy, Durkheim's proposed solution to the anomie inherent in modern societies was the promotion of the idea of occupational guilds and other intermediate institutions that would stimulate value cohesion.

Durkheim's second book, *The Rules of Sociological Method* (1895), attempted to establish a clear method for the new discipline. He argued that it: had to be based on observation (rather than the generation of abstract philosophical schemes); had to provide both causal and functional explanations; and had to study social rather than psychological facts. By this he meant that proper sociological data were observations about features of societies, not about the individuals who peopled them. He was firmly opposed to **methodological individualism**.

He tried to demonstrate his method in his third major work, *Suicide* (1897). Unlike previous scholars who had treated **suicide** as an individual act, Durkheim studied the relationship between suicide rates and other aspects of a society. Whatever the reasoning of an individual suicide, regular patterns could be discerned in suicide rates and changes in these could be explained without recourse to individual motives. The fallibility of his data and his inconsistent shifting between individual and social levels of analysis explain why few scholars now find his treatment of suicide convincing, but the approach was profoundly influential, particularly on the **structural-functionalism** associated with Talcott **Parsons**.

Durkheim's fourth seminal work (summarised by Maurice Halbwachs (1930) as *The*

Origins of Religious Sentiments) was *The Elementary Forms of the Religious Life* (1912). This study of aboriginal religion was influential in describing and explaining religious ideas and practices in terms of the latent or hidden functions they performed for the society. At the heart of much primitive religion was the creation of social cohesion; by worshipping totems, primitive peoples were worshipping their own societies.

Durkheim also wrote on education, socialism and morality and founded the journal *L'Année Sociologique*.

DYSFUNCTION   The use of 'function' (as in 'the primary function of the family is to produce and socialise the next generation') gives a certain grandeur missing from 'consequence', 'effect' or 'purpose' and implies a biological metaphor. Just as we understand the kidney by the part it plays in keeping the rest of the body working, so the significance of any social institution is the part it plays in maintaining the whole society.

Activities that are injurious to a society are unlikely to become institutionalised. Almost by definition, function is positive because we look for the contribution to the maintenance of the social body. For that reason the prefix 'eu' (meaning good) died from neglect; but its opposite 'dys' is used to describe some patterned activity that has harmful or unpleasant consequences.

E

ECOLOGICAL FALLACY   This is the mistake of drawing false conclusions about individuals from information that refers only to a collectivity. For example, that Washington DC, is a wealthy city does not mean that all, every or the typical Washingtonian is wealthy: the aggregate characteristic could be made up of very rich people and very poor people. The mistake of drifting from one level of analysis to another can also be made for different scales of group. For example, at the level of the nation-state, the USA has greater religious diversity than the UK. But most US towns, cities and counties are more religiously homogenous than is most of the UK. The USA's religious pluralism is a mosaic of places that are very largely one faith or another. The ecological fallacy is particularly important in statistical analysis since it is quite possible to find that two factors are statistically associated even though they may in fact be unconnected. An example often given is that, in the USA, the wealth of residential districts appears to be positively correlated with the proportion of foreign-born people in the local population. But this association gives rise to an ecological fallacy. The correlation does not mean – as first appears – that foreign-born people tend to become wealthier than the average US resident. It means that foreign-born individuals choose to settle where the richer (US-born) residents already are. Foreign-born individuals remain less wealthy than locals. Thus wealth and the proportion of foreign-born individuals may be ecologically correlated even if foreign-born individuals are not wealthier than average.

ECONOMIC DETERMINISM   'Causation' might be a better word than 'determinism'; economic determinism is the idea that social structure and social change are primarily to be explained in terms of economic factors. Determinism is an approach to human behaviour which supposes that it is not a matter of free choice but is completely, mostly or somewhat a consequence of forces other than choice. **Marxism** is the primary example of an approach to social action and social evolution that supposes people are mostly shaped by their place in the economy.

ECONOMIC MAN   At the heart of economics is the assumption that people seek to maximise their returns (or satisfaction or utility). If we can buy an identical product in two outlets at different prices, we will buy the cheaper because it satisfies us every bit as well as the alternative and leaves us change to spend on something else. The problem is that many people do not seek to maximise in the obvious sense. For example, they will pay a premium to have the name of a famous designer emblazoned on their clothes or they will work voluntarily for charitable organisations. The economist can salvage the starting assumption by saying that the return that is being 'maximised' is the pleasure of owning something expensive and exclusive, or the warm feeling that results from people admiring your charitable efforts. However, if whatever someone does can be described as maximising their 'returns', then the claim that people are basically economically rational becomes vacuous.

See **rational choice theory**.

ECONOMIC TRADITIONALISM　　At the heart of Max Weber's **Protestant Ethic Thesis** and many other attempts to understand the rise of modern capitalism, is the problem of an apparently radical change in attitudes to work and industry. Most pre-modern people had relatively fixed notions of their traditional, customary or expected standard of living and, given the choice, preferred less work to more money. In Weber's own example, there was no point in doubling the wage-rate for a Silesian grass cutter in the hope that he would work harder; he would simply work half as long. Tasks were often performed in a fixed traditional manner, with some notion that ritually correct performance would be rewarded with success. The pursuit of wealth was often flamboyant. Merchants staked their fortunes on single ships that could make or break them; lords invested in foreign wars on the same principle.

What were conspicuously missing was the cautious search for the calculable steady rate of return and the rational experimental attitude to improving work methods. It was the power of economic traditionalism that led Weber to suppose that modern attitudes to work and accumulation could not have evolved from it but must have originated in some radical new ideas about the importance of work and the virtue of rationality.

EGALITARIANISM　　Generally this is a value system that supposes that all people are in some sense of equal worth. It is the basis for the modern belief that all people should

enjoy the same basic human rights. More particularly it is a political creed that promotes greater **equality**, either of opportunity or of outcome. In the first case the goal is greater fairness in the competition to get on in life; in the second it is a more even distribution of the prizes.

EGO　　The Greek word for 'self' or 'I', 'ego' appears in a variety of compound terms relating to the self, such as 'egotism' for selfishness. It has a particular meaning in Sigmund **Freud**'s three-part model of the personality. The ego is the part that deals directly with reality, the id demands immediate pleasure or gratification, and the superego is the internalised conscience. The ego tries to reconcile the demands of the id with what the superego will permit and with what the world seems likely to allow.

EGOCENTRISM　　In common usage this denotes selfishness. According to Jean **Piaget**'s developmental psychology, children go through a stage of egocentrism in which thought is focused on the self.

See **solipsism**.

EGOISTIC SUICIDE　　See **suicide**.

ELABORATED AND RESTRICTED CODES　　The British socio-linguist Basil Bernstein made a powerful contribution to the study of social class with his analysis of the background features of language. It is obvious that we can ascribe class to strangers by their vocabulary and accents. Bernstein was concerned with a subtler and less apparent connection. A restricted code is a type of speech in which meaning is implicit and telescoped and **indexical**. For example, 'How did it go for yer man?' can only work in the intimate context of a conversation between people who know what the 'it' is and who 'yer man' is. The same question between relative strangers would take the elaborated code form (which assumes no shared knowledge and is thoroughly explicit): 'How was your husband's hernia operation?'. Each code has its proper place: excessive formality between intimates would ring as false as excessive informality between strangers. Bernstein links codes to social class by arguing that the educated middle classes, because they are thoroughly familiar with elaborated codes, can readily adopt the code appropriate to the setting while less-well-educated working-class people have difficulty functioning with an elaborated code and thus operate less effectively in public and formal settings. For example, unfamiliarity with elaborated codes prevents working-class children performing as effectively in school as their middle-class counterparts, particularly in abstract disciplines that require the use of elaborated modes of expression.

Although there is clearly a great deal of value in the distinction, some socio-linguists dispute that we can identify codes underlying speech, that codes can be associated with class, and that different types of language can be regarded as more or less efficient ways of communicating.

ELECTIVE AFFINITY　Finding a plausible model of explanation which combines appropriate degrees of free will and causation is a persistent problem for sociology. Max **Weber** used this phrase to describe the links between novel doctrines promoted by the Protestant Reformers (the **Protestant Ethic**) and attitudes to work, capital accumulation, spending and investment (the spirit of capitalism). The former were certainly not intended to cause the latter and in the historical record we find very few people who explicitly made the connection in their own lives. This is no surprise; very large but slow changes in culture are often obscure to those

who live through them. Yet for good reasons, Weber believes there is a connection and uses 'elective affinity' to suggest that bodies of ideas and assumptions (or more precisely the people who adhere to them) fit more or less well together. Although not commonly used, the term is valuable because the word 'elective' reminds us of the element of choice in social life.

See **Protestant Ethic thesis**.

ELIAS, NORBERT (1897–1990)　Elias left his native Germany when Hitler came to power and worked first in England and later in Ghana and Holland before returning to Germany. He called his approach to social analysis **figurational sociology** because he analysed changing social configurations (the unintended outcomes of the actions of interdependent individuals) rather than societies. His first major work, *The Civilising Process*, attracted little attention when it was first published in German in 1939 but by the time an English edition appeared in the late 1970s, Elias had built a considerable following in England and the Netherlands. In that study and *The Court Society* (1969) Elias explored the links between the evolution of European states and changes in individual behaviour and personality (in particular the imposition of new forms of morality and increasing self-control through developments in etiquette and manners). Later works included *What is Sociology?* (1970), *The Loneliness of Dying* (1982) and *Involvement and Detachment* (1986).

ELITE　A term borrowed from French, this is useful for describing a small group that dominates a society, an organisation or a social group without committing yourself to any particular explanation for that domination. Hence it is a broader term than 'ruling class', which explains the power of such a group in terms of its economic position. In the 19th century (and later in very conservative hands) use of the word elite rather implied that the rulers deserved their position because they were innately superior. It is the cohesion implied in the term that explains why C. Wright **Mills**'s classic 1950s study of power in the USA was called *The Power Elite* (1956). Social scientists had depicted the USA as being governed by a number of relatively autonomous elites that acted to check and balance each other. Mills claimed to find a well integrated and partly self-perpetuating elite of political, business and military leaders who were closely linked by kinship and friendship ties and who shared a common social background.

ELITE THEORY   Less a theory than an observation, this terms refer to the work of various analysts (starting with the 19th-century Italians Vilfredo **Pareto** and Gaetano **Mosca**) who have taken the fact that in almost all known societies the mass of people have been ruled by a small elite, as warrant for supposing it will always be so and as the starting point for explanations of this phenomenon. Robert **Michels**, for example, argued that the frequently repeated pattern of initially left-wing parties and trade unions becoming increasingly rightwing was explained by the fact that as soon as a formal organisation was created it became dominated by a small oligarchy of bureaucrats. Later, social scientists argued that the democratic competition between rival representative elites, which we see in most parliamentary democracies, offers the best practicable form of democratic government.

See **iron law of oligarchy.**

EMBODIMENT See **body, sociology of.**

EMBOURGEOISMENT   Literally the French for 'the process of becoming middle class', the term was popularised in the 1960s by Polish sociologist Ferdynand Zweig who argued that increasing affluence was causing many industrial workers to adopt the lifestyle and culture of the middle class and hence weakening traditional class loyalties. In essence it was the alternative to the Marxist claim that the working class would get poorer and that class conflict would become more severe. The major empirical test of the idea – John Goldthorpe and David Lockwood's **Affluent Worker** research – produced a more complex finding: there was certainly class convergence in patterns of consumption but there were still clear differences in values.

EMERGENT   This term is most commonly found in the expression 'emergent property', where an emergent property is a characteristic that cannot be explained or understood in terms of the sum of its parts. The functioning of a clockwork watch, for example, can be understood in terms of how the parts operate together. One can see how the springs and gears make the hands turn at a steady rate. The brain, by contrast, does not seem to operate in this way. We may understand how brain chemicals work but this does not allow us to grasp consciousness. Emergent properties cannot be reduced to the operation of the systems of which they are made up and biologists commonly assert that biological phenomena are emergent to stress that biology cannot be reduced to chemistry and physics. For similar reasons, sociologists have been attracted to this terminology to emphasise their view that sociological phenomena cannot be boiled down to the aggregation of psychological occurrences.

EMIC AND ETIC   A distinction fashionable in the late 1970s, this pair comes from linguistics where 'phonemic' refers to a speaker's own recognition of patterns of sound, whereas 'phonetic' refers to the professional observer's modelling and measurement of differences in sound. By extension 'emic' came to mean 'internal' or 'indige-nous' and etic 'external'. An emic approach to analysis involves describing a situation or pattern of behaviour from the standpoint of those involved in it while an etic one is based on the external observer's accounts. Often the distinction is used for moral purposes; the emic or indigenous being preferred to the etic. In practice the distinction is hard to maintain because in most social settings there are major differences within the group and major similarities between some insiders and some outsiders.

ÉMIGRÉ   Emigration denotes leaving one's homeland for good, but describing someone as an émigré carries the additional sugges-tions of having been forced abroad, of con-tinuing to look to the old world for identity, and of being unable to return.

EMOTION WORK   One of those terms that straddle social science and feminist polemics, this signifies the work that wives and mothers and other female partners and relatives are said to do in making up for men's inability either to express their emotions or to respond adequately to the emotions of others.

EMOTIONAL LABOUR   With the shift from manufacture to service industries in western economies, an increasing number of people are employed in positions that require not only face-to-face interaction with customers but also the sustained presentation of certain emotions. Arlie Russell **Hochschild**'s (1983) *The Managed Heart* coined the term to refer to jobs which require the expression of 'commodified emotions'. Bar tender, with its requirement for the regular projection of friendly concern and sympathy, is an example of emotional labour.

EMOTIONS, SOCIOLOGY OF   Just as the typical sociological actor has always been

rather disembodied, so he or she has usually been emotionally arid. Sometimes emotions are assumed; for example, George Herbert Mead's theory of socialisation and Charles Horton Cooley's **looking-glass self** use pride and shame to link the actor's impression of how she or he appears in the eyes of the 'other' (significant or generalised). Likewise Erving **Goffman**'s thoughts about the impor-tance of maintaining 'face' in social inter-action assume actors are strongly motivated by shame and pride. But generally sociology has explained purposive action by thoughts, values and beliefs rather than by emotions and it has rarely considered emotion as a topic in its own right. In the 1990s there was some sociological writing on emotions but much of it, like much in the sociology of the body, is simply criticism of social theory for not taking emotion seriously and the pro-grammatic assertion that we should.

One good reason why emotion is rarely the focus for sociological research is that it is hard to gain access to emotions through sys-tematic methodological approaches. For example, we can often back our beliefs up with reasons and justifications; beliefs can be scrutinised in interviews and through opin-ion polling. But emotions are typically raw and unreflected-upon. Worse still, it is often very difficult for us to understand our own emotions, let alone those of others, in a deci-sive and certain fashion.

EMPATHY   Although often confused with sympathy, this is importantly different. To have sympathy for someone is to align your-self with that person's fortunes and reac-tions; it is very similar to 'feeling sorry for'. Empathy signifies imaginatively feeling what others are experiencing or mentally putting yourself in the other person's shoes. Accuracy is important with empathy in a way it is not with sympathy. Or to put it another way, to sympathise with someone is a purely per-sonal state: I may not fully understand what it is like to lose a son but I may sympathise nonetheless. If I say that I empathise with someone who has lost a son, I am making an empirical claim about the closeness of correspondence between what that person feels and my imaginative reconstruction of it. The empirical issue is important: **interpretive sociology** insists that we be concerned with how things appear to those whose actions we are trying to explain (what W.I. **Thomas** called 'the **definition of the situation**'). Most sociologists take seriously Max **Weber**'s insistence that sociology be concerned with discovering the meaning in meaningful social action and many would argue that in most instances to explain an action is to uncover its meaning to the actor. The point of interviewing people, observing them, and participating in their lives is to arrive at an adequate understanding of what their world looks like from the inside. That is, interpretative sociology assumes that empathy is possible.

EMPIRICAL   Usually forming a contrast pair with such terms as conceptual, theoretical, abstract or philosophical, this suggests an observation or assertion rooted in firm evidence. Too often one reads articles in which authors claim that their work is based on 'empirical evidence', implying that there is any other kind. All evidence in the social sciences is empirical, although that is not to deny that there is room for conceptual analysis.

There are two common exceptions to this rule about empirical evidence. First, is **phenomenological** research, which is based on reports of perceived experiences (of religious fervour and so on). Since these reports are inevitably about private phenomena they are not open to empirical checking in the ordinary sense. Second, in some branches of social philosophy, people make use of 'thought experiments', that is considerations of what would happen in a hypothetical situation that illustrates a philosophical dilemma (e.g. what would parents do if advances in reproductive technology allowed

the genetic character of their children to be manipulated at conception?). Such studies have empirical ambitions but since they deal with fictional situations they cannot be viewed as thoroughly empirical.

EMPIRICISM   This can have a neutral meaning: a philosophical doctrine about knowledge that says that the only true knowledge is derived from experience or evidence. But it is generally used as an insult to refer to a style of sociological work that is, in the eyes of the person writing, insufficiently informed by theory or insufficiently aware of the difficulties of collecting reliable data, or both.

ENCOUNTER   Everyday life is made up of a large number of episodes of face-to-face interaction. Some are with people we know well but many are brief encounters. Erving **Goffman** analysed the social rules governing such features of encounters as the correct positioning of the body and appropriate and inappropriate attention and gaze.

See **interaction ritual**.

ENCULTURATION   Meaning the formal and informal acquisition of cultural norms and practices, this term, favoured by anthropologists, is pretty well synonymous with what sociologists call **socialisation**. The disciplinary divide in usage reflects the greater weight that anthropology gives to culture.

END-OF-HISTORY THESIS See **end-of-ideology thesis**.

END-OF-IDEOLOGY THESIS   Daniel Bell's (1960) *End of Ideology* argues that major changes in the nature of capitalism (such as diffusion of the ownership of capital, the incorporation of the working class in the polity, and the growth of the welfare state) have robbed the old clash between right and left of much of its force. An increase in public militancy in the 1960s and 1970s, with the anti-Vietnam war protests and industrial conflicts, seemed to refute the thesis but it regained popularity in the late 1980s when, with the effective end of state communism, it was restated by Francis Fukuyama as the 'end of history'. By that he meant that, while liberal democracy still had faults, there was no longer any credible alternative and hence there could be no more of the great ideological revolutions that had previously shaped human history.

It is certainly the case that the left–right divide which dominated political and social thought in the 19th and 20th centuries has largely gone. Even left-wing parties accept capitalism, the collapse of the Soviet Union in 1990 ended the global contest between right and left, and radical politics is now somewhat diffused across globalisation, the environment, the rights of indigenous peoples and a variety of lifestyle issues that do not fit neatly into simple ideological categories. Fukuyama himself has lately announced that the end of history may have been proclaimed prematurely, not because there are new ideological challenges to liberal capitalism, but because the possibility of genetic transformations of humankind may result in such differences between people that old assumptions about **universalism** and **egalitarianism** would no longer apply.

ENDOGAMY   The Greek for 'within' (endo) is here coupled with the Greek for marriage (gamy) to describe the institution of marrying within a particular group. Social groupings of various scales – tribes, clans, castes, nations – can require it. The alternative is exogamy (from exo meaning 'without').

ENDOGENOUS   From the Greek meaning 'caused from within', this adjective has been applied to a variety of social and human phenomena. For example, endogenous depression is that form of depression which is internally generated and is not a reaction to external stimuli.

ENGELS, FRIEDRICH (1820–95)   A German-born industrialist whose family owned a textile business in Manchester, Engels spent much of his adult life working in England. He contributed greatly to the development of Marxist thought in two ways: with his own ideas and with his financial support for his close friend Karl Marx. In the 1840s Engels collaborated with Marx on some of the foundation texts of Marxism: *The Holy Family* (1925), *The German Ideology* (1974), and *The Communist Manifesto* (1967). After Marx's death, he revised and prepared for publication volumes 2 and 3 of *Capital* (1886). Engels suggested a less deterministic model of social organisation than had Marx when he allowed that elements of the 'superstructure' such as law and ideology could on occasions be free from and even shape the economic base. On the other hand he was more responsible than Marx for the grand claims to scientific status. His *Anti-Dühring* (1877–8) provided the basis for what was later called **dialectical materialism** and, influenced by **Darwinism**, he became more committed than Marx had been to the idea that social evolution was unilinear.

Engels also wrote on history and anthropology. His *The Condition of the Working Class in England* (1845), based on his close observations of life around his family business in Salford, was profoundly influential, although many modern historians think he was mistaken in supposing that the dire conditions he observed represented a decline in living standards from those obtaining in pre-industrial rural England.

Perhaps the greatest contribution Engels made to Marxism was that he funded it. Critics are fond of pointing out the disjuncture between the high place that Marx gives labour in his theories and the fact that he lived as a 'remittance man', supported by Engels from the profits of exploiting the English working class whose condition so disturbed him.

ENLIGHTENMENT, AGE OF   This denotes the second half of the 18th century when a number of thinkers attacked tradition, autocracy and the Church and promoted rational analysis as the proper basis for the ordering of human affairs. The term probably exaggerates what writers such as Voltaire (1694–1778), Montesquieu (1689–1755), Diderot (1713–84), the organiser of the mammoth *Encyclopédie*, and Jean-Jacques Rousseau (1712–78) who coined the slogan 'Liberty, Equality, Fraternity', had in common. But it was nonetheless an age of impressive innovation in thought and in public life. It is conventionally held to have terminated with the bloodshed of the French Revolution in 1792 and the subsequent rise of Napoleonic imperialism.

Since the 1980s it has been fashionable to dismiss much sociology as being informed by 'the Enlightenment project'. Usually one of two points is being made with this perjorative. Either sociologists have exaggerated the rational and progressive elements of modernisation, which has been as bad as it has been good, or their social analysis is distorted by them being standard bearers for the Enlightenment (for example, in exaggerating the extent of secularisation or mistaking its causes). In most case the criticism is irrelevant. It is true that the Enlightenment (especially in its Scottish form, see below) provided some of the earliest sociological writings, but by the end of the 19th century much sociology was moving away from a vision of social evolution as being driven by a conscious desire for this or that change to an acceptance that much social change was the result of unintended and inadvertent consequences.

ENLIGHTENMENT, SCOTTISH   Coincident with the Enlightenment in France, Scotland produced, for its size, a disproportionate number of scholars who made major contributions to modern thought. Adam **Smith**, Adam **Ferguson** and John Millar were key figures, as was David **Hume**. Less well-known but also significant were Lord Kames, Lord Monboddo, Dugald Stewart and Frances Hutcheson. Because they were much less closely tied to the church and to the ruling class than were Oxford and Cambridge in England, the universities of Glasgow, Edinburgh and Aberdeen were centres of ideological innovation. Like the French, the Scots had their compendium of modern knowledge: the *Encyclopaedia Britannica*, edited and printed by William Smellie, first appeared in 1771.

Common ideas of the Scottish Enlightenment were: (a) the importance of empirical study of social institutions; (b) the assumption that society must be studied as a natural and moral order (rather than, for example, being seen as divinely ordained); (c) an assumption that laws underlying social realities (like those explaining the natural world) would eventually be discovered; and (d) the progressive nature of the world. A common interest was the centrality to human action of **unintended consequences**. As Smith noted, the individual in pursuit of his own interest frequently promotes that of society 'more effectively than when he really intends to promote it'.

ENTREPRENEUR   Economists have long been interested in business leaders who innovate because they believe that those who find new things to do or new ways of doing existing things (such as expanding the market for air travel by drastically reducing air fares) hold the key to economic growth. Max Weber's **Protestant Ethic thesis** was a pioneering attempt to relate social values, personality and economic growth. Interest in the conditions for stimulating an entrepreneurial personality periodically re-emerges in studies of comparative economic development.

More generally the term signifies someone who works hard to develop something new; hence the phrase 'moral entrepreneur' to describe people such as anti-pornography campaigners, environmentalists and animal rights activists who try to effect a radical change in opinions.

ENTERPRISE CULTURE Generally speaking this is a societal culture that emphasises and encourages individual initiative, energy and self-reliance. Societies that have such a culture are thought to demonstrate greater economic growth and to give greater freedom to individuals than societies with a high degree of state regulation of economic activity, extensive state welfare provision, and a high degree of public ownership and control of productive capital. The 1980s saw a general swing in many industrial societies away from the state control that had developed in response to the economic crises of the 1930s and the restrictions of the Second World War era. Conservative governments in the UK, the USA and elsewhere removed much government regulation, introduced commercial competition into many sectors of the welfare state (such as health and education) and privatised (i.e. sold off) state-owned transport and other public utilities.

As well as liberating producers to innovate, such reduction of state control was designed to increase consumer choice, to make services more efficient by subjecting them to the rigours of free market competition and to give people greater opportunity to take responsibility for their own welfare. In many European countries the encouragement of enterprise involved a direct attack on the power of professions to regulate themselves.

The most radical introduction of an enterprise culture has occurred since the late 1980s in the economies of the former communist countries of eastern Europe (and, to a lesser extent, in China). In the space of a few years, entire **command economies** were dismantled and state enterprises sold off. Generally speaking, those countries that were most advanced before the imposition of communist rule (e.g. what is now the Czech Republic) have made the smoothest transition to free market economies. In Russia privatisation has not yet created the hoped-for enterprise culture because the communist **oligarchy** used its political power to convert its previous managerial control of state monopolies into outright ownership of what were still monopolies.

The experience of the former communist countries offers a powerful reminder of Weber's insight, sometimes overlooked by students who know his Protestant Ethic thesis but are unfamiliar with his related work on the conditions other than personality necessary for rational capitalist development. Entrepreneurship requires not just an absence of state regulation of economic activity but also political stability and a law enforcement system that can safeguards assets and ensure the enforcement of contracts.

ENTROPY See **systems theory**.

EPIDEMIOLOGY The study of the prevalence and distribution of disease and illness in human populations has its origins in a recognition that, although illness presents itself as a characteristic of the sick individual, many diseases are in various ways group properties. Susceptibility to certain illnesses may be a group characteristic. An example of a gender-based ailment is haemophilia (the lack of the clotting agent that prevents excessive bleeding), which can be carried by women but afflicts only their male offspring. An example of a 'racial' disease is sickle-cell anaemia which primarily affects people of African origin. In these examples, the group characteristic is biological and genetic but epidemiologists also trace patterns of disease that are in two senses social in origins. First, social properties such as poverty create a disposition to suffer from certain ailments. Second, the origins of diseases can often by illuminated by working backwards through the social pattern of spread. Obviously the transmission of diseases that pass from one person to another is clearly a social matter and, as in the case of AIDS, the study of patterns of spread can be extremely useful in allowing us to understand the causes of some illnesses. But even where the agent is acquired directly from a non-human source, epidemiology can be important in understanding illness. The discipline's first great success was of this nature. Dr John Snow mapped the incidence of cholera in an 1854 London outbreak. He showed first that almost all the victims lived closed to a water pump in Broad Street and second that the exceptions could be explained. A large workhouse close to the pump had no cases but it had its own well. Two elderly ladies who lived 10 miles away died; it turned out that they liked the taste of the Broad Street water so much they had a large bottle delivered every day. When the handle was removed from the pump, the epidemic subsided.

EPIPHENOMENA   With 'epi' meaning on top of, upon or in addition to, this term is contrasted in **Marxist** thought with 'phenomena': the surface appearance of something and its underlying reality. To describe something as epiphenomenal (religious conflict in Northern Ireland, for example) is not to say that it is unreal; rather it is to claim that it disguises a deeper determining reality: Marxists would say that the epiphenomenon of religious conflict is produced by the phenomenon of class conflict. A general problem with such a distinction is that it is rarely supported by any evidence. The actors in question are not expected to be aware of the underlying causes of their actions and so

evidence cannot be sought from their own accounts. Usually the analyst asserts the true explanation on the basis of his or her claimed knowledge about action in general.

EPISTEME   The Greek for a piece or structure of knowledge, the term was popularised by Michel **Foucault** as a synonym for **discourse** formation: a body of ideas that shapes the way the world is seen or experienced. In that sense it is similar to **paradigm**.

EPISTEMOLOGICAL BREAK   Thomas Kuhn (1962) in his *Structure of Scientific Revolutions* argued that the development of science proceeds not by the steady improvement of ideas but through a series of dramatic breaks. For long periods work in a particular field of scientific research ('normal science') is conducted on the basis of an agreed set of principles or **paradigm** which come under increasing pressure from anomalous results until the field is forced to accept a radical revision of its central ideas. Underlying this model is the claim that a paradigm can be so closed that alternative ways of seeing evidence are **incommensurate**: that is, the ideas of a new paradigm cannot be stated in the language of the old. Accordingly, paradigm succession is marked by an epistemological break.

Louis **Althusser** used the idea of an epistemological break to separate radically the humanistic work of the younger Karl Marx from the supposedly scientific theories of the mature Marx.

The term also appears in anthropological arguments over whether an outsider can truly understand an alien culture.

EPISTEMOLOGY   This is the science or discipline ('ology') of knowledge (**episteme**) and in philosophy denotes that field concerned with how we know what we think we know about the world. In sociology the term is used more loosely for investigations into the status of sociological knowledge and for considerations of the links between scientific method and sociological knowledge.

EPOCHÉ   This term, originally from ancient Greek, refers to the placing of some aspect of thought or reality in parentheses or brackets (hence the anglophone alternative of 'bracketing'). Sociological discussion of epoché chiefly dates from Edmund **Husserl** and his work on **phenomenology**. In an attempt to get at the phenomenon of pure consciousness, Husserl claimed that we must set aside (or bracket off) how consciousness or individual personhood appears at any particular historical time, since that appearance is likely to be contaminated by cultural factors that are historically variable. Subsequently, writers from within the tradition of **ethnomethodology** argued that Husserl had got his argument the wrong way round. As far as they were concerned, the important material for understanding the experience of social life was precisely all the taken-for-granted cultural assumptions that make life regular and dependable. They were more interested in bracketing off abstract philosophical considerations and macroscopic sociological assumptions (for example about **class**) and examining the residual elements of **intersubjective** reality.

EQUALITY   In general there is no mystery: equality is the state of being equal or the same. The difficulties come when we consider how similar and in what. Giving everyone the right to vote appears to allow equal participation in the choice of government but the vote of a Democrat living in a state with a large Republican majority has less impact than one living in a marginal state. Does providing a lawyer free to those defendants who cannot afford one ensure equal access to the law if private lawyers are generally better than public defenders? Given that

absolute identity is rare in social phenomena 'equal' usually means 'roughly similar'.

Then there is the 'in what' question. A major divide between social democratic and socialist policies is encapsulated in the difference between equality of opportunity and equality of outcome. Social democrats believe that social justice requires that we give all people an equal chance to succeed in life and to make the best of their talents: hence the stress on equal opportunities. For a genuinely **meritocratic** society a degree of positive handicapping is required to compensate for disadvantages such as a poor family background, racial discrimination and the like but, provided the race is run fairly, social democrats have no objection to it having winners and losers. Socialists are more concerned with equality of outcome and argue that social justice requires an equal distribution of whatever is valued rather than an equal distribution of the chances to compete for what is valued. Social democrats, liberals and conservatives would all object that, even if equality of outcome were possible (and the failure of communist regimes to prevent new dimensions of inequality such as political power replacing capitalism's social class suggests it is not) that itself would be grossly unfair because it would mean that individuals who begin life with some advantage (such as being brighter or born into a wealthy family) would be punished for something that was not their fault. That is, positive discrimination in favour of one group of people designed to redress one sort of inequality inevitably creates another. The problem for liberal democratic societies is striking the balance between the two imperatives.

EQUILIBRIUM   In mechanics this is the state of being at rest because the forces of action and reaction are equal. In chemistry it is the point in a reversible reaction when in a mixture of substances no apparent change takes place. The notion was taken into models of society (such as that promoted by

Talcott **Parsons**) as a system of inter-connected elements that tended towards equilibrium, even if they did not reach it. As one element of a social system changes, the whole becomes unbalanced and others will change to restore the balance in a new state. While this idea of dynamic equilibrium has a certain intuitive appeal, it has the weakness of much social science that it gives an air of precise explanation to what is often little more than after-the-fact renaming. In mechanics and controlled chemical reactions we can specify the equilibrium point. In the study of social systems the notion can only be a loose metaphor.

ESSENTIALISM   In philosophy, this may denote the view (a) that it is possible to know the essence of something or (b) that definitions are intended to capture the essence of the thing described (and hence can be right or wrong rather than just more or less useful). So many sociologists now suppose that knowledge can only ever be provisional and that definitions are matters of social convention rather than discovery, that essentialism in either sense is used only about the work of others and as an insult.

However, we need to be wary of going too far in the other direction. If definitions have no connection with a reality beyond words, and, if we can never confidently know enough about the world to distinguish between, for example, democracy and dictatorship, then social science becomes impossible.

ESSENTIALLY CONTESTED CONCEPT When it comes to describing some attribute of a society (**equality**, for example), the sociologist will typically hope that analysts can agree about what the term means. If there is disagreement about the concept, then the plan is that further research should lead to clarification. However, some political philosophers have argued that there are some terms in social science whose meanings may never be agreed. This is because it is in the nature of these terms to have differing interpretations. The entry on **equality** illustrates the problem here: if one wants to assess how far different societies have got in producing equality, one needs to know what equality means. Yet there are persistent differences over whether an 'equal society' is one with equality of outcome or equality of opportunity. Since these political and ideological disputes are not likely to go away, neither will the problem of how to assess or measure inequality. The concept is disputed and will remain so; it is, in the phrase coined by W.B. Gallie, essentially or inherently contested. Democracy is often also cited as an essentially contested concept.

ESTABLISHMENT, THE   Like **elite**, this term is useful for denoting a small group of people with considerable power and influence without committing yourself to an explanation of that power and influence. It neatly captures the sense that complex modern societies have a variety of sources of power: economic, military, political, social, legal and cultural. Wealthy businessmen, higher civil servants, controllers of mass media, senior educators, politicians, church leaders, top military officers and policemen all enjoy considerable power though their interests may not always be sufficiently similar to make them act in concert. Nonetheless, the term 'establishment' conveys the sense of a relatively integrated group (often bound by kinship ties) and one that does not have to struggle to maintain its position. This second point makes the term more appropriate for stable societies (such as the USA and UK) than for societies such as are common in the Third World where elites deriving their power from different sources (owning capital, leading the country's army or leading a powerful social movement, for example) compete.

See **Mills**.

ESTATE Many feudal societies were stratified (i.e. divided horizontally) by divisions based on statuses, defined in law, which had attached to them complex rights and responsibilities. Each estate or 'station' had its prescribed way of life, which included rules of etiquette and often extended to rules about appropriate consumption. A common system was a three-fold division of clergy, nobility and commoners. The important point about estate as the basis for stratification is that, like the religiously-sanctioned **caste**, it allows far less flexibility and social mobility than **class** and hence discourages social change and economic growth.

ESTEEM Sometimes used loosely as a synonym for status, this term is better kept for the positive (or negative) evaluation of the characteristics or performance of an individual so that 'status' can be used for the evaluation of a role or position within a social system.

ET CETERA PRINCIPLE This term is used in **ethnomethodology** to refer to a problem with mainstream sociology. In the mainstream, social action is usually interpreted in relation to a variety of factors (such as class or educational background). But in any given instance there are innumerable factors possibly at play, depending on which social scientists one asks. Hence, according to ethnomethodologists, sociology is confronted with the 'et cetera problem' of not knowing which factors to take into account in any given instance: there is class, educational background, gender et cetera. By contrast, ethnomethodologists argue, people in the ordinary course of their interactions with each other are not plagued by the et cetera problem. People have their own practical procedures for working out what is going on and what needs to be attended to. Ethnomethodologists assert that the interesting

phenomenon is the non-issue of the et cetera problem in everyday interaction. They see this as a reason for preferring the study of people's 'ethnomethods' to the more abstract business of mainstream sociology.

ETHICAL DEPRIVATION It has been common to explain various sorts of involvement in religious and social movements by deprivation: those short of status might be joining in movement activity to try to resolve 'status deprivation'; others might be trying to compensate for their poverty or 'economic deprivation'. Charles Glock and Rodney Stark used the phrase 'ethical deprivation' to describe the problem of those respondents who believed that the world would be a better place if everyone accepted the same severe moral code. It seems curious to describe an ideological preference as a form of deprivation (would we have 'art deprivation' or 'jazz deprivation'?) but it is of a piece with a deterministic streak in sociology that minimises the role of individual consciousness by explaining (or better, explaining away) preferences as mere reflections of antecedent, usually-socio-structural conditions.

ETHICS OF RESEARCH Strictly speaking, ethics is the branch of philosophy concerned with distinguishing the right from the wrong. Almost all social groups, from the smallest voluntary association to whole societies, generate and promote ethical codes; that is, they socialise their members into a conception of moral and immoral action.

Until the 1970s it was common for medical researchers to use patients as research subjects without their knowledge or consent. During the 1939–45 war, German scientists used concentration camp inmates as subjects for experimental work that would have been unacceptable on free citizens. What we know about the effects of exposure comes from studying subjects who were slowly murdered by being immersed in freezing water. Less barbarously but with similarly little consent, US doctors were funded by drug companies from the mid-1950s to the mid-1970s to conduct covert experiments on the inmates of Holmesburg, PA, prison.

Public opposition to such medical arrogance led to a major revision of ethical principles so that most medical research in the West is now underpinned by the notion of informed consent. For examples, new drugs can only be tested on people who have the likely benefits and costs fully explained to them.

Although few forms of social research have consequences for their subjects anything like as severe as those of much medical research, social scientists have become increasingly concerned about the ethics of their work. It is very widely agreed that research should not harm those studied but harm may not always be obvious. An anthropologist may study a previously isolated society with no intention of changing its way of life yet, simply by having joined, irreversibly change that world.

The effects of intrusion are not generally a problem for sociologists because even those who use covert participant observation normally study worlds in which their presence is not an anomaly or a source of alien contamination. The greatest damage we can normally do to people is to present them in an unfavourable light (and we may do that without intending to simply because, as the Scots poet Robert Burns noted, it is a rare gift to 'see ourselves as others see us'). Hence a major principle of the ethics of social research is the protection of anonymity. In two cases (John Lofland disguising the Moonies as 'The Divine Precepts' and the Lynds calling Muncie, Indiana 'Middletown') researchers have stuck with the false name even after the real identity was widely known.

Some radical and feminist sociologists create an additional ethical problem by asserting that sociologists have an obligation to assist those they study. We can imagine cases where this is quite compatible with normal ideas of reciprocity: if the inhabitants of a women's refuge are willing to help us with our research, why should we not also help them raise funds, campaign against domestic violence or help them better understand themselves and their predicament? But it is hard to imagine western liberals suggesting that someone studying a group that attacks abortion clinic staff should assist it to better achieve its goals.

See **covert research, ethics of**.

ETHNIC CLEANSING   A translation of a Serbo-Croat phrase first used in 1991 to describe Croats sacking Serbs from their jobs, this has since come to be used as a synonym for genocide. It might be called a euphemism except that, far from making more palatable what it denotes, to English ears at least, it is every bit as brutal as genocide. Cleansing, with its suggestion of tiled public lavatories, strong disinfectant, of something repellent suppressed, implies that the other is not just the enemy but also an affront, so alien that their presence contaminates the land and the society. With its suggestions of 'clinical' hygiene, it also suggests the thoroughness with which people engaged in the task.

ETHNIC MINORITY   This signifies a population within a society that is clearly identified by distinctive origins and culture: migrants from Pakistan to Britain and their descendants, for example. As with most social categories, this entity is defined from at least four different perspectives: from within the ethnic minority, from without by lay members of the wider society, by policy experts and officials, and by the professional social scientist. Because such definitions are themselves acts of social construction that may carry a large political charge, they will often not match. Members of certain castes or from particular regions may resent being lumped together with those they regard as very different (and possibly inferior). Outsiders may use categories that make little sense to insiders. Government officials may use categories (in censuses, for example) that fit awkwardly with the interest of academic scholars. It seems that the term is here to stay although more and more of the practical problems associated with its use come to light each year and every time there is a census.

ETHNIE, ETHNIC GROUP Much confusion is caused in the social sciences by inconsistent use of terms such as race, nation, ethnie (or ethnic group) and caste. Some of the inconsistency results from people being casual with terms, but much of it results from competing assumptions about what matters most in the creation of group identities.

Ethnie or ethnic group denotes a group on the scale of a people or a nation, the members of which claim descent from common ancestors and are usually united by a common language, religion, culture and history. Like nation it is generally self-defining. There is little value in pointing out that the descent from common ancestors is almost always fictional and that boundaries change. What defines the ethnic group is its members' belief in common ancestors.

It differs from the **nation** in that it does not immediately imply a common political identity or purpose. Most nationalisms demand for the people the right to be ruled only by their own kind. In practice most nations have an ethnic core and base their political claims on the supposed integrity and superiority of the ethnie, but it is possible for nations to be based on shared territory and loyalty to a state. For example, although there are Americans who assert that only Anglo-Saxon Christians can be true patriots, most Americans subscribe to a civic nationalism in which a wide variety of ethnic groups can co-exist, united by common residence and a common loyalty to the state.

Ethnic group has largely replaced race because race (a) is felt to be offensive; (b) implies a degree of blood relationships that is incompatible with what we know about inter-breeding; and (c) implies that important social and personal traits are differentially distributed between distinct races. For example, those southern US states that passed laws prohibiting miscegenation (originally a biological term for cross-breeding) did so in the belief that whites possessed superior characteristics (such as intelligence) that would be diluted by breeding with inferiors. The advantage of ethnie is that it focuses more on the cultural and elective nature of the group than on its supposed genetic integrity.

ETHNOCENTRIC, ETHNOCENTRISM It is a natural weakness of human thought (but one that can be overcome with effort) that we take our own experiences as normal, inevitable or paradigmatic. Ethnocentrism is the practice of taking one's own people, society and culture to be the vantage point from which all else is viewed and judged. At its mildest, ethnocentrism can make us blinkered (as when some Europeans supposed that Australian aborigines did not have religion because they did not have churches and clergy). At its most extreme it takes the form of making inappropriately negative judgements about other peoples; New Yorkers may suppose southerners to be stupid because they speak more slowly.

One major issue for comparative social science is whether analysts can distance themselves from their own cultures sufficiently to understand those of others; the answer is that they can and do so everyday in their successful interactions with others who are not identical. The 'Can-we-understand-Pygmies?' problem is much exaggerated by people who forget that, given the similarities between many features of our lives and the lives of Pygmies and the many differences within any culture, it is not that different to the 'Can I understand my mother?' question.

ETHNOGRAPHY   Literally 'writing about the people', this denotes research which concentrates on directly observing and describing in detail the activities of some people. The term is often used with a hint of judgement. People describing their own work as ethnography are often asserting that, in contrast to others, they have really captured the essence of group life. It can also be used in a negative sense to label work which is thought to be merely descriptive or to have no explanatory content. Because the authority of ethnography lies in the ethnographer's ability to describe and write down how a culture 'really' is, ethnography has been strongly attacked by **postmodernist** critics.

ETHNOMETHODOLOGY   Ethnomethodologists tend to devote a lot of time to defining and arguing over what they see their programme as offering or being about. But a common definition would suggest that ethnomethodology is the systematic exploration of the techniques used by members of a society to perform the ordinary social tasks that make up that society's life. Examples of ordinary social phenomena studied by ethnomethodologists include the orderliness of a queue and the regularities of turn-taking in conversation.

Ethnomethodologists insist that they are interested in the 'incarnate' production of social life; for example, the orderliness of a queue is generated by the people doing the queuing as they queue. A conversation is assembled by the speakers as they talk. These phenomena are orderly without being pre-scripted or governed by explicit, external rules; this insight has been developed most successfully in **conversation analysis** (an outgrowth of ethnomethodology). Thus it is the practices and skills that are used

spontaneously to produce the orderliness of social life that interest ethnomethodology; ethnomethodologists assert that mainstream sociology takes these practices and skills for granted and thereby denigrates them.

Some early enthusiasts for ethnomethodology argued that it was the only viable approach to studying social life since mainstream sociology was an institutionalised procedure for telling stories about society that were ungrounded in everyday social practices. Lately, ethnomethodologists have tended to soften these claims and some ethnomethodologists have worked collaboratively with mainstream social scientists.

ETHOLOGY   This is the comparative study of animal behaviour, especially of its innate or non-learned elements. Attempts to apply lessons learnt from studying primates to people have never been very successful with academic social scientists but they have entered the popular consciousness through television programmes and popular non-fiction. It is clear that humans are close biological relatives of primates but the explanatory value of ethology for studies of human behaviour are widely thought to be limited.

ETIC   See **emic and etic**.

ETIOLOGY   This is the study of causation, especially the causes of diseases.

ETYMOLOGY   This denotes the study of the sources and development of words. Etymology has often been undertaken purely as a branch of linguistics but since words and cultures tend to develop and migrate together, etymology has become increasingly integrated into cultural history and historical sociology. People may re-write their histories for ideological reasons but, since words often seem so natural, it is common for historical changes to leave unnoticed linguistic traces. Etymology is therefore a powerful complement to more traditional historical research methods.

EUFUNCTIONAL   See **dysfunctional**.

EUGENICS   The term was coined by Francis Galton in 1883 for his proposals to improve the human race by selective breeding. As a social movement, eugenics was popular in the early part of the 20th century. The American Genetic Association was formed in 1913 with the aims of promoting positive selection (by, for example, giving financial support to parents who were thought to be particularly intelligent or in some other sense excellent) and negative selection (by, for example, constraining the fertility of people thought to be inferior or in some manner defective). Leaving aside for a moment the vexed issue of to what extent we are a product of our genes or our environment, the parallel with animal husbandry shows the obvious difficulties of human eugenics. The characteristics of cattle that a farmer wishes to develop (for example, speed of weight gain or ease of calving) are often simple, observable and calculable. The characteristics of a bull's offspring can be measured within a year. And there are few ethical obstacles to selecting mates for your bull or sending unsatisfactory calves for slaughter. None of that is true for people. Worse still from the viewpoint of advocates of eugenics, human genetic inheritance seems more complex than had been supposed a century ago.

It is now believed that the kinds of measures Galton proposed would have been ineffective. Recent advances in genetic understanding have given rise to new calls for selective breeding with, for example, genetic testing available for parents to ensure that children at risk of genetic defects can be assessed before birth and selectively aborted. Many campaigners view this as a new and stealthy form of eugenics since it is unclear what should count as a defect. People with disabilities fear that this procedure may further stigmatise those with congenital disabilities. Equally, it is logically possible that being female (or in some cases male) might be seen as social disadvantageous and female embryos might be terminated in a eugenic fashion.

See **Darwinism, Social**.

EVOLUTION   Evolution refers to the idea that something – an animal, an idea, an institution, a religion – developed out of something else rather than came into being fully formed. In that sense, all social phenomena have evolved. In the biological realm the idea was originally contentious because it suggested that one species evolved into another; this conflicted with the traditional view that distinct species were separately created by divine purpose. Early on, biologists generally suggested that life forms evolved from simple to more advanced kinds. It seemed self-evident that the best came last. On this basis, it came to be common to use the term evolution to signify a form of development that moves in the direction of progress or towards complexity.

Modern Darwinian understandings of biological evolution do not share this latter assumption. Evolution by natural selection argues simply that species tend to evolve to fit their environment better; there is no necessary expectation that they become better in some absolute sense: smarter or more sophisticated, for example. Bacteria continue to evolve in response to changes in the environment but they do not become better bacteria. Having left the ocean, mammals then returned to it in the form of seals, manatees and dolphins, though they are not necessarily better in the sea than fish are. Indeed, since they cannot breathe under water, sea-going mammals are in a sense worse off than fish.

When sociologists write about social evolution they are seldom thinking strictly in this modern Darwinian way. They usually mean that **feudal** societies developed into **capitalist** ones, simpler societies into more complex ones and so on. Societies change and develop; they most likely tend to become more complex as time goes by because people learn and knowledge accrues. But they do not evolve in a Darwinian sense. Individual human beings themselves are, of course, the product of biological evolution too. But the importance of culture and social learning in humans means that human animals are unusually well insulated from the forces of natural selection. Biological evolution is barely significant as a force on human development in most contemporary wealthy societies even if natural selection was an important influence during human prehistory.

EVOLUTIONARY SOCIOLOGY   W.G. Runciman argues that any substantive social theory must be evolutionary in the sense that: (a) human social capacities are biologically-based; (b) while no simple single model of human development in the past can be described or projected into the future as prediction, nonetheless there is a history to development such that later changes depend on earlier ones; and (c) it is sensible to use the idea of selection to explain why certain social practices become established. The first and second of these propositions are widely accepted; even theorists such as Anthony **Giddens**, who explicitly reject the idea of historical sequencing and prefer to see the past as a series of episodes, nonetheless end up presenting what seem rather like evolutionary models. It is the third proposition, the use of selection, which causes most difficulty for social scientists. The idea can be applied with some precision in biology because what an animal needs is relatively simple. Needing less food, surviving longer with less water, having more offspring; it is often fairly clear

just what would count as a competitive advantage for an animal. It is much less easy to see what characteristics of a society are advantageous. If we cannot specify advantages in advance of change occurring and simply suppose that every change must have been advantageous, then we are not explaining anything.

See **evolution**.

EVOLUTIONARY UNIVERSALS   In his latter years, Talcott **Parsons** re-worked his functionalist theory into an evolutionary perspective. He believed that societies progress through their capacity for adaptation to their environment. Increasing adaptive capacity comes mainly through increased structural differentiation: societies evolved ever more specialised institutions and ways to integrate these. Evolutionary universals are the practices and institutions that increase adaptive capacity: bureaucratic organisation; a universalistic legal system; money and a market structure; democratic association; and science.

EXCHANGE THEORY   Most associated with George **Homans**, this approach shares with classic economics the assumption that individuals seek to maximise their personal gratifications. Its starting point is Georg **Simmel**'s assertion that all human contact is based on reciprocal giving and receiving. Exchange theory has generated new ideas by applying economistic analysis to areas of social life previously thought to operate on very different principles. An example is Peter **Blau**'s application of it to intimate relationships such as marriage. He argued, for example, that people tend to marry partners who can offer matching social assets. The more controversial arguments have generally been unconvincing. Much social action is patently guided by tradition rather than maximising calculation. Much is altruistic. In much social interaction there is very little reciprocity because one party is vastly more powerful than the other. Relationships between superiors and subordinates must either be exempted from the exchange framework (in which case it is so limited as to have little value) or notions of utility and reciprocity must be stretched so far as to be worthless as tools for explanation. Exchange theory inspired little work after the 1960s though it was revived in some fields in the 1990s as a more ruthlessly economistic **rational choice theory**.

EXOGAMY   See **endogamy**.

EXPERIMENT   Much research in the physical sciences proceeds by creating a highly artificial setting for two purposes. An experiment is usually designed, first, to drastically simplify reality to just the variables that interest the researcher and, second, to cause what interests the researcher to be varied in a controlled fashion so that effects can be observed and accurately measured. For practical and ethical reasons, sociologists are very rarely able to experiment with their subjects and instead must make the best of naturally occurring phenomena. It is important to recognise that this places enormous constraints on the confidence that we can have in even the most rigorous social research. If we are interested in the effects of higher education on religious beliefs we cannot assess people's religious beliefs, educate them to a certain level, re-test for religion, then wipe their memories clean and start again, this time giving them less education. Instead we have to compare the religious beliefs of people with different experiences of education. We try to control for extraneous variables; for example we can remove gender from the equation by comparing only men or only women. Ditto for age and so on. However we can never strip out all the other possible sources of influence. Hence we can never be

sure that whatever results we find are the effects of education.

See **et cetera principle**.

EXPERIMENTAL EFFECT   See **Hawthorne effect**.

EXPLANANDUM, EXPLANANS   These two abstract, Latin terms have long been used in logic to designate the two parts of an **explanation**. The 'explanandum' is the occurrence or observation that is to be explained; the 'explanans' is the general law that does the explaining. Such terminology is seldom used in the course of research when everyone is fairly clear about what is to be explained. The terms are used in philosophical debate about the nature of explanation when – for example – philosophers are comparing explanation in physics to explanation in sociology. Probably because Latin is so little understood these days, the terms are now used less and less frequently; when used they tend to promote confusion rather than clarification.

EXPLANATION   In the natural sciences, explanation is not simple but it becomes even more complex in the social sciences where our subjects possess motives, intentions and reasons. There are a wide variety of ways of explaining which are often combined.

(a)   Causal explanation involves identifying the general law and conditions immediately prior to the thing needing explaining. Metal expands when heated. This bar is being heated. That's why it expands.

(b)   Meaningful explanation is what we often refer to as 'understanding' (or in Max Weber's language **Verstehen**); to appreciate why members of the Heaven's Gate flying saucer cult committed suicide in 1997, we access their beliefs and knowledge and show how, starting with those beliefs, it was sensible to see the passage close to the earth of the Hale-Bop comet as a sign that the time was right to leave their temporary bodies to move on to a higher plane of existence.

(c) Deductive explanation (which would probably not be seen by most lay people as explanation) is the logical deduction of a conclusion from other propositions in the system. Much mathematical reasoning takes this form.

(d) Probabilistic explanation is the presentation of a statistical generalisation regarding relevant cases for the matter in hand. For example, we may explain why this widow was likely to have outlived her husband by pointing to the different life expectancy of women and men.

(e) Borrowing from biology, where the existence and nature of an organ such as the liver may be explained by its part in meeting the needs of the organism as a whole, **functionalist** explanation begins with a social system and then explains a particular social practice or institution by showing how it meets 'functional requirements' of the social system.

(f) Evolutionary explanations show how the interaction of adaptive features of the organism and characteristics of its environment result in its survival.

(g) Teleology is the study of purposes, intentions or goals. A teleological explanation follows the 'in-order-to' form and involves showing that the action being explained resulted from a desire to achieve a particular end: Why did I get my hair cut? In order to appear more serious.

Of these types, it is the 'because' (which can be (a) or (b)) and the 'in-order-to' types (as in (g)) that are most common in sociology.

EXPLOITATION   We could define exploitation neutrally as 'making the most of' or 'extracting the most from' but the term usually carries either positive (as in 'exploiting renewable energy sources') or negative (as in 'exploiting the rainforests') connotations. It is a mark of how attitudes to extraction and manufacture in the West have changed, that what was a term of praise (as in the heroic exploit), is now commonly a term of condemnation. Like 'expropriation', the term is widely used by Marxists.

EXPONENTIAL GROWTH OR DECLINE   see **linear growth**.

EXPRESSIVE AND INSTRUMENTAL   This is one of the most useful contrast pairs in social science. Although it is always difficult to untangle them, there is great analytical value in distinguishing actions that express sentiments and feelings from actions that are designed to produce a particular outcome. If I embrace my son to show my affection, I am being expressive; if, in full view of the TV cameras, I embrace the retiring politician whom I privately loathe but whose seat I wish to win in the election, I am being instrumental. A recurrent theme in the sociology of modern societies is the frustration that people periodically feel about being constrained by the rational bureaucracy that dominates much of modern life and hence the need for outlets for expressivity.

EXPRESSIVE LEADER   Talcott **Parsons** believed that for the modern nuclear family to function effectively there should be a sexual division of labour and that women were genetically pre-disposed to take primary responsibility for nurturing. Hence women were the expressive leaders. Few would disagree with Parsons's description of the **domestic division of labour** but many question whether such a division is functional and whether its origins are genetic (rather than social).

See **family**.

EXTENDED FAMILY   See **family**.

EXTRA-DISCURSIVE   This ungainly term is used in two senses. First, it is used as a fancy way of saying that something is 'real', that it is not merely a product of the discourse in which it is named. For example, analysts who study claims and counter-claims about climate change may want to emphasise that there is some truth about climate beyond the cacophony of media claims. The second use is similar though a little less pretentious.

Some writers, notably followers of **Foucault**, argue that our understanding of the world is shaped to a very large (though maybe unspecifiable) extent by the predominant **discourses** of the cultures we inhabit. None the less, they argue, this does not commit them to arguing that there is nothing but discourses. They use the term extra-discursive to refer to factors or changes outside of the discourse, even if one cannot be clear about exactly what those factors may be – since from within the discourse one cannot quite be certain of its limits.

F

FACTOR ANALYSIS Factor analysis is a statistical technique that seeks to reduce a large set of variables to a small number of key attributes. For example, we might find that most people who are opposed to abortion are also against women working outside the home and in favour of mild corporal punishment of errant children. Rather than describe such individuals by listing all their attitudes, it is more economical to suggest that they possess a single 'factor'; we might call it social conservatism.

This approach can be very useful, but we need to pay attention to two things. The first is that the factors really do summarise major differences between individuals; there is no point using the new factors instead of the old variables if they do not provide most of the information more concisely. The second concern is that we have to be able to interpret the factors; it is not very helpful to find them if we cannot say what they mean. Statistical software often allows us to choose between different sets of factors.

Although factor analysis frequently helps to simplify a large set of variables, it can sometimes reveal complexity that we did not expect. For example we could analyse the answers to a number of questions about political attitudes, starting with the idea that dissatisfaction with the government is a single property. We might discover that negative opinions do not form a single block but instead divide into feelings about domestic issues, foreign policy and trustworthiness.

FACTORY SYSTEM The term 'manufacture' originally came from the Latin words for hand and making. Hence a manufactory was a place where things were made and 19th-century abbreviation gave us our word. It derives its significance from a contrast with independent craft working and with the 'putting out' system in which middle-men distributed raw materials to workers in their homes and then collected the finished goods for sale. Grouping together workers in large units allowed the use of new forms of inanimate power (such as the water wheel and later fossil fuels), large machines and a complex division of labour. Factory owners also came to realise that by bringing lots of workers together, factories – along with mines and docks – provided the conditions for employees to organise themselves and take industrial action.

Factories came to symbolise industrial development and a kind of modernity so perfectly that the term circulated much more widely. Thus, the New York studio of 1960s US pop artist, Andy Warhol, was known as The Factory.

FACT–VALUE DISTINCTION It is common to distinguish between factual assertions (e.g. it is raining) and moral assertions (e.g. it is wrong to kill). Max **Weber** and the mainstream of social scientists accept this distinction and regard it as central to sociology's claim to be a social science (rather than, for example, a social philosophy). On a wide variety of grounds, others have argued that the distinction between fact and value is impossible to maintain. Recent philosophical analyses suggest that there can be a fact–value distinction but no fact–value dichotomy; in other words there is no sharp dividing line even if it is easy to distinguish between highly factual and highly evaluative assertions.

This apparently rather abstract, philosophical issue matters to sociology in two principal ways. First, **critical theory** authors suggest that the very business of rational social enquiry presupposes certain values (of impartiality, openness to reasoned criticism and so on). These values may be present or absent in the societies we study. For this reason – they argue – sociologists cannot concern themselves with facts alone since sociology itself has a commitment to specific value orientations. On this view, sociologists will inevitably have a moral perspective on the societies they study. Second, when studying social action, sociologists are interested in people's own reasons for action. Sociologists try, for example, to understand why terrorists use violent means to achieve political ends. The answer will be given not only in factual terms but in value terms also: the advocates of terror will typically argue that the circumstances justified abnormal tactics. Some anti-abortion campaigners believe that abortion is so repugnant that they are justified in attacking or threatening to kill doctors who perform terminations. In such circumstances sociologists have to work out whether the moral justification and reasoning given represent the actual reason or whether there is some deeper or ulterior consideration at work. In other words, sociologists have to figure out whether the reason proffered is a good enough reason to 'in fact' explain the action. And part of the judgement about whether the reason is 'good enough' is a value assessment of the grounds for action. Sociologists face this problem in a way that chemists (say) do not, because

molecules do not have reasons for action while people do.

See **critical theory, objectivity, value-neutrality**.

FALLACY OF MISPLACED CONCRETENESS
See **reification**.

FALSE CONSCIOUSNESS
It is common for social scientists to suggest that this or that group of people is on specific occasions unable to understand correctly the world, its place in it, or the causes of its actions. Marxists tend further to argue that most people are unable fully to recognise their true interests most of the time; ruling class **ideology** has made them partially blind to their objective circumstances.

A version of the idea has long been influential in sociological accounts of popular or **mass culture**, which after the **Frankfurt School**, is taken to be a bad thing because, like the gladiatorial circuses organised by the Romans, it distracts the working classes from seeing the true nature of their oppressed position.

No doubt people do not understand their situations objectively and comprehensively. But the problem with the concept of false consciousness is that it rests on the analyst's claim to have a privileged insight into the objective interests of others. No plausible defence of such privilege has ever been made.

FALSIFICATION, FALSIFICATIONISM
At its simplest, falsification is the disproof or refutation of some scientific law or explanation by presenting empirical evidence which it cannot accommodate. It has a particular place in Karl **Popper**'s philosophy of science. He made the point that falsifying and verifying are not mirror images of each other. In his

famous example, the proposition 'All swans are white' is not much aided by us seeing yet another white swan. A truckload of observations of white swans may make us feel more confident of the truth of the proposition but no amount of verification will absolutely fix the claim. However, it only takes one black swan – one counter-instance – to falsify the proposition. Hence as a method for moving knowledge on, falsification is much more effective than verification. The methodological doctrine that scientists should therefore seek out stern tests of their theories, that they should look for counter-instances, is known as falsificationism.

Popper's elegant insight is, however, not quite as compelling as he initially thought. If ones sees a black swan one may actually doubt that it really is a swan; or it may be that it is a swan that has had an accident in an ink factory. People may quite reasonably question the observation and thus keep their hypothesis or theory intact. Popper and his followers have never been able to devise a set of rules for working out when a falsification should be treated as compelling. Further cold water has been thrown on the methodological doctrine of falsificationism by historical researches that suggest that leading scientists (Newton, Pasteur, Darwin, Einstein) were not, in practice, great falsificationists.

FAMILY　At its simplest the family is an intimate domestic group of people related to each other by blood and legal ties and sexual relations, in which adults are responsible for the care and raising of their children (natural or adopted).

There have been and still are a very wide variety of forms of the family. Sociologists usually distinguish between the nuclear and the extended type: the former being just the parents and their dependent children; the latter being a larger group made up of more than two generations and/or less immediately-related kin (such as cousins, uncles and aunts). George Murdock was right to make the basic point that most known societies have something like the nuclear family at their core.

Much modern sociology of the family could be described as an argument with the ghost of **functionalism**. Murdock's explanation of the popularity of the nuclear family is that it is particularly good at vital social tasks: regulating sexual relations, reproduction, the socialisation of children and economic co-operation between the sexes. Talcott **Parsons** added an historical element to the case by arguing that the nuclear family was better suited than the extended one to the geographical and social mobility associated with industrialisation: two adults and their children can move more easily than an extended kinship group. He also added a further function: providing close affective ties in what otherwise is an impersonal world.

Inspired by feminist critiques, sociologists increasingly questioned who benefited from the nuclear family. What Murdock called economic co-operation could easily be described as exploitation and patriarchal oppression. While men had a wide variety of ways in which to be the breadwinner, homemaker was a much narrower role. There is also an obvious imbalance in that wives are supposed to nurture their husbands but no-one nurtures wives. What is also missing from the functionalist family is any recognition of domestic violence, whether actual or threatened. With some justification, Parsons could respond that domestic violence has increased with the break-up of the family, but even for the 1950s affluent American family, the Parsonian 'safe haven' seems a little utopian.

Scholars have also questioned the evidence for the decline of the extended family. Historical research since the 1960s has shown greater variation in family forms in industrialising societies than was previously thought, and elements of the extended family have survived. Young couples often move a long way from their parents but many maintain frequent contacts through phone calls and visits. Retired couples often move to be close to a married child and their grandchildren. Single mothers will often move close to their mothers for support.

English sociologists Peter Wilmott and Michael Young (1972) in *The Symmetrical Family* argued that relations within families were becoming more symmetrical as the domestic division of labour weakened and as home became more important for male identities and social life. Feminist sociologists challenge this view. In the USA in 1950 less than one-fifth of mothers with a child under six were in the US labour force; in 2000 it was two-thirds. The greater involvement in work outside the home and decline in the typical number of children in a family may have reduced the salience of family relations for women's lives but it remains the case that most housework is done by women. Family decision-making is now more equitable but the division of work is not.

By the end of the 20th century the family had become considerably more complex than in 1950 as the consequences of increased rates of illegitimacy, divorce and unmarried co-habitation were worked out. The growth in the number of openly gay families, with their own or adopted children, and the increasing extension of legal recognition to gay families has intensified this complexity. As adult couples separate and reform it is increasingly common to find family units composed of adults and children from previous relationships. The instability of the family has, according to Arlie Russell **Hochschild**, 'hyper-symbolised' the role of mother, who is now seen as the last stable prop in the family and caring business: 'the more shaky things outside the family seem, the more we need to believe in the unshakeable family and failing that, in the unshakeable mother-wife'.

FAMINE   A famine is a widespread shortage of food that kills, directly from starvation and indirectly from increased vulnerability to sickness and diseases. Rapid collapses in levels of food consumption often result from failures in distribution rather than a long-term decline in the production of food. In fact, some authors would claim that in the contemporary world where emergency food stocks abound, famine can only result where there has been a failure to intervene. Some modern famines have been precipitated by climatic conditions (drought in the Horn of Africa; flooding in Bangladesh) but many have been caused by warfare or by deliberate government action. For example, Stalin deliberately starved the people of the Ukraine in 1932–3 because they refused to accept his policy of replacing private family farms by collective enterprises; between six and seven million died. In 2003, the government of Zimbabwe precipitated a crisis of agricultural production by confiscating land from white farmers.

FASCISM   Italy gave the world the word (from the Latin 'fasces': the bundle of sticks with projecting axe which signified the authority of a Roman consul) and the first example: the movement founded by Benito Mussolini in 1919. Fascism rejected liberal democracy, asserted racial superiority and promoted the cult of the dictator. The term is used for Adolf Hitler's Nazism in Germany, for the Falange led by General Francisco Franco in Spain and a variety of imitative right-wing authoritarian movements of the 1930s in Europe. The word has come to be widely used as a pejorative term for someone thought to have authoritarian leanings, though this is inaccurate since the criticized person seldom advocates fascistic views.

FATALISTIC SUICIDE   See **suicide**.

FECUNDITY   This denotes the physiological or biological ability to reproduce and it is distinguished from **fertility**, which is fecundity as it is shaped by a wide variety of social and cultural forces.

FEMININITY   The characteristics associated with the female sex (e.g. nurturing, passivity, gentleness, a maternal 'instinct') were for centuries assumed to be caused by female biology and hence innate. Most social scientists now recognise that while the biological differences between women and men have some effect on their attitudes and character, what we might call femininity is influenced as much by culture as by biology. The simplest reason for doubting that biology contributes much to supposed feminine characteristics is cross-cultural comparison. Although most cultures have clearly divided gender roles, the content of those varies considerably from culture to culture while the female biology, we may suppose, remains the same. Even within the same society, women of different social classes were viewed in very different ways. In the Victorian and Edwardian upper-class home, the wives and daughters were regarded as sufficiently frail as to need protecting from the rougher aspects of life; the female servants were treated like workhorses.

The idea that femininity is primarily a cultural construction is somewhat compromised by the fact that some feminists do attribute to men and women fundamentally different characters. For example, in discussions of the role of women in politics and management, it is sometimes asserted that women are more caring, less confrontational, more collegiate and more likely to seek compromise than are men. Such general behavioural differences need not rest on biology; they could be explained by social expectations and socialisation into different roles. However, that such differences are treated as if they can (and should) survive the greater incorporation of women into what were previously male domains suggests that at least some elements of the cultural construct 'femininity' are seen as having deep roots.

See **Butler, Chodorow, Irigaray, Kristeva.**

FEMINISATION OF LABOUR   This is the process in which certain jobs or sectors of employment (especially ones previously monopolised by men) come to be dominated by women. An example would be clerical work, which is so called because it was once the preserve of ordained clergymen or 'clerks' before being taken over by laymen. In the mid-to-late-19th-century world portrayed in the novels of Charles Dickens, the clerks in manufacturing and trading houses were all men. Now most clerical work in Europe and North America is performed by women. School teaching (especially at junior levels) has also been heavily feminised. Sociologists often point out that the feminisation of a particular occupation coincides with a decline in its relative status and income, though it is often difficult to work out which causes which.

FEMINISM   The term has a very wide variety of meanings which can be divided into four: (a) an over-arching theory about the nature of women's oppression by men; (b) a political theory (and associated practices), which aims to liberate women from male exploitation; (c) a modern social movement that promotes specific changes in the legal, social, economic, political and cultural condition of women; and (d) an ideology that opposes all misogynist (i.e. 'women-hating') ideas and behaviour.

Sociology has been particularly influenced by the first and third of these. The women's movement has attracted a great deal of sociological attention, both because of its worldwide impact and because of the way it changed common conceptions about the appropriate point of focus for political activism. Feminism made interpersonal relations, reproductive rights and domestic violence into issues of wide political significance. At the same time, feminism changed sociology by demanding that sociologists investigate the reasons for the perpetuation of men's social advantages, studies that gave rise to various theories of **patriarchy**.

FEMINIST EPISTEMOLOGY; FEMINIST METHODOLOGY Some feminist social scientists have argued that traditional **epistemology** has understated the importance of areas of knowledge that have been uppermost in female experience. Conventional epistemology is held to be too empiricist and too rationalistic. Hilary Rose, for example, has argued that feminist research methods must place greater emphasis on 'affectual rationalities'.

We must distinguish between research agendas, methods and epistemology. There can undoubtedly be a feminist research agenda: any vision of the world, any coherent set of assumptions about how it works, and even very specific interests can usefully generate a new series of research questions. Feminism has been extremely useful in alerting us to important questions that were previously overlooked. For example, in the 1980s the feminist critique of the convention in social mobility studies of attributing to wives the social class of their husbands brought a halt to a practice that by then had little justification; furthermore it led to interesting analyses of the social classes of partners.

It is less clear that there can be feminist research methods. It is true that qualitative methods are disproportionately popular with feminist scholars but this probably reflects the disciplinary background of such scholars and the topics they study. Feminist studies, like most good sociology, are often concerned with questioning everyday beliefs and assumptions (about the 'naturalness' of customary

gender roles, for example) and accordingly feminists may favour qualitative methods for trying to get behind 'common sense'. Still, if a topic requires mass survey data, it is hard to see how a feminist questionnaire would differ in its technical construction from a conventional one and the techniques of multi-variate analysis do not vary according to ideological preference. Some feminists argue that **quantitative research** is in some sense 'masculine' and thus to be avoided, but the case is not convincing.

The claims for a feminist epistemology, though often repeated, face insuperable difficulties. Though there are some speculative philosophical arguments in its favour, no such epistemology has yet been set out. The best case for a feminist epistemology comes from a general relativism: if perception can never be other than perception from a certain point of view, then a feminist standpoint is more likely to serve women's interests than any other. However, to prevent this collapsing into an individualistic relativism (in which any one view was as good as any other), it would have to be the case that women form a single coherent group with one set of interests that form a single standpoint. Just as the real working class disappoints Marxists by failing to form the class-for-itself demanded by the theory, so real women disappoint feminists by having diverse interests. Some feminists solve the problem in the same way as Marxist intellectuals: by claiming to perceive correctly the interests of women. The feminist standpoint epistemology then reduces to simply what the writer wishes to believe.

FEMINIST METHODOLOGY See **feminist epistemology**.

FEMINIST SOCIOLOGY As with **feminism**, feminist sociology is broad and varied but it has some common concerns and assumptions. It routinely raises the often-neglected topic of gender so that feminist sociologists working in, for example, the sociology of education or religion, will not assume that male and female experiences are the same but will research the differences. In this sense, feminist sociology is a research agenda. It is also, like other 'isms' such as Marxism and functionalism, a general orientation to explanation. Feminist sociologists will begin with the expectation that patriarchal oppression or something like it is of major explanatory significance.

Some feminist sociologists object to the fact that sociology remains dominated by the conceptual apparatus of its founding fathers. The frequency with which this dictionary refers to Karl **Marx**, Max **Weber** and Emile **Durkheim** suggests they are right. But it is hard to see how we can abandon our past or why we should criticise a scholar for studying one thing rather than another (unless, of course, that neglect leads to errors in the understanding of what is studied). In any case, our experience of the way the discipline has changed over the time of our careers, suggests that respect for social science produced by the patriarchs of the subject is quite compatible with openness to new agendas and ideas. It is a vindication of feminist sociology that it is now taken-for-granted that gender is as potent a source of social division as class, religion or ethnicity.

It is noticeable that feminist sociology has been influenced by a large number of philosophers, literary critics and psychoanalytical writers: Jacques **Lacan**, Judith **Butler**, Luce **Irigaray**, Julia **Kristeva** are examples. The difficulty with these sources is that they promote quite incompatible views of the self, of gender and of society. In some feminist sociology, themes and propositions are selected from their work and from that of others largely on political or programmatic grounds: for how well an idea fits with what the writer wishes to believe. Such ideas are very rarely supported by any body of empirical research; nor are they subjected to

detailed tests in empirical research. The result is that, more than many other fields of sociology, feminist sociology seems fashion-driven and fragmented into competing perspectives that have no hope of finding common ground through empirical research.

FERGUSON, ADAM (1723–1816) One of the great thinkers of the **Scottish Enlightenment** who has been unfortunately over-shadowed by Adam **Smith** and David **Hume** and whose rediscovery is long overdue, Ferguson was an early pioneer of historical sociology. His (1767) *Essay on the History of Civil Society* discusses the emergence of civilised societies from prior barbaric and savage stages. **Civil society** – refined, morally sensitive and politically sophisticated – was precarious. Ferguson believed that the institution of private property was progressive in that it allowed the evolution from barbarism to savagery to civil society but as self-interested individualism became embedded in a complex division of labour there was a danger that egoistic individualism would weaken the bonds between the individual and civil society and open the way for political despotism. He anticipated Emile Durkheim's interest in the problems of social order caused by economic individualism; he also anticipated Karl Marx (who was much influenced by him) in understanding the alienating effects of a capitalistic division of labour.

FERTILITY; FERTILITY RATE For many reasons social scientists and policy-makers are interested in understanding and predicting population changes. To allow comparisons we need a standard measure of how many children are being produced and this is usually given as the number of live births per thousand women or per thousand women of child-bearing age.

Although fertility is obviously affected by health it is not just a matter of **fecundity**; it is also affected by social and cultural factors. Fertility rates changed considerably with industrialisation (see **demographic transition**) as standards of living improved and children became less important as guarantors of material support in old age. Fertility rates vary between religious cultures; for example, the opposition of the Catholic Church to artificial contraception has kept Catholic fertility higher than that of non-Catholics in some countries. They can also be influenced by government policy. Since the 1960s the Chinese government had tried to improve living standards by forcing families to have only one child.

FEUDAL MODE OF PRODUCTION

In Marxist models of economic evolution, feudalism is the **mode of production** that precedes the rise of **capitalism** and its **relations of production** are characterised not by exchange in a market but by landlords using their political and legal power to extract a surplus from unfree labourers.

FEUDALISM

In the Europe of the Middle Ages a 'feud' or 'feu' was an estate or large unit of land given in return for military service. Feudalism was a system of social stratification and economic organisation with the monarch at its head, who gave land to his major nobles in return for them raising armies and keeping the peace. The major nobles in turn granted land to lesser lords in return for the same service and so on down to the smallest estate. The result was an elaborate system of reciprocal obligations that bound lords and their 'vassals' together; the vassals produced various services for the lord; in return the lord protected the vassal and promoted his interests. The lowest orders, the serfs, were not free to sell their labour to the highest bidder but were bound to their lord and were often treated as his property. For example, if a serf's daughter married a

freeman or someone from another estate, the serf would have to pay a penalty to the lord as compensation for the loss of his property. The status of the feudal serf is perfectly indicated by the fact that many medieval documents use the Latin term for 'litter' rather than that for 'children' to describe the offspring of a serf.

FEYERABEND, PAUL K. (1924–94)

A philosopher of science, Feyerabend became famous because of his favoured methodological slogan, 'anything goes'. His books, most notably *Against Method* (1975), were designed as smart and satirical attacks on authors such as Karl **Popper** who claimed that there was a universal scientific method. Feyerabend aimed to debunk these universalistic claims by showing how much diversity there was in scientific procedures and how even the best scientists used 'tricks' – rhetorical techniques – to win the audience over. He was also keen to argue against naive enthusiasts for scientific progress by trying to document how much knowledge was lost during scientific 'progress'; new theories are often associated with the forgetting of a lot of details associated with past beliefs. In a similar way, Feyerabend was also cautious about, and critical of, the arrogance of scientific and technical experts. His view was that their expertise was commonly exaggerated and he argued, particularly in his later work, for more public scrutiny of expert judgements. He was a pioneer in offering in-principle, philosophical reasons why lay-people must, as he put it, supervise science.

FIEF, FIEFDOM

Meaning much the same as 'feu' (as in **feudalism**), a fief was an estate held in return for military service. Although in its proper use, the term signifies a complex set of reciprocal obligations between a lord, his superiors and those he controlled, the term is often used metaphorically to refer to an enterprise or part of an organisation run by someone who acts as if he or she has unlimited power.

FIELDWORK   This denotes any face-to-face methods of data collection, for example, observing people by participating in their activities, informal interviewing, or interviewing with a questionnaire.

FIGURATIONAL SOCIOLOGY   See **Elias**.

FIRST-ORDER CONSTRUCTS   See **phenomenology**.

FIRST WORLD   See **Third World**.

FLANEUR   We suspect that even at the time of writing, this term (strictly speaking the French for one who strolls, loafs, lounges around) is disappearing, but in the 1990s it was extremely popular. Derived originally from the work of the 19th-century French poet Charles Baudelaire, it was popularised by Walter **Benjamin** (1949) in his *Arcades* project. It signified a new metropolitan character, the man in the crowd, someone who is shaped by the diversity and rapidly changing nature of urban experience and who has to decode its complex meanings.

FLEXIBLE SPECIALISATION   First formulated by Michael J. Piore and Charles F. Sabel (1984) in their *The Second Industrial Divide* the theory of flexible specialisation is one of the clearest attempts to conceptualise the form of manufacturing that has supposedly replaced **Fordism**.

Flexible specialisation is the production of small volumes of a wide and rapidly changing range of products. 'Flexible' refers to the nature of production systems. Unlike their predecessors of the early 20th century,

modern machines are clever enough to be programmed to make a wide variety of different products. Multi-skilled workers, often designing computer applications, are needed to get the best out of flexible machines. 'Specialisation' refers to the nature of modern product markets. In many industrial societies people are affluent enough to be able to afford variety. Hence an automobile producer can no longer make a profit (as Henry Ford did) by making one model. It must offer a wide range of models and within each model, sufficient customising scope for potential customers to express themselves in their purchase.

As with all such attempts to depict a major change, flexible specialisation has been criticised for exaggerating changes in the world of work.

FOCUS GROUPS   Telephone interviewing with a questionnaire allows market researchers and opinion pollsters to collect fairly shallow responses from very large numbers of people. Such research is often complemented by lengthy and detailed discussions with small groups of people. For example, a political party's pollsters might have two or three groups that meet frequently over the course of an election campaign to give feedback on the campaign's progress. In the last decade focus groups have become a favoured research strategy in sociology. Focus groups, typically made up either of a random selection of people or of invitees from a particular background (all genetic counsellors, for example) are used to try to gain an insight into popular understandings and views. In particular, it is claimed that in focus groups respondents will have their views challenged and corrected by the opinions of other group members. They will thus be more informative and reliable as informants than would be the case in individual interviews. Group members may also serve to remind each other of salient information, though there is also the danger that people may not express in public, views thought to be embarrassing or unpopular. For this latter reason, many sociologists choose not to rely on focus group results alone and may use them only at an exploratory stage of research.

FOCUSED INTERACTION   Erving **Goffman** coined this term to distinguish what we normally think of as interaction from the sort of gestures and signals that occur merely because two people are co-present. The body language by which people in a crowded lift signal their awareness of others is 'unfocused'; a couple talking to each other is 'focused'.

FOLK DEVILS   Drawing on an idea that originates in Emile **Durkheim**'s functionalist theory of **deviance**, the term came to prominence with Stanley Cohen's (1972) *Folk Devils and Moral Panics*   a study of British mass media responses to 1960s youth sub-cultures. Cohen argues that a society creates an array of social types to demonstrate what sorts of social roles should be avoided and what imitated. That process invariably dramatises, so that in describing a deviant type (such as the street graffiti artist or the user of recreational drugs) small differences are made large and the threat of such people is greatly exaggerated.

See **labelling theory, moral panics**.

FOLKWAYS   William Graham Sumner's major contribution to US sociology was his interest in folkways and **mores**. The former are habits (for individuals) or customs (for groups); largely by trial and error, societies develop shared ways of acting that are well-suited to their environment. Mores are a particular form of folkways that include specific moral imperatives. Not only do we do things this way because we have always done them this way; this way is also felt to be right and proper.

FOOD, SOCIOLOGY OF   Sociological analysis of food has not yet become an established sub-discipline, though it is a topic of increasing interest. There are four principal routes by which sociologists have approached the topic of food. First, **figurational sociologists** and other historical sociologists have been interested in the ways that food preparation and consumption have been a source of manners and a vehicle for the refinement of taste and the making of social distinctions. Second, sociologists interested in health issues have become alerted to questions about diet and food consumption. For example, it is clear that in North America and much of Europe, children are given more sweet foods than dietary guidelines would recommend. Studies of family conduct suggest that often parents understand and accept the official dietary advice but chocolates may be used to reward children for good behaviour or be exchanged for docile behaviour in the supermarket. There may be strong sociological reasons for nutritionally poor diets. A third topic, overlapping with the concerns of rural sociology, focuses on food production, in particular its environmental consequences (because of the use of pesticides, genetically modified seeds and so on) and the treatment of farm animals, particularly in intensive production where animals can be treated very oppressively. Finally, in the last decade, well-known problems for human health have arisen from the way that food is grown and processed. The most notorious example is bovine spongiform encephalopathy or BSE (mad-cow disease), an incurable and deadly infection in cattle that is believed to have arisen from the cost-saving procedure of feeding unwanted pieces of dead cattle to live cows. This disease has now spread to a (relatively small) number of people who ate beef and has come to symbolise the way that food can be a source of **risk**. Sociologists are accordingly now interested in the regulation and safety-testing of food.

FORCES OF PRODUCTION Although used inconsistently by Karl Marx and Frederich Engels and by later Marxists, this term is useful in distinguishing between those elements of the production process that are necessary irrespective of the context in which work takes place and the social relations of production (which refers to such 'political' aspects of work as social domination and exploitation). Among the forces of production are raw materials, the tools or machinery used to work those materials, labour power and skills.

FORDISM Taking the mass production methods developed between 1908 and 1914 in Henry Ford's automobile factories to be typical, Italian Marxist Antonio **Gramsci** used the term to denote the following features of advanced capitalism: scientific management (see **Taylorism**), the moving assembly line, standardised outputs, and the stimulation of demand for goods by skilful advertising and marketing. Although the term is often used to criticise (particularly the way that industrial work is regimented), that was not Gramsci's intention. He was breaking with the Marxist tradition that supposed capitalism would make the lives of workers worse and recognising that industrial capitalism was markedly improving living conditions for many workers.

Since the 1980s the term has mostly been used in a contrast with 'post-fordism'. With machines taking an ever-greater role in production and reducing drudgery, and with service industries displacing manufacturing, work is supposedly becoming more flexible and individual creativity is becoming more important than regimentation.

See **de-skilling**.

FORMAL ORGANISATION The term was first used by the **Human Relations School** for the managerial blueprint that showed the structure of authority and communication in an organisation. It is often used in an illuminating contrast between the way in which an organisation is supposed to work and the reality of its 'informal organisation'. Many sociological studies of work document the ways in which people subvert or work round organisational rules, either for their own benefit or because the formal structures are a hindrance to achieving the organisation's goals.

See **bureaucracy**.

FORMALISM, FORMAL SOCIOLOGY The contrast here is not between formal and informal but between form and content. Usually taken to have been founded by Georg **Simmel**, this type of sociology is concerned with capturing the underlying forms of social relations; what Simmel called a 'geometry of social life'. We might divide social life by its superficial concerns (the family, education, politics) but underlying these divisions are 'forms' (such as conflict) that pattern all areas of life. Simmel identified a variety of forms, including the consequences of numbers for group alignments (isolated individuals, 'dyads' or pairs, and 'triads' or triplets). He also pointed to patterns of domination, group relations (conflicts, competitions and coalitions), identities and roles (the stranger, for example), disclosures and evaluations (such as prices and exchanges).

FOUCAULT, MICHEL (1926–84) One of the most popular 20th-century French theorists, Foucault was responsible for introducing a number of terms to sociology (e.g. **discourse**, **episteme** and **panopticism**) and for creating a widespread concern with the way that knowledge can act as a source of social power and domination. His work is hard to place. At first sight it appears historical though he is usually more concerned to make a philosophical point with his histories than to provide compelling evidence for his claims.

Underlying his specific studies of madness (*Madness and Civilization* [1989]), imprisonment (*Discipline and Punish* [1979a]) and sexuality (*History of Sexuality* [1979b]) is the claim that the Enlightenment thinkers were wrong in assuming that increased knowledge is essentially liberating and progressive. The knowledge that forms the basis of new disciplines (such as medicine, psychiatry and social work) acts as a subtle basis for new forms of control and domination. Foucault's method is to document the increasing rationality of some field of human life and then expose the alienation and oppression hidden inside what others had taken to be a considerable improvement. For example, his history of punishment contrasts the informal power over the body symbolised by the public executions of the classical era with the regulatory systems of the modern prison, which aim to control not just the body but also the soul.

Foucault's interest in such changing **discourses** of health and morality coincided with a concern with the historical emergence of ways of being. For example, it was only possible to be 'mad' or 'depraved' or 'perverted' in anything like the modern sense once new discourses of mental health and morality were in place. Foucault and his followers emphasise that these identities could only emerge at specific historical junctures; in this sense, Foucault is a **Hegelian** thinker. His point is not just the general social constructionist claim that identities are constructed (and could therefore have been constructed in other ways) but the more specific claim that certain identities, certain ways of being human, are only available under particular historical circumstances.

One major problem with Foucault is that, like many French intellectuals, he delights in deliberately opaque and allusive prose. Another is that he generalises in an unwarranted way from his selective histories. For example, to sustain the case that **surveillance**

is a dominant feature of modern societies, he makes great play of Jeremy **Bentham**'s panopticon ('all-seeing') design for a prison: the cells were in spokes radiating outwards from a central observation point, hence prisoners would potentially be constantly under the eye of prison guards. This is then taken as a metaphor for the pervasiveness of surveillance in modern society. What Foucault does not tell the reader is that Bentham's panopticon was never built (nor anything like it) and that even in the most modern and well-staffed prison most prisoners are rarely supervised. Far from being sites of constant surveillance, most prisons are run as medieval fiefdoms by the most powerful prisoners using brutality and wealth to maintain systems of patronage that are little different to the crime families and gangs found outside.

Like much grand theorising, Foucault's work suffers from the weakness that it pays little attention to how people actually live within any of his discourses. For example, his idea that modern scientific medicine offers radical new techniques for controlling people misses the point that the beliefs and attitudes of consumers may be very different from the beliefs and attitudes of doctors. Very many patients feel quite free to ignore medical advice or to supplement official discourses with their own recourse to 'alternative' medical practices.

See **genealogy, confessional technologies**.

FOURTH WORLD   This is one of the many ideas in Manuel Castells's voluminous writings on the **information society**. He believes that the increasing importance of information technology and its attendant networks is causing parts of the **Third World** to become largely irrelevant to the global economy, now that unskilled labour and certain raw materials are of less economic significance. Parts of Africa, Asia and Latin America now form a

'Fourth World' that is falling ever further behind in economic development and that will feature mainly as a source of drugs, criminal gangs, contraband arms sales and political instability.

FRAME, FRAME ANALYSIS *Frame Analysis* (1975), was **Goffman**'s last major work and in many ways his most theoretical. The basic idea, that of the frame, refers to the way in which in everyday life there are widely held, small-scale assumptions that allow us to recognise and sort out social phenomena. For example, one well-recognised frame is that of the joke. The joke frame allows us to see that, for example, apparently offensive remarks made by our friends are just teases or fun. Our working knowledge of the frame means that, usually, we immediately see these remarks as jokes. Goffman defined a frame as 'definitions of the situation [that] are built up in accordance with the principles of organisation which govern events – at least social ones – and our subjective involvement in them'. So far so straightforward. However the main problem with the idea lies in knowing how many frames there really are: are jokes separate from irony or is there only one frame? No-one has yet been able to devise a way of categorising all the social frames; indeed no such list probably exists since frames are inherently flexible and fuzzy at the edges. Second, frames do not always work automatically. Sometimes we don't know whether our colleagues are teasing or being hurtful; they may not even know themselves. Thus, empirical reality does not exist in pre-labelled frames. A joke may turn sour. An orderly queue may break down. Goffman clearly identified something important about the intersubjective interpretation of social life. But it remains unclear whether frame analysis is the best way to explore this topic further.

See **inter-subjectivity**.

FRANKFURT SCHOOL The Frankfurt Institute for Social Research was founded in 1922 by Felix Weil, a wealthy Marxist political scientist. When the Nazis came to power in Germany, it moved to New York and returned to Frankfurt in 1949. It was disbanded 20 years later but remained influential primarily because of the work of Jürgen **Habermas**.

Many leading left-wing theorists were associated with the School: Theodor **Adorno**, Herbert **Marcuse**, Walter **Benjamin**, Erich **Fromm** and Max Horkheimer. A number of features of its work made the Frankfurt School popular in the 1960s and 1970s. It augmented **Marx**'s interest in structures with **Freud**'s interest in the personality. It argued that the social sciences could not borrow their epistemology from the natural sciences. Rather they had to find a method suited to their own distinctive subject matter and to sociology's potential for ethical engagement with society as a **critical theory**. Finally, the School was equally likely to criticise western capitalism and Soviet communism. Generally the Frankfurt School thought mainstream Marxism too concerned with the economy and too deterministic.

Particularly interesting is the way that theorists associated with the School reacted to the political changes of the 20th century: in particular the rise of fascism in the 1930s and the decline in political radicalism in the second half of the century. One pessimistic strand, exemplified by Adorno's writings on mass culture, concluded that the revolutionary potential of the working class had been drained by the subtle oppression of popular culture. Marcuse managed to retain some hope of revolution by finding new sources of revolutionary consciousness in groups such as ethnic minorities and those that made up the 1960s student movement. As these groups in turn failed to stimulate revolution, others in the same tradition have identified the women's movement and environmentalism as the new proletariat.

FREE MARKET See **market situation, market conditions**.

FREE RIDER This signifies someone who accepts the benefits of collective provision without contributing to it. The term comes from economics but it figures on the fringes of sociology; for example, in Mancur Olson's (1965) *The Logic of Collective Action*. Olson concluded that where a group is large enough for people to avoid censure and where the benefits of collective action cannot be withheld from shirkers, it would be rational to free-ride. The notion is of limited value to sociology because much social action quite happily tolerates and even encourages free-riding. Political parties and churches, for example, naturally wish to turn all potential support into cost-bearing members but would rather have free-riders than be unpopular.

FREQUENCY DISTRIBUTION See **distribution**.

FREQUENCY POLYGON See **histogram**.

FREUD, SIGMUND (1856–1939) The founder of psychoanalysis as we know it today, Freud's fame rests on his treatment of prosperous, middle-class patients, mostly from Vienna, who were suffering from neurotic disorders – they were troubled by irrational fears or strange compulsions. Freud's innovations were essentially two-fold. He initiated a form of treatment through intensive individual discussion with the therapist (the 'talking cure') in which, by the analysis of patients' personal histories and their dreams and other unconscious thoughts, the analyst and patient would come to recognise the source or cause of the problem. Second, he argued that the source was commonly a sexual conflict or anxiety, often stemming from a period in childhood not normally associated with sexual

impulses. Thus, Freud shocked many of his contemporaries by suggesting that young boys might have a form of sexual attraction to their mothers and thus be jealous or afraid of their fathers, leading – in some cases – to suppressed desires that emerged as neuroses later on. By emphasising the role of unconscious desires, desires that we do not acknowledge to ourselves, Freud is often said to have dealt a further blow to Enlightenment conceptions of rational humankind since it appears that we may not consciously understand some of our deepest emotional urges.

Freud continued to develop and elaborate his thinking and never formally codified his views, though his followers tried to systematise his views around the ideas of the **ego**, **id** and **superego**, respectively the conscious self, the source of urges and the regulator of admissible desires.

Many sociologists have looked to Freudian theory for an account of the operation of the human psyche that would match their structural theories about the social environments in which people live. Thus **Parsons** used Freudian ideas to flesh out his structural functionalist account of the social system since Parsons's theory contained no specific theory of the individual human actor. Neo-Marxists such as the members of the **Frankfurt School** have also used Freudian ideas extensively in an attempt to understand how the economic inequalities of capitalism could interact with individual psychological tendencies in ways that might explain the docility of workers and the attractiveness of authoritarian leaders. Finally, **Habermas** drew on the psychoanalytic therapeutic encounter for his model of social emancipation. Just as the neurotic recovers from neurosis by recognising the neurosis him- or herself, Habermas suggested that sociology could help to emancipate people by helping them see the sources of their own exploitation and discontent.

Though still read by sociologists and literary theorists, Freud is less accepted by mainstream psychologists (the psychoanalytic community aside). In part this is because they are sceptical about the lasting therapeutic value of his recommendations. It is also hard to reconcile Freud's theory of human psychology with Darwinian interpretations of human evolution and urges. Nonetheless, Freud's emphasis on the pervasiveness of sexual motivations and on the importance of unconscious thought is widely accepted, even if his rather 19th-century assumptions about the differences between women's and men's sexuality now appear implausible.

FROMM, ERICH (1900–80) German-born, this radical social psychologist, theorist of psychoanalysis and member of the **Frankfurt School** moved to the USA in 1934. Like others of his generation he was concerned to explain the appeal of fascism. His explanation, given (1941) in *Fear of Freedom*, was that people often lack the psychological resources to live with freedom and are attracted to authoritarian movements for the certainty and direction they provide. Fromm's rather unconvincing alternative solution was love: people needed more positive affirmation from others.

FRONT REGION AND FRONT STAGE See **back stage or region**.

FUNCTION This term is not quite a synonym for 'consequence' or 'purpose' but combines elements of both. In **functionalism**, institutions and actions are explained in terms of their functions. Thus, religious beliefs about divine reward and judgement after death may help people deal with the persistence of unfairness in this life. But these functional consequences are not mere accident. Rather it is because those consequences are beneficial for the system as a whole that the action occurs or the institution exists. Hence functions have a purpose

but it is not necessary for functionalism that actors be conscious of the functions of their actions. Robert K. **Merton** distinguished between manifest (those of which the actors are aware) and latent functions (the unintended consequences of action).

FUNCTIONAL EQUIVALENT The idea of a functional equivalent is both essential for, and a threat to, functionalism. One of the best justifications for asserting that some institution performs an important function is to show that when that institution declines, something else that performs the same function takes its place. For example, we might bolster the argument that religion is functional in the sense of providing social cohesion through opportunities for collective **catharsis** by showing that some other institution takes its place in secular societies: sport and class politics have both been offered as candidates. At the same time, functional equivalence weakens the ability of function to explain the existence of any particular social institution of collective pattern of behaviour because, if it is possible for the same societal need to be met in a variety of ways, we need another explanation for why any society meets any particular need in a particular way.

FUNCTIONAL IMPERATIVE OR PREREQUISITE In full-blown **functionalism**, these are the basic needs that must be met for the social system to survive. Some method of socialising children into the norms of the society would be a functional imperative in this sense. The term may be used more loosely as a pompous way of saying that something is very important.

FUNCTIONALISM Although functionalism in modern sociology is most obviously associated with Talcott **Parsons**, it has a long history. It was particularly popular with anthropologists such as Alfred R. Radcliffe-Brown and Bronislaw Malinowski. In modified forms it continues to influence much sociological thought.

The key to understanding it is to appreciate the organic analogy. If biologists wish to understand the nature of some element of the body, they typically ask what part it plays in maintaining the whole organism. We understand sweating when we appreciate that the human body operates most effectively within a fairly narrow temperature range and that sweat glands play an important part in keeping body temperature stable in a changing environment: when it gets hot; we cool ourselves by sweating.

Social institutions can be understood in the same way. For example, Emile **Durkheim** explains the fact of crime by arguing that it allows us to mark out and reinforce the boundaries of acceptable behaviour: crime has the function of maintaining social cohesion. Kingsley Davis and Wilbert Moore similarly argued that social **stratification** had positive social benefits in ensuring that the most able people compete for the most important jobs.

The most detailed elaboration of functionalism was in the Parsonian systems theory that dominated a large part of US sociology in the 1950s and early 1960s. The greater the power of a ruler, the greater the vilification after his fall. It is a mark of the enormous influence of Parsons that, for decades after his star waned, ritual denunciations of the errors of functionalism were commonplace. Some of the criticisms were misplaced. It is not true that functionalism could not account for social change or social conflict. Parsons presented an evolutionary theory in which systems and sub-systems became increasingly differentiated and then reintegrated. Conflict could then be explained as a feature of the periods before reintegration was successfully completed. It is also not true that functionalism is innately conservative.

The basic research question (if something is common, there must be a good reason for it) does encourage analysts to justify the arrangements of the present but, as with Durkheim's treatment of crime, it is possible to have a functionalist explanation of apparently radical, deviant and disruptive features of society. As the fondness for functionalism among Soviet Russian and Polish sociologists in the 1960s shows, it is also possible for Marxists to adopt the model.

Far more damaging to functionalism are two rather abstract criticisms. First there is a good reason for saying that functionalist **explanation** is no explanation at all. Normally, that which explains something comes before the thing it is explaining. In the proposition that economic depression explains the rise of Hitler, the depression precedes the rise of Hitler. Generally we only allow consequences to explain an action when a desire for those consequences motivates the action. So becoming thin only explains my dieting because it is the desire to be thin that impels me to cut down my eating. But in this model there is a conscious agent who anticipates the consequences and acts to bring them about. It is less easy to see how the latent functions of a social institution can explain its existence. Do criminals really commit crimes in order that their punishment may increase social cohesion? Functionalist explanation works in biology because it is coupled with natural selection. Organisms that do not possess appropriately functioning organs die out.

This difference leads to a second compelling critique. Many would dispute that 'society' exists in the same sort of way that the human body exists. The body is bounded and finite in a manner that allows us to talk about it as a single thing and to specify fairly simply what counts as success, survival, adapting to its environment, and the like. Hence we can ask what the liver does for the body and we have the crucial test of death to confirm our suspicions: without the liver (or some **functional equivalent**); the body dies. It is open to the critic of social functionalism to argue that what benefits one part of a society may be so obviously to the detriment of some other group that we cannot assign functions for a society as a whole. To take a dramatic example, a high rate of unemployment may be beneficial to those who employ labour because it keeps costs down and reduces the likelihood of strikes but it is hardly beneficial to the unemployed or to those who fear losing their jobs. It is also hard to see, for societies, the equivalent of death as a crucial test. Societies constantly change and what would count as success is so much more complex (and difficult to free from ideological preferences) than in the case of an animal, that we can reasonably question the value of the biological metaphor.

See **postulate of universal functionalism**.

FUNCTIONALIST THEORY OF DEVIANCE   See **deviance**.

FUNCTIONALIST THEORY OF RELIGION See **religion**.

FUNCTIONALIST THEORY OF STRATIFICATION See **stratification**.

G

GADAMER, HANS-GEORG (1900–2002) German philosopher and student of **hermeneutics**, Gadamer is best known to sociology for his analysis of interpretative understanding (**Verstehen**) in *Truth and Method* (1960). This work aims to clarify the rather abstract question of what it means to understand something properly – whether it be a person's utterance, a play, a religious text or a legal document. He argues against the position that to understand something properly is to understand it objectively, on the grounds that any contact with the unfamiliar is influenced by our pre-judgements (a word that is often translated as 'prejudices'). As these pre-judgements cannot be transcended, there cannot be a single, objective version of what a play or religious doctrine (etc.) means. Gadamer's position is often characterised as being anti-objective and therefore relativistic, although this was not how he viewed things. He wished to emphasise how much interpretation depends on the pre-existing beliefs and commitments we bring to any interpretation. In this sense he proposed that we are confined by a hermeneutic circle: every text (and pretty well everything is a 'text') can only be understood as a manifestation of an entire worldview and any worldview is a synthetic product of texts. In developing his own views on interpretative understanding **Habermas** drew repeated contrasts with Gadamer, thereby introducing Gadamer to many sociologists who would not otherwise have come across his work.

GALBRAITH, JOHN K. (1908–) See **affluent society**.

GALLUP POLL US social researcher George Gallup (1901–84) was so much the pioneer of the application of modern sample survey techniques to the study of political attitudes and public opinion that such surveys are now often called 'Gallup polls'. He developed many of the techniques used in polling and established the legitimacy of the exercise by showing that surveys of samples of voters could accurately predict voting behaviour.

GAME THEORY This is the general study of rational behaviour in situations where two or more people, whose interests conflict, at least partly interact; it is a sub-field of **rational choice theory**. First elaborated by economists John Von Neumann and Oskar Morgenstern (1947) in *The Theory of Games and Economic Behavior*, game theory attempts to model mathematically the options available to participants and the outcome of competition and choice in such settings as marriages, employer–employee bargaining, war and political party contests.

One of the best-known exemplars in game theory is the prisoner's dilemma. Two prisoners, against whom there is evidence of possession of illegal firearms but insufficient evidence to convict for the big crime of which they are suspected, are kept apart.

Each is promised a very light sentence if he confesses and implicates the other in the big crime that police are eager to solve. If both remain silent, the two of them will be convicted of lesser offences that nonetheless carry a prison sentence. If both confess, both serve moderate sentences for the bigger offence. The odd thing about this set-up is that for each of the prisoners separately, it is more rational to confess than to stay silent whatever the other one does. If you stay silent and I squeal, I get a very light sentence, lighter than the one I would have got anyway for staying silent. If you choose to inform, I am better off confessing than not since we both get reduced punishments that way. Thus for each individual it is rational to do the thing that – overall – is contrary to them achieving the best outcome. This is what makes it a dilemma.

Another common example is the 'tragedy of the commons', which neatly illustrates the point that pursuing rational self-interest may be self-defeating if you do not consider the actions of others. A number of farmers share rights to graze their beasts on common land. One farmer reasons that he can increase his herd slightly without damaging the shared pasture. But if many or all of them do the same the pasture becomes exhausted and everyone loses. In repeated laboratory versions of these games, two-thirds of people choose the selfish option, though it has to be borne in mind that these are only experimental simulations, not people's real-life behaviour.

Sociologists rarely use the mathematical versions of game theory, largely because most naturally occurring problems are too complex to be modelled in this way. Nonetheless, the language of game theory is common and some situations, for example, when members of an association, political party or board of governors can vote for the candidate to be their leader, do closely resemble such mathematical games. More generally, game theory illustrates the way in which the structure of institutions within which choices are made can shape the outcome of those choices.

See **strategic interaction**.

GARFINKEL, HAROLD (1917–) Acknowledged as the founder of **ethnomethodology**, Garfinkel is celebrated for a number of studies that illustrated his claims about the richness of everyday knowledge, which is often implicit, and the ways in which people **reflexively** monitor their performance of social tasks. Early on, he encouraged his students to undertake 'breaching' experiments where people would violate everyday patterns of interaction by, for example, treating their parents as hotelkeepers or responding to ordinary conversational queries as though they were scientific investigations. These studies revealed the moral orderliness underlying all interaction and highlighted the crucial, though routinely unnoticed, knowledge and understandings that sustain everyday interaction. He also set exercises in which students were asked to spell out all the background knowledge that was alluded to in everyday conversations between intimates; students were never able to specify this knowledge comprehensively, thus demonstrating the enormous depth of mundane, ordinary knowledge. Considering his enormous influence, Garfinkel has written comparatively little and his more programmatic statements about ethnomethodology are wilfully difficult to figure out. His best known work is *Studies in Ethnomethodology* (1967).

GATE-KEEPERS The term is used metaphorically in a number of fields to signify those who can grant or refuse access. In research methods, it is used of those people we need to win over in order to have access to our chosen respondents.

GAZE A term which was first used in film criticism in the 1970s, this denotes the assumptions underlying specific cultural products or the viewpoint or perspective built-in to them. The claim was that, as most films were made by men, their 'gaze' viewed women stereotypically and voyeuristically. It has since been used for a variety of particular ways of seeing the world: for example, in the phrase 'tourist gaze'. While the term seems proper for a product, such as film, where the makers are entirely responsible for the content of the product, it seems less so for complex experiences, such as tourism, which we cannot control, even if the leisure industries often try to promote a particular view of tourist 'sights'. There is also a danger that the term misleadingly suggests a unity of vision.

GEHLEN, ARNOLD (1904–76) Although extremely influential in his native Germany, Gehlen was not translated into English until 1980 and is mostly known through the work of Peter L. **Berger**. Gehlen believed that humans were set apart from other animals by the lack of a set of instincts strong enough to provide a stable environment. Born with an 'unfinished character' humans create social institutions to give direction and purpose to what would otherwise be a formless life. However, technology and other elements of modernity undermine those institutions and create a wide variety of socio-psychological problems. Whereas the institutions of archaic life seemed 'objective' and could thus be taken-for-granted, the modern world advertises its socially constructed nature. In place of a 'character' rooted in the social structure, the modern human is obliged to develop a 'personality' which, because it is not rooted in a relatively stable environment, is fluid and unreliable.

GEISTESWISSENSCHAFTEN AND NATURWIS-SENSCHAFTEN These German terms denote, respectively, the social and the natural sciences; 'Geist' means 'spirit', 'Wissenschaften' means

'sciences' and the meaning of 'Natur' is obvious. The distinction is frequently used in debates about the appropriate methods for the social sciences and the extent to which they must be modelled on the natural sciences.

See **hermeneutics, Verstehen, Weber**.

GEMEINSCHAFT   See **community**.

GENDER   In common usage this is the distinction between females and males on the basis of anatomy. Sociological usage is importantly different in that sociologists often use 'sex' for the biological differences between women and men and 'gender' for the packages of social characteristics that are culturally associated with the sex difference. The same distinction can be maintained by using the terms female and male when focusing on the biological components of difference, and feminine and masculine when writing about the socially-created differences.

Precisely what of masculinity or femininity is caused by biology is a contentious issue, both in the social sciences and in the world at large. It is of a piece with the general sociological perspective (which stresses **social construction**) to see gender differences as owing relatively little to biology and a great deal to culture. Most sociologists would argue, that while maternity is a biological fact, a 'maternal attitude' is a socially-specific cultural construct: different cultures specify different sorts of roles and attitudes as being appropriate for mothers. For example, women in societies with high rates of infant mortality are generally less emotionally attached to their young children than are mothers in modern industrial societies where almost all children reach maturity. However, as with a lot of sociological thought on the importance of biology for determining human nature and behaviour (e.g. in our understanding of inheritance and **mental** illness), there is always a danger that advances in biology may reduce the scope for sociological explanation.

GENDER DIFFERENTIATION   This is the social process by which biological differences are given social and cultural significance and used as the basis for social classification. That cultures can make more or less of biological differences shows that we cannot take gender differentiation as being merely the working out in social life of sex differences. However, we should be cautious of the extreme social constructionist view that gender differences have no biological basis. While societies differ in precisely what characteristics are imputed to the sexes and in the extent to which social roles are 'gendered', there is a good deal of consistency across time and space. Put it this way: we can think of very few societies which reverse roles and characteristics so that males are expected to be 'feminine' and females 'masculine'.

GENDER IDENTITY   This term usually refers to the sense of self associated with **gender**; it denotes the psychological internalisation of feminine or masculine traits. Gender identity arises out of complex patterns of interaction between the self and others. Some people can reject the gender specified by their biology by, for example, passing as members of the other gender and even changing their sex by radical surgery. Some people are born with a mixture of the typical biological traits from both sexes; in such cases medical professionals may decide on the 'proper' sex and intervene accordingly. This suggests that biology does not always determine gender identity but we need to be cautious of making too much of extremely rare cases.

GENDER ROLE   This is the external partner of **gender identity**: the social expectations that a society attaches to gender and their

expression – for example in speech, demeanour, gesture posture and dress. In many societies gender roles are radically divided and form the principal categorisation within social life.

GENDER STEREOTYPING   The term 'stereotyping' implies making unwarranted generalisations from sex differences and making too much of them. For example, it is a fact that women are typically shorter than men. Whether it is equally true that women are naturally more emotional or affectionate than men is not clear. This may well be an improper generalisation from the facts that raising children gives most women more opportunity than men to display affection and that most societies teach women to be affectionate towards their offspring. An example of making too much of a real sex difference would be the exclusion of women from physically demanding forms of work. That in times of necessity (such as major wars) women have perfectly adequately replaced men in every form of manual work shows that the segregation of the labour market is a product of socially-constructed gender differences and not a matter of biological necessity.

GENEALOGY   Conventionally this is the tracing of our ancestors and it is of considerable importance in societies where properties of importance (such as wealth or social position or membership of a ruling family) are inherited.

The term is also used by Friedrich **Nietzsche** and Michel **Foucault** for their own particular kind of alternative and debunking history in which bodies of ideas or perspectives that are now assumed to be obvious, unquestionably correct, rational and progressive are challenged by showing that such views are under-pinned by unscientific, partial and irrational assumptions. In Nietzsche's

(1887) *On the Genealogy of Morals* the point was to demonstrate through historical reconstruction that the dominant Christian values of the West were neither God-given nor inevitable; that the development of a particular moral ethos involved contests and struggles in which the outcomes could have been different. Few scholars would now dissent from the view that morality is a historical human product. More radical is Foucault's view that scientific knowledge, especially in the social sciences and in medicine, is also genealogically derived and that therefore, with a different history, our scientific beliefs could also have been significantly different.

GENERALISATION This is central to the sociological enterprise; we study one event, activity, person, group or institution in the belief that what is learnt there can be extended or generalised to a larger number of cases of which the one we have studied is representative. The persistent problem for social researchers is that, because we must study what is naturally occurring and cannot experiment, we can rarely be confident that the instance we have studied is truly representative. Or to put it the other way round, we always need to be careful how far we generalise from the case studied.

GENERALISED OTHER This term was coined by George Herbert **Mead** for a crucial component of his model of socialisation. He believed that people (children especially) draw out of every particular encounter with a variety of others (especially **significant others**) a series of abstract principles that come to form a generalised other. For example, if a child finds that a large number of others respond to loud and boisterous behaviour with various signs of disapproval, it gradually constructs a generalised other who embodies the principle 'Don't be boisterous'. It is through imaginary interaction with this

abstraction (in particular by playing at taking its place) that the child internalises social values and thus becomes capable of engaging in complex co-operative interaction.

GENERATION Most generally this is a body of people born in the same period, however that period is defined. As a rule of thumb, we take the period between the birth of one cohort and it producing its own children to be 30 years; hence that figure is conventionally used to define a generation.

GENETICISATION As knowledge of genetics and of genetic disorders has grown, this unattractive word has come into widespread use. It refers to the way in which conditions, disorders and diseases which were once understood in rather vague and flexible ways can be made more concrete by pointing to their actual or supposed genetic basis. For example, many biologists argue that schizophrenia has a genetic basis, even if the genes and processes that give rise to it have not yet been identified. If we begin to think of schizophrenia in genetic terms it will change both how the disorder is thought of – whether you are a sufferer or not will now depend on whether you have the gene, not the associated behaviours – and how policy towards the problem is shaped. Parents might be offered screening tests in order to rule out the possibility of having 'schizophrenic' children. Other attributes, that have nothing to do with unwellness, might come to be thought of in the same way, including homosexuality (and, of course, heterosexuality). Given that there are only a few conditions that are coded for directly by a small handful of genes, the geneticisation of most characteristics seems bound to remain contentious.

GENOCIDE From the Greek 'genus' or species, this term refers to the deliberate attempt to eradicate an entire people, nation, race, or ethnic or cultural group. It is sometimes argued that genocide is a peculiarly modern phenomenon: a consequence of the desire of the modern nation-state to be culturally homogenous and of its unprecedented power to impose its will over large areas. This overstates the case: over the centuries many small peoples have either been eradicated or reduced to shadows of their former selves. Muslim destruction of the Chaldeans, the Copts, the Arameans and the Assyrians in the Middle East are examples. And many recent late 20th-century genocides (in Rwanda and Cambodia, for example) have been medieval in their methods. But the modernity point is an important one. Between 1939–1945 the Nazi German state killed some six million European Jews (as well as thousands of Romanies): these extermination programmes were made possible not so much by developments in the technology of death but by efficient bureaucratic organisation.

GENOTYPE AND PHENOTYPE The genotype of any organism (plant, insect, human and so forth) refers to its genetic make-up. Two individuals of the same species, unless they are twins or clones, will thus have different genotypes. The phenotype refers to the individual's actual physical characteristic: how big it is, how hairy and so on. The development of the phenotype is shaped by such considerations as nutrition, exposure to illness and other environmental factors. Accordingly 'identical' twins, though they share a genotype, are not phenotypically identical. In the natural world, some organisms are enormously similar in appearance and characteristics (i.e. they are phenotypically similar) despite considerable differences in the underlying genetic make-up. In others, variations during phenotypical development can alter the final appearance dramatically even for genotypically similar individuals. The human animal is at neither extreme in this regard.

However, human cultural practices (of dress, training and grooming) further shape the appearance of the adult individual in a way that is very rare among other organisms.

GENTRIFICATION This term became fashionable in the 1970s to describe one part of a cycle of urban degeneration and regeneration. In many major cities, high-earning, salaried professional people took advantage of low property values to move into unfashionable and decaying areas and renovate the existing housing or redundant factories into high-valued, desirable properties.

GENTRY
The precise meaning varies with time and place but this generally signifies a class of landowners below the **aristocracy** whose wealth is nonetheless great enough to allow them a degree of leisure and education.

GEOGRAPHICAL DETERMINISM There is an ancient tradition of explaining social organisation and human behaviour by geographical features such as climate and terrain and, although rarely used now by sociologists, geographical determinism is still found in popular talk. For example, southern and northern Europeans are often given the personality characteristics of 'hot' and 'cold' and this is taken to be caused by the climate of their respective regions.

GEOGRAPHICAL MOBILITY This is the real counterpart to the metaphorical **social mobility** and it means what it says: the movement of people from one place to another.

GEOGRAPHY Geography is that science which describes the earth's surface, its forms and physical features, its natural divisions and its climate and distribution of natural resources. It is conventionally divided into physical and social (or human) geography and the latter comes very close to sociology (especially to the work done by urban and rural sociologists). Towards the end of the 20th century, geographers became very interested in examining new phenomena using their customary methodological focus on places and spaces; for example, there were geographical studies of people's working and private spaces (such as bathrooms). Around the same time, sociologists became interested in the significance of spatially defined relationships for social structure and social processes; an example is Anthony Giddens's theory of **structuration**.

GERONTOLOGY   The study of the old and ageing, this field, like the sociology of deviance, changed markedly in the 1970s. Initially it was thoroughly social policy-oriented and was concerned with managing the problems of the elderly. By the end of the 20th century, scholars were studying the politics and experience of ageing and the way in which ideas of ageing were socially constructed. The assumed characteristics of the elderly vary from one culture to another so that there must be a cultural component to what the elderly are typically like.

GESELLSCHAFT   See **community**.

GHETTO   This was the term originally applied in the Middle Ages to the parts of European cities in which Jews were forced to live and by extension it came to mean a segregated part of a city inhabited by one ethnic or religious group. Since Louis Wirth's (1928) classic of Chicago urban sociology *The Ghetto*, the term has also implied social disadvantage.

GIDDENS, ANTHONY (1938–)   Probably the most renowned sociologist in Britain today, Giddens has shaped the discipline not only through his writings but through his influence on academic publishing in the social sciences and through the recognition he has won from leading political authorities including the current UK Prime Minister Tony Blair. Despite this renown, Giddens is not associated with a single theoretical position and it is not easy to be a 'Giddensite' in the way that one could be a follower of, say, **Elias** or **Foucault**.

Giddens's sociological reputation rests primarily on three rather separate achievements. Following his early work, which concentrated on re-assessing the value of sociology's 'founding fathers' for analysing present-day capitalist societies, in the 1980s he worked on the theory of **structuration**. Most fully expressed in *The Constitution of Society* (1984), structuration theory was intended to clarify how social structures were continuously reproduced by social action while – at the same time – the possibilities of social action were set by social structures. Giddens pointed out that social structure was not only constraining but also enabling. In short, he was attempting to resolve the 'micro–macro' problem of structure and agency. Scholars agreed that Giddens had expressed the problem with great clarity though opinions varied as to whether he had solved or merely re-stated the central difficulties. Though the term structuration is still relatively frequently seen, it is by no means universally used, not even by Giddens himself in his later writings.

By the 1990s, Giddens was working chiefly on the nature of modernity. He noted how in modern, heavily rationalised societies more and more things had become the subject of choice. Fewer decisions can be left to 'nature'; we have to take more and more responsibility for our diet, our ageing, our fitness, the education and psychological well-being of our children. In most of these areas one cannot even choose not to choose. At the same time our technological societies mean that we are more routinely dependent on others: they service our airplanes, look after air-traffic control, maintain airport security and so on. Ordinary people cannot look after their own interests in these matters. Hence there is a paradoxical quality to late modern life. We are enjoined to choose but in much of our lives have no control over the choices that others make on our behalf. This, he suggests, is the principal cultural problem of advanced modernity and leads to specific kinds of anxieties and unease. A metaphor he used to characterise this feeling was that of riding in an out-of-control juggernaut.

Later in the same decade, after the election of Tony Blair as the new leader of the UK, Giddens began to write on the **third way** – the attempt espoused by Blair (alongside former US President Clinton and other European Social Democratic leaders) to steer a political course between state control and the free market. Giddens wrote a powerful defence of third way-ism and followed it up with a book of responses to critics. In this way Giddens became a very public intellectual, a rare creature in Britain. As Blair's Labour government continued in office it began to drop talk of the third way which was no longer fresh and newsworthy. Clinton and other third-way political leaders lost out in an international move to the right. Sociological interest in the topic also declined.

In every stage of his career Giddens has been outstandingly prolific but it is hard to present his successive analyses as integrated or cumulative.

GIFT RELATIONSHIP   Less relevant to sociologists than to anthropologists, gift-giving can be an important social phenomenon: as either a way of creating strong social bonds or of displaying superior wealth. Marcel Mauss's (1925) *The Gift* remains a classic text well-worth reading.

GLASS CEILING   This metaphor, used frequently by feminists, perfectly captures the sense that there is an invisible and unacknowledged but nonetheless real barrier to the upward social mobility of women.

GLOBALISATION   For much of the 20th century, sociologists tended to treat societies as if they were relatively isolated entities; relations between nation-states was largely the preserve of the academic discipline known as International Relations. From the late 1960s we became much more aware of the connections between societies and of the emergence of an increasing global cultural system brought about by the following changes: increasing economic dependency and trade; the creation of global patterns of information exchange; the development of global patterns of consumption; increase in the number of international cultural and sporting events (such as the football World Cup); cheaper travel and hence more frequent tourism; the decline of the sovereignty of the nation-state; the rise of global political movements (such as Marxism and more recently religious fundamentalism); the development of world-wide health problems (such as the spread of AIDS); and increasing awareness of environmental problems. Faster and more contentful means of communication has increased knowledge about life elsewhere and has intensified pressure on governments to act in pursuit of common values: for example, we now become very quickly aware of suffering caused by famine in North Africa, flooding in the Indian subcontinent, or genocide in the former Yugoslavia and press our governments to intervene. In brief, we are now often aware of the world as a single place.

Globalisation theory differs from **world-systems theory** in being concerned with more than economic inter-dependency. It should also not be confused with the idea that all states are evolving towards a common form of **industrial society**. Globalisation theorists argue that there are two contradictory processes in play simultaneously. While in some respects societies are becoming more similar, there can also be cross-national exploitation and inequality: for example, polluting industries may relocate from richer countries to poorer ones taking the globe's pollution burden with them. Globalisation may also stimulate a local reaction through, for example, the celebration of local sports and cultural products. That paradox is sometimes expressed in the term 'glocalisation', which is a translation of a Japanese business term that means to tailor a single product for a variety of local markets.

GLOCALISATION   See **globalisation**.

GLOSSING   According to **ethnomethodology**, all utterances and actions gain their meaning from their context (that is, in the jargon, they are **indexical**). As it is not always obvious what the context is and hence what some utterance or action means, people are forever checking that they have got it right. In a conversation, one person will produce an abbreviated description or 'gloss' of what he/she takes to be occurring and the other can either confirm that or modify it.

GOAL   Anything which we consciously seek to achieve is a goal or an end. The contrast is with 'means': the things we need to attain our goals.

GOAL ATTAINMENT   See **subsystems model**.

GOAL DISPLACEMENT   Though Robert Michels's **iron law of oligarchy** formulated in the 1920s is a perfect example of the phenomenon, this phrase was first used in 1949 by Robert K. **Merton** to explain how overly-rigid organisational rules could encourage bureaucrats to pursue their own survival rather than the goals of their organisation. The term remains useful because the phenomenon endures. It

is common for organisations to lose sight of the purposes for which they were established and to replace the founding goals with self-preservation.

GOFFMAN, ERVING (1922–82)   Probably the best known and most accessible microsociologist, Goffman's approach centred on his analysis of **dramaturgy**. In other words, he emphasised the ways in which people routinely mould and monitor the presentation of their selves – almost like actors on a stage – in social situations. Goffman's approach to his task was rather unusual. He was frankly unsystematic about how he collected his materials and was nearly as open to fictional materials and reports plundered from the press as he was to scientific investigation. He commonly gave insufficient detail to allow others to check his observations, and yet his observations were extremely insightful and full of resonance for most readers who were also attracted by his easy and entertaining style of writing.

In addition to studies of routine interaction he wrote tellingly of behaviour under special circumstances, for example about what happens to inmates in prisons and psychiatric facilities where the normal courtesies and 'decencies' are suspended or about what happens to people with 'spoiled' identities and how they manage their stigmas in public.

Goffman largely avoided theory, though in his **Frame Analysis** he sought to set out the basis for a systematic framework for studies of everyday life. However, theory writers, including **Giddens**, have been attracted to his work – in Giddens's case because Goffman conveys such a strong feel for the way in which people's knowledge of social institutions feeds into the reproduction (or **structuration**) of everyday life.

See **frame analysis, back stage or region, interaction ritual, stigma, strategic interaction, total institution**.

GOING NATIVE We might have expected this term to have died with the British Empire that spawned it but it survives because it neatly describes an enduring problem for the social sciences. In many styles of research we wish to get well-acquainted with our subjects and to observe them closely. To make sense of their worlds, we need to imagine ourselves in their places. Researchers often choose to study people for whom they feel a certain sympathy. The danger is always that the researcher will shift from being an interested and informed outsider to becoming an insider.

GOLDTHORPE, JOHN H. (1935–) Goldthorpe first came to prominence with the **Affluent Worker** studies: the first serious attempt to test the **embourgeoisment** thesis. In the 1980s he became a leading student of class structures and social mobility. In contrast to the US approach to mobility, which concentrated on the individual and family characteristics associated with changes in class location, Goldthorpe focused on the relative chances of people from varying socio-economic backgrounds moving up or down the class ladder. He has also been highly influential in promoting international comparative studies of mobility. His lasting contribution has been to persuade a majority of those working on social mobility to use a model based on a Weberian understanding of class.

See **class structure, social mobility**.

GOODNESS OF FIT This is the degree to which any data conform to the pattern of distribution predicted by whatever model is being tested.

GRAMSCI, ANTONIO (1891–1937) An Italian Marxist who was leader of the Communist party from 1924–26 when he was imprisoned by Mussolini, Gramsci was influential for his criticisms of **economic determinism** and for his use of the term 'hegemony'. In response to his contemporaries who stressed the coercive power of the capitalist state, Gramsci argued that at least as important as physical domination was the ideological effect of the Catholic Church, the legal system, education and the mass media that together, by taking-for-granted certain ideas, managed to create a cultural hegemony for the ruling class. Although rarely read or studied in detail now, he is still frequently cited by those who want a humanistic Marxism.

GRAND NARRATIVE AND META-NARRATIVE These terms are used by postmodernists to describe (and often to deride) what they take to be the big ideas that permeate orthodox social science treatments of modernisation. By 'grand narratives' they mean accounts of historical development which present history as having a theme: for example, the ideas that history is 'really' about the growth of knowledge or the rise of personal liberty. According to **Lyotard**, 'the emancipation of the subject' is one such meta-narrative which, untenably, presents human history as the story of the growing recognition of the centrality of the human subject. A central claim of postmodern writing is that it and other grand themes have lost their legitimacy.

There are three difficulties with this assertion. First, it is in danger of self-refutation in that Lyotard's postmodernity itself looks pretty much like a grand narrative. Second, it runs together two very different claims and provides evidence for only the less important one. If the claim is that ordinary people no longer value such benefits of modernisation as the increase in individual liberty or the improvements in medical science, the evidence would have to concern general attitudes and preferences. If the claim is that intellectuals have lost faith in the grand narratives of modernity, that is quite a different matter. The difficulty with much recent writing on postmodernism is that it has evidence only for the second assertion but claims it for the first. Third, the criticism of 'metanarratives' exaggerates the extent to which sociologists believe that modernisation resulted from the specific intentions of people as summarised in grand narratives. Most sociologists would regard social change as, most often, the result of unintended consequences; in other words, mainstream sociologists are typically sceptical of grand narratives (even if Marxist sociologists are not).

GRAND THEORY   Only ever used pejoratively, this term was coined by C. Wright **Mills** to refer to highly abstract sociological theories such as the **structural-functionalism** of Talcott **Parsons**.

GRANOVETTER, MARK (1943–)   A leading US economic sociologist, Granovetter made an important contribution to **network** theory with his (1973) article 'The strength of weak ties' and book (1974) *Getting a Job*. These demonstrated the value of an extensive network of fairly shallow social connections in alerting people to job opportunities and showed that such weak ties may be more consequential in many ways than strong (such as family) ties.

GROSS NATIONAL PRODUCT (GNP)   This is the total value of the finished goods and services produced in a country (including income from overseas but minus the domestic production that gets counted for overseas economies) in one year. It provides a simple and reasonably standard way of describing and comparing the overall wealth of countries. Very different countries may have similar GNPs: for example Turkey and Denmark have similar GNPs even though the population of Turkey is about 13 times larger than that of Denmark.

GROUNDED THEORY   This term was initially coined by Barney G. Glaser and Anselm Strauss (1968) in *The Discovery of Grounded Theory* to describe fairly concrete ideas and explanations that were generated in the process of analysing (usually qualitative) data. Although Glaser and Strauss offer a very detailed model for the process in which explanations are gradually constructed and repeatedly tested against observations, like the middle ground beloved of politicians, grounded theory is often used in self-description merely to signify that the work is neither data-free abstraction nor mindless empiricism.

GROUP   Used narrowly the term denotes a number of individuals, defined by informal or formal criteria of membership, who have some shared sense of identity or are bound by relatively stable patterns of social interaction. By pointing to some real association, these last two characteristics distinguish the group from aggregates or social categories that are created by outsiders (as when, for example, a sociologist writes about 'men' or 'junior doctors'). More commonly the term is used as an all-purpose term for any collection (actual or abstract) of people.

GUATTARI, FÉLIX (1930–92)   See **Deleuze**.

GUILD   Medieval guilds were self-governing bodies of craft workers that controlled entry to the craft, set standards and provided mutual aid. Periodically (for example, in Europe in 1930s) conservatives have promoted the idea of a polity made up of trade guilds and professional associations as an alternative to the class competition of socialism.

See **corporatism**.

GUTTMAN SCALE   See **scale**.

HABERMAS, JÜRGEN (1929–) The leading author in **critical theory** today, Jürgen Habermas has pursued a complex path in trying to show how sociology can be both a valid description of social reality and a critique of social life – both empirically rich and normatively justified. He thus presents himself as a direct heir of Karl **Marx** in the sense that Marx aimed to describe capitalism as 'scientifically' as he could while also revealing how the alienating economic system could be overthrown. Habermas realized that Marx's own approach failed to live up to its original ambitions: it was neither empirically very accurate nor philosophically precise in its critique. He sought to do better.

His first approach was rooted in the study of **epistemology**. Habermas claimed that, while the natural sciences unquestionably produced empirically rich knowledge, their methods held no promise for critique. Such knowledge was inevitably based on an interest in prediction and control. Any sociology modelled on the natural sciences was doomed to fall short ethically and politically since it was oriented to the prediction and control of human behaviour. Sociology had to find an alternative template. In *Knowledge and Human Interests* he (1968) proposed that the psychoanalytic encounter offered a better model. In psychoanalysis the patient learns more about themselves but with a view to emancipating themselves rather than to predicting their future behaviour.

Subsequently, Habermas acknowledged numerous difficulties with this suggestion and switched his style of argument. He moved away from the idea of interests towards reflection on the process of analysis itself. He claimed to find value criteria within the very language of academic analysis. According to Habermas academic inquiry, and more generally the search for truth, presupposes an 'ideal speech situation' (ISS) of unfettered interaction. In any inquiry, speakers implicitly make claims to speak – for example – truthfully, sincerely and comprehensibly. Of course, people may in fact lie or attempt to deceive. But lying only works because the background 'norm' is that one tells the truth. The important point for Habermas is that within this ISS we can find ethical values already presupposed by the way we conduct our analysis. The values do not come from outside; they are already inside – they are 'immanent'. Much of his subsequent work took the form of debates with other social theorists, legal scholars and philosophers about the refinement of this fundamental framework which in many respects resembles the outlook of many contemporary North American philosophers such as John Rawls.

Alongside this rather abstract analysis, Habermas also undertook some more concrete work on social institutions. Just like Marx he is interested in the historical development of society. Given his emphasis on discourse and interaction, Habermas differs from Marx in stressing not only economic development but also social learning and the emergence and refinement of ethical discourses.

His interest is not in writing histories of the way particular societies develop but in trying to reconstruct the generalised 'logic' of social development.

HABITUS   This complex and often obscure idea represents the attempt of Pierre **Bourdieu** to solve the perennial problem of balancing **agency and structure**. The key is 'habit', as in 'habitual'. Habitus is the 'durably installed generative principles': a set of acquired principles of thought, behaviour and taste ('classificatory schemes' and 'ultimate values') that generates social practices and is particularly associated with a certain social class. It is described as a person's own knowledge and understanding of the world, which in part constitutes that world. It is also described as 'systems of durable transposable dispositions', the 'embodiment in individual actors of systems of social norms, understandings and patterns of behaviour' and the 'basic stock of knowledge in people's heads'. The habitus is inherited with class position but it may be modified by experience. Some users of the notion take it to offer considerable leeway for individual freedom. Others see it as micro-Marxism: an account of how ruling class culture is reproduced. In all it is thought by many to be a useful descriptive term though its imprecision has prevented it being widely adopted by sociologists.

HACIENDA   The mainstay of agricultural production in Latin America in the 19th and early 20th centuries, this is a large landed estate that combines subsistence production and production for local and regional markets. One of the most important social characteristics of the hacienda is the use of various forms of unfree labour. In the medieval European **feudal** estate, serfs were almost as much the property of the lord as his cows and horses. In the hacienda the workers have greater theoretical freedom but are in practice tied in various forms of debt peonage ('peon' being the term for an unfree labourer). The landlord incurs various – sometimes fictional – costs on behalf of his workers, who are tied to him until such debts are cleared. Where the debt (and the obligation to labour) are passed from one generation to another, we can talk of 'debt slavery'.

HALÉVY THESIS   In the late 18th and early 19th centuries, when much of Europe was in political upheaval, Britain remained relatively calm. The French historian Elie Halévy believed such lack of revolutionary turmoil was largely a consequence of the pacifying effects of Methodism. This form of evangelical Protestantism diverted revolutionary sentiment into harmless channels allowing people to criticise their social superiors for immorality and impiety. It also provided a real solution to many of the social problems of the industrial age. It encouraged in the working classes, a new personality suited to urban capitalism: sober, thrifty, diligent and responsible. It also provided such valuable resources for individual social advance as literacy, the opportunity for lay leadership roles, and the support of like-minded people. By preaching personal rather than political change and individual rather than social salvation, Methodism defused incipient revolution. By allowing the lower classes to develop a form of the dominant religion well-suited to their social circumstances it prevented the growth of the anti-Church spirit that became so widespread in Catholic countries such as France and Italy.

The thesis acquired new relevance in the 1980s when it was used to explain the rapid growth of Pentecostal Protestantism in Latin America and Africa.

It is plausible that a puritanical and individualistic faith will attract people making the transition from the community-oriented life of rural agriculture to urban capitalism. What is contentious is the claim that without

Methodism there would have been revolution. There is little evidence that Britain had been on the point of revolution. The same applies to Latin America at the end of the 20th century. We suspect that, even without Pentecostalism, Marxists would have been disappointed in the politics of central and South America.

HALO EFFECT This denotes our common habit of assuming that people who impress us on one score possess a whole range of other virtues and are generally admirable. One form of the **self-fulfilling prophecy**, it is particularly relevant in the sociology of education where it has been found that an initial positive judgement of a child often leads to subsequent bad behaviour being over-looked by teachers or school authorities.

HARAWAY, DONNA (1944–) Cultures reveal a lot about themselves through the way that they view primates, humankind's closest relatives. Haraway is widely admired for being the first social scientist to appreciate the value of analysing primatology (the scientific study of primates) in the same light. Her 1989 book, *Primate Visions: Gender, Race and Nature in the World of Modern Science*, was a large-scale study of the way that assumptions about gender and inequality are written in to scientific stories about primates. Primates supposedly show us something akin to our 'natural' selves but she argues that narratives about primates are always infused with cultural assumptions drawn from contemporary human society. Subsequently, Haraway wrote extensively about 'cyborgs', the idea that our extensive reliance on technology means that we can no longer understand ourselves independently from electronic and mechanical devices. We cannot live as 'natural' humans because we cannot get by without our technological counterparts: the PC, the phone, the pace-maker, our contact lenses and so on. Both of her major projects are thus examinations of nature and the impossibility of telling (non-ideological) stories about 'natural' human beings.

See **hybrids**.

HAUTE BOURGEOISIE Now rare, this French term was used by 19th-century Marxists to identify the wealthiest and most powerful sections of the middle class and is a contrast with the **petite bourgeoisie** (typified by the small-shopkeeper).

HAWTHORNE EFFECT Named after the Chicago suburb in which the Western Electric Company had its plant, this turned what would otherwise have been a failure into one of the best-known pieces of sociological research. In the 1920s, researchers studying the effects on productivity of varying such working conditions as the levels of lighting, pay rates and hours of work came to the remarkable conclusion that variations in output were caused less by the experimental variables and more by the fact of the research itself. The special attention of the researchers convinced the workers that the management was interested in them and thus raised morale, which in turn increased productivity.

The phrase was later widely used to denote any unintended modification of behaviour that stemmed from being the subject of investigation.

In later work, Elton **Mayo** showed that the pace of industrial work is regulated by informal social norms among the workers; he also clarified how this process operated. He concluded that productivity was driven as much by management style and informal work organisation as by pay rates. Increasing productivity required management sensitivity to, and manipulation of, work-place human relations.

See **observer effect**.

HAYEK, FRIEDRICH A. (1899–1992)

Born in Austria, Hayek spent the middle part of his career at the London School of Economics (1931–50) before moving to the University of Chicago. His best-known work, *The Road to Serfdom* (1944), was a passionate defence of the political benefits of free market capitalism. The free market he envisaged was much more individualistic and unregulated than any form of capitalism witnessed during the 20th century. At a time when economics was dominated by Keynesian theory and many governments accepted an obligation to moderate the market for social purposes, Hayek argued that such state intervention would lead to impoverishment and totalitarianism: a view that was very popular with right-wing politicians such as Margaret Thatcher and Ronald Reagan (respectively the UK Prime Minister and US President in the 1980s). He was joint recipient of the Nobel prize for Economics in 1974, curiously having to share the award with an economist of nearly opposing views.

HEAD OF HOUSEHOLD

This phrase, which is becoming less common as families become more diverse, is used to denote the senior male (who was normally also the principal earner) in a family. Since the 1980s there have been arguments about taking the occupation of the male head of household to stand for the social class of the whole family. In defence of what might seem like male chauvinism, it is worth noting that, as it is still common for upper-class married women to have part-time occupations that are less-well rewarded and of lower status than their husband's jobs, ranking each individual separately can easily create a misleading impression.

HEALTH AND ILLNESS, SOCIOLOGY OF

The sociological interest in health and illness has three strands. It is concerned with the measurement and distribution of ailments, with social components of the causes of illness, and with the social definition of illness. In the first two strands, social science complements medicine; in the third it presents a challenge.

As with crime, there are basically two ways of measuring illness. We can collect and collate information from the agencies that deal with the phenomenon (such as health centres, hospitals, clinics). As official statistics do with crime, this will miss cases that are not reported and treated. Or we can survey a community: an expensive but useful way of trying to discover the extent of some illness that may be systematically under-reported. Measuring the extent and distribution of any illness is useful because it provides health services with information to plan responses (such as screening or inoculation programmes or ensuring enough doctors and nurses are trained in particular specialisms). It is also useful in identifying social causes of health and illness. It has long been obvious that both general ill-health and specific ailments are socially patterned. Age, gender, race, social class, religion and occupation all play a part. Much sociology of health and illness is concerned with trying to identify the causal connections between such patterns of characteristics and people's vulnerability to certain ailments.

The third strand – the social definition of health and illness – is the most radical contribution. Comparative studies by historians, anthropologists and sociologists show very clearly that cultures differ markedly in how they respond to physical and psychological problems (for example, what western medicine now treats as mental illness is in many cultures regarded as a spiritual problem to be managed with religious therapies). Such studies also take us one stage further back to appreciate that the very definition of a problem is also a matter of considerable cultural variation. What Europeans in the 1930s diagnosed as hysteria might in Polynesia be regarded as evidence of valuable spiritual gifts. Similarly, in the USA in the 20th century homosexuality was officially classed as a mental disorder until campaigners managed to persuade the medial authorities to revise the manual of disorders.

HEGEL, GEORG WILHELM FRIEDRICH (1770–1831)   Though very difficult to read, the work of Hegel marked an important innovation in modern philosophy. Previous philosophers had sought to arrive at ultimate answers. For example, Hegel's forerunner Kant had tried, once and for all, to explain the basis of moral law and also to introduce a systematic framework for understanding the different types of human knowledge (mathematics, religious understanding and what is now called science). Hegel took a different approach. He argued that the possibilities for understanding can grow and develop. It is not therefore possible to arrive at a complete system of philosophy because future developments in culture and human understanding may overthrow or transcend what we think of as the best answers. For example, earlier philosophers investigated the concepts of freedom and justice. But new forms of social order make those earlier philosophical enquiries out of date. In this sense Hegel was a 'historicist' thinker because he believed that the potential for philosophical reflection about justice or truth or ethics would be enhanced as culture and society themselves developed. Understanding of, for example, justice develops through a contest between different interpretations of the potential for justice; Hegel referred to such contests as dialectical conflicts.

None the less, Hegel appears to have convinced himself that historical development was reaching maturity in the society in which he lived, so that he tended to see contemporary political arrangements as the culmination of cultural development. Obviously, this was comforting to the status quo. But he had more left-wing followers (so-called Young Hegelians) who used his approach to look forward to even more

perfect forms of the state and of political order. This style of thinking was very influential on Karl **Marx** who accepted the idea that the possibilities for cultural and social development might be radically different in the future. What passed for obvious 'rights' in 19th-century Prussia would come to be seen in the future as injustices, as institutions of exploitation. Where Hegel and most of his left-wing followers suggested that radical change was introduced by new ideas and new forms of culture, Marx argued that the changes were brought about by developments at the material (that is, economic and productive) level. In this way Marx is often said to have turned Hegel on his head. Marx viewed the dialectic as an economic and political struggle, not a contest of ideas. More recently, Michel **Foucault** too is in many ways a Hegelian analyst since his work tends to focus on, for example, the different notions of sexuality and sexual health that flourish at particular times. He too adopts **historicism**.

HEGEMONY   This term was introduced by Antonio **Gramsci** to describe a particular form of social class domination but it is often now used to mean simply 'considerable influence over'. It is narrower than 'dominance' in that it is concerned with ideological influence and implies a lack of dispute.

HEREDITY   This is the genetic transmission of characteristics from one generation to the next. It has long been clear that parents, whether human, animal or plant, pass on certain features to their offspring. The young of fast race horses tend to run fast and so on. But two things have generally been less well understood. The first is the issue of how much of an attribute is passed on through heredity and how much derives from the conditions under which the child is brought up. The second issue concerns the exact mechanism through which characteristics are inherited biologically.

In relation to the first point, it is now almost universally agreed that most significant human characteristics are in part hereditary and in part to do with the environment, nutrition and so on. On average, the children of tall parents are likely to be tall, though if they have a poor diet or contract childhood diseases they may turn out to be much shorter. With some complex characteristics, such as academic ability, the environmental factors involved may be very numerous, ranging from nutrition and exposure to disease, through their parents' attitude to learning, the availability of books and computers at home, the quality of the school and the nature of the peers the child chooses as friends. In such cases it does not even make much sense to ask about the relative importance of genetic and environmental factors since there will not even be a fixed ratio for their relative significance. One cannot state that academic ability is, say, 60 per cent due to heredity since a child that gets a bad childhood disease may have their ability overwhelmingly influenced by that disorder whereas a luckier child will have less of an environmental influence. Of course, this is not to deny that some human features are straightforwardly genetic. The children of parents with blue eyes will (barring chance mutations and other unlikely effects) themselves have blue eyes.

The second issue concerns the mechanism by which inheritance occurs. This has become a great deal clearer in the last quarter century. For creatures such as mammals that reproduce sexually (unlike greenfly and other insects that can reproduce by a form of cloning) one can approximately state that every individual carries equal amounts of genetic material from their mother and from their father. In turn, they then pass on 50 per cent of this to each of their children. But this 50 per cent can be made up of virtually any mixture of the material they received from their parents. The resulting children can thus end up with a complete mix of attributes or they may strongly resemble one of their forebears. It is largely a matter of chance, conditioned by a few rules of genetic transmission.

As knowledge of the laws of inheritance grows and as our understanding of the biochemistry of genetics increases (so that we know which bits of genetic 'code' are responsible for colour blindness and so on) it is conceivable that parents will wish to select which genetic attributes their offspring inherit from the mother and which from the father. In the future parents may even be able to purchase genetic material that is thought superior to their own natural stock. This would give rise to so-called designer babies. Parents would then be more directly responsible for the genetic endowment of their children and children could come to blame parents for giving them the 'wrong' hair colour or leaving them to suffer from baldness. The potential dilemmas for parents serve as good examples of Anthony **Giddens**'s point about the juggernaut of modernity.

See **Darwinism, eugenics, evolution, genotype**.

HERMENEUTICS   In the early 19th century this denoted the branch of Christian scholarship that was concerned with reconstructing the original (and hence authentic) meaning of the Bible from the many divergent versions of the texts that were available. Scholarly arguments developed about whether there was only one original meaning or whether the meaning of a text arises from an interaction between the reader and the text. The sophisticated later 19th-century reader, approaching the Bible centuries after the Reformation and with knowledge of Darwinian and other challenges to the literal interpretation of the scriptures, has a different relation to the text than an eigth-century monk would have had. That interest led in turn to the general question of how the experiences and interests of the author shape a text, and gradually hermeneutics moved from a search for the correct reading to the view that there is no one correct interpretation of the text. Of course, this is not to say that the text can mean just anything one likes but that we cannot read the New Testament or Shakespeare plays in precisely the way that near contemporary readers would have done.

In social life there are many texts; we read books but also advertising material, bureaucratic records and so on. Film and television programmes are also a kind of text. Hence the concern about the reader's shaping of the text takes on a much broader life within sociology and cultural studies. Unlike in the natural sciences where – it is assumed – an experiment has only one meaning, in the humanities the subjects of study have manifold meanings.

HETEROSEXISM   Developed on the model of **sexism**, this refers to the ways in which social institutions and everyday practices disadvantage people who are not heterosexual. Thus, very few countries permit marriages except between women and men, and thus systematically deny the advantages of marriage to, among others, lesbian and gay couples. The advantages in question relate to such things as inheritance and recognition as 'next of kin'. As advocates of **feminism** have often been determined critics of marriage, there is a clear irony to lesbian and gay demands for the 'right' to marry, an irony that has not been lost on proponents of **queer theory**.

HEURISTIC DEVICE   This signifies a concept or idea that is used, not so much because it is well-supported by the evidence, but because it helps us to think about the problem. Max Weber's **ideal-type** is a heuristic device. By definition, nothing in the real world is exactly like the ideal-type but such artificial constructs allow us to see clearly what features of the matter in hand are

important for our purposes. Another heuristic device is the 'rational economic actor' proposed by economists. No actual person behaves as this imaginary actor does, but the hypothetical behaviour of the rational economic actor throws light on the conduct of actual shoppers and consumers.

HIDDEN CURRICULUM   Schools have an obvious curriculum: the content of the subjects they teach. In the 1960s it became popular to point out that they also have a hidden curriculum. In addition to teaching chemistry, biology and the like, schools teach pupils to respect authority, to accept being told what to do, to compete with each other and to get used to being judged. It is a sign of how much the political climate has changed that what educationalists once exposed and denounced, was, by the 1980s, being championed as an important part of preparation for the world of work.

HIERARCHY OF CREDIBILITY   Howard S. **Becker** made the point that those at the top (of an organisation or a society) usually appear much more credible than those at the bottom. The underdogs might be so completely discredited as effectively to have no voice at all. In the title of an essay that now seems romantic to the point of exemplifying the hippy culture of the 1960s, Becker asked 'Whose side are we on?' and argued that sociologists had an obligation to help the marginalised to find their voice. The problem with the idea of sociologist as advocate is the selection of those for whom we speak. We might sympathise with marijuana users or jazz musicians but it is hard to imagine many sociologists feeling obliged to assist users of child pornography or crack cocaine dealers.

HIERARCHY OF NEEDS   The phrase was popularised by psychologist Abraham Maslow, who believed that we had various needs, each of which became pressing when the more basic one was met. Most basic were the physiological: food, water, shelter. Then comes safety, security and structure. Third comes the need to love and to belong. Fourth is the need for self-respect and the approval of others. Finally, once all those are met, comes the need for self-actualisation. Maslow supposes that we have within us something (his examples relate to creative expression) that we need to live out in order to truly be ourselves. There is no evidence that our needs present themselves pressingly in this order, or even that we have 'needs' (as distinct from desires) much beyond the very basic; nowadays few sociologists mention the self-actualisation stage of the model. But the distinction between the first two and the rest is frequently made, though usually in the negative. It seems sensible to suppose that people whose material lives are a struggle rarely think about fine art. Within the last decade sociologists of the environment have drawn on the suggestion about the hierarchy of priorities to try to explain why environmental awareness developed first in prosperous countries. In most respects the environment was better in these countries than elsewhere and yet people in North American and Northern Europe were the pioneers in activism and nature protection. It seemed that, having met basic and security needs, they were free to attend to a 'need' to enhance their environment.

See **post-materialist values**.

HIGH MODERNITY   See **modernity**.

HISTOGRAM   Also known as bar charts, histograms are ways of representing the distribution of data by having columns of equal width whose height represents the frequency of the occurrence of that thing. One could display the differential take up of child vaccination programmes by displaying a histogram of the percentage of children inoculated against common diseases in each socio-economic class.

HISTORICAL DEMOGRAPHY   This is the study of past patterns of population structure, fertility and the like using historical source material such as early censuses and parish registers. As much sociology is concerned with the supposed unique features of modern industrial society, it is important that we understood pre-industrial social formations. Historical demography has played a major part in re-appraising some of our basic assumptions; for example, we now know that many pre-industrial families were not of the extended type even though the extended family was part of the 'stereotype' of pre-modern living.

HISTORICAL MATERIALISM   Karl **Marx** used this term to describe his theory of social evolution. It was historical in the sense that it was concerned with the order in which social forms unfolded. It was materialistic in the sense that, in contrast to G.W.F. **Hegel**'s idealism, it stressed the primacy of the economy (and the social relations created in that realm) over culture and the development of new ideas.

See **economic determinism, evolution, forces of production, mode of production**.

HISTORICISM   In Karl **Popper**'s usage, historicism is that type of social science which supposes that there are fixed laws of historical development, the grasp of which allows us to predict and manipulate the future. An example would be **Marxism**.

Popper faults historicism for making unconditional prophecies; good social science, if it predicts at all, hedges its predictions with conditions. He also argues that human history is always unpredictable because it depends on advances in knowledge that are themselves unknowable. We cannot know now what we will know in 100 years' time. As well as being wrong, historicism is dangerous. With good reason, Popper argues that historicists are loath to subject their theories to hard testing. Like the adherents of a **millennialist** religion, they cling to them despite the failure of their predictions. And because they are convinced of the correctness of their predictions, historicists are willing to support extremist politics in order to hasten the assuredly-coming **utopia**; we could cite Adolf Hitler, Joseph Stalin, Chairman Mao and Pol Pot as examples.

See **falsification, Hegel, open society**.

HISTORIOGRAPHY   This term was once used to prevent confusion between history as the facts of the past and historiography as the scholarly discipline of studying the facts of the past. As we now use the word 'history' for both these meanings, this term has been 'moved upstairs' and now refers to reflection on or writing about the craft of studying history.

HOBBES, THOMAS (1588–1679)   Hobbes had such an influence on social thought that the student of sociology is likely to come across the adjective 'Hobbesian' while Cartesian and Platonic are barely seen. His major work *Leviathan* (1651) presented a reasoned justification for authoritarian politics derived from assumptions about human nature. Hobbes believed human action to be driven by two concerns: fear of death and a desire for power. If people were allowed to subsist in a state of nature, without laws or government, each individual, expecting little or no good will from his fellows, would relentlessly pursue more power. Each person's desire for security would create perpetual personal antagonism and instability and it

was this state that Hobbes described with his famous (and usually mis-quoted) phrase: 'solitary, poor, nasty, brutish and short'. But because people are gifted with rationality and foresight, they appreciate that if they gave up some or all of their power to one individual or group, that agent would guarantee peace and security, by exercising sovereign power over them. In the present-day world, Hobbes's arguments seem most applicable to nation-states which often seem to confront each other in solitary competition. Generally, the term 'Hobbesian' (normally applied critically) refers to his pessimistic vision of what people would be like if left to themselves.

See **social contract**.

HOCHSCHILD, ARLIE RUSSELL (1940–)
In *The Managed Heart: the Commercialization of Human Feeling* (1983), Hochschild added to Erving **Goffman**'s concentration on external appearances by distinguishing surface acting, in which people pretend to feel, and 'deep acting' in which they actually manage their real feelings. As well as simulating emotions in playing a part, workers such as air hostesses often have to control alternative emotions. Emotional work requires not only that the appearance of socially-required feelings is produced but also that real alternatives be suppressed.

In *The Second Shift* (1990) and *The Time Bind* (1997), Hochschild explored the family-work link, focusing on the ways that two-job families struggle to find enough time for family life. *The Second Shift*'s analysis of gender relations described the advance of women as a 'stalled revolution'. Her *Commercialization of Intimate Life* (2003) was more negative. Capitalism had drained intimate life of meaning by commercializing it. Detailed analysis of manuals offering advice on personal relations leads her to conclude that the trend is for women to approach male norms: more detachment, thicker psychological armour, and more compartmentalisation. 'Women are encouraged to be cooler, men are not encouraged to be warmer'.

See **family**.

HOLISM   See **methodological individualism**.

HOMANS, GEORGE C. (1910–89)   In his 1964 presidential address to the American Sociological Association, Homans argued that social phenomena could only be explained in terms of individual motivation and that sociology should be based on elements of what he regarded as two highly successful branches of social science: behavioural psychology and elementary economics. Though he regretted the name, his work came to be known as **exchange theory**.

HOMEOSTASIS   This denotes a process that regulates or maintains any system in relation to its external environment. An obvious example from human biology is the sweat system, which helps to cool the body and thus keep us at a constant temperature when the world around us heats up. The idea that social systems act to keep themselves in equilibrium is one of the more contentious parts of **structural-functionalism**.

HOMOPHOBIA   By the normal derivation rules this should be 'homosexual-phobia' as it refers to an extreme hatred or fear of homosexuals. The term was coined in the 1970s by George Weinberg to denote a deep-seated psychological fear of homosexuality. These days it is used simply to mean a very strong dislike for homosexuals.

HOPE–GOLDTHORPE SCALE   See **occupational scales**.

HORKHEIMER, MAX (1895–1973)   See **Frankfurt School**.

HORTICULTURE   Horticulture is the cultivation of plants. Agriculture is broader and includes the breeding and rearing of animals. The former is generally less technically advanced, relying on hoes and digging sticks.

HOUSEHOLD   This denotes a group of people who share living space, pool their incomes and, a common marker, eat together.

HOUSEWORK, SOCIOLOGY OF   One of the benefits of the feminist movement of the 1960s was that it caused people to study areas of social life that had been previously regarded as of little interest. One such is housework, which has rarely received the attention accorded to paid work outside the home. Helene Z. Lopata's (1971) *Occupation: Housework* and Ann Oakley's (1974) *The Sociology of Housework* were pioneering works in the field.

Questions studied include the self-image of houseworkers, the organisation of housework, changing standards of cleanliness, and job satisfaction. One important conclusion of research is that greater gender equality in the paid labour market has not been matched by greater equality in the home. British women do almost four times as much housework as their male partners. Only when the male is not in work and the female works full-time outside the home is housework evenly divided. When both partners work full-time the male generally does only a third of the domestic labour. Although the gender gap is diminishing, this is largely because women are spending less time on domestic work and not because men are doing more.

An enduringly contentious issue in the sociology of domestic labour is how we explain the apparent high levels of satisfaction with a gendered distribution of tasks that are regularly reported by women. There is a parallel with approaches to a lack of radical class consciousness in the working class. If we assume that workers are objectively exploited, high levels of work satisfaction are mysteries to be explained (possibly by **false consciousness**). If we assume that women should regard their levels of housework as exploitative, then we may be drawn to explanations that stress **patriarchy**. On the other hand we could assume that couples apply a degree of rational choice to domestic decision-making and note that some conclude that an inequitable division of housework is fair because they take account of work commitments outside the home.

HUMAN–CAPITAL THEORY　　In classic economics the two main forces of production are capital (the factory, the money to buy raw materials and the like) and labour. Human–capital theory aims to add more detail to our understanding of labour by noting that labour is not all of equal value or productivity. People who invest time and effort and money (for example, by foregoing earnings to stay in education) can be said to have increased their human capital by improving their knowledge and skills. According to the Nobel prize-winning economist Gary S. Becker, other things being equal, personal incomes vary according to the amount invested in human capital because hirers of labour will not pay more than they have to and sellers of labour will want to recoup their investment in human capital. One weakness is that there is no independent measure of increased value or productivity; it is assumed that highly-paid people are more productive and useful than poorly-paid ones. There are other explanations of wage differentials.

HUMAN ECOLOGY　　Now only of historical interest, this described the approach to

urban development of members of the **Chicago School**, who applied ecological principles derived from plant biology (for example, competition, invasion and succession) to understanding patterns of change in cities. Eventually these processes created a series of concentric rings: an inner city of commercial prosperity and decaying private houses, then an area of established working-class housing, and then the outlying suburbs to which the affluent retreated. As groups could afford to leave the inner rings, they were replaced by new social groups (such as recent immigrants). Although it produced an illuminating description of Chicago in the 1920 and 1930s, the ecological metaphor was not widely taken up. In many respects this pattern seems peculiar to a particular time and place and not a universal rule of 'succession' in urban development.

HUMAN NATURE　　The phrase denotes those characteristics that are fundamental to humans as a species: what is left once the clothes of civilization we have acquired through socialisation are stripped away? Sociologists are generally agreed that, compared to other species, humans have very little 'nature'. Most animals act as they do because their instincts set the responses to their environment. Hunter bees are instinctively programmed to perform a dance in front of the hive that shows other bees which way to fly to find the honey. It is not a matter of conscious choice. We talk casually about human instincts such as 'the will to survive' but some people commit suicide. There may be a reproductive imperative but some people choose to remain childless. Seeing how differently people can behave in different societies shows us that whatever species nature we have as humans is remarkably plastic: sexual activity may be universal but there are wide differences between cultures and sub-cultures in what forms of intercourse are permitted (or encouraged) and with whom.

That human nature does not set for us specific behaviour patterns is important in the social sciences because it explains why so many scholars are interested in the twin problems of social order and personal stability. Emile **Durkheim** and Arnold **Gehlen** among many others argued that the 'world-openness' of the human, unconstrained by instinct or environment, was a cause of both psychological and social problems. Because our nature did not specify the limits to desires, however much we acquired we could feel deprived. Because nature did not direct behaviour in detail, even the simplest co-ordinated activity would be difficult for large numbers of humans. The solution to both sets of problems is the creation and imposition of a culture of rules and values that, like the external skeleton of a beetle, compensates for the plasticity of human nature. This, of course, does not explain the content of any social order but it does explain the necessity for one.

HUMAN RELATIONS SCHOOL　From the late 1930s to the early 1960s this interdisciplinary approach to the study of work (associated particularly with Elton **Mayo**) largely replaced the earlier school of scientific management that treated workers as isolated individuals. The Human Relations approach stressed the importance of work-based group norms, communication and the behaviour of supervisors.

HUMAN RIGHTS　The idea of a right is clear enough; the adjective 'human' signifies not a distinction from animals or gods but the entry qualification. These are rights for which being human is the only requirement. Although it is fashionable to deride modernisation, one of the great benefits of the last three centuries has been the expansion of the rights that societies accord to all people.

See **civil rights**.

HUMANISM　This may refer to an ideological alternative to religion, in which human needs and human fulfilment are considered without recourse to gods or divine agencies. With the decline of the Christian churches in the West, humanist associations have attempted to fill the ritual gap by creating non-religious alternatives to church baptisms, weddings and funerals. It may more broadly mean an emphasis on human creativity and the basic worth of human beings.

In debates about Karl **Marx** 'humanistic' refers to his early writings (for example on **alienation**) which structuralists such as Louis **Althusser** criticise for giving undue weight to the autonomous human subject.

HUME, DAVID (1711–76)　A leading philosopher of the Scottish **Enlightenment**, Hume wrote on a wide variety of topics but is now known mainly for his influence on modern **empiricism**. As a uncompromising empiricist, Hume made the case that whatever people know they learn from experience; they do not come 'pre-packaged' with knowledge. Taking this position to its logical limit created problems for Hume, notably about the analysis of causation and about the problem of induction. One cannot be certain of the inevitability of causation from observation and experience since what one observes is 'constant conjunction' not causation. Flicking the light switch is routinely followed by the light coming on, but one cannot see that one event is the cause of the other, only that bright light always follows the movement of the switch. Equally, the fact that we have seen the sun come up every morning in recorded history does not guarantee that it will come up tomorrow; we cannot be certain of our inductive generalisation that the sun will continue to rise. In this way Hume is credited with having pushed empiricism as far as it can logically go, leading to uncomfortable and hardly sustainable scepticism about causation and induction.

Hume was also insistent that knowledge about facts (what is) and knowledge about values (what ought to be) are radically different kinds of thing. In his view, one cannot infer from an 'is' to an 'ought'. He is regarded as the first philosopher to spell out what is now seen as the **fact–value distinction** in something like its modern form.

HUNTER-GATHERERS　　As the name suggests, these are people who do not cultivate or domesticate their food but hunt wild animals and collect wild plants. Because resources tend to be scarce, hunter-gatherers are normally nomadic and live in small kinship bands. Once we were all hunter-gatherers; now there are only a few thousand left.

HUSSERL, EDMUND GUSTAV ALBERT (1859–1938)　　See **phenomenology**.

HYBRID IDENTITY　　Although they place the point of change in different eras, many sociologists suppose that social identities used to be relatively simple and derived from all-encompassing roles and membership of stable groups, and are now complex and fluid. 'Hybrid identity' was coined by Ulrich **Beck** to describe the condition of moving (at least partly at will) between a number of identities. If we take identity to mean 'social identity' then the greater our freedom the less certain our identities.

HYBRIDS　　Related to **hybrid identities**, sociologists including adherents of **actor-network**

theory, have recently argued that sociology is wrong to think of its subject matter as the study of people. Societies are not 'peopled' only with humans but also with machines, symbols and increasingly with agents of mixed identity (known as hybrids or, following Donna **Haraway**, as 'cyborgs'). In the most extreme case, hybrids would be technologically enhanced humans or robotic beings, but in the current world we can think of people who have implanted micro-chips or pilots in fly-by-wire aircraft as hybrid actors. They are neither machines nor conventional human actors.

HYDRAULIC SOCIETY　　See **Asiatic mode of production**.

HYPER-REALITY　　See **Baudrillard**.

HYPOTHESIS　　This is a proposition (usually containing the two elements of a cause and an effect) that is framed in such as way as to be appraised or tested; 'Catholic states are more repressive than Protestant ones' is an example. The important point about an hypothesis is that it should be formulated in such a way that it is clear what would count as a test. In this example, the supposed 'cause' (the religious culture of the state) is relatively straight-forward but the effect ('being repressive') would require considerable elaboration before we could agree on what would count as appropriate measures.

HYPOTHETICO-DEDUCTIVE METHOD　　See **induction**.

I

IATROGENIC DISEASE   In standard usage, this term refers to illness that is caused by the medical profession. Thus, medical intervention can have harmful side-effects: the 18th-century practice of bleeding patients and the 19th-century use of mercury to treat syphilis are illustrative cases. A spectacular example is puerperal fever. This was an often-fatal disease acquired by women, we know now, in the delivery stages of childbirth and common in the 19th century. Because it was carried by doctors from one patient to another, those women who could afford to be attended by physicians were far more likely to contract puerperal fever than the poor. The term iatrogenic was broadened by Ivan Illich (1926–2002) to describe two other ways in which illness in society may be caused by the medical profession. At the social or definitional level, western medicine may create illness by encouraging people to see themselves as needing expensive medical interventions. Illich also argued that our general capacity to deal with physical and psychological problems was sapped by a medical profession that encouraged us to seek a medical solution to every difficulty.

ICON   Originally this meant a sign that resembled the thing it represented (as distinct from those such as the mathematical signs for divide and add, the meaning of which is purely conventional). It was used mostly to describe the paintings of Christ, saints and angels that decorated Greek and Eastern Orthodox Churches. This meaning has been carried into computer design where an icon is a small button with a stylised representation of the action that it triggers. The term is also loosely used to mean any celebrity who is an object of hero-worship and emulation.

ID   This is one of three parts of the personality in Sigmund **Freud**'s theory. It contains the inherited elements (in particular **instincts**) and from it grow the **ego** and **superego**. The id is the unconscious part of the mind, is closely associated with human biology, and, according to Freud, operates on the 'pleasure principle'; that is, it seeks to gratify the instincts. According to Freud there are two main instincts: sex and aggression. The ego operates to shape the desires of the id into forms which are socially acceptable.

IDEAL SPEECH SITUATION   The critical theorist Jürgen **Habermas** introduced the term 'ideal speech situation' (or ISS) to describe the ideal of human interaction which, he believes, is presupposed by the language of academic analysis and other systematic inquiries. According to Habermas, academic debate, and more generally the search for truth, presuppose an ideal speech situation of unfettered interaction. In any inquiry, speakers implicitly make claims to speak – for example – truthfully, sincerely and comprehensibly. Of course, people may in fact lie or attempt to deceive. But lying only works because the background 'norm' is that one tells the truth. The important point for Habermas is that within this ISS we can find ethical values already taken for granted and assumed to exist by the way we conduct our analysis. The values do not come from outside our social research; they are already inside: they are '**immanent**'. Thus the ISS shows how sociological inquiry can be factual and objective while also supporting particular value orientations. In other words, through the ISS, Habermas seeks to overcome the **fact–value distinction**. Critics of Habermas query the manner in which he derives particular values from the way that he envisages the ideal speech situation; they also doubt whether the immanent values he claims to discover actually get one very far in elaborating a social and political programme. The value of truthfulness for example is compatible with virtually any modern political ideals.

See **Habermas, critical theory**.

IDEAL-TYPE   Even though we know that they can never be attained, it is often useful to imagine pure or ideal forms: a total vacuum, for example. Simplifying the world allows the natural sciences to construct laws which, although they do not represent the world with complete accuracy (because of the simplifications), give us a very good understanding of how the natural world operates. By investigating how far reality diverges from the pure models we can improve those models.

The use of the ideal-type in sociology was championed by Max **Weber**, who was influenced by its popularity in economics. It is important to appreciate that in laying out the characteristics of the ideal-type of **bureaucracy**, for example, he was not implying any moral judgements nor was he claiming that

any actual bureaucracy would display all those features in just those idealised forms. He was trying to grasp the essence of bureaucracy by logically teasing out and exaggerating its defining characteristics.

A crucial difference between Weber's use of ideal-types and that of the natural sciences is that he does not suppose that further research will eventually bring consensus about the nature of reality or produce workable 'laws'. Rather he sees ideal-types as **heuristic devices**: as products of the sociologist's imagination that help us grasp what the researcher thinks is analytically important. By linking the value of an ideal-type to the analyst's success in making his or her point rather than to the degree of accuracy of the ideal-type, this position gets us away from endless arguments about whose ideal-type is better. However this stance could be interpreted as a warrant for relativism. If the test of the description of any phenomenon is how well it fits a body of thought rather than how well it fits the real world, then we seem to be abandoning social science in favour of accepting competing explanations as equally valid. That is, no ideal-type would be better than any other.

An alternative is to see ideal-types as a best starting classification with further research intended to modify them to better accord with reality, but that rather gets away from Weber's distinctive understanding of the methodological value of ideal-types.

IDEALISM   In everyday usage this describes the state of mind in which people think inappropriately well of the world or have unusually high-minded aspirations. In the social sciences and in philosophy it refers to an emphasis, not on ideals, but on ideas, and it is usually contrasted with **structuralism** or **materialism**. The issue is the extent to which social change and human conduct should be explained as a result of 'ideas', that is, reasons and thoughts. As an example, Max **Weber**'s suggestion that Protestant beliefs were important in providing the motivation for capitalist accumulation by the wealthy (who invested rather than engaging in conspicuous spending) is an idealist account of the development of modern capitalism. A non-idealist account would place most emphasis on economic and technical factors rather than on the autonomous significance of ideas and beliefs. For this reason, 'idealist' is usually used pejoratively, as, for example, when Marxists damn the entire discipline of sociology for giving insufficient weight to economic conditions in explaining human behaviour.

In the philosophical literature too, idealism refers to philosophical positions that give priority to ideas over things. In this sense **Hegel** was an idealist since he viewed the development of society as driven primarily by changes in the leading political and cultural beliefs. As an opponent of Hegel's followers, Karl **Marx** was thus an anti-idealist both philosophically and sociologically.

IDENTITY   One meaning of this term refers to the sense of self that develops as the child separates from parents and family and acquires a place in society. Sociology's view of identity is distinctive in giving great weight to socialisation and social interaction. The work of George Herbert **Mead** and Charles Horton **Cooley** was significant in developing an understanding of the self as a social product. Sociologists often draw attention to the situational or contextual nature of identity. Whatever endures it is clear that we can choose from a wide variety of emphases depending on the matter in hand. Father, son, worker, countryman, Virginian, fundamentalist, American; which of these identities is given priority will vary according to circumstance.

More recently, sociologists have argued that, in very highly modern societies, the sense that one's identity stems from early socialisation may be changing. There may be two processes at work here. First, in

advanced **modernity** there is greater scope for people to revise their identities through choice of lifestyle and through the way they adorn and comport themselves. Increasing numbers of people are resorting to cosmetic surgery to change their apparent identity at the bodily level. In this way, nearly every aspect of the self is seen as malleable and open to deliberate choice. Second (and contrastingly), with increasing understanding of our genetic backgrounds, people are increasingly thinking about their own identities in genetic terms. Of course, human identity is not genetically programmed but people are now increasingly self-conscious about the influence of their genetic inheritance on their sense of identity.

IDEOLOGICAL CLOSURE   In cultural and media studies, this denotes the use in the production of texts (including films and television programmes) of strategies which lead the reader or viewer inexorably to one interpretation rather than another.

IDEOLOGICAL STATE APPARATUS   Now rarely used, this term was coined by the French Marxist Louis **Althusser** as half of a contrast pair with 'repressive state apparatuses'. The point is a simple one and parallels the common distinction between authority and power. The state maintains itself in part through such repressive institutions as the army, police, courts and prisons which can coerce conformity and punish dissent. But in one sense, the need to deploy such agencies shows weakness. The effective state uses ideological state apparatuses such as the church, schools, and the mass media to ensure that people think the right way and do not want to deviate or dissent.

IDEOLOGY   Most generally an ideology is a coherent set of ideas but more often than not it has the narrower meaning (which distinguishes it from 'belief system') of some body of ideas that justifies the domination of one group by another. Although some users disclaim this implication, the term (especially in its adjectival form 'ideological') usually also suggests untruth. Hence 'gender ideology' indicates a body of ideas about differences between women and men, some or all of which are false, which justifies male domination.

See **false consciousness, knowledge, sociology of**.

IDIOGRAPHIC AND NOMOTHETIC These terms represent yet another version of our old friend: the general argument about the extent to which the study of social phenomena can be scientific in the sense of imitating the methods of the natural sciences. Idiographic methods (from the Greek 'idio' meaning 'one's own' and 'graphein' meaning 'to write') focus on cultural and historical particulars and stress accurate description. Nomothetic approaches (from 'nomos' meaning 'rules') seek, after the fashion of physics, to establish general laws.

IMAGINED COMMUNITIES Benedict Anderson's (1983) seminal *Imagined Communities: Reflections on the Origins and Spread of Nationalism* made the point that, although the nation could engender strong feelings of belonging, it was 'imagined' in the sense that no member can ever have real relationships with all or even many of the other members (especially not with the previous generations, a vital part of the nation). The implied contrast is with the classic **community** in which the majority of relationships are face-to-face and social identity is created and sustained through those relationships. The phrase has since been widely adopted and used rather loosely for any association or social entity where communication is mediated rather than direct. Both terms may end up being

used carelessly. Almost all social entities involve a degree of imagination' in the sense that people act on the basis of their perceptions of reality rather than in immediate response to the reality itself, but most also have a firm reality independent of what particular actors think of, for example, their nation or their village. And 'communities' is often used in place of other words which would tell us more about the groupings in question. To call something an 'imagined community' may mistakenly imply we can change its nature by changing our thoughts.

See **nation**.

IMITATION EFFECT See **copycat effect**.

IMMANENCE Most often used in religious and theological contexts, immanence usually refers to the idea that God is in some sense in the world rather than being located entirely outside of it in His or Her own transcendent sphere. In philosophical writing the term has a related meaning: an argument about the validity of a philosophical system derived from within the standpoint of that system is referred to as an **immanent criticism** or critique.

IMMANENT CRITIQUE A critique is usually used to refer to a criticism of a system of thought, and an immanent critique is a criticism that is based on the precepts or founding assumptions of the system itself. Thus Marxists often referred to Karl **Marx**'s critical analysis of capitalism as an immanent critique since it was allegedly based on identifying contradictions within capitalism itself. The capitalist system claimed to liberate workers but only liberated them to the extent of allowing them to choose the master that would enslave them. In the case of Marxism, the main issue has turned out to be not whether the critique was immanent or not but whether

Marx's arguments were sound; by and large they were not. More recently **critical theorists** have been attracted to immanent arguments: for example **Habermas**'s suggestion that interaction presupposes an **ideal speech situation** (ISS) is a form of immanent argument.

See **immanence**.

IMMIGRATION   See **migration**.

IMPERATIVE CO-ORDINATION   This is one possible translation of Max **Weber**'s *Herrschaft*. Although more clumsy than the more commonly used 'domination', it conveys better Weber's sense of the likelihood that a command will be obeyed and it is contrasted with power (or *Macht*), which is the ability of an actor to see his or her will prevail despite the resistance of others. When Weber wishes to stress domination that was widely accepted as legitimate, he wrote 'legitime Herrschaft', which Talcott **Parsons** translated as 'authority'.

IMPERIALISM   Derived from the noun 'empire', this denotes the political and economic domination of one or more countries by another. The classic empires of modern times were the Ottoman, which at the start of the 19th century covered the Balkans and the Middle East, and the British, which at the end of the 19th century extended over enough of the globe for its officials to boast that the sun never set on the empire.

Empires have differed in the way that the imperial centre has ruled its overseas territories. The French, for example, imposed their language and culture on their colonial possessions and treated some of them (Algeria, for example) in many respects as if they were parts of France. The British generally remained distant from those they ruled, preferring to work through existing social and political structures.

One of the main reasons for imperial expansion was economic: a cheap source of raw materials, an outlet for surplus population, and a captive market for finished goods. The European nations abandoned their overseas possessions, in part, because they had become a financial drain and because liberation movements were raising the costs – military and economic – of continued rule. They were also an embarrassment in that even the best-run colonies denied to native people the civil and political rights which in the 20th century were taken-for-granted at home.

Critics of US foreign policy and cultural expansion from the 1950s onwards talk of 'American imperialism' but this is a rather casual usage. What is clear is that the influence the USA exercises over large parts of the world is quite different from Ottoman or British imperialism in that it does not rest on constant military presence or the formation of permanent colonies but can be exercised through preferential trade terms, local military proxies and the rapid deployment of military force. Unlike the popular British support for its empire, Americans are highly ambivalent about direct involvement in the affairs of foreign countries.

See **neo-colonialism**.

IMPLICIT RELIGION   Some analysts responded to the obvious decline of Christianity in western Europe in the second half of the 20th century by suggesting that the spirit of religion endured in (or its social functions were performed by) a variety of activities that were not at first sight religious. Various forms of collective social activity (such as spectating at a football match) were described as being 'implicitly religious'. This seems a rather pointless piece of re-naming. It is quite sensible to ask to what extent and in what ways non-religious activities share common features with religious ones. For example, the reverence of celebrities may have some similarities with the reverence of saints. But the concept is unhelpful because there are no limits to its application. When used as a way of asserting that people or societies are innately religious, implicit religion has the further fault of prejudging the sociologically important question of whether people or societies in some sense need religion.

See **civil religion**.

IMPRESSION MANAGEMENT Erving **Goffman** (1959) introduced the term in his classic *The Presentation of Self in Everyday Life* when he was describing the many ways in which people in company seek to manage the impression they make on others. The point he wished to make was that the human self is not so much a set of adjectives as a series of verbs. For example, it was not enough to possess the character of being virtuous; one had to act in ways that dramatised one's virtue. For Goffman, the self was a performance.

INCARCERATION From the Latin meaning 'to be imprisoned', this term is now used to describe a wide variety of ways in which people may be confined against their will. For example, it would include forced hospitalisation. When used in an unexpected way (for example, to describe the condition of being required to attend school), it is always pejorative.

INCEST TABOO All societies prohibit sexual relations between certain classes of relations, although the prohibitions vary. Sex between parents and children and between siblings is almost universally banned but some cultures also ban sex between cousins while others actively encourage it. Why incest is prohibited is not entirely clear. We know now that in-breeding, by concentrating genetic material, can generate a variety of

physical and psychological problems but, as is clear from the preference for cousin-marriage, many societies would not have made this connection. Sigmund **Freud** believed that the origins of incest taboos lay in the strong appeal of incest (particularly between mothers and sons). There was already enough conflict inherent in the family without its members competing for each other's sexual favours. Claude **Lévi-Strauss** argued that the point of banning in-breeding was to force 'out-breeding' and thus create bonds with wider social groups.

INCOMMENSURABILITY Generally speaking, two things can be said to be incommensurable when no common measure or language exists through which they can be compared. We can, for example, compare the costs of television sets in different economies by calculating how many hours the typical worker has to work in, say, Russia and Belgium, to buy one. Incommensurability is a problem for **rational choice theories** of human action because we can only make rational choices when we can compare the costs and rewards of alternative courses of action. We cannot make rational choices between two competing religions because, until after death (when it is too late to switch), we cannot be sure if either religion will deliver the promised rewards.

One particular use of the term derives from the work on the history and philosophy of science of Thomas **Kuhn**. Kuhn is celebrated for his argument about the role of **paradigms** (large-scale theories such as Darwinian natural selection) in the development of science. Kuhn seems to believe that all observations are 'theory-relative'; that is, how things are seen depends on the ideas one brings to the observation. It therefore seemed to follow that paradigms are truly incommensurable since what one can observe depends on which paradigm one inhabits. Because there is no neutral language of observation, it cannot be the case, as philosophers such as Karl **Popper** suppose, that science evolves gradually as experimental observation allows scientists to choose between better and worse explanations. More generally the idea that bodies of thought are incommensurable has been used as a justification for **relativism** and, in anthropology, for the claim that we cannot really understand people of other cultures.

See **Feyerabend**.

INCORPORATION   Most generally this means simply bringing some body of people into a group which they were previously outside, but it usually has the more specific sense of signifying the removal of a potential threat to a dominant group's position by bringing on board either an entire body that threatens it or the potential leaders of that body. Although this can be entirely benign, as when the British parliament extended the franchise to bring working-class people into the mainstream of democratic politics, there is often a suggestion of trickery: those incorporated seem to have been bought off cheaply.

INDEPENDENT AND DEPENDENT VARIABLES The distinction here is between cause and effect. In an experiment to examine the effects of heating a bar of metal on its length, heat is the independent variable and the length of the bar (the thing that changes with temperature alterations) is the dependent variable. Where we cannot create clean experiments but have to rely on naturally occurring data, we are often unsure about which, of two things we know to be connected (or, to put it formally, two variables that are correlated), is the cause and which the effect. As 'being paid less' will not turn a man into a woman, we may be confident that in the correlation between gender and average income, the former is the independent

variable and income the dependent one, but the direction of causation is often less obvious. For example, we know that mixed-religion couples are less likely to be church-goers than couples of the same religion but it is not clear which comes first. Is marrying someone of a different religion proof that you have already lost faith or does being in a mixed-religion marriage undermine faith?

INDEX   In survey analysis this refers to the combination of a variety of variables into a single measure. For example, we could combine questions about frequency of church attendance, beliefs about God, church membership and self-image as a religious person (or otherwise) into a single index of conventional religiosity. The term may also refer to something that is not measured directly. So we might refer to voting for pronouncedly left-wing parties as an index of political militancy.

INDEXICAL   EXPRESSION,   INDEXICALITY This is a central concept in **ethnomethodology** and derives from a specialist term in linguistics. Some words derive their meaning from their context of use; for example, 'here' (as in 'I can see the castle from here') only has meaning in relation to the location of the speaker. Such words are said to be indexical. Most linguists regard only a few words as indexical in this sense. In linguistic terms, the meanings of the majority of words do not depend on context. However, by extension the term applies to a key assertion of ethnomethodology: that utterances and actions do not have single unchanging meanings but derive their meanings from the contexts in which they are made. The single expression 'Do you like pizza?' can be both an invitation and a request for information and only the context would tell us which. The indexicality of everyday interaction underlies one of ethnomethodology's key claims: that the orderliness of social life does not follow from a script or set of rules. Rather social order is constantly being constructed as we go along.

INDIGENOUS   From the Latin for 'native', this term has displaced terms such as 'aborigine' as a way of designating the original inhabitants of some land, usually with the added implication that the natives have been swamped by colonisers or migrants and now form a minority. As part of a general cultural trend to distrust western science and globalised culture, the usage of phrases such as 'indigenous knowledge' often carries the implication that what is taken to be native or aboriginal is better, more authentic, than more recently imported culture, knowledge and social forms.

INDIVIDUALISM   This has a very wide variety of meanings but either as a description or as a political preference, it implies contrast with characteristics that come from nonvoluntary membership of some sort of group. For example, the Protestant Reformation's insistence that each of us had to answer to God for our piety was an individualistic attack on two aspects of Catholic teaching. It denied that a priest or other official was necessary for our salvation and hence was an assertion of individual right. It also denied that the piety of the people as a whole could compensate for personal failure: it was thus an assertion of individual responsibility. As a political programme, individualism stands for the rights of the individual against the power of the state or some ruling elite. As we can see from the popularity of constitutional safeguards of individual rights and of politics based on equal citizenship, individualism is now universally accepted, in rhetoric at least.

Contemporary cultures differ in the extent to which individual freedom is celebrated and encouraged. However, all modern cultures experience some difficulty over the exact extent of individual liberty. For example,

in the USA many conservative Christians use individualistic arguments to say that they prefer their children not to be taught about current biological views on evolution. In this way, individual rights may come into conflict with other features of modern culture, such as the idea that there are scientific experts whose views are well founded and are not just an expression of an individual, personal opinion.

Individualism may also refer to one side of two enduring arguments about the nature of the social sciences. The first argument concerns method. Against scholars such as Emile **Durkheim** who argue that the proper concern of sociology is the explanation of **social facts** (that is, data which relate to societies and social groups), methodological individualists assert that social phenomena can ultimately only be explained in terms of facts about individuals. Hence although we can, as a matter of convenience, compare the suicide rates for classes of people, we should remember that such rates are merely the accumulation of the acts of individuals and thus any explanation must be convincing at the level of individual actors. The second argument is closely related and concerns the extent to which individuals are as they are because of individual, personal factors or because of their membership of social groups. The individualist stresses the voluntary components of beliefs, actions and identity.

See **determinism**.

INDUCTION   This is the thought process by which general regularities are derived from repeated observations of connections between two or more variables. On one warm winter's day we see ice melt. We see ice cubes melt in the glass we hold in our hand. We gradually induce that ice routinely turns to water when it is heated. In discussion of research methods, induction is contrasted with deduction: the deriving of new propositions by logical inference from starting premises. Induction is the basis of social and natural science though it has repeatedly caused problems for philosophers who have been troubled by the lack of certainty associated with inductive generalisations: that the sun has risen every morning of my life is no logical reason to expect it to rise tomorrow.

See **falsification**, **Hume**.

INDUSTRIAL CONFLICT   There are many expressions of conflict between the owners (or managers) of industry and the workforce. Absenteeism, sabotage, and deliberate output restriction may be individual or collective expressions. Strikes are collective manifestations of conflict.

The **Human Relations School** movement argued that industrial conflict could be prevented by better management incorporating the workers into a socially supportive community. Most sociologists of work see a degree of conflict as inevitable, especially during difficult periods – for example, when the economy is in recession or when technological innovations may transform the nature of work. For Marxists, capitalist work is essentially exploitative and workers will periodically realise that fact. Weberians do not see paid work as inevitably exploitative but they make the obvious point that the interests of workers and managers often diverge.

INDUSTRIAL REVOLUTION   This describes the major technical, economic and social changes that first occurred in Britain between 1760–1850 as manufacturing moved from a craft basis to machine production in a **factory** environment. Its primary features were a greatly increased division of labour, increased control by capitalist business owners over the labour process, the invention of new machines to aid production and the use of inanimate (first water and then steam)

power in manufacturing industries (such as textiles and iron and steel), extractive industries (such as mining), and transportation (by road, rail and sea).

Economic productivity increased greatly and the population became urbanised. Although the long-term effects were a major increase in prosperity and social welfare, in the short term, life in industrial cities was often miserable. Additionally, a number of skilled craft groups suffered (such as hand-loom weavers) and there was considerable resistance to the new disciplines (strict time-keeping, for example) that were required to co-ordinate large workforces in the factory system.

Industrialisation in Britain was quickly followed by similar changes in western Europe and North America.

INDUSTRIAL SOCIETY   Although analysts argue about which of these are necessary for industrialisation and which are more or less accidental by-products, it is a matter of historical observation that industrial societies differ from their agrarian predecessors in the following ways. By definition, industrial societies are ones in which the mass of the workforce is engaged in industrial production and only a small part is employed in agriculture. Production is mechanised and organised in factories. It is also commercialised; that is, goods are intended for sale rather than for subsistence. Agriculture itself is based on large units, is highly mechanised, and is oriented to serving the market. The mass of the population is literate. A majority of the population live in large towns and cities. The exchange of goods and services between very large numbers of people over large areas encourages the creation of an effective state and that is usually accompanied by the development of a shared sense of national identity: the development of a national economy stimulates the evolution and imposition of a common language and culture. There is also the growing influence of science and the rationalisation of large areas of thought and action. Finally, industrial societies normally have democratic political systems which incorporate the entire population in the body politic through mass parties.

The phrase is not only descriptive; in the 1960s and 1970s it also denoted one point of view in a controversy over how best to characterise modern societies. Marxist writers argued that North America and western Europe were as they were because they were capitalist societies. 'Industrial society' authors claimed that most aspects of these societies – the distribution of power, the inequalities in wages, the control over technological change – stemmed from the fact that they were industrial societies. Marxists wanted to separate industrialisation (good) from capitalism (bad). Many non-Marxists thought that the major features of industrial societies were primarily a consequence of them being industrial rather than of their particular pattern of ownership. This was not just a debate between historians; it had implications for the future development paths open to non-capitalist economies.

While there were in existence societies that were industrial in most of the senses given above but not capitalist (whether the USSR, East Germany or Czechoslovakia were **communist**, **socialist** or **state socialist** is another matter), it was possible to explore the effects of industrialisation, aside from the effects of capitalism. We could ask, for example, if work in East Germany was any more or less alienated than in West Germany. That non-capitalist industrial societies showed a tendency to divide into social classes suggested that industrialisation contained other sources of social division as important as those which Marxists thought were unique to capitalism. As the organisation of manufacturing in capitalist economies shifted from the owners of capital to a class of professional managers and as spending on social welfare rose, so analysts started to talk of a

convergence between capitalist and socialist societies.

History never had a chance to test properly the idea that common reliance on industry would create convergence because political changes removed one side of the comparison. Between 1989–91 the Soviet Union and the communist states of eastern Europe collapsed. Once free to do so, the former communist states in Europe revived the civil, social and political institutions of their pre-communist pasts or borrowed from the West.

See **technological consciousness**, **de-industrialisation**.

INDUSTRIALISATION   This is the general process in which agriculture and handicrafts are displaced in economic importance by large-scale manufacturing and extraction. The **Industrial Revolution** occurred first in the UK and was soon repeated across western Europe and North America. Industrialisation is central to sociology because it necessarily brought with it (that is, the connections are not accidental) a wide variety of changes that created modern societies, the distinctiveness of which was the central focus of the founders of sociology as an academic discipline.

INEQUALITY   See **equality**.

INFANT MORTALITY RATE (IMR)   The number of infants who die within one year of their birth, per thousand live births, is the infant mortality rate and it provides a convenient way of comparing a vital social statistic across societies and social groups. A rapid decline in the IMR is a feature of industrialising societies and a good mark of prosperity. In the UK in 1901, the IMR was 150. In 1950 it was 31. In 1999 it was 5.7. In the USA in 2000 it was 6.9. The single figure disguised major internal differences. For US blacks in

1980 the figure was 24; for whites it was 11. Twenty years later both had improved but the distance between the two was as big as ever: 14 for blacks and 5.7 for whites.

INFANTICIDE   Like all 'cide' words, this refers to the 'killing of' people or creatures: in this case, the killing of children. Child killing has been systematically used in non-industrial societies to control population in times of great scarcity and to eliminate children who possess unacceptable characteristics (such as deformities) or whose birth is in some respect **taboo** (for example, twins or breech births). Infanticide also appears to occur in the animal world where newly dominant males may kill off their predecessors' young so that their own young stand a better chance of survival and success.

INFERENTIAL STATISTICS   See **statistics**.

INFORMAL ECONOMY   This term denotes three sorts of work that do not feature in the formal economy of paid and taxed employment. It includes the 'black' economy of people whose work is hidden (because it is illegal, because they wish to avoid taxation, or because the employer wishes to evade responsibilities), the domestic economy of unpaid household work and the 'communal economy' of people who do jobs for friends and neighbours as part of a complex web of reciprocal relationships.

See **commodification**.

INFORMATION SOCIETY   Primary extraction (farming, mining, fishing, logging) and the manufacture of physical objects formed a much smaller part of the economy of most modern societies at the end of the 20th century than at the start. Daniel Bell (1973) in *The Coming of Post Industrial Society* used

'knowledge society' to draw attention to the growth in professional occupations and high technology work and the rising power of the educated, technological elite. With the invention of the computer micro-chip and the subsequent boom in information technology, 'information society' became the fashionable term. In the title of the first volume of his trilogy *The Information Age: Economy, Society and Culture*, Manuel Castells (1996–98) uses the term 'network society'. Castells believes that three major changes at the end of the 20th century combine to create a new type of society: the information technology revolution, the crises of capitalism and communism, and the rise of **new social movements** such as environmentalism and feminism. He believes that 'networks constitute the new social morphology of our societies'. Networks create a new kind of economy, in which power is no longer concentrated in institutions, corporations or states but is diffused. It now lies in codes of information and images of representation lodged in people's minds. There is now a split between the 'abstract universal instrumentalism' of the network society and old particularistic identities. Religious fundamentalism, nationalism, localism, environmentalism, feminism and sexual identity movements are all elements of resistance to the new network logic.

Stripped of its new abstruse language ('the edge of forever' and 'the annihilation of time') much of this is the old neo-Marxism: capitalism is in crisis but the working class has failed in its historic task and so a new radical force must be discovered and it is found in new social movements. What makes Castells's vision novel (apart from the sheer length of the trilogy) is the **postmodern** take on the effects of networks. The 'space of flows' and 'timeless time' create a culture of 'real virtuality': a 'system in which reality itself is entirely captured, fully immersed in a virtual image setting, in the world of make believe, in which appearances are not just on the screen through which experience is communicated, but they become the experience'.

As with most of the fashionable single-idea characterisations of the modern world, Castells's notion of the information age exaggerates sensible specific observations into a misleading whole. For example, it is true that information technology weakens some aspects of the state (such as the ability to control news and knowledge) but the **nation-state** remains immensely powerful. Much of the economic development of Asian countries has been driven by the state, international relations continues to be driven by state interests and the nation-state remains a powerful dream for submerged nations. There is also little evidence that religious fundamentalism, feminism, environmentalism and the like, form coherent movements engaged in 'defensive and offensive struggles'.

See **Fourth World, Negri**.

INITIATION RITES   Classically this refers to rituals associated with passage from one age group to another (particularly from childhood to adulthood) and with admission to various forms of secret society. Such rituals usually involve some sort of humiliation and pain. The term is often used more loosely to mean rituals associated with entry into any sort of group.

INSTINCT   See **human nature**.

INSTITUTION   See **social institution**.

INSTITUTIONAL RACISM   In the 1990s a major public enquiry into the working of London's Metropolitan police force concluded that the force was characterised by institutional racism: 'the collective failure of an organisation to provide an appropriate and professional service to people because of

their colour, culture or ethnic origin. It can be seen or detected in processes, attitudes and behaviour that amount to discrimination through unwitting prejudice, ignorance, thoughtlessness, and racist stereotyping which disadvantage minority ethnic people'.

The character of an institution or organisation is primarily a consequence of the attitudes and actions of its staff. As **ethnomethodological** studies of organisations have shown, even in the apparently most-rule bound settings, staff make creative choices in their implementation of rules and procedures. Nonetheless, for a variety of reasons institutions are more than the wishes of their staff: the collective effect of individual actions may be other than the effects desired by each individual taken separately, and rules which are properly designed for the matter-in-hand may inadvertently have unanticipated consequences. In particular, organisations may inadvertently sustain inaccurate assumptions about their environments by selective perception. For example, if inner-city police officers suppose that the typical drug dealer is a young black man, they are more likely to stop and search young black men who will thus form a disproportionate part of those arrested (hence charged and convicted). That selective action then generates a body of evidence that proves that the typical drug dealer is a young black man and in turn justifies and sustains the original selective perception. Although individual staffers may feel free of discriminatory attitudes, they may be socialised into a work culture that is implicitly informed by prejudicial stereotypes.

Although the idea of institutional racism offends those who (largely because they want to assign moral responsibility) wish to focus on the individual agent, its two main points will be familiar to sociologists. Those are, first, that actions may regularly have inadvertent and unintended consequences (for example, a minimum height barrier for entry to the police force may effectively discriminate against an ethnic minority though that was never its intention) and, second, that the effects of an organisation's operations are often other than those desired by any or all of the individuals who comprise it.

INSTITUTIONALISATION   When applied to activities, this refers to the process in which social practices become sufficiently popular and continuous to be described as social institutions. When applied to people (such as prisoners and long-stay hospital patients) who inhabit institutions for a long time, it means losing the ability to manage on one's own and becoming dependent on the institution.

INSTRUMENTAL   See **expressive and instrumental**.

INSTRUMENTAL COLLECTIVISM
See **Affluent Worker**.

INTEGRATION   This can mean the extent to which individuals experience a sense of belonging to a collectivity by virtue of sharing its norms, beliefs and values. It can also describe the extent to which the activities or functions of social institutions and societal sub-systems complement rather than clash with each other. For example, we can describe the way that the national church in 18th-century England supported the monarchy and the army, supplied service in the local magistracy, and provided education and social welfare as an example of a high degree of integration of religion with other social institutions.

It is a common observation in all models of social evolution that, as societies become more complex, they increasingly need institutions that co-ordinate and integrate other institutions and spheres of life (a written language is one such; a state-wide legal system is another).

INTELLIGENCE   The nature and measurement of intelligence is one of the most controversial subjects in the social sciences. Early theories were united in taking for granted a narrow range of cognitive abilities (such as abstract reasoning, comprehension and memory) but were divided between those which assumed that a single, general property of intelligence lay behind all skills and those which supposed distinct mental abilities. More recent views have tried to broaden the concept to include practical problem-solving, artistic creativity and social skills. The question about whether intelligence is one thing or many is now being rephrased in the language of genetics, though the question is still far from being answered. The great fault line is between those (primarily psychologists) who see intelligence as a product of our biology and those who see it as a matter of socialisation and environment. The majority of sociologists would be in the second camp.

See **heredity**.

INTELLIGENCE QUOTIENT, IQ   This is intended to be an impersonal measure of relative intelligence and was introduced in order to give a straightforward numerical expression to the results of **intelligence tests**. For children, it can be employed to indicate how well a child is doing in relation to their age group. A 'ratio IQ' is calculated by administering a common test to a large number of children and calculating from those results the typical score for each age. Then one can ascertain an individual's mental progress by seeing how their test performance compared with the typical score for someone that age. Setting the average score to 100, this means that the feeble-minded and the unusually bright would score below and above 100 respectively. There is another measure – the deviation IQ – which assumes a normal distribution of IQ and expresses any individual's distance from the mean in terms of **standard deviations**. Adults' scores are assumed to be less age-dependent so that grown ups of different ages can be compared on the same scale.

INTELLIGENCE TESTS Intelligence tests were devised as a rapid and impersonal way of assessing someone's intellectual ability. The ideal was to find questions that reflected the innate ability of the person being examined, questions that were as independent as possible of the training and socialisation of the candidate. Intelligence tests have thus been based on the assumption that intelligence is some sort of experience-free inherited competence and that cultural and environmental factors can be eliminated by careful test design. Critics argue against all those assumptions. That professionals offer to coach children in taking IQ tests and that coaching improves scores does rather weaken the case that such tests measure something innate. However, such tests continue to have wide popularity because performance in other forms of test – school examinations, for example – is clearly related to how well the person has been taught and is thus not a measure of underlying ability, or 'aptitude' as it is often known. If universities wish to admit the most able school-leavers they may find that using applicants' performance in school examinations favours the children of the affluent. In such cases, tests of aptitude can appear comparatively attractive.

Intelligence tests have proven most politically controversial when they have been deployed to make the argument that intelligence and 'race' are related. Since ethnic differences are nearly always associated with cultural differences and since people from different ethnic groups typically have widely differing access to high-quality schooling, the idea that cultural and environmental influences can be eliminated from the tests has generally seemed suspect. Claims that race and intelligence are strongly associated have accordingly tended to appear dubious and highly partisan.

INTENTIONAL COMMUNITY This signifies artificial communities created for a specific purpose; monasteries, residential drug-rehabilitation centres and army training camps are all examples. The phrase is rather awkward because in the conventional distinction between a community and a voluntary association, the community is naturally-occurring (rather than deliberately created) and all-encompassing in its 'purposes'. It was simply the environment in which people lived out every facet of their lives. However, some term is needed to distinguish a residential drug-rehabilitation centre, for example, from a voluntary association such as a political party because, even if it is for a fixed time period and the initial decision to join is voluntary, people are immersed in the former in a way that they are not in the latter.

INTENTIONALITY This is a term from the discipline of philosophy that is often used loosely by social scientists. Philosophers use the word intentionality to refer to what is sometimes called 'aboutness'. Novels can be about London but London is not about anything. More generally, mental states are about things while physical phenomena lack the property of 'aboutness'. Some philosophers have used this point to argue that mental phenomena are thus radically distinct from physical ones and that the mind must therefore be different from the brain. Given that the social world is partly made up of people's ideas, beliefs and perceptions, intentionality is a property of part of the world investigated by sociology. People's awareness that they have beliefs and ideas about the world means that there is a widespread awareness of the phenomenon of intentionality even if people are not generally interested in its philosophical ramifications. When **symbolic interactionists** or **ethnomethodologists** study how actors make sense of the social world, they are therefore studying intentionality empirically. It should be noted however that intentionality does not mean simply that people have intentions (in the sense of purposes or objectives); intentionality refers to a much wider range of mental phenomena.

INTERACTION ORDER, INTERACTION RITUAL
Social scientists have long been interested in social interaction but the work of Erving **Goffman** in the 1960s was pioneering in that he concentrated not on the surface specifics of encounters and interaction but on the general and trans-situational features of interaction. An interaction order is the result of there being a set of norms, the equivalent of a body of traffic rules or Highway Code for the interaction of people (**civil inattention** is one element of that code). Interaction ritual is that part of the order that allows actors with whom one interacts to preserve 'face' through maintaining a common social reality in interaction.

INTERACTION, SOCIAL   This widely used term has no single precise meaning. It is often used to emphasise the point that when people interact they do so in the light of the social expectations and background assumptions which they bring to the encounter. People make assumptions about the motivations, experience, intentions and abilities of others. In that sense interaction is always social, though there is a great deal of sociological detail to the social aspects of any specific interaction. Sociologists also disagree on the best way to explore this sociological detail: **conversational analysis, ethnomethodology** and symbolic interactionism are

alternative approaches to the systematic investigation of the social aspects of interaction.

See **Goffman**.

INTERACTION, STATISTICAL   In statistics this denotes the combined effect of two or more **independent variables** on a dependent variable. In analysing survey data, for example, we may find that class and age, considered separately, each account for a certain amount of voting behaviour. But when considered together they account for more because the two variables 'interact'.

INTEREST GROUP   See **pressure groups**.

INTERGENERATIONAL   MOBILITY   See **social mobility**.

INTERNAL COLONIALISM   Marxists V.I. Lenin and Antonio **Gramsci** used this term to explain major disparities between regions of a single state, the point being that the metropolitan centre can treat the peripheries of its home territory much as it treats distant colonies: extracting their raw materials, denying them opportunities to develop, stemming rebellion by drawing their most talented people to the centre and selling them finished goods. The relationship between centre and periphery thus distorts the economic development of the periphery to the advantage of the centre. Michael Hechter's (1975) *Internal Colonialism: the Celtic Fringe in British National Development 1536–1966* is still the most impressive attempt to test the idea rather than just use it in political journalism and it is widely cited as supporting the concept. However, British historians find it inaccurate and shallow and subsequent social research has not supported Hechter. For example, analysis of the distribution of employment sectors in Britain found that there was more difference in the nature of economic activity between parts of England than there was between England and Scotland. The profession has not been convinced that the claim of exploitation at the heart of the Marxist internal colonialism model is an improvement on the much less contentious (but also less contentful) point that there are major differences between centre and peripheries, some of which arise from the vagaries of the local context and some of which stem from the relationship between the two regions.

More because of the political advantages of claiming this particular kind of deprivation than because it is applicable, race relations in the UK and USA have sometimes been described as a form of internal colonialism.

INTERNAL COLONISATION OF THE LIFE-WORLD   According to Jürgen **Habermas**, it is characteristic of modern capitalist societies that forms of economic rationality spread beyond the economy to penetrate those areas of 'communicative practice' which focus on cultural transmission. They thus impoverish cultural life. This is similar to the point made by Peter L. **Berger** that the economy is such a powerful part of modern societies that the **instrumental** orientation, which is the ethos of economic activity, now distorts other spheres. He argued, for example, that many Americans now view their leisure pursuits and emotional lives with the same eye to efficiency and productivity that they use at work.

See **technological consciousness**.

INTERNALISATION   This is the process in which individuals learn and come to accept as binding the social values and norms of conduct of their society (and those particular to their social positions). Most sociologists would see effective internalisation as crucial to the development of a stable self.

See **socialisation**.

INTERPELLATION   Louis **Althusser** introduced this idea to describe how ideology works to shape people and place them in social structures. Rather than see ideology as a set of beliefs inside consciousness, which rather implies people could choose to believe something different, we should view ideology as a social process that 'picks out' people and gives them a particular subjectivity. We suspect that this sounds more plausible in French.

INTERPRETATION   See **empathy, hermeneutics, Verstehen**.

INTERPRETATIVE SOCIOLOGY   Often a synonym for **qualitative** sociology, this identifies those types of sociology that treat meaning and action (rather than social structure) as the primary objects of the discipline. They vary in the extent to which they regard interpretation as problematic. Weberian sociology and **symbolic interactionism** generally treat interpretation in a common sense, almost casual manner. **Phenomenological** sociology presents an elaborate theory of interpretation and **ethnomethodology** makes the practical skills involved in interpretation a central focus for its approach.

INTER-SUBJECTIVITY   People unfamiliar with the social sciences are liable to suppose that the relationship between ideas and the material world come in only two forms: the objective and the subjective. A student memorably and with no irony concluded an essay that argued there was no objective basis to mental illness by saying: 'So we can see that mental illness is all in the mind'! We can readily see that the Grand Cooley Dam has an 'objective facticity' and that the beauty of my cat is a matter of personal preference. But for the sociologist there is, between these extremes, a vast world of ideas and opinions that are so widely shared that they have a degree of solidity. These things are our inter-subjective reality. If people challenge these inter-subjective understandings it can be as disturbing as if they call into question aspects of the objective physical world.

INTERTEXTUALITY   This signifies the characteristic of one text containing references to another. Any one text (which here includes visual images as well as the written word) will usually contain a wide variety of cross-references. Some will be inadvertent, as when one text implicitly draws on previous conventions. The intertext for any film that features attacks by aliens is every previous film on that theme. Others will be quite deliberate, as when one film borrows or parodies a sequence from another. The deliberate borrowing for effect is sometimes called 'hypertextuality'. Although the term is most useful when it is clearly in the author's intentions, it is also used to describe expectations that an audience may bring to a text, irrespective of what the author intends. Television advertisements are commonly highly intertextual since that provides the advertiser with a way of presenting complex ideas and sentiments within the few seconds of air-time available. Accordingly modern audiences are often thought to be more accustomed to reading intertextual details than was true a few decades ago.

INTERVAL SCALE   See **measurement, levels of**.

INTERVENING VARIABLE   This is a variable that mediates the effect of one variable on another; identifying them is often the hard part of inducing explanations from data. For example we know that there is a strong connection between the occupational status of fathers and that of their sons: that is, a large part of social class is inherited. But only a small part is directly passed on (as when a father chooses his son to succeed him as manager of the firm). Most of it is to some extent achieved: educational attainment is one of the intervening variables. For a variety of reasons, the sons of high-status fathers do well at school and that success gives access to high-status careers.

INTERVIEWER BIAS   This signifies not that social researchers who conduct interviews may distort the results by their own prejudices (though they may) but that an interview may be distorted by the subject's response to the interviewer. Although this is so quirky that it is very hard to measure, we know that even in telephone interviews, where the interviewer's presence is reduced to a voice, subjects may react sufficiently strongly to an interviewer that we can suspect different answers would have been given to another person. One response to the problem is to have interviewers read from the same script but this itself creates problems because interviewers vary in their acting ability. As managers of call centres are increasingly finding, people on one end of a phone can become distinctly hostile when they realise that the other end of a conversation is pre-programmed.

INTIMACY   See **emotions**.

IRIGARAY, LUCE (1932–)   One of a number of psychoanalysts who have influenced feminist sociology, Irigaray tried to re-write Freud to remove the masculine bias, particularly in relation to the way in which sexual desire is understood. As a follower of Jacques **Lacan**, she placed emphasis on the importance of language, asserting that female language patterns differ from those of men. She tried to link those differing language patterns to the distinctive erotic imagination and experiences that are characteristic for women and men, although she also tried to avoid the essentialistic implications that would seem to follow from this position. Her (1993) *Ethics of Sexual Difference* was popular but, as with other psychoanalytically informed social theory, Irigaray's work provides no systematic evidence to support its fanciful assertions and even a supporter described the work as aimed at effective change rather than aiming to be an accurate representation of some state of affairs.

IRON LAW OF OLIGARCHY   Oligarchy is rule by 'a few'. In *Political Parties* Robert Michels (1911) documented many examples of left-wing trade unions and political parties that were initially democratic becoming gradually less so. The longer they lasted and the larger they became, the more the original radical purposes of the organisation were moderated. That even organisation that want internal democracy end up being led by a small professional leadership seems good grounds for supposing that Michels had identified a general social process when he wrote: 'He who says organisation, says oligarchy'.

Michels grouped the elements of this process in three. First, there were technical considerations: To improve the chance of attaining their goals, the members create what they hope will be an efficient bureaucracy but this means that a small number of officials (the people who staff the committees, draft the regulations, edit the paper, run the education programme) will acquire disproportionate knowledge and hence power. The second element concerns the character and motives of those officials: That they became leaders suggests they already differed from the mass membership but their position gives them interests which are at odds with the founding goals of the organisation. They want to maintain the organisation and the benefits to them in status and satisfaction that come with their high position in it; hence the gradual re-orientation from pursuing radical goals to reproducing the organisation. The officials also mix more with officials of other parties than with their own rank-and-file and are thus drawn into (if they were not already recruited from) a cross-party political elite. The third element of the complex story concerns the 'psychological characteristics of the mass': Put bluntly, Michels thinks the drift to oligarchy is encouraged by the sheep-like nature of the rank-and-file: easily swayed by oratory and only too willing to let someone else take charge.

By the end of the 20th century, the political centre of social science had moved enough to the left for the tone of Michels's comments about the docility of the working class to seem out-of-place. There had also been many case studies that pursued parts of the story in detail and clarified them. But there remains broad support for the view that organisations have a tendency to become oligarchic and such ideas as **goal displacement** have proved useful in the study of **social movements**.

J

JAMES, WILLIAM (1842–1910) See **pragmatism**.

JAMESON, FREDERIC (1934–) A US Marxist literary critic and cultural theorist, Jameson crops up in sociological debates because of his arguments with Jean-Francois **Lyotard** and Jean **Baudrillard** over **postmodernism**. As a Marxist he wishes to retain one particular **meta-narrative**: Marxism. He also wants to resist relativism. The argument he puts forward is that postmodernism – far from being an autonomous development within the realm of culture – is in fact the 'cultural logic' of late capitalism. In other words, he argues that the postmodern aesthetic in design and architecture and so on is engendered by developments in capitalism. He thus inverts the usual postmodernist account.

JAPANISATION Before the Japanese (and other East-Asian economies) faltered slightly in the early 1990s, it was axiomatic that Japanese management was superior to that of the West; hence the borrowing signified by this term. Among the ideas thought worth borrowing were just-in-time supplying (where the manufacturer does not hold stocks of parts but has such effective relationships with suppliers that parts can be delivered when needed) and belief in continuous improvement and the realistic possibility of zero-defects. Another popular theme was 'total quality management': control activities based on the leadership of top management and the involvement of all employees and all departments – from planning and development to sales and service – in quality assurance.

Observers differ as to just how much Japanese methods have influenced the West and what their effects are. Some see great benefits in replacing class antagonism with co-operative work relations, in greater flexibility in working practices, and in workers gaining a greater say in production. Critics see mainly a new **Fordism** in greater supervision, peer-group pressure on workers and increased workloads. They also believe that just-in-time supply systems simply export costs from the assembler to the companies that supply parts. The net result is a dual economy in which workers for the main assembling company enjoy improved conditions and job security but those who work for the suppliers lose protection and get paid less well.

JOB SATISFACTION As the phrase suggests, this is the fit between what employees seek from work and what they get out of it. Studies often distinguish between intrinsic sources of satisfaction (for example, whether a worker can feel pleasure at 'a job well done') and extrinsic ones (for example, the status outside the work place that comes with the position and the pleasure that can be purchased with the income). Analysts differ in the weight they give to enduring psychological needs as against shifting cultural expectations and in their conclusions about the extent to which job satisfaction rests on the nature of the job itself or on outside considerations. It is important to appreciate that job satisfaction is concerned primarily with subjective psychological states and is thus significantly different to the Marxist notion of **alienation**.

See **orientations to work**.

JOINT CONJUGAL ROLES   The contrast is with 'segregated conjugal roles' and the phrase means a division of labour within a household where partners share tasks instead of having clearly demarcated roles for husbands and wives. We might expect that the increasing number of women in paid employment outside the home and a general cultural shift in attitudes to gender would have made joint conjugal roles more common, but detailed research shows that, while decision-making may now be more co-operative, women – particularly in families with young children – still perform the bulk of domestic labour.

JUNG, CARL GUSTAV (1875–1961)   The most famous of Sigmund **Freud**'s followers, the Swiss psychologist Jung started by working closely with the founder of psychoanalysis. By the second decade of the 20th century their views had diverged in large measure because Jung did not agree that unconscious symbolism was primarily rooted in sexual desires. Jung began to stress the role of universal symbols, known as archetypes. Drawing on accounts of religious and mythical stories from around the world, he proposed that there was a 'collective unconscious' to which all people subscribed in some manner; he agued that this shared inheritance could be used therapeutically. There are relatively few Jungians today though his idea of a collective unconscious is often alluded to in works of fiction and in other cultural spheres.

JUVENILE DELINQUENCY   See **delinquency, delinquency drift, delinquent subculture**.

K

KANTIAN The adjective derives from the name of the 18th-century German philosopher Immanuel Kant (1724–1804). Kant was probably the last great systematic philosopher: the last thinker to try to develop a universal analysis of ethics, of epistemology (the foundations of knowledge), of aesthetics and so on. He tried to overcome persistent problems in philosophy by showing that the make-up of the mind must have a role in organising knowledge. Minds cannot just start blank and be filled up with perceptions since it is unclear how those perceptions would be arranged and sorted if the mind were not pre-organised to some degree. In this vein, Kant tried to resolve the epistemological problems of his day by categorising the kinds of knowledge that exist: some things we know because they are true by definition; other things we know by observation and experiment. But there are other forms of knowledge, knowledge about the geometrical properties of triangles or about the properties of numbers, that fit into neither of these categories. Such things – the so-called synthetic *a priori*s – enable us to derive innovative knowledge about our experience of the empirical world but are not learned exclusively from observation; we can discover things about all triangles (or squares, hexagons, etc.) just by thinking. Such knowledge is testimony to the significance of the pre-organisation of the mind. Kant undertook a parallel study of ethical knowledge elaborating an ethical position based on universal principles, most notably the 'categorical imperative': that one should always behave in such a way that one's actions correspond with rules that could be made into universal requirements. One should never lie because one would not want to live in a world where lying was generally tolerated.

Subsequent writers have departed from Kant in two main ways: some have detected problems with specific claims. Others – such as **Hegel** – have suggested that Kant was wrong to aim for universal truths since our knowledge inevitably changes with the historical development of human culture.

These days, the term Kantian usually refers to the universalistic philosophical project. For example, Jürgen **Habermas**'s attempts to base contemporary **critical theory** on the universal ideal of an **ideal speech situation** is a Kantian strategy.

KINSHIP Kinship – the social relationships that derive from blood ties (real or imagined) and from marriage – is universal and in almost all societies plays a major part in the socialisation of individuals and in the maintenance of social groups. In small-scale societies kinship ties may be so extensive and so important as to constitute the entire social system; hence the anthropological interest in the subject. In modern societies, kinship plays only a small part in the social system. Indeed, because it offends against **egalitarian** principles, undue favouritism to kin (known as nepotism, after the Latin for 'grandson') is often scorned and in some sectors specifically outlawed.

KNOWLEDGE SOCIETY   See **information society**.

KNOWLEDGE, SOCIOLOGY OF   Initially the sociology of knowledge was concerned with explaining mistakes. It operated an explanatory dualism. Although there were interesting things to be said about the social conditions that encouraged, for example, the pursuit of science, correct knowledge was not thought to need any explaining. It triumphed or was accepted because it was true. What needed explaining was why people got it wrong. Karl Mannheim's work on **ideology** is an example: people were misled by their own interests or the interest of those who manipulated them. In the 1970s, largely because of the ideas of Alfred **Schutz** (presented by Peter L. **Berger** and Thomas Luckmann (1967) in *The Social Construction of Reality*) sociologists turned to mundane everyday knowledge and abandoned the dualism so that all forms of knowledge were held to be in equal need of explanation.

See **social studies of science**.

KRISTEVA, JULIA (1941–)   Like Luce **Irigaray**, Kristeva combines linguistics and psychoanalysis to produce difficult ideas that defy easy summary but have nonetheless been influential on feminism and hence feminist sociology. Kristeva's work is not directly sociological; in fact, most of her published studies have been analyses of modern literature. She departs from mainstream psychoanalysis by stressing the importance of maternal influences (including pre-natal influences) and from mainstream **semiology** by emphasising the role of bodily functions in prefiguring certain forms of symbolic relations. For example, the ingestion of food can be viewed as a bodily template for 'identification', the merging of one thing into another. For her, abstract symbolism is thus underpinned by very early developmental experiences; this is a key part of her rationale for linking psychoanalytical studies with the business of literary criticism.

KUHN, THOMAS (1922–)   A US historian of science, Kuhn rose to fame because of *The Structure of Scientific Revolutions* published in 1962. Kuhn pointed out that, rather than proceeding in a regular linear fashion, the development of scientific ideas occurs in relatively sudden leaps interspersed with periods of tranquillity. An example that was almost contemporaneous with the publication of Kuhn's book can illustrate this point. For most of the 20th century geologists assumed that the continents were stable masses of rock fixed in place on the earth's surface. But then opinion shifted and a new way of thinking about the continents – a new **paradigm**, Kuhn would call it – was introduced. Accordingly to this new paradigm, the earth's surface is composed of a number of plates, many carrying continents on them, and these slowly move around relative to each other driven by the heat energy of the molten centre of the earth. When continents happen to collide, as Africa and Europe did, mountain chains (the Alps) are built up through the collision.

The history of any science will typically consist of long periods of 'normal science' punctuated by occasional 'scientific revolutions'. Kuhn presents normal science as a puzzle-solving activity. Scientists share the fundamental commitments of the prevailing paradigm (for example, that the continents move) and attempt to solve particular problems using the conceptual tools of the paradigm. Things that fail to fit the paradigm are explained away or set aside as anomalies to be explained later on. When a paradigm is challenged, the challengers often use the accumulated anomalies to throw doubt on the overall viability of the existing beliefs. According to Kuhn there is no set method for overturning a paradigm. The process is more like a political coup than a formal debate. In the extreme, followers of competing paradigms may view the world so differently that their views are literally **incommensurable**. Other well-known examples of paradigms include the **Darwinian** idea of evolution by natural selection, Newtonian theory in physics, the atomic theory in 18th- and early 19th-century chemistry and Einstein's theory of relativity. Within sociology itself one can also point to large-scale theories that resemble paradigms: to **structural-functionalism**, for example.

Kuhn's views about the development of scientific thought became very influential in sociological studies of the scientific community. They encouraged social scientists to study the social processes involved in scientific revolutions and other major episodes of controversy. Kuhn's term 'paradigm' is very widely known although it has become clear that it is difficult to define precisely and analysts are more and more reluctant to use it unquestioningly. One author claimed that Kuhn himself used it with 22 different meanings. Other scholars have pointed out that Kuhn's central claim about paradigms was very similar to an argument about 'thought styles' in science advanced independently by a Polish scholar named Ludwik Fleck in the 1930s.

L

LABELLING THEORY Howard S. **Becker** made a distinctive sociological contribution to our understanding of deviance when he drew together a variety of ideas (many from **symbolic interactionism**) to make two radical assertions. First, acts are not of themselves evil, criminal or deviant: these are social comments on acts. Hence deviance is not a property of the act but of the societal reaction to the act. Second, borrowing a distinction from Edwin Lemert, when people's primary deviation is negatively labelled by powerful social agents, they may well become what the labellers thought they already were. Denied opportunities and positive self-conceptions in the conventional world, people might find themselves attracted to a deviant sub-culture and a deviant identity and hence commit more deviant acts. Secondary or career deviation may thus be caused by societal reaction or labelling.

Where many official agencies see their labelling as merely correctly identifying existing characteristics (for example, 'She is a thief'; 'He is a schizophrenic'), Becker sees labelling as causing deviance in both a definitional sense and a real sense. The labellers say what counts as deviant and they push people to become deviants.

The labelling perspective became immensely popular in the sociology of crime and deviance in the 1960s where it appeared as a liberation from the narrow **positivism** that had previously dominated the field. Labelling raised vital questions about how rules were made and enforced. Because it was concerned with such basic sociological notions as the effect of social interaction on the sense of self, labelling theory brought crime and deviance back into the sociological mainstream from the dull social policy backwater where it has rested since the days of Durkheim. It should also be said that it had considerable appeal because its underlying assumptions chimed with the briefly radical spirit of the times. If people were sent to prison, forcibly confined in mental institutions or punished for indiscipline in school, this was not their fault; they were victims of 'the system'.

There is much of value in the labelling perspective. To say that society creates deviance by creating the rules the infraction of which constitute deviance may seem trite but the study of rule-formation is as important as the study of rule-breaking. The way the definitions are applied is also important. Apparently very similar acts may attract very different responses; for example, rowdiness on the part of rich college students may be viewed as 'high spirits' while the same trouble from working-class youths is taken as evidence of underlying criminal tendencies. The causal part of the theory is also reasonable for some sorts of behaviour; labelling can change people's self-images and, when accompanied by systematic exclusion from the mainstream, it can create further deviance. This is widely recognised in the common reluctance to place young offenders in adult prisons.

However, there are also many falsehoods in labelling. First, many deviants are not naive victims of labelling but are perfectly aware that their behaviour is rule-breaking and indeed are motivated precisely by a desire to be recognised as outsiders. Second, some deviant characteristics are present before any acts of labelling. Forty years on we know that some forms of mental illness (a favourite site for the labelling approach) do indeed have biological causes. Third, some deviants wish to engage in their chosen deviance irrespective of how others regard it; the increasing acceptability of homosexuality has not (as one might infer from the labelling approach) reduced the number of homosexuals. While the punitive behaviour of social control agencies might have made the lives of homosexuals difficult, it is hard to see how social control created homosexuality.

A possible defence of labelling theory is that it never set out to explain 'primary deviation' (why someone deviates in the first place), only to show how societal reaction can create 'secondary deviation' (the stabilised self-image as a deviant and subsequent deviant career). That may be true. But putting it that way hides the radical innovation: the implied claim that primary deviation was largely irrelevant to secondary deviation (either because no rule-breaking has occurred or because it is so widespread that why this person is selected for labelling must be due to something other than the rule-breaking). If we admit that primary deviation is more often than not a precursor to secondary deviation, labelling is of little consequence.

Applied carefully to certain types of crime and deviance, the labelling perspective is of considerable value but it lost plausibility and popularity because it was over-sold.

LABOUR PROCESS This denotes the process of production in which labour power is applied to machinery and raw materials to produce finished commodities and was promoted by Marxist analysts as an alternative to the term 'production process' in order to imply that all value was created by labour.

Harry Braverman's (1974) *Labor and Monopoly Capitalism: the Degradation of Work in the Twentieth Century* argues that the labour process in advanced capitalist economies is shaped by capitalist social relations and not, as most people thought, by technological or organisational requirements that have their own logic irrespective of the pattern of ownership. For example, new technologies may be introduced into the factory not because they are more efficient or more economical but because they break the power of particular key groups of workers. The way work is organised reflects the conflict that arises inevitably from the fact that capitalists exploit workers. Because managers cannot rely on workers to voluntarily labour diligently and effectively, they must find ways to tighten their control and weaken the labour force. The key to this is **de-skilling**. By making work even more routinised and mechanised, the power of the workers to reduce the extent of their exploitation is weakened.

Braverman's pessimistic analysis of changes in the labour process has not been supported by subsequent studies or validated by actual changes in the nature of work. The de-skilling of some jobs has usually been accompanied by the creation of even more skilled jobs elsewhere in the process (for example, in the design and maintenance of technology). Although some managers have sought to increase control over their workers, particularly those in declining sectors of the economy or those threatened by competition from countries with lower wage costs, others have found it more profitable to increase worker autonomy and give the workforce a greater say in the structuring of production. While we may want to retain the use of the term 'control' this can only be done by extending it to cover a very wide variety of ways in which managers seek to motivate workers. For example, trying to ensure compliance by increasing wage rates seems rather a benign form of control.

LABOUR THEORY OF VALUE　This notion is at the heart of **Marxism**'s attempts to present a political programme as social science. Like many economists of his time, Karl **Marx** argued that, as all commodities are made by labour, the value of any commodity would be expected to be tied to the amount of labour time put into its production. A suit that takes two days to make should (all things being equal) cost twice the price of a one-day suit. The owner of a business, the capitalist, can thus sell goods at the price of the labour embedded in them. But in the capitalist system, the capitalist can purchase workers' time at a cheaper price. All that the capitalist has to pay the worker is the amount required to keep the worker going, a sort of subsistence. According to Marx, labour is thus a unique commodity since one regularly pays less to buy it than one receives on selling the things that the labour has produced for you. For Marx this was the key to capitalist **mode of production**. It was also the source of the conflict endemic to capitalism since the capitalist's profits depended directly on the exploitation of employees' labour.

It should be noted that this way of thinking about the issue is at odds with mainstream economic thought. In current, neo-classical economics, the price of a good depends on the demand that exists for it, not on the amount of work that went into producing it. The labour theory of value makes the value of a commodity a characteristic of the thing itself rather than a characteristic of what someone wishes to do with it. Nonetheless it was a vital idea for Marx. It allowed him to talk about surplus value (the difference between what workers had to be paid to cover their subsistence and what their labour contributed to the value of goods) and thus to talk about exploitation in a manner that appeared objective. It also allowed him to produce mathematical analyses that suggested that the rate of profitability had to fall and that therefore, in the end, the capitalist mode of production would inevitably run out of steam. Of course, no workers in capitalist societies are paid at the meagre levels Marx implied; trade union activism and competition for skilled workers have seen to that. So the labour theory of value approach now seems erroneous both empirically and conceptually.

LACAN, JACQUES (1901–81)　Charismatic but often difficult to understand precisely, Lacan helped to revive the standing of psychoanalytic theory in France from the 1950s. His innovation was to combine Sigmund **Freud**'s ideas with the linguistics' approach stemming from Ferdinand de **Saussure** and the **structuralists**. Lacan proposed that the best way to understand the unconscious was to approach it as though it were a language. In normal language, signs are typically arbitrary. The word for tree has nothing tree-like about it; similarly aspects of the unconscious might be arbitrary or metaphorical or idiosyncratic. This approach freed him from some of the dogmatism of Freudian psychoanalysis and allowed him to suggest that Freud's ideas should be interpreted symbolically rather than literally. Of course, reinterpreting Freud in this way made the scope for the analyst's interpretations even wider than it had been before but it did offer to make Freudian thinking less male-centred and to make Freud's ideas about – for example – penis-envy less restrictive. Lacan also developed novel ideas about childhood development and the interplay between the growth of language and the acquisition of a sense of self. Lacan was a controversial practitioner of psychoanalysis. Nonetheless he represents an influential strand in the re-thinking of the modern relevance of psychoanalysis.

See **Irigaray, Kristeva**.

LAISSEZ-FAIRE   From the French for 'let it be done', this is the economic theory that governments should not interfere with the market forces that result from self-interest and the profit motive. Originating in France, the idea was promoted by Adam **Smith** among others and was orthodox until the end of the 19th century when governments began to accept that the free market produced its own vices (monopolies, cycles of boom and bust, grossly inequitable distributions of wealth, and vicious exploitation of labour) and had to be controlled. All subsequent argument has been about the appropriate form and extent of government intervention.

LANGUAGE   Language is so central to human culture and social interaction that it is easy to take it for granted. In many cases, the language one speaks is taken to be an indivisible part of one's culture: speaking Norwegian is a large part of being Norwegian for example. However there are five principal ways in which the study of language matters to sociology. First, sociologists – notably Erving **Goffman** and the exponents of **conversation analysis** – have studied the role of language in everyday interaction. The maintenance of even the most ordinary conversation requires developed social skills, and social scientists have made considerable progress in analysing these skills. Such work turns out to have wide implications since many specialised jobs in modern society (counselling, questioning in court, air-traffic control) are jobs which are largely conducted through talk; such professional talk turns out to depend on everyday patterns of linguistic communication.

Second, other social scientists, often known as socio-linguists, have been interested in charting the distribution in society of language patterns. While most people in France, say, speak French, they don't all speak the same French; there are regional, ethnic and class differences. Socio-linguists are concerned with the social implications of linguistic differences, for example in relation to the way people are treated by the educational system (see **elaborated and restricted codes**).

Third, a more general trend has been for sociologists to use the idea of language in an analogical fashion. For example, the way people dress is in some respects like a language: clothes are intended to convey a meaning particularly among certain sub-cultures. Sociologists have drawn on the vocabulary of linguistics to try to understand how these meanings are produced and communicated (as in **structuralism**).

A fourth line of investigation comes from the discipline of linguistics. Noam **Chomsky** and others have argued that all languages are underlain by a common deep structure and that children's brains must in some way be pre-programmed for the acquisition of language. This matters to sociology mostly because it contributes to the **nature–nurture debate** the suggestion that some important social skills may be closely tied to our biological make-up. Finally, anthropologists who are interested in language differences point out that language and perception are closely related. For example, among arctic peoples there are complicated vocabularies for describing varieties of snow. In most of Europe people can only recognise ice, snow and sleet. In some arctic cultures, where there are up to a 100 words for kinds of snow, ordinary people obviously see things that we 'southerners' do not. Taken to the extreme, this view suggests that our language is not just a medium for describing the world. Rather, it shapes what we are able to observe and conceptualise; this is the **Sapir-Whorf hypothesis**.

The word 'language' is also used to describe computer-programming protocols that have their own 'grammar' or sets of rules: for example html (HyperText Markup Language) or FORTRAN. Such artificial languages lack the flexibility and potential for creativity that characterise natural human languages.

See **semiology**.

LANGUAGE CODE See **elaborated and restricted codes**.

LANGUE AND PAROLE These terms were introduced by the Swiss linguist Ferdinand de **Saussure** to distinguish between the system of a language (*la langue*) and actual speech or speech acts made possible by that language (*la parole*). He regarded the former as a social property and the latter as an individual one. This distinction became central to **structuralist** analysts who carried the terminology over into the study of other aspects of culture and society (symbols, literature, dreams and so on) and chose to focus their attention on the structure rather than on what individuals do with the symbols or dreams. It should be noted that this distinction is not equivalent to linguists' other distinction between **competence** and performance since much of parole (as well as all of langue) would be included in competence. This can be illustrated in relation to pronouns. The terms 'you' and 'I' exist only as formal possibilities with langue. If I say, 'I am in my office', that is an aspect of parole since its value depends on whether or not I am in my office. But to form the utterance correctly would normally be thought of as part of linguistic competence.

LATE MODERNITY See **modernity**.

LATENT FUNCTION This is a synonym for the unintended and unrecognised consequences of actions and is contrasted with the manifest function of actions. A collective act of religious worship will have the manifest function of pleasing God. It may also have the latent function of increasing the sense of solidarity among the group that engages in such worship. The term comes from **functionalism**, where social institutions are analysed in terms of their functions; in particular the part they play in maintaining the society as a whole. Although the term is useful, it has the danger of confusing **causation**. We may mistakenly think that because we have identified a latent function of some action, we have explained it, which is usually not the case. If the solidarity-building consequences of religious worship are genuinely unrecognised, they can hardly explain why people engage in it. Furthermore, people are hardly likely to continue with the action in question unless they believe in it; if they realise they are just building social solidarity, they may well find other ways to do that and give up with the God-worshipping distraction. The point is that, whatever the unintended consequences of people getting together for worship, we still need an explanation of why they worship God.

LATIFUNDIA This denotes large agricultural estates in Latin America (originally imperial grants from the Spanish crown to settlers) on which labourers are subject to authoritarian control, which, although less binding than that of the medieval feudal estate, is nonetheless coercive.

See **hacienda, debt peonage**.

LAZARSFELD, PAUL (1901–76) One of a generation of European social scientists who moved to the USA in the 1930s, Lazarsfeld was a pioneer of empirical social research. The Bureau of Applied Social Research which he established at Columbia University in New York was in the forefront of the statistical analysis of social phenomena. Among his major fields of work was the analysis of voting behaviour: *The People's Choice* (1944) and *Voting* (1954). He was also influential in promoting the scientific study of mass communication and sponsored the early work of Robert K. **Merton**.

Lazarsfeld was one of the scholars criticised by C. Wright Mills for the sin of **abstracted empiricism** but this seems rather harsh. He did not simply gather up social data and then try to make of it what he could, but encouraged the design of surveys to test hypotheses that were the result of sociological reasoning. Like politicians who describe alternatives to the right and left of themselves so as to claim for themselves the middle ground, many sociologists (Mills included) construe abstracted empiricism and fact-free theory in such a way that what they do can be presented as the proper middle way. Lazarsfeld has a better claim than most to that middle ground.

LEFT REALISM   This denotes a 1980s development in British sociology of crime and deviance. Jock Young, who had been involved in the 1960s promotion of **labelling** approaches to crime and deviance before espousing a Marxist position similar to that of Richard Quinney in the USA, later shifted again. He argued that those who sentimentalised crime or construed it as some elementary form of revolutionary activity were missing the crucial fact that most working-class crime was directed against other weaker sections of the population. 'Realism' was used to establish distance from romantic views of criminal behaviour; 'left' to show that the origins of crime should still be found in the inequities caused by capitalism.

LEGAL-RATIONAL AUTHORITY   With **traditional authority** and **charisma**, this forms the trio of forms of **authority** which Max **Weber** used in his comparative sociology. It is typical of modern societies that instructions are taken as legitimate and binding if they come from the appropriate office and are issued under the appropriate regulations and by due process. The authority of officials (such as the staff of a local council) depends not on tradition or on their personal charisma but on consensus about the validity of the rules that the officials follow. In advanced modern societies the number of such rules multiplies enormously and most rules are not challenged in the course of everyday life. Accordingly the implicit claim that the rules are legally well-founded and rational is seldom tested.

LEGITIMATE AUTHORITY   See **authority**.

LEGITIMATION   This can refer either to the specific grounds that are offered to justify a particular action or to the general process through which power is given moral grounding.

See **authority**.

LEGITIMATION CRISIS   The term was popularised by Jürgen **Habermas**, a German neo-Marxist, to describe the problems western democracies face (or should face) in maintaining their legitimacy while managing the conflict between the demands of capitalist accumulation on the one side and increasing demands for social welfare, social equality and increased participation in the polity on the other side. What makes this a Marxist analysis is the assumption that the governments of states with capitalist economies have a particular problem reconciling competing demands and that the problems will get progressively worse (and eventually trigger a major reconstitution of the economy and the state). The three decades since the publication of *Legitimation Crisis* (Habermas, 1975) have disappointed the book's central thesis. Some states under popular right-wing governments (the UK and the USA in the 1980s, for example) responded to problems by cutting back the welfare state. They shifted the problems on to individuals and on to the private sector, encouraging private health care and private pension plans. The return of economic growth after the 1970s assisted other countries (notably France and the northern European states) that rejected the Anglo-American strategy. While governments have come and gone as ever they did, there has been no major crisis of legitimation in the West in the sense that Habermas foresaw. In some areas where the state retained a lot of control, for example over food production and food safety, there has been widespread popular concern, particularly in relation to BSE or 'mad cow' disease. However such issues are now more commonly discussed in relation to the theory of the **risk society** than Habermas's concerns with legitimation, though one could with some justice describe the mad-cow episode as a crisis of legitimation. Ironically it was not the capitalist economies that suffered a fatal crisis of legitimation: it was the communist states of Eastern Europe that passed into the dustbin of history.

LEISURE AND LEISURE SOCIETY Leisure is conventionally defined as time left over after paid work, though this is little awkward in the case of those such as children, unpaid domestic workers and the elderly who do not have clearly delineated employment.

The most obvious feature of leisure is its growth. Over the 20th century the typical working week of manual industrial workers fell from about 55 to around 40 hours and paid holidays became more common and more frequent. Most leisure time is spent at home, with watching television the most common activity (if it can be called that).

Early studies of leisure made interesting connections between people's occupations and how they spent their non-work time. For example, it was noted that men such as coal miners who worked in filthy, dark and cramped conditions often spent their leisure time cycling, rambling, gardening, and pigeon racing – all outdoor pursuits – or singing in choirs and playing in brass bands: hobbies which allowed artistic expression, denied in their working lives.

Modern commentators are less likely to see leisure as an antidote to work; indeed some analysts think that work now plays such a small part in people's lives (beyond providing income) that we can sensibly describe modern industrial societies as 'leisure societies'. Often linked to a wider **postmodernism**, this position argues that people now derive their sense of identity more from individually chosen programmes of leisure consumption than from social class. As always with such sweeping claims, an element of truth becomes false by exaggeration. There remain socially structured differences in how people spend their time off. Men are more likely than women to have pursuits outside the home. Professional and managerial classes spend more time on leisure outside the home than other classes (which is partly a reflection of wealth and partly a matter of cultural preferences).

LEISURE CLASS Thorstein Veblen's (1899) *The Theory of the Leisure Class* might better have been called *A Critique of the Leisure Class* because it does far more condemning than explaining. His target was a particular section of the US upper classes in the second half of the 19th century that disdained any kind of useful work and devoted itself to **conspicuous consumption**.

LESS DEVELOPED COUNTRY (LDC) Social scientists have struggled to come up with a term to refer to the majority, less prosperous parts of the world. To refer to them as 'developing countries' often seemed blithely uncritical since some of them, some of the time, do not seem to be developing at all.

The new euphemism, less developed country, was promoted in the 1990s and has been taken up by the World Bank and other international bodies. It is still far from universally adopted by sociologists.

LÉVI-STRAUSS, CLAUDE (1908–) A pioneering social anthropologist, Lévi-Strauss's principal innovation was to suggest that systems of classification – such as kinship – and enduring customs and myths should be understood as symbolic structures. All cultures, he believed, built up structures of symbolism ultimately based on pairs of binary opposites, such as the raw and the cooked. Thus the key elements of all cultures should best be understood as a kind of code or structure, susceptible to objective, scientific analysis. This view was labelled **structuralism**. When pressed on the source of these binary structures, Lévi-Strauss argued that they were rooted in patterns in the human mind. Though there are few present-day advocates of Lévi-Strauss's own structuralist methodology, the idea that myths or systems of classification can be read as a system of signs or a set of symbols is widely supported.

See **structuralism**.

LIBERAL DEMOCRACY This denotes the type of representative political system typical of western European states and North America in the 20th century: based on universal voting rights, competition for power between political parties and the protection of the rights of citizens. The details of the structure of the polity are less important than the (to borrow a card game metaphor) 'no trumps' principle. At the heart of liberal democracy is the basic equality of all citizens: the liberal democracy does not give preferential treatment to those of the majority religion or to one ethnic group. Universal egalitarianism may be infringed by patterns of discrimination (against an ethnic minority or women, for example) but there is still a fundamental difference between those polities that aspire to universal egalitarianism (such as the UK and the USA) and those that deliberately constrain it with some other principle (such as the Iranian insistence on the supremacy of Islam).

LIBERALISM There are two common meanings of liberalism, which unfortunately clash. In the history of political thought, liberalism is a doctrine developed in Europe from the late 17th century onwards (most closely associated with the British philosophers John Stuart **Mill**, John Locke, David **Hume** and Jeremy **Bentham**) which argued against authoritarian and **absolutist** forms of government and in favour of freedom of speech, association and religion, and the right to private property. These are the men of the **Enlightenment**, now scorned as representing the sort of exhaustive and comprehensive worldview that is impossible in **postmodern** societies. Their thinking was grounded in rationality; it assumed that a liberal society was one that self-interested right-thinking people would choose. It was also firmly linked to capitalism and the laissez-faire economics of Adam **Smith**.

Liberalism is also used loosely to mean an attitude of general toleration and a position on the left wing of any contemporary debate.

The clash between the two meanings arises because the world has moved on a long way since the time of Mill. The rights which the first liberals argued for are now almost universally taken-for-granted and the state, insofar as it interferes in the operations of the free market, does so not to protect a small landed aristocracy but to safeguard working people and promote the interests of minorities excluded from full citizenship. Hence the basic terms of political debate have shifted. To be a liberal in the 1780s was to be radical. In the 1980s economic liberals such as Margaret Thatcher (UK Prime Minister 1979–90) and Ronald Reagan (US President 1980–88) were reactionary: keen to reverse the 20th century expansion of the state.

LIBERTARIANISM　　The libertarian wishes to reduce the functions of the state to the bare minimum of maintaining law-and-order and providing those services which individuals cannot provide for themselves, and opposes almost all forms of government interference in personal behaviour. This extreme liberalism often puts political conservatives into an uneasy alliance with radicals. For example, libertarians are often in favour of such radical measures as the de-criminalisation of recreational drug use and homosexuality, not because they think these are good things to be encouraged but because they insist that the state has no right to tell people what to do in their private lives. They believe the private sphere should be as large as possible.

LIFE-CHANCES　　Max **Weber** used this term to refer to the common consequences of class situation: the ownership of property and scarce skills determine the chances that any individual can realise his or her goals in social action. More generally it is used to refer to the chances of educational attainment, health, prosperity and status mobility.

LIFE CYCLE, LIFE COURSE　　Both terms are used to denote the process of personal change from birth through infancy, childhood and adulthood to old age and death, that results from the interaction between biological and biographical events on the one hand and social events on the other. In the 1990s, life 'course' was preferred to life 'cycle' because the latter (with its reminder of the cycle of the seasons) was held to be too deterministic. There is a great deal that is common in our progress from infancy to old

age. Human biology creates a common order as does our culture and our laws. But there is still considerable variation by social group (rich old people's lives are not like those of poor old people) and by individual preference, competence and circumstance.

LIFE-EXPECTANCY　　This is the number of years that the average person of a social group can expect to live. It is largely determined by environmental factors, though gender is a major consideration; women typically live longer than men. Life-expectancy at birth is a very useful standard measure for comparing the health of societies, and for noting progress and regress in economic development. In Norway in 2000 it was 79 years and in the USA 77 years. In Sierra Leone it was 35 years. As an example of regress we can note that for Russia, life-expectancy fell between 1986–94 from 70 to 64 years. Some of that reflects the economic problems of the collapse of communism but experts believe it was already falling because of the failure of the communist regime in the 1960s to invest in medical care.

LIFE-HISTORY　　W.I. Thomas and Florian Znaniecki's classic (1918) *The Polish Peasant in Europe and America* was one early example of a style of research that rested on a highly detailed study of documents (some 700 letters, newspaper reports and one very lengthy biography) that purported to allow deep insight into the lives of people who were taken to be typical of a wider population. Clifford Shaw's (1938) *The Jack-Roller* was another product of the Chicago School of sociology that used detailed life-histories.

Unlike the social survey, which gathers rather shallow information about a large number of people, the life-history uses lengthy unstructured interviews, letters, diaries and the like to learn a great deal about a very small number of people. This raises the issue of representativeness. How confident can we be that the Polish peasants in Thomas and Znaniecki's work were typical? Or, to put it the other way round, how far can we generalise from a very small number of cases? It also raises the issue of validity. As Herbert **Blumer** pointed out, autobiography always involves retrospective revaluation. With the best will in the world we cannot simply reconstruct our pasts; how we now **account** for earlier stages in our lives will be influenced by our subsequent lives and our current concerns.

Life-history research declined in popularity in the 1950s and 1960s as American sociology became dominated by the rather abstract theorising of Talcott **Parsons** and the large-scale survey work pioneered by Paul **Lazarsfeld**, among others. It enjoyed something of a revival from the 1970s as more interpretative and interactionist sociology came into fashion.

One interesting response to the methodological issues is to regard them as a resource rather than as a problem. Recently, scholars have studied the ways in which people create and re-create their biographies.

LIFE-WORLD   A direct translation of the German *Lebenswelt*, this term is used by social **phenomenologists** such as Alfred **Schutz** to denote the everyday material and social world that ordinary people construct in the course of their routine interactions. The life-world is taken for granted; it usually only becomes noticeable when it is challenged. Harold **Garfinkel** proposed **ethnomethodology** as an empirical exploration of the life-world. He encouraged his students to undertake 'breaching' experiments in which people would violate everyday patterns of interaction by, for example, treating their parents as hotel-keepers. They would then observe how strongly people reacted to challenges to the taken-for-granted details of the life-world and thus come to understand its pervasive importance.

LIKERT SCALE   See **scale**.

LIMINALITY   This term was popularised by Arnold van Gennep's (1960) classic *The Rites of Passage*, published in 1909, where it described the curious, in some cases almost sacred, status of those who are in transit across the symbolic boundaries between statuses. It was extended by the Scottish-American anthropologist Victor Turner (1920–83) to describe the unreal socio-psychological state that was induced by rituals that have the power to transform everyday realities into a symbolic 'commitarian' experience. Exposure to this experience thereafter affects the individual's lived reality. It is this meaning which has been carried into contemporary cultural studies where it is sometimes attributed to people who 'lose themselves' in collective effervescence at mass musical events such as concerts and raves.

LINEAGE   See **descent groups**.

LINEAR GROWTH   The contrast here is with exponential growth. 'Linear' is the adjective for 'in a straight line' and it would describe, for example, the growth in the amount of cash under my mattress if I salted away the same sum every week. Drawn on a graph of two axes (cash under mattress × date) this would give a rising straight line. An example of exponential growth would be the change in my income if every year I was given a 2 per cent pay rise. Because the total on which any year's 2 per cent was calculated was bigger than that for the previous year, the pay rise would get steadily and evenly bigger and so, when added to my pay, the result would be a smooth upward curve. The two types are often called arithmetic and geometric growth to signify the difference between adding the same amount (straight line arithmetic change) and multiplying by the same amount (curved line geometric change).

LINEAR REGRESSION See **regression analysis**.

LINGUISTICS This refers to the systematic or scientific study of **language**. Linguistics is important to sociology firstly because some linguistic phenomena are of direct sociological relevance. For example, patterns of linguistic interaction are central to a great deal of routine social conduct; **conversation analysis** represents the clearest and most systematic study of such phenomena. Second, **structuralist** linguistics – especially as outlined by Ferdinand de **Saussure** – has been adopted as a methodological platform by many influential social theorists including Claude **Lévi-Strauss** and Jacques **Lacan** among others.

LIPSET, SEYMOUR MARTIN (1922–) Lipset is the only person to have been chair of both the American Sociological Association and the American Political Science Association, a mark of the range and nature of his interests. Although *Social Mobility in Industrial Society* (1959), co-authored with Reinhard Bendix, was an important early work in the field, his main interest has been democracy: its pre-conditions, character and consequences. *Agrarian Socialism* (1950) explained the rise to power in 1944 of the Co-operative Commonwealth Federation in Saskatchewan, the only occasion a socialist party has gained power in North America. *Political Man* (1960) was an international comparative study of the bases for democracy. *Consensus and Conflict* (1985) examines how democracies were shaped by social divisions. With Earl Raab he co-ordinated a major research project on extremist movements such as the Klan and the John Birch Society in *The Politics of Unreason* (1970). Central to his work is the theme outlined in the title of a 1959 article 'Some social requisites of democracy: economic development and political legitimacy'. Development aids democracy by promoting democratic values and attitudes, reducing class conflict, creating a large middle class, and encouraging a vigorous association life or **civil society**.

LIQUID MODERNITY This phrase encapsulates Zygmunt **Baumann**'s attempt to characterise what is distinctive about the world of the 21st century. 'Liquid' is used to suggest fluidity and lack of substance. Baumann believes that 'territorially plotted identities' (for example, being a Scot or a Virginian) are eroded by modernity. Old distinctions of time and space collapse. Competing 'discursive sites' undermine reality. State boundaries are made porous and border guards are rendered impotent by new technologies of communication. Our existence is increasingly fragile, 'precarious, insecure and uncertain'. As with all such sweeping characterisations, we are tempted to say 'only to an extent'. The globalisation of cultural resources certainly allows the Virginian to experiment with Feng Sui or Buddhism but the Afghani Muslim who tries to holiday in the USA will discover that boundaries are not that porous and border guards far from impotent. As for the precariousness of identities, we suspect that the experiences of the cosmopolitan middle classes are being generalised to humanity at large.

LITERACY Meaning basic competence in reading and writing, this term was first widely used in the 19th century when, with the expansion of formal education, illiteracy was seen increasingly as a social problem. In most pre-industrial societies such books as existed were extremely expensive, writing was the preserve of a small group of professionals (usually the clergy) and there was no medium for writing in many of the languages people spoke. Much writing was for the purpose of international communication between elites and the classical languages of Latin and Greek were used because these were widely known throughout Europe. This was not, as some have suggested, a matter of deliberate social exclusion. There was simply no great need for ordinary people to be able to read and write. Indeed, far from wishing to retain a monopoly over writing, Christian clerics were in the forefront of developing scripts for indigenous languages. That used in Slavonic Eastern Europe was the invention of a Greek monk, St Cyril and his student St Climent, who named his simplified alphabet Cyrillic in honour of his teacher.

The Protestant Reformation of the 16th century was a major stimulus to the spread of mass literacy. By shifting the centre of religion from correctly performing rituals to knowing the teachings of the Bible, and by undermining the power of the clergy in favour of ordinary people taking responsibility for their salvational fate, the Reformers created a new demand for literacy.

By the 19th century, two further concerns were driving the campaign for mass literacy. There was the obvious technical requirement: the machine-age and the mass market required that ordinary people be capable of being instructed and of keeping records. But as important was the drive to create national identities to give legitimacy and cohesion to the new nation-states. One element of that was the creation of national school systems; another was the development of an heroic literature.

LOG LINEAR ANALYSIS Many statistical techniques require us to use variables measured on an interval **scale**. However, much sociological information cannot be expressed in that way; we may be dealing with attributes that can be categorised (e.g. what is your favourite colour?) but not measured with some kind of yardstick. Variables of this kind are usually analysed in tables that allow us to see whether there is an association between one characteristic (colour preference) and another (favourite kind of music). Log linear analysis is a sophisticated tool for analysing the relationships between such categorical variables.

Although simple tables with a small number of rows and columns are easy to understand, things quickly become complicated when we have three or more variables each with several possible values. An analysis of church-going, for example, might involve looking at church attendance, age, gender, social class and region. A log linear analysis allows us to quantify the main effects (what is the impact of social class?), the two-way interaction effects (perhaps being female makes more difference if you are old than if you are young) and even three- or four-way interactions. Our aim is to identify which effects need to be considered without making the model more complicated than necessary. Computer-based statistical packages help in finding the best model.

See **regression analysis**.

LOMBROSO, CESARE (1836–1909) Lombroso, an Italian army physician, is one of the clearest exponents of the view that, while some crime is learnt, the majority of serious criminals are degenerates whose deviant behaviour is caused by defective biology. He argued that such defectives could be recognised by physical characteristics such as the shape of the skull. His perspective was utterly discredited long since but he is still frequently mentioned in the sociology of crime and deviance because his mistaken views provide a convenient way of introducing sociological perspectives.

LONELY CROWD, THE See **Riesman, David**.

LONGITUDINAL STUDIES These are studies of the same people over a long period of time. They have a number of advantages over cross-sectional studies (that is, studies of different people on every occasion). First, because they are repeatedly current, they rely less on recollection. In a cross-sectional study of changes in voting we can ask how respondents vote now, how they voted in the past, and how their parents voted, but for the second and third we rely on recollection. With longitudinal studies we repeatedly collect information that is current or recent.

Second, with cross-sectional studies our evidence for change (e.g. 'Support for gay marriage has risen by 10 per cent over the decade') rests on the conviction that our sampling techniques are reliable and that questions mean the same now as they did then because we are not interviewing the same people. Support for gay marriage may not have changed at all; we may simply have hit upon more of those people in favour with the second survey sample. Because in a longitudinal study we follow the same people, we can have much greater confidence that we are observing real change.

Longitudinal studies have weaknesses. First, we may create a **Hawthorne effect**: the very fact of being regularly studied may make our respondents unrepresentative. For example, in response to our repeated questioning they may become more thoughtful than the rest of the population which we take them to represent. Second, we have to wait a long time before the study produces useful information and research funders like results. Third, they are expensive. It is extremely costly to maintain contact with a large number of people for a long time and, because people die, move away, or lose interest in co-operating, to ensure that we have a large enough number of people at the end of the study, we have to begin with an unusually large number.

LOOKING-GLASS SELF Symbolic interaction was much influenced by the view of Charles Horton Cooley (1864–1929) that the sense of self was not self-generating but developed through interaction with significant others. Other people act like a mirror (or 'looking-glass' to use the 19th-century term) in which we see ourselves. The notion has

three components. (a) I imagine how I appear to someone else; 'appear' is shorthand for every way in which I and my actions can come to someone's attention. (b) I guess how that person judges me. (c) I feel either shame or pride (or something in-between). I may then change so as to alter the imagined responses of others to something more pleasing.

To develop this into a theory of learning requires adding all sorts of additional considerations (such as my relations with and estimation of any particular 'other' and the role of abstract 'others') but Cooley's model perfectly captures a simple but vital part of the development of the sense of self.

See **Mead**.

LUHMANN, NIKLAS (1927–98)   A leading German sociologist who spent most of his career in Bielefeld but studied briefly with Talcott **Parsons**, Luhmann is celebrated for his work on sociology as **systems theory**. He famously proposed that modern society was characterised less by its social divisions than by its division into numerous independent sub-systems such as education, the law, science, the arts and the economy. He attracted criticism for seeming unwilling to consider that these sub-systems might not be fully autonomous. For example, when a scientist gives evidence in court, is that part of the legal or the scientific sub-system? Nonetheless, Luhmann explored such novel resources for the development of systems theory as the biological sciences (from which the idea of self-organising systems or **autopoiesis** derives).

LUKÁCS, GYÖRGY (1885–1971)   A minister in the short-lived 1919 revolutionary government of Hungary, Lukács is known to social science for contributions to Marxist theory. Particularly in *History and Class Consciousness* he (1923) argued that the working class (because its triumph would end class struggle and thus did not contain within itself the origins of false consciousness) uniquely had a correct understanding of social and historical reality. Or at least it would have if it was not misled by distracting arguments within itself and by false consciousness induced by ruling class ideology. Hence it was the job of the political analyst to deputise for the working class in the role of possessor of truth. Quite why anyone outside the circle of professional communist ideologues took this remarkably arrogant position seriously is not clear but he was popular with some sociologists in the 1970s and his works remain in print.

LUMPENPROLETERIAT   From the German 'lumpen' meaning 'rags', this term was coined by Karl **Marx** and Friedrich **Engels** to describe a class of people on the margins of society, without regular employment and engaged mainly in crime. This population of swindlers, hoodlums, tramps, vagabonds, ex-prisoners, pimps and brothel-keepers was regarded with disdain by Marx and Engels who saw them as a threat to the revolutionary potential of the working class.

See **underclass**.

LYOTARD, JEAN-FRANÇOIS (1924–98)
Though his writings are sometimes painfully obscure, Lyotard is the main proponent of the idea that we have entered a period of postmodernity (*La condition postmoderne*, 1979). The central idea can be illustrated through the example of artistic representation. From the Renaissance, European artists became increasingly interested in making better representations. But the 20th century saw the overthrow of that ideal. Early in the century the artist Marcel Duchamp introduced the 'ready-made' and displayed not a still life depicting flowers and jugs on a tablecloth but an actual, shop-bought urinal and a pot rack. His 'representation' was more life-like than anything else because it was the

very thing. He was thus simultaneously the most extreme exponent of the modern ideal of representation and its assassin. Lyotard argues that a similar process infects all modernist culture, including the ideals of scientific and political representation. In the postmodern age earlier ideals have to be discarded and new aesthetics invented.

In Lyotard's view this process appears as autonomous development within the realm of culture. Critics, such as Frederic **Jameson**, argue that postmodernism is in fact the 'cultural logic' of late capitalism. Inverting the usual postmodernist account, critics argue that the postmodern aesthetic in design and architecture and so on is engendered by developments in capitalism.

See **performativity**.

LYSENKO, TROFIM DENISOVICH (1898–1976)
This Russian geneticist appears in sociology texts only to exemplify the way that science can be ideologically distorted. When most biologists had accepted that only material already present in the genes could be passed to the next generation (and hence that evolution worked by selecting the most effective of random variations), Lysenko was still arguing for the position developed by Jean Lamarck: that traits learnt or acquired by an organism during its lifetime could be transmitted genetically. In the accepted view, giraffes have very long necks because those with short necks fed less well and less often raised successful off-spring. In the Lamarckian model, giraffes lengthened their necks by stretching a lot and in each generation the effects of stretching were passed on. This latter view appealed to Stalin because by stressing learnt experience it resonated with the Soviet Union's claim to be developing a 'new man'. Because of political patronage, Lysenko enjoyed enormous power over Soviet science and was able to retard Soviet work in plant genetics for 30 years.

M

MACHIAVELLIAN After Niccolo Machiavelli (1469–1527), a diplomat and political theorist from Florence who argued that statecraft could not be conducted on the same moral principles as private relations, this word has two meanings: broadly used it means manipulative and narrowly used it means acting unethically in pursuit of some socially desirable end.

MAFFESOLI, MICHEL (1944–) French sociologist Maffesoli is best known in the Anglophone world for his (1988) *The Time of the Tribe*, an ambitious attempt, influenced by Walter **Benjamin**'s Arcades Project, to characterise modernity and postmodernity. Unlike most theorists he does not see social evolution as a reasonably linear move from communitarian orders to an individualistic world. Instead there is perpetual flux between mechanically structured social orders that allow for **individualism** and organically structured ones that confine people by social **roles**. He sees late modernity as being similar to late antiquity (hence the 'tribes'). In common with many glum French theorists, he sees the present as intensely problematic. Apparently we are passing from the 'rational era' into the 'empathetic' or 'passional' era in which individualism is replaced by local networks of people playing social roles with a degree of aloofness, artifice and detachment. As we recognise that the political and economic order is 'saturated' we reject the social order imposed from above and find ourselves through a variety of over-lapping tribes (which can be hobbyists, interest-based collectivities, lobbyists and enthusiasts of every sort) and create a new social order through personal interaction. The new social cement is the 'gossip of the coffee house'.

Though there is something clearly recognisable about the idea of modern tribes (some environmental protestors for example have even cultivated a 'tribal' image), the lack of precision about what exactly constitutes a tribe means that one cannot tell whether Maffesoli is correct or not. The deliberately poetic nature of his prose and his method of supporting grand claims with illustrative snippets from everyday life contribute to making his theses more or less impossible to evaluate.

MAGIC The use of ritual to activate, arouse or manipulate supernatural or spiritual agencies in order to achieve a specific goal is not always easy to distinguish from **religion**, with which it overlaps. But there are clear differences. Success in magic is entirely technical: get the spell right and the appropriate outcome occurs. In the major religious traditions this-worldly benefits might flow from pleasing God but in his infinite wisdom God might well decline our request. He is not beholden to us.

Magic is not only instrumental; it is also narrow in time and in purpose. There is rarely a need to be enduringly obedient to the supernatural agencies and no sense of ethical codes or ways of life that must be followed to qualify the supplicant for the favour. The request is normally very specific; it is not for a good life but for the cure of a sore leg, the return of a lost pig or the production of a marriage partner.

Social scientists have also been interested in what separates magic from science. In many traditional societies what we call magic is seen by the users as both science (in that it provides explanations of events in the natural world) and technology (in that it provides a vehicle for changing the material world). Arguments within anthropology about the nature of magic have informed debates in the philosophy and sociology of science about the demarcating line between **science** and pseudo-science. The most salient feature is its resistance to refutation and to change. While few scientists and technologists are keen to admit their ideas are mistaken or can be much improved on, the admission of error is often made and the body of ideas and practices changes, sometimes very rapidly. Magic has in common with religion that it is impervious to refutation. The consumer believes that the spell has worked (the sore leg clears up) or, if it does not heal, then the spell has not been properly performed or someone has invoked an even stronger counter-spell.

MALTHUS, THOMAS (1766–1834) This British clergyman, demographer and economist is of interest to sociology primarily for his dismal (and, as it turned out, inaccurate) view of the relationship between food and population. In his (1798) *An Essay on the Principle of Population* he argued that population grew at a geometric rate while food supply showed only arithmetic or **linear growth**. Unhindered, population would inevitably grow to the point where people could not feed themselves. What maintained the balance between population and food were such 'positive checks' as disease, famine and violence and such 'preventative checks' as late marriage, moral restraint and chastity. He was wrong both about population growth (which in many industrial societies is now negative) and food production (which has come close to geometric growth thanks to the industrialisation of agriculture).

MANAGERIAL REVOLUTION James Burnham's (1943) *The Managerial Revolution* identified a major change in the nature of capitalism: the growth in the number of professional managers who controlled companies that they did not own. This was a product of two sorts of change. First, ownership was changing as enterprises divided their capital into shares, which became widely distributed. An increasing amount of capital was owned by institutional investors (pension funds, insurance companies, investment companies and the like) and through them, by ordinary people. What Andrew Carnegie sold in 1901 to J.P. Morgan for $480 million was entirely his own steel company. Now such concentration is rare and very rich industrialists are likely to have spread their own wealth across a large number of enterprises. Second, management also changed a great deal over the 20th century. As the typical enterprise grew and became more complex, control passed to a large stratum of middle-class managers trained in accountancy and business studies.

While these core changes are clear enough, the consequences are less so. Burnham hoped first that, because they were under less pressure to maximise profits, professional managers would be more socially responsibly than owner-managers and second that there would be less antagonism with the workforce. Neither hope has been realised. Senior managers normally have their own rewards tied to the share price, are share-holders themselves and are beholden to those who own shares. Capitalists remain and can exert considerable control with only a minority share-holding because the rest of the capital is widely spread. It is true that work place militancy is less common now than in the 1930s or even 1960s but this has many causes more significant than the managerial revolution.

See **capitalism, transformations of**.

MANIFEST FUNCTION   See **latent function**.

MANNHEIM, KARL (1893–1947) Hungarian-born, Mannheim moved via Germany to England where he spent most of his working life at the London School of Economics. He is principally known for his work on the sociology of **knowledge**. He argued for a firm association between forms of knowledge and social structure in an attempt to understand how differences in belief arise and persist within societies. Although rejecting the Marxist view of **ideology**, he did believe that membership of particular social groups conditioned beliefs. He tried in two ways to avoid the **relativism** that seems a logical consequence of such a position. Initially he tried to distinguish between different sorts of ideas and beliefs so that, while much of what we knew was class-conditioned, some forms of knowledge (science especially) were independent of class location. Later he weakened the supposed link between social position and belief.

His major difference with Marxism was that he did not confine the group (membership of which shaped receptivity to ideas) to class or even to the Weberian status group. He believed that religious affiliation, gender and especially generation were all major sources of a predisposition to see the world one way rather than another.

MANUAL AND NON-MANUAL LABOUR The distinction between physical and mental work (or blue-collar and white-collar or working-class and middle-class occupations) is central to most applications of the idea of social class. It is common for social surveys, which begin with more sophisticated distinctions of occupational grade, to reduce them to just this binary divide. This is partly a matter of technical convenience: even large samples run out of cases in any category if, to the obvious divisions of age (say 3 bands), marital status (2), gender (2), education (say 4 bands), rural/urban (2), we add five different sorts of occupational status. That is 480 cells; with 1000 respondents we have only 2 in each cell; too few for most statistical tests to be reliable.

It also reflects the well-observed fact that in industrial manufacturing economies, the distinction between manual and non-manual work maps very well onto other important differences in **life-chances**. Manual workers are generally paid weekly, attain their highest earnings early in life, seek improvements in their working conditions through collective action and share a common culture that marks them off from non-manual workers. White-collar workers generally have longer periods of education before starting work, can expect income to rise over their working lives and pursue careers in which they compete with each other for personal advancement.

Although the manual–non-manual divide is often described in class terms, it does not correspond well to the contours of Marxist class analysis theory. Although manual workers could accurately be described as Marx's proletariat, few white-collar workers would fit neatly into his idea of the bourgeoisie in that their privileged position is due not to the ownership of capital but, as Max **Weber** noted, to their **market situation**.

MANUMISSION Although **slavery** is the most constraining system for the control of one group of people by another, most systems have included various devices for freeing slaves, known as manumission. For example, slaves might be freed on the death of their master, on becoming a kept sexual partner (or concubine) or as a reward for military service.

MARCUSE, HERBERT (1898–1979)

One of the leading 'glums' of modern sociology, Marcuse fled Germany for the USA in 1933 with other members of the Frankfurt Institute of Social Research. He wrote on a wide range of subjects from the perspective of someone who recognised all the flaws in classical Marxism (particularly its failure to deal adequately with the individual; hence his interest in Sigmund **Freud**) but wished to remain radical. Like that of Theodor **Adorno**, his analysis of the western working class was elitist and damning; he believed that it had been successfully incorporated by consumerism and **mass culture**. As the workers could no longer be expected to act as the vanguard of the revolution, that role would have to be performed by an alliance between radical intellectuals such as himself and, as he (1991) put it in *One-Dimensional Man*, 'the outcasts and outsiders, the exploited and persecuted of other races and other colors, the unemployed and the unemployables'. None of those groups took up the challenge but Marcuse was briefly very popular with affluent middle-class students in the late 1960s who were attracted by his criticism of the one-dimensional character of affluent consumerism and by his depiction of the affluent West (and their parents!) as controlling by 'repressive tolerance'. Repressive tolerance referred to the idea that the USA was so superficially attractive and tolerant that people were prevented from seeing just how horrible it was and rebelling.

MARKET SITUATION, MARKET CONDITIONS

Karl Marx's model of social **class** was based on the ownership (or otherwise) of the **means of production**. Max **Weber**, while fully accepting the importance of the worker–owner divide, also attended to differences between groups of workers in their market situation. Those with scarce and valued skills could command a higher price for them; that price typically including not just financial rewards but also conditions of work such as flexibility, promotion prospects and ability to determine how to perform their jobs.

Market situation can be altered by the exercise of political power. Trade unions have tried to improve their bargaining position by insisting that only workers who join the union can be employed in a particular job or factory. Since the 1970s many western governments have outlawed such closed-shop agreements as violating individual rights. The senior **professions** have been better able to protect their privileges by insisting that the preservation of quality requires that candidates experience extensive university-based education and be tested for competence by the profession.

MARRIAGE

This is the legally-ratified union, normally of a man and a woman (although a number of societies are now being led by the logic of their commitment to **human rights** to introduce a marriage-like status for same-sex relationships).

Societies vary considerably in rules and methods for selecting marriage partners. In many pre-modern societies marriage is used as a way of creating advantageous links between families, clans, tribes and royal households; personal attraction and sexual and emotional satisfaction (sometimes called 'affective individualism') are not major considerations. In modern societies marriage is usually a free choice though it remains the case that most people tend to choose partners who are similar in religion, class, educational background and the like.

For a large number of subtle reasons, marriage is becoming less common in many affluent societies. Greater prosperity reducing the need for a spouse; the popularity of sexual relations outside marriage; improvements in health allowing later pregnancies; decline in the popularity of the Christian view that marriage is pleasing to God; all of these have contributed to greater flexibility in the organisation of intimate relations.

MARSHALL, THOMAS H. (1893–1981) For many years professor of sociology at the London School of Economics, Marshall is best known for his pioneering writings on the concept of citizenship. In *Class, Citizenship and Social Development* he (1963) argued that modernisation had been accompanied by an expansion of the rights of the **citizen**: from legal rights (such as the right to a fair trial) in the 18th century; to political rights (such as the right to vote) in the 19th; to welfare rights (such as safety-net social security benefits) in the 20th century. The implied model of the attainment of successive rights has been criticised by some feminist authors who have noted that women sometimes acquired rights in a different order with, for example, many legal rights coming after the right to vote.

MARX, KARL (1818–83) Although his work is cited as often by those who disagree with him as by his supporters, Marx has had an enormous effect on sociology. After finishing his education in Germany, Marx became a journalist but, unable to find employment writing the kind of articles that concerned him, emigrated to Paris in 1843. There he mixed with other émigré radicals, became a socialist and met Friedrich **Engels** (who was his colleague as well as financial backer and should be credited with much of what follows below). Expelled from France, Marx moved to Brussels and then to London where he spent 34 years in writing and political activity.

In his early work Marx was interested in **alienation**, by which he meant the workers' lack of control over the production and disposal of their product. He also wrote extensively about the relationship between the economy and other elements of society. With the theory of the **base and superstructure**, he argued for a consistent relationship between the way that the means of production were owned, the way work was organised and everything else of importance in a society. Although he permitted that institutions such as the state and the family could sometimes be independently influential, what was distinctive about his social analysis was the primacy given to the economic base. In this sense he was an advocate of **materialism** and opposed to **idealist** accounts of social change which emphasised the importance of novel ideas.

For Marx all societies are **class** societies with people set against each other by their differing relationship to the means of production. In capitalist economies this takes the form of a central divide between those who own capital (the factories, the machines, the money to buy raw materials) and those who have to live by selling their labour power. Although Marx recognised the complexity caused by the apparent existence of other classes, these are dismissed as survivals from earlier economic forms.

Marx's model of class is not just a description and explanation of current social divisions. It is also the key to a general theory of social evolution, often referred to by Marx's supporters as his 'theory of history'. Class conflict is the motor which drives change. In any stage of evolution the economy can only develop so far within a particular set of class relations. Eventually there is upheaval with the new rising class casting aside the old and creating a new set of relationships. Just as the bourgeoisie had overthrown the old feudal aristocracy to create capitalism, so the working class would overthrow the capitalists to create a socialist economy. And there history would end because socialism, as it is based on common ownership of the means of production, cannot have class divisions; hence there can be no more class struggle and no further change.

Marx was not just an analyst; he was a political agitator (and was cattily scornful of mere philosophers). Although confident of the way history was going, he spent much of his life encouraging others to hasten its progress.

Were Marx a chemist or biologist he would have long been forgotten because he was wrong far more often than he was right. His key claim about the exploitative nature of capitalism depended on out-dated assumptions derived from the **labour theory of value**. Subsequent advances in our knowledge have shown much of his historical and anthropological knowledge to have been faulty (and hence cast doubt on the pre-capitalism stages of his evolutionary model). And his predictions could hardly have been more wrong. Capitalist societies did not become increasingly polarised between labour and capital: instead the middle-class grew and the importance of **manual labour** steadily declined. Class conflict did not intensify; capitalist societies proved enviably stable. Far from becoming ever-poorer until they were driven by despair into radical action; the industrial working classes of capitalist economies prospered. There were no revolutions in capitalist economies: the two most important countries to experience revolution (Russia and China) were largely agrarian and feudal.

Still, Marx was correct about a good deal. His emphasis on the endlessly competitive nature of capitalism is reflected in present-day concerns over globalisation, for example. But he was right about the things that were least unique to his work and similar claims can be found in many other authors' writings. He remains important to sociology because his work exemplifies the keystone of the discipline: that to understand people we must understand their relations with each other and with social structures; because his body of work is so large that people with widely divergent interests can find in it something that inspires them and locates their work in a tradition which gives it some legitimacy; because his mixing of conceptual analysis and political activism appeals to many; and because his generally critical view of modern societies remains popular.

MARXISM   The legacy of Karl **Marx** can be divided into two parts: practical politics and social analysis. For much of the 20th century a large number of states were ruled by communist parties that legitimated their rule by claiming to represent Marxism-Leninism (a body of ideas originally formulated by Marx and Friedrich **Engels** and developed by V.I. Lenin, one of the leaders of the 1917 Russian revolution). Far from confirming Marx's predictions, the spread of communism in eastern and central Europe was entirely due to warfare and state political power. In the final years of the 1939–45 war the Soviet Union was able to take control of eastern Europe and impose communist regimes in Poland, Hungary, Bulgaria, Czechoslovakia, the Baltic states and the eastern half of Germany. In the period from the 1950s onwards, as liberation movements challenged European imperialism in Africa and Asia, many nationalist parties adopted the language of Marxism; not because its ideas suited their conditions particularly well, but because it justified a general anti-western posture and because it ensured financial backing from the Soviet Union.

As Marxist parties seized power by force in circumstances quite unlike those which Marx regarded as essential for revolution, it is a little unfair to regard the regimes that were so created as exemplars of Marxist political thought but it is not entirely accidental that all such regimes were totalitarian and oppressive. While the communist leaders of the Soviet Union, Poland and Bulgaria quickly forgot (if they ever knew) the intricacies of Marxism, they were, like messianic religious leaders, reinforced in their actions by the belief that history and virtue were on their side. Once private ownership of the means of production was replaced by 'social' ownership in the hands of the state, there could no longer be legitimate differences of interest; hence there was no need for political structures that permitted competing voices to be heard. Being convinced that they had a monopoly of the truth they felt quite justified in taking control of every means of public expression and treating those who disagreed with them as enemies of the people rather than as political opponents.

Marxism as a political reality collapsed in the late 1980s, destroyed by the manifest corruption and dishonesty of communist party leaderships and by the inability of state-owned economies to match the growth in productivity of their capitalist rivals. The European states with a history of parliamentary institutions prior to the imposition of Soviet rule fairly painlessly reverted to being liberal democracies. The new creations in the south and east of the Russian empire became unprincipled dictatorships. In Africa and Asia the Marxist rhetoric was replaced by nationalist and ethno-religious discourses (with radical Islam being particularly attractive).

As a form of social analysis, Marxism declined in popularity from its highpoint around 1970, in part because the real world was not conforming to Marx's expectations but also because various forms of postmodernism were claiming the high ground of radicalism. Ironically, the political failure of communism has cleared away one obstacle to the return of Marxist social analysis. Without any non-capitalist industrial economies to serve as a comparison, it is easier to suppose that any unpleasant feature of the modern world must a consequence of capitalism.

MASCULINITY   See **femininity**.

MASLOW, ABRAHAM (1908–70) See **hierarchy of needs**.

MASS CULTURE   Being Marxist did not stop the **Frankfurt School** being elitist to the point of snobbery. Herbert **Marcuse** and Theodor **Adorno** both wrote very critically about the commercialised popular culture of the USA in the 1940s and 1950s. They thought it not only superficial but also oppressive in that it created false needs and maintained **false consciousness**.

There are many sensible ripostes to the critical view of mass culture. The commercialisation of culture does not discourage people from producing their own 'subsistence' culture: the response of many young people (men certainly) to buying their first rock record was to form their own band. Nor does it displace something more worthwhile (however one makes such judgements). The cinema did not take people away from the opera house; more often it gave access to a popularised version of high cultural products to those who would never have been able to afford such access. The success of public service broadcasting and the proliferation of mass media has brought high culture to a much wider audience than had access to it in the 19th century.

The claim that the glossy products of mass culture prevented the oppressed masses from appreciating the extent of their exploitation (and thus defused the potential for revolution) is untestable but, given that there is little independent evidence of any revolutionary potential that needed to be defused, it seems unlikely. If one needs to explain the absence of radical politics in countries such as the UK and USA, legitimate and effective government and increasing prosperity seem better contenders than the stupefying effects of mass culture.

MASS MEDIA   This signifies all impersonal vehicles of mass communication such as newspapers, magazines, radio, television, cinema, record music and the Internet. Sociological interests in the mass media could be summarised under content (is it shaped by audience demands or by producer imperatives?) and effect (to what extent are people's attitudes, beliefs and behaviour shaped by the mass media?). As part of a general concern about the disappearance of effective small groups and the supposed rise of **mass society**, early responses tended to be driven by a fear that people would be readily manipulated by radio and television. Research to assess the effects of mass communication suggests that such fears are exaggerated. It is clear that audiences are selective in what they take from the mass media; attending to those presentations that fit well with what they already believe and simply not noticing or re-interpreting ideas that might challenge their existing attitudes. Mass media products such as religious programmes tend to be influential only when they are endorsed by personal relationships; as when a newcomer watches a television evangelist in the company of others who support the programme's message and add their positive commentary.

The collapse of Soviet communism is a major challenge to those who see the mass media as effectively persuasive. For 70 years the communist party exercised complete control over the mass media and systematically used newspapers, radio and television as instruments of propaganda. And yet when the party relaxed its oppressive control in the late 1980s, its popular support collapsed. All that ideological work had failed to win the hearts and minds of the Soviet people.

The current major concern is over violence and the possibility that young people (very young children especially) are being brutalised by the violent behaviour they regularly see on television. It has proved very difficult to produce definitive research findings because the sources of influence on children are many and varied.

See **two-step flow of mass communication, uses and gratifications**.

MASS SOCIETY Popular from the late 1930s to the 1950s, this gloomy depiction of modern society asserted that a variety of recent developments (universal voting, mass education, the growth of mass media, urbanisation and mass production) was undermining many forms of local community bonding and thus creating a society of isolated atomised individuals who (and this was the topical part of the analysis) were vulnerable to political manipulation by unscrupulous elites. The term was widely used and acquired a variety of importantly different meanings but familiar to many was C. Wright **Mills**'s argument that modern societies were becoming increasingly homogenised as what had previously been a large number of centres of influence and opinion were becoming concentrated. This is something of a perennial theme in sociology and can be found in Emile **Durkheim**'s concern with changing forms of social solidarity and Ferdinand **Tönnies**'s loss of Gemeinschaft or '**community**' thesis but the mass society formulated owed much to attempts to explain the widespread success of **fascism** and **authoritarianism** in 1930s Europe.

Empirical tests of the idea found it much too sweeping. For example, studies of the influence of mass media discovered that the radio and television audience was not an undifferentiated mass but was actually highly segmented, that mass media tended to be influential only when their messages were mediated by and reinforced through personal communication and that both high art and community were surviving the growth of mass **popular culture**.

See also **social capital, two-step flow of mass communication**.

MASTER STATUS It is a consequence of the complexity of modern life that all of us occupy a number of statuses – shop owner, mother, keen sportswoman and the like – and shift between them. Symbolic interactionists use the term 'master status' to describe a status that may come to dominate all others to the extent of making them irrelevant in our social interactions. The idea is important for the **labelling** approach to crime and deviance as it allows one effective way of describing how societal reaction may turn primary deviation into secondary deviance. 'Criminal' may become the master status that denies the person so labelled other statuses and so increases the temptation to be drawn further into a criminal sub-culture and further crime.

MATERIALISM   Normally this signifies the Marxist view that economic relations are the base, or basic cause, of social relations and institutions and is contrasted with **idealism**. More generally, a materialist claims that the most important entities in explaining social change are material concerns and alterations at the material level, for example changes in techniques or the availability of new material resources. Materialists ascribe changing ideas only a small role; extreme materialists deny ideas any influence. In the philosophical literature materialism has a slightly different meaning: philosophical materialists claim that there is only matter and energy and that the apparently distinct worlds of the mind or the soul are only the consequences of material phenomena.

See **Engels, dialectical materialism, historical materialism, Marx**.

MATERNAL DEPRIVATION   The work of psychologist John Bowlby on the role of early relationships in the development of the personality was extremely influential in the 1950s and 1960s. He argued that for a young child to be separated from its mother, for any extended period, created emotional and psychological problems in later life. The theory was attacked by feminists as an ideology of **patriarchy** intended to keep women out of the labour force. Recent research has suggested that stable relationships with a number of adults (including, importantly, fathers or other male **significant others**) may be as important for social development.

MATRIARCHY   Narrowly meaning rule of the family by the mother (as opposed to the father or patriarch), matriarchy is also used to mean any form of social organisation based on female domination. John Ferguson McLennan's (1865) *Primitive Marriage* claimed that the earliest human social organisations were matriarchal. Friedrich **Engels** (1902), in *The Origin of the Family, Private Property and the State*, argues that the patriarchal nuclear family was preceded by the primitive matriarchal clan. Women were displaced by men who created the monogamous family unit so there could be no doubts about paternity and inheritance rights. The modern family evolved to safeguard private property. Our lack of evidence about the social organisation of pre-historic peoples means such accounts must remain speculative but they were an important inspiration for many feminists as they could be claimed for the case that gender need not determine social relationships.

MATRILINEAL   This means 'from the line of the mother' and describes a system in which property, titles or some other asset is inherited through the female rather than, as is more common, the male line.

MAYO, ELTON (1880–1949)   See **Human Relations School**.

MCDONALDISATION   The clever use of the methods of a hamburger chain to symbolise the dominant ethos of modern society in George Ritzer's (1993) *The McDonaldization of Society* gave a new popularity to an idea which has its roots in Max **Weber**'s 'iron cage of rationality': that formal rationality taken too far produces irrationality. McDonald's offers a very limited range of standardised products cheaply and effectively by imposing a strict order on its staff, its raw materials and its customers. According to its critics, the result is good profit and bad food. Ritzer's secondary claim that McDonald's-like methods are permeating large parts of the social world beyond the fast food restaurant (and thus corrupting what should be original and authentic life) is a particular instance of the general point made by Peter L. **Berger**: that the techniques and values of industrial production (such as an extensive division of labour, standardisation of outputs, the search for predictability) were spreading into other areas of life.

In later work, Ritzer added further indictments to the charge sheet. New means of consumption (such as credit cards, shopping malls, Internet shopping) were making people consume more than they needed and more than they could afford. He borrowed Jean **Baudrillard**'s idea of '**simulacra**' to describe (and condemn) the scripted interaction between staff and customers. He also added an explicit globalisation element: the USA was McDonaldising the rest of the world.

Ritzer's sweeping characterisation of modern society, while insightful, lacks solid research foundations and can degenerate into polemic (as, for example, when he condemns articles in sociology journals for being as standardised and homogenised as a Big Mac burger). In viewing McDonaldisation as something that US capitalism is doing to people, he overlooks an alternative interpretation of the success of McDonald's: one which presents a more plausible voluntaristic view of human choice. McDonald's may have succeeded, in part at least, because people prefer the assurance of decent food and efficient service to the gamble that may produce either the great or the ghastly.

MEAD, GEORGE HERBERT (1863–1931)
The University of Chicago philosopher and social psychologist credited with creating **symbolic interactionism** called his position 'social behaviourism' to distinguish it from the psychological **behaviourism** of John B. Watson. Mead emphasised the conscious mind, self-awareness and self-control of social actions. He believed that the **self** emerged from social interaction in which people, by 'taking the role of the other', internalised the attitudes of real and imagined others. Models of the self, mind or personality that posit an internal tension between the natural and the social are common enough but, by borrowing Charles Horton Cooley's idea of the **looking-glass self**, Mead was able to suggest a plausible model of how the external came to be incorporated in the self. The I (myself as I am) is in constant interaction with the Me (myself as I imagine that others see me). The Me represents the attitudes of the social group: an imagined **generalised other** formed by amalgamating our experiences with a series of **significant others**. By role-taking in play and in imagined internal 'rehearsal' of interaction, we come to internalise the group's beliefs and values as a generalised other. By continually reflecting on ourselves as others see us, we acquire the ability to produce and deploy social symbols.

The key difference with classic behaviourism is that, in Mead's view, our ability to use language and symbolic communication allows us to transcend the limits of our biology.

Mead was crucial in the **Chicago School**'s treatment of the relationship between the self and society. When he died in post, Herbert Blumer took over his lectures, refined his social theory and named it symbolic interactionism.

See **pragmatism, significant other.**

MEAD, MARGARET (1901–78)   From the publication of her (1928)*Coming of Age in Samoa*, Mead was a major figure in cultural anthropology. The central theme of her early work was the demonstration that gendered patterns of behaviour (including sexual behaviour) were a product of socialisation, not of nature. This made her an important source for progressives in child-rearing debates and for early feminism in the USA. In the 1980s critical re-examination of her field work (for example she did not learn Samoan) rather dented her reputation as an anthropologist though her standing as a social reformer remained high.

MEAN   See **measures of central tendency**.

MEANINGLESSNESS   Robert Blauner used the term for one indicator of **alienation**: assembly-line work created a sense of meaninglessness because it denied workers the opportunity to feel pride, purpose and ownership in their work. Note that here alienation is a psychological state created by objective circumstances; in most Marxist writings alienation is held to be an objective condition.

MEANS OF PRODUCTION   Prominent in Marxist thought, this signifies what is required to produce goods and services. It includes the obvious material resources but adds the social relations between workers and owners (or labour and capital).

MEASUREMENT, LEVELS OF   Phenomena that are of interest to the sociologist come in a variety of shapes that are more or less amenable to measurement. A common way of sorting these is as nominal, ordinal, interval and ratio level data. Which of these best describes any data is crucial for choosing appropriate statistical models for investigating their properties and relationships.

Nominal data is what we have if we simply replace names by numbers. When coding responses to a census we assign numbers to religious groups, but replacing the labels Baptist, Presbyterian, Episcopalian and Catholic by the numbers 1, 2, 3, 4, does not allow us to do sums with the data; two Baptists does not equal one Presbyterian.

Data is ordinal if we can place it in some sort of order. For example, we might persuade ourselves that these four varieties of Christian can be arrayed in terms of how hierarchical they are: with the Catholic at the high end and the Baptist at the low.

Interval-level measurements are ordinal ones with the added refinement that the distances between categories are fixed and equal. Temperature is a good example. We can say that the change from 29 to 30 degrees centigrade is of the same magnitude as the change from 19 to 20 degrees. However, the assignment of a zero point on everyday measures of temperature is purely arbitrary; it could have been put anywhere. Hence we cannot compare intervals proportionately. We can say that the distance between 0 and 10 and between 10 and 20 is the same but we cannot say that 20 degrees centigrade is 'twice as hot' as 10 degrees.

To do that we need levels of measurement that make use of real numbers and have a naturally-occurring, fixed zero point: height is a good example. Because zero height is a real point we can describe a 30 cm (12 inch) plant as being twice as big as a 15 cm (six inch) plant. This is 'ratio-level' because we can sensibly use ratio terms such as 'twice as big'.

The main point of recognising these different levels of measurement and placing them in the order nominal, ordinal, interval and ratio is that statistical tests are applicable to the right of the positions for which they are designed but not to the left. That is, a test which works with ordinal data will also work with interval and ratio data but one which is designed for the specific properties of interval data will not work with the simpler forms of ordinal and nominal data. For example, tests that require the calculation of a mean (see measures of central tendancy) cannot work with ordinal data because the idea of mean is inappropriate with such data.

Sociologists need to be aware of these distinctions because once we replace words by numbers we are liable to forget the limitations of the data (for example, treating ordinal data as though it were interval-level) and we need to select statistical tests that are appropriate.

MEASURES OF CENTRAL TENDENCY   The 'average' is a crucial notion in the social sciences, where we are often concerned more with common tendencies than with the purely individual or idiosyncratic. But there is more than one way of picking out the average case, also known as the 'central tendency'. The three different ways of identifying it are the mode, mean and median.

Imagine 15 families; 3 of them own 3 cars each, 3 of them own 2 cars each, 3 each own only 1 car while 5 families have no cars and 1 family has 4. Between them, the families own 22 cars. If we want to express in a figure the average or typical car ownership, we can do this in different ways. The mode is simply the most common position: in this case owning no cars. More families are in this position than in any other position. The mean (what we most often have in mind when we talk of an average) is nearly 1.5 (22 cars divided by 15 families). The median is in many ways similar to the mean though (as noted below) it may sometimes be importantly different. It is the score that occurs in the middle position. In this case there are 15 families so the middle case is the 8th one along. Thus, in this case the median value is 1 car.

Each measure has its uses. The median is especially useful when the inclusion of a small number of deviant cases would skew the mean (as in the above example if we add a new family that owned 22 cars – that family alone would double overall car ownership and raise the mean to nearly 3). A sociological example

is income. There is little point in trying to describe the typical income in a society by presenting the mean if our population includes a small number of people who earn vastly more than the rest. This would make the average income appear higher than the experience of the typical person.

MEASURES OF DISPERSION   Just as there are a variety of ways of describing the centre of a range of observations (see **measures of central tendency**), there are different ways of describing their spread. The range is the largest number minus the smallest. For example, if the tallest in a group of 10 children is 180 cm (5' 11") and the shortest 160 cm (5' 3") the range is 20 cm (8"). The variance is a measure of how far the values are spread from the mean and should be used only with **interval**-level measures. It is an average of the squared deviations from the mean. Once the mean of the heights is calculated, the extent to which each child is taller or shorter than that mean is calculated, squared and the mean of those values calculated. The point of squaring the numbers is to ensure that the small number of big deviations have a large impact on the final figure. The standard deviation is the square root of the variance. We use it in preference to the variance to describe dispersion because, being in the same units as the original data (rather than their squares), it seems easier to interpret. The standard error is an estimate of how far the mean for a set of scores from a sample differs from the true mean score for the whole population.

MECHANICAL AND ORGANIC SOLIDARITY According to Emile **Durkheim**, how societies hang together can be described in relation to two polar types. Simple small-scale societies cohere because everyone is much the same; they work in the same way, have the same lifestyles, see the world the same way, share common standards of conduct and the like. This is mechanical solidarity. Modern societies are clearly not like that. The complex division of labour, differences in **life-chances** and lifestyles, differences in beliefs and values preclude mechanical solidarity and instead require integration on the basis of differences between individuals and groups being inter-locking and complementary. While the distinction is clear and sensible, the names chosen can mislead; to many readers the mechanical car seems more complex than the organic frog.

One simple way of appreciating the difference is to compare the contributions of individuals to team performance in the case of a darts team and a football (soccer) team. In a darts team, each player does the same thing; the team performance is simply the aggregate of the scores of the individuals. A football team is composed of players with very different roles. Goalkeeper, defender and striker do very different things; what is virtue in one role (handling the ball, for example) may be vice in another. The success of the football team depends on each player performing her or his special task well and the various specialisms being well co-ordinated.

MEDIA　　See **mass media**.

MEDIAN　　See **measures of central tendency**.

MEDIATED CLASS LOCATION　　The term was proposed by Erik Olin Wright in the 1980s but it described a commonplace: many people's social class is determined not by their own 'relation to the means of production', as a Marxist would put it, but by that of their relatives. For example, because art dealing is seen as glamorous, daughters of wealthy and even aristocratic families are willing to work as secretaries and PAs in that sector but their class position is clearly not that of the secretary whose salary is his or her only means of support. Leaving aside such

occupational mobility as she may enjoy, a woman's class location may change four times in her life: twice through her own circumstances of working or not working and twice through her mediated class as she shifts from her father's to her husband's class. Given that women form half the population, such potential volatility has important implications for the development of **class consciousness**.

MEDICAL MODEL　　Since the development of the germ theory of disease in the 19th century, the principal form of explanation in scientific medicine has assumed some or all of the following: all diseases are caused by a specific agent such as a virus, parasite or bacterium; because illness is a characteristic of the body as a machine rather than of the person in a wider social context, the patient is treated as the passive target for medical intervention; and restoring health requires the use of medical technology and advanced procedures.

Although the medical model has been immensely successful, the last quarter of the 20th century saw an increasing demand for more 'holistic' approaches to health and illness. In part this demand can be understood in terms of the impersonal nature of many medical encounters and the social gulf that sometimes separates people from medical professionals. In part it is a perverse result of the success of medicine and improvements in diet. As people live longer they come more commonly to experience problems (many cancers and degenerative diseases, for example) about which the medical profession can do little. One of the appeals of alternative or complementary medicine is that its practitioners claim to treat the entire person rather than just the single presenting symptom. These supposed benefits should not be taken for granted: in reality a Reiki healer who spends only 30 minutes with a stranger is less likely to have a sense of the whole person than the family doctor (if one is lucky enough to have one) who has treated that person's symptoms for 20 years and kept detailed records. Nonetheless the medical model, like science generally, has an image problem among those drawn to **New Age** spirituality.

MEDICALISATION   This denotes the treatment of morally unacceptable or socially undesirable behaviour as though it were an illness to be cured. It is important both as a characteristic of modern societies and as identifying a discipline boundary dispute. The success of the medical model in treating what are uncontentiously diseases has made it an attractive metaphor. Those who disapprove of something and wish to portray it as beyond the normal range of choices label it as a disease in need of (forced, if necessary) treatment: this attitude to homosexuality was common in the 1950s. But medicalisation is not always hostile. People may wish to portray themselves as ill in order to win sympathy and deflect criticism about their moral responsibility for their conduct; for example, most self-help groups for alcoholics assert that alcoholism is an illness.

MELUCCI, ALBERTO (1943–)   In *Challenging Codes: Collective Action in the Information Age* (1996a) and *The Playing Self: Person and Meaning in the Planetary Society* (1996b) Melucci outlines a theory of social movements. In contrast to the US approach, which distinguishes social movements from other social phenomena by their structure, Melucci follows the continental model of defining them by their purpose: they challenge the ends, values and power structure of a given society. However, unlike those (such as Antonio **Negri**) who see youth protest, the women's movement, environmentalism and gender politics as forming some new oppositional 'class', Melucci does not find a deep-seated unity underlying new social movements. They do not form a single symptom of social-structural malaise; rather they are active

constructions of collective identity. His analysis of specific movements builds into a characterisation of the modern world. Melucci believes that we live in a world 'without centres' where it is not possible to seize the central instruments of power. In social systems that are networks of relations, information is the crucial resource. Hence collective active which is designed to change the way we think ('public discourse') is more effective than that based on force and violence.

MEMBERS' METHODS   See ethnomethodology.

MEMBERSHIP CATEGORISATION DEVICES See **Sacks**.

MEMMI, ALBERT (1920–)   In common with many French social theorists, Memmi held a chair of sociology but was, by training and inclination, a philosopher and writer. A Tunisian Jew, educated in Algiers and in France, Memmi settled in France in 1956 when Tunisia gained its independence. He is best known for *The Colonizer and the Colonized* (1957) and *Racism* (1999). He argued that colonisation affected the colonised in every aspect of social and psychological organisation. He went beyond the racism inherent in colonial institutions to examine in detail the ideology of colonial culture that dehumanised the colonised and legitimated their oppression. He concluded that the revolt of the colonised was the built-in conclusion to the process of colonisation and that, as part of that revolt, the colonised had to reject the language and knowledge of the dominant culture and rediscover their own identity.

MENDEL, GREGOR (1822–84)   See genetics.

MENTAL ILLNESS   Diseases of the mind can vary from the brief and mild to the permanent and severe. The sociological contribution to our understanding of mental illness has broadly taken two forms. There is a tradition that takes as given conventional psychiatric diagnoses and seeks social explanation of the distribution, onset and severity of such illnesses. As with most diseases, psychiatric disorders follow social inequalities and there have been many studies examining the differential rate of occurrence of psychiatric problems among women, the poor and people from ethnic minority backgrounds. There is also a more radical sociology that considers the role of social interaction and **labelling** in the creation and maintenance of mental illness. In the 1960s and 1970s this radical position was taken as far as to suggest that there were no mental illnesses as such but that they were created by the **medicalisation** of unusual or deviant behaviour. Subsequent advances in the medical understanding of some psychiatric illnesses has rendered this position more or less untenable though it is clear that a great deal of uncertainty surrounds medical classifications of mental ill-health. Undoubtedly the sociological claim that the treatments of patients as insane added to their problems was fundamentally correct and most western countries have greatly reduced the numbers of psychiatric patients confined in hospitals, even if this trend has been assisted by the cost savings it also brings.

MERCANTILISM   From 'merchant' meaning 'trader', this term describes both a political doctrine of the 16th and 17th centuries and the type of economy that prevailed under such a doctrine. Then foreign trade was largely controlled by the state and the general aim was to accumulate assets (gold and other valuables) by selling manufactured goods and only importing raw materials. In the late 18th century, economists and politicians argued against such control and in favour of free trade and

a **laissez-faire** approach. They claimed that the key thing was to increase the overall size of the economy and that this was more important than acquiring riches from others. Mercantilism came to be the pejorative term for the earlier outlook, an outlook that was said to be highly favourable only to the merchants and manufacturers who benefited from it directly.

MERITOCRACY   Like all '-ocracies' this means 'rule by': in this case, rule by those who have earned their position by some combination of innate ability and individual endeavour. The implied contrast is with a structure in which social positions are inherited rather than earned. Modern liberal democracies are committed, in rhetoric at least, to meritocracy as the proper way to distribute social positions, on grounds both of fairness and of efficiency. A major concern of studies of **social mobility** is to test the extent to which our societies are genuinely meritocratic. As with the notion of **equality** of opportunity, there is a major rift between those who believe that meritocracy can be created merely by ensuring that the rules of the competition for scarce rewards are fairly applied (e.g. by preventing inappropriate discrimination in hiring policies) and those who argue that the influence of inherited advantage is so great that procedural fairness is not enough: there must be positive assistance for those of less privileged backgrounds to make the race fair.

While it is easy to identify 'unmeritocratic' procedures (for example when parents' social contacts offer easy access to desirable jobs), it is more difficult to demonstrate meritocracy because identifying and measuring innate ability (for example, in the form of **intelligence**) is no easy matter.

MERTON, ROBERT K. (1910–2003) From the start to the finish of a long life, Merton had an immense effect on sociology, though his work is better known than his name. His doctoral thesis (1970) (published in 1938 as *Science, Technology and Society in 17th-century England*) helped establish the sociological study of science as a legitimate exercise. The same year the *American Sociological Review* published his essay 'Social structure and anomie' (1938). Seventy years on it is still reprinted and read with benefit. From 1942–71 he was deputy to Paul **Lazarsfeld** at the Columbia University Bureau of Applied Social Research and there he played a major role in encouraging scholars to develop what he called theories of the **middle range**.

Unlike his teacher Talcott **Parsons**, Merton did not develop a school of followers but arguably his influence has been greater. Few scholars now use Parsonian concepts but the following is a list of terms associated with Merton that are still part of the sociological vocabulary: self-fulfilling prophecy, reference groups, focus groups, opportunity structure, manifest and latent functions, unanticipated consequences, role-models, status-sets, social dysfunctions and the norms of science. Though his commitment to **functionalist** analyses meant that he fell from favour after the 1970s, many of his detailed studies are highly regarded.

MESSIAH   Initially the promised saviour of the Jews, this title was applied to Christ in the Christian tradition. By extension it has since been applied to charismatic leaders in any religious tradition (and in secular fields) who promise either to liberate the oppressed or bring the world to an end.

MESSIANISM   See **millenarianism**.

MEŠTROVIĆ, STJEPAN (19??–)   In *Postemotional Society* (1997), Meštrović argues that most sociology is defective because it neglects the emotions. Other sociologists have frequently issued programmatic calls for more work on the emotional aspects of action but Meštrović's innovation is to tie

this claim into a sweeping characterisation of the contemporary situation. He asserts that our world is not **postmodern**; it is postemotional. Society's contradictory trends to order and to chaos creates a new hybrid world of 'McDonaldised emotion'. Postemotionalism is a system designed to prevent loose ends in emotional exchanges, to civilise wild areas of emotional life, to prevent emotional disorder and to 'tidy up' emotional debris. As with many suggestive but very broad theories, Meštrović is not able to adduce enough evidence to make this characterisation completely persuasive.

META-ANALYSIS   Deriving its sense from the Greek 'meta' meaning 'over', this is a style of study in which the results of many detailed case studies or surveys are brought together and analysed to produce an overview of a field. It is very common in medical research where, for example, scholars periodically evaluate the success of a particular therapy by collating the results of a number of evaluations from different countries. The technique is beginning to be used in the applied social sciences.

META-LANGUAGE   In order to talk about language, we need a 'second order' language of technical terms (such as noun, verb, sentence and so on); this is an 'over' or metalanguage. Other symbolic systems – such as those used in logic or in mathematics – also have meta-languages which govern how the symbols may be used.

META-NARRATIVE see **grand narrative and meta-narrative**.

METAPHOR   In common use, metaphor is the use of a descriptive term or phrase that strictly speaking does not apply, but which brings out some vital feature of the thing so described. Thus 'the war against poverty' is intended to suggest how seriously the government treats the problem, not its intention to kill rich people. Metaphor is essential to forms of social analysis (indeed, to all human life) but it carries an obvious danger: while drawing our attention to one aspect of a phenomenon it may cause us to overlook or misconstrue something almost as important. For example, in treating social roles as if they were parts in a scripted play, Goffman's **dramaturgy** is immensely useful. It reminds us, for example, that 'being virtuous' will not have the desired effect unless we are seen to 'act virtuously'. However, dramaturgy has the potential danger of suggesting that all social performance is insincere and that any role can be shed merely by leaving the stage.

METAPHYSICAL   Narrowly speaking metaphysics is that branch of philosophy that deals with the fundamental nature of reality; it is tied to questions of being (**ontology**) and related to questions of knowing (**epistemology**). It was formerly thought of as the loftiest form of enquiry. These days, the adjective is frequently used pejoratively to mean 'speculative' or without any supporting evidence.

METATHEORY   As with **meta-language**, this means a theory about theories and refers to the general background of philosophical assumptions that provide the rules for the construction of particular theories and justifications for particular research methods. An example is **hermeneutics**.

METHODENSTREIT   This German term meaning 'dispute over methods' refers to a major debate in German sociology in the 1890s over the methods appropriate to the social sciences. Then as now, the key issue was the extent to which methods which had proved so successful in the natural sciences could or should be imitated in the study of

people and societies. These issues re-surfaced in the 1960s as sociologists aimed to find a new analytical orientation after **functionalism**. The term was revived in German debates between Jürgen **Habermas** and others over **hermeneutics** and **critical theory**.

See **positivism, Verstehen**.

METHODOLOGICAL INDIVIDUALISM   This can have two importantly different meanings. It can mean simply that, as a matter of technical limitation, social researchers interested in institutions and other supra-human are confined to studying individuals. For example, while we may suppose that 'government' has some sort of being greater than, and more enduring than, the individuals who at any one time people it, we can only study the actions of a government by studying the actions of the ministers, officials and others who compose it.

There is a further meaning that is theoretical rather than technical. Many sociologists maintain that a convincing sociological explanation must involve reference to the interpretations, meanings and actions of individuals. Abstractions such as social class are a useful shorthand but a social class is in the first and last analysis a collection of real people; if we had the time we could name all the people who we take to form the working class of Arkansas in 2003. A good example of the dispute between methodological individualists and those who believe that characteristics of such collectivities as societies and features of social systems have a 'facticity' that allows us to explain the relationships between them without reference to individuals, is that over Durkheim's explanation of **suicide**. With good grounds the individualists would argue that the suicide rate for a society is only an adding up of individual suicides. This is not simply a practical point: as the sole difference between suicide and other forms of death is the intention of the deceased, any one death can only be accurately described as suicide if we ascertain the intentions of the deceased. If that is true for any one death, it remains true when we add them up.

The standard objection to methodological individualism is that, as many of the characteristics of individuals that interest sociologists are derived from such common sources as gender, social class, religion, age and the like, there is no need or value in reducing analysis from the social level to the individual. The individual can be treated as a corridor in which social cause becomes social action and social consequence. While any sociologist must accept the first part of the proposition, the methodological individualist can reasonably respond that frequent 'unpacking' to the level of the individual actor is a good way to ensure that the explanation is sensible. For example, one **rational choice** explanation of why churches (such as the Scandinavian Lutheran churches), whose clergy are paid out of public taxes, are less popular than self-financing churches of the USA, is that clergy who do not need to recruit and sustain a congregation to make a living will prefer empty churches: less work for the same money. When put as a general proposition about the incentives and rewards for a class of workers this may seem credible but when we unpack it to the level of a real (or imagined) Lutheran pastor we should immediately see that it rests on an implausibly narrow view of motivation. Most clergy are ideologically inspired. They believe in what they do and find comforting reinforcement in persuading others to believe the same. The income-effort ratio may be a small consideration for some people but its limitation becomes obvious when the social level of analysis is complemented by unpacking to the level of the individual.

METHODOLOGICAL PLURALISM   As the term suggests, this is a commitment to the idea that a wide variety of different research techniques and approaches is likely to be more productive than faithful adherence to just one method or perspective.

METHODOLOGY   This is the study or knowledge ('-ology') of methods and includes, on the one hand, technical instruction in research methods and, on the other, philosophical reasoning about methods and technical study of the operations and consequences of various methods. Thus one finds methodologists both teaching methods and arguing about their appropriateness.

The major issue in social science methodology remains as ever it was: the extent to which the social sciences can and should follow the methods of the natural sciences.

MICHELS, ROBERT (1876–1936)   A friend of Max **Weber**, German sociologist and political philosopher, Michels is best known for his (1911) *Political Parties* and its central theme of **oligarchy**. His interest in the subject stemmed from his personal frustration with the leadership of the German Social Democratic party. In later work he developed a theory of the social advantages of representative democracy, which can be seen as a precursor of the theory of stable democracy.

MIDDLE CLASS   Often used in the plural to reflect its internal diversity, this term identifies non-manual workers: 'middle' in the sense of enjoying a wide variety of advantages over most manual workers but clearly subordinate to those whose wealth means they need not work. Although wealth and status usually go hand-in-hand, the initial division between middle and working class is not economic; it is social and cultural. A skilled plumber in most industrial societies may well earn more than an infant school teacher but not be middle class.

In the early 19th century the numbers employed in non-manual or professional work were few but, especially over the 20th century, there has been a steady rise in the size of the old professions (such as medicine and the law), in the number of new professions (accountancy, social work and public administration, for example), and in the number of non-manual workers in industry (such as supervisors and managers). In 1900 in the USA or the UK about 80 per cent of workers were manual; in 2000 it was well below half.

The huge growth in this class and its internal diversity cause a major problem for Marxist models that associate major social dividing lines with relationship to the **means of production**. One response has been to argue that middle-class work is being **deskilled** and that, in a process of **proleterianisation**, the status, pay and working conditions of white-collar workers are being reduced to those of blue-collar workers. Another is to suggest a radical revision of Karl Marx's original class schema to reflect the way the bases of wealth and power have changed.

The Weberian model of class also needs qualification, although unlike the Marxist one, its framework can be left intact. As the middle class has grown, so has the internal variation in **market situation**, the principle that Weber uses to define class. There are major sector and status differences: there is a wide gulf in the earnings and conditions of routine clerical retail workers and lawyers. Additionally, many sociologists now argue that there is a divide within the middle class between those whose occupations are tied to manufacturing and production (for example, surveyors and accountants) and those in the knowledge class. The latter group includes social workers, regulators, therapists and so on whose professions are concerned with remedying problems caused by capitalist modernity. These middle-class groups owe their positions to qualifications and they are likely to be receptive to criticisms of unfettered free markets: for example, they are more likely than the classic middle class to join environmental groups or organisations that campaign for animal welfare or prisoners' rights.

See **bourgeoisie, occupational scales**.

MIDDLE-RANGE THEORY   More politely than C. Wright **Mills** with his condemnation of **abstracted empiricism** and grand theory, Robert K. **Merton** also suggested that sociology would be much improved if it could develop more theories that lie between the 'minor but necessary' working hypotheses that are tested in much empirical work and the all-inclusive theories of everything that are the domain of social theorists.

MID-LIFE CRISIS   A term used more in popular than in professional sociology, this refers to the doubt and anxiety that is held to beset some people when they enter middle age (usually defined as years 40–60). Around this age people in western industrial societies usually have a good idea of the limit of their career advancement and may reflect ruefully on it. They also begin to shed active parental responsibilities and contemplate the first signs of the physical deterioration associated with **ageing**. The realisation that opportunities are running out may prompt various forms of soul-searching and returns to youthful behaviour. For men, buying a motor-bike is a classic symptom.

MIGRATION   The movement of people from one country to another, with the intention of staying, is further described as either 'emigration' (leaving) and 'immigration' (entering). Peoples have always moved around the world but migration has some particular associations with modernisation. In a strictly logical sense there can be no immigration or emigration until national boundaries and national identities have been introduced. European empires encouraged their citizens to populate new outposts. The Afrikaners of South Africa are descendants of Dutch settlers. Many Canadians, Australians and New Zealanders are descendants of British people offered free or assisted passage and settlement grants. Although the former imperial centres have been less keen to receive their overseas subjects than to export their surplus population, former colonial relationships explain some modern patterns of movement. For example, thousands of Ugandan Asians (descendants of workers brought to Africa by the British to help staff new imperial outposts) were expelled from independent Uganda in 1972 and settled in Britain. Africans from former French territories are attracted to France by the common language.

Another connection with modernisation is the increased ease of long-distance transportation. In the 19th century it took weeks to travel across Europe; now it takes less than a day.

Economic opportunities and disasters have always provided one powerful reason for people to move, political violence another. Political violence is not new but the ready availability of modern weapons and the fragility of many new states has given it a new intensity that frequently creates mass migrations.

MILITARY-INDUSTRIAL COMPLEX   It is ironic, given that it is usually used by left-wing critics, that this phrase came to prominence when it was used in a 1950s speech by the Republican president of the USA (and former soldier) Dwight Eisenhower to refer to what he saw as a dangerous side-effect of the Cold War competition with the Soviet Union: the increasing influence on US life of the military and of the industrial companies they commissioned to build weapons. C. Wright **Mills**, in his 1956 *The Power Elite*, explored the close links between military, economic and political power. The phrase has a certain ring of plausibility. The death of the

Soviet Union ended the Cold War threat but it was replaced as a justification for increased military spending by Islamic terrorism.

Analysts have detailed many of the factors that favour the development of military-industrial relationships at the highest level. For example, national security considerations provide a ready excuse for secrecy and the making of private and furtive deals. The need to have weapons that are as good as possible nearly always leads to over-ambitious design and overspending. But the more extravagant claims made by some neo-Marxist authors about the role of the military-industrial complex in the US economy have not been supported by detailed evidence and in recent years a number of steps have been taken to increase transparency and competition in weapons procurement. The term military-industrial complex is, however, widely enough known that it has been adapted for other purposes. For example, the close relationships between national health services and drugs companies have given rise to talk of a medico-industrial complex and such borrowings of the term are likely to continue.

MILL, JOHN STUART (1806–73)   A prolific author and wide-ranging intellectual, Mill is probably the most well-known liberal theorist. Aside from his arguments for liberalism and tolerance, he is of interest to sociology for two main reasons. First, he was concerned with the development of empirical social sciences. He publicised Auguste **Comte**'s work and wrote extensively on the possible methods to be used in the human sciences. For example, he sought to set out the logic for using pairs of case studies to try to identify the causes of social phenomena. Though his classification is quite exhaustive it is not greatly used today. Second, Mill is of continuing interest because of his contribution to **utilitarianism**. He tried to refine this theory of ethics in the face of criticisms levelled at early versions of the doctrine. His refinements are important to the way that utilitarian thinking is used in public policy.

MILLENARIANISM It is a popular belief among Christians that when Christ (the Messiah or saviour; hence messianism) returns, he will usher in a reign of 1000 years (or a millennium) of righteousness before the world ends. The Christian world has seen many millenarian movements. Often triggered by a major social or economic crisis that could be interpreted as a sign of the 'end times', such movements often have serious political overtones. They are critical of the status quo that has either caused the problem or cannot resolve it and they believe that dramatic action will encourage the Messiah to come sooner rather than later.

Millenarian movements can be found in all religious traditions, though they are most common in the **monotheisms** such as Christianity, Islam and Judaism where a creator God made the world and will at some point end it. An Islamic example is the support for the Mahdi in Sudan in 1884–5.

There was a fashion in the 1960s for interpreting such religious upheavals as 'prepolitical' or 'proto-revolutionary'; they were what cultures which had not yet evolved proper politics (or were denied them by their colonial masters) did when they were distressed. In many cases this seems an unwarranted re-writing. It is quite possible to recognise the political roots and consequences of radical religious movements without denying religious ideas and aspirations the central place that the people in question give them.

See **cargo cult**.

MILLENNIALISM AND MILLENNIAL MOVEMENT
See **millenarianism**

MILLS, C. WRIGHT (1916–62) Unusual in early US sociology in being a radical, Mills produced a number of influential works. *White Collar* (1951) examined the characteristics of the US middle class. *The Power Elite* (1956) studied the detailed inter-connections between what he argued were largely self-perpetuating economic, military and political elites. He was a sympathetic commentator on Marxism in *The Marxists* (1962). His best-known work remains *The Sociological Imagination* (1959), still reprinted, in which he criticised most of his colleagues for either **abstracted empiricism** or **grand theory**, both of which had failed the mission of sociology. For Mills, that was to draw out of the connections between personal troubles and social institutions. More of a populist than a clear thinker, Mills is probably best remembered for his demolition of the academic pretension of Talcott **Parsons**. By translating passages of his long-winded prose into simple English, Mills showed its triteness and thus suggested that the entire structural-functional model was merely bad prose disguising shallow thought.

MIMESIS See **mimetic desire**.

MIMETIC DESIRE This term, derived from the literary analysis of René Girard, has been taken up by some psychologists and cultural critics. Girard claims that mimesis or imitation turns out to be a central strategy or motivation for characters in works that have great cultural significance. He thus claims that mimesis is a stronger human motivation than is customarily recognised. His point about mimetic desire is that the things that are sought after are typically desired, not so much for their own sake, as for the sake of enjoying and possessing what another person desires. This speculative idea can be applied to politics, anthropology and even theology.

MIND The mind is our name for the component of humans this is responsible for thinking, willing and consciousness. For nearly 3000 years, thinkers have been aware that there is a problem of the following sort: our body is a physical thing but our mind feels different. We feel that we would still be ourselves if our brain were put in a different body. But it is unclear, as René **Descartes** and many other philosophers have noted, how our mind and body interact. Until comparatively recently, the mind (often thought of as the same as the soul) seemed to be just as real as the body but to exist in a different realm of being. Psychologists and philosophers now mostly reject that view, believing that our consciousness must somehow arise from our body rather than sitting in some parallel dimension giving it orders. But exactly how this works is the leading remaining philosophical and scientific puzzle.

Sociologists do not contribute much to this puzzle directly. However, inspired by work in **ethnomethodology**, numerous commentators have pointed out that we do not even have pure, immediate access to our own minds. Our conception of mind is learned through socialisation and even our inner dialogue with ourselves draws on patterns of interaction that we have acquired from social interaction with others. This supports the observation, famously associated with the philosopher Ludwig **Wittgenstein**, that there cannot be a strictly private language. The mind is more social than common sense would lead us to suspect.

See **Cartesian**.

MIXED ECONOMY   A **free-market** economy is one in which there are very few controls on the production and distribution of goods and services; we say 'very few' because all modern state intervene to some extent. The polar contrast is the **command economy** typical of communist states where the government allocates resources and determines the priorities for production and the price of products. The mixed economy lies between these two extremes: the state takes a role in managing the environment for the free market (by, for example, regulating the quality of foodstuffs), plays some part in manipulating certain forms of production (modern states are the main customers for the arms industry, for example) and provides social welfare to protect people from the full effect of market forces. During the Second World War (1939–45) all states took a major hand in controlling the economy and extensive state intervention remained common until the 1980s when the political pendulum swung decisively back to liberal economics. In many countries this was marked by the selling of (or privatisation) of major state enterprises in power generation, telecommunications, transport, extraction and manufacture.

MODE   See **measures of central tendency**.

MODE OF PRODUCTION   If sociologists had a sense of humour this would denote industrial clothing. Instead Marxists use the term to describe a historically specific combination of **forces of production** and **relations of production**; or the economic basis of work and its social organization. So we have the **feudal mode of production** and the **Asiatic mode of production**.

MODERNISM   This denotes an artistic and cultural movement (1880s–1950s) represented by such figures as Pablo Picasso in painting, James Joyce and T.S. Elliot in literature, Igor Stravinksy in music and the Bauhaus movement in architecture. Modernism marked a confident break with earlier notions of good taste and style. In art and literature, modernist work tended to be deliberately unrealistic and non-representational: words were used in unusual ways and pictures did not look like conventional depictions of their subjects. In architecture, modernism tended to mean machine-like and functional. Buildings were unadorned and starkly attractive. Many modernists were inspired by new technologies, the strength and speed of the industrial age and the availability of new industrial materials; they celebrated the wonders of **modernity**. This is mentioned here only to clarify that **post-modernism** is the 'ism' of the postmodern rather than the 'post' of 'modernism'.

MODERNITY   The term denotes that package of characteristics that define modern societies and distinguish them from early formations. There is some dispute about when we date the onset of modernity but there is widespread agreement about the following list of characteristics: industrial capitalist economies, democratic political organisation and a flexible social structure based on **class**. The implied contrast is with agrarian **feudal** economies which had autocratic polities and a rigid social structure based on **estates**. There is more disagreement about the socio-psychological or cultural correlates of those structural changes but many scholars suggest that modernity involves the **commodification** and **rationalisation** of many spheres of life, a fragmentation of experience, and an acceleration of daily life. Since the 1980s it has been argued by some that contemporary societies have acquired a distinctive **postmodern** quality while others see only a steady intensification of the characteristics of modernity itself. This latter view is sometimes described as 'late' or 'high' modernity.

MODERNISATION   This can mean just the process of becoming modern but it may also refer to the expectation, common in US sociology in the 1950s, that other parts of the world would follow the path taken by the societies of the West: that is, that the changes that created the modern world the first time round would be repeated elsewhere. In the 1960s and 1970s this view was commonly criticized for being unthinkingly **ethnocentric**;

for missing the point that the first countries to modernise did so without the aid (or hindrance) of global powers and a global economy; and for over-looking the negative effects on traditional societies of western-inspired modernisation.

All of these points are well-founded but they do not completely refute the central idea of modernisation theory: that changes come in non-accidentally-related clusters. For example, economic modernisation (increasing division of labour, manufacture for commercial markets, improved technology, professional management) brings with it urbanisation, literacy and a decline in traditional authority. While it may not be necessary for economic modernisation to be accompanied by the growth of representative democratic political institutions, the failure of the Soviet economy suggests that a democratic deficit hinders economic development. This was certainly the view of 1980s reformers such as Mikhail Gorbachev who believed that low productivity was a consequence of mass alienation from the polity and hence that *perestroika* (or restructuring) required *glasnost* (or openness). One positive connection between economic and social aspects of modernisation is revealed in the various editions of the World Values Survey, which find a regular strong correlation between increasing prosperity and increasing individualism.

MONOGAMY, BIGAMY AND POLYGAMY These terms indicate marriage to one, two and many spouses, respectively. Rather quaintly, the USA custom of having many spouses – usually wives – in quick succession is called 'serial monogamy'.

MONOPOLY   This signifies a market for a particular good or service in which one provider so dominates that it is able to control prices (both those it will pay for raw materials and those it can charge for its products). A complete monopoly is the opposite of perfect competition. Monopolies are most common when the state is the provider. Social research has indicated that monopolies are not always undesirable. For example, in Britain, radio broadcasting is virtually a monopoly run by the BBC and yet the quality of the services is agreed to be very high.

MONOTHEISM　　This denotes a belief in the uniqueness of God and identifies those religions that have a single creator God (which are principally Judaism, Christianity and Islam). Whether a religion has one or many Gods (polytheism) has important sociological consequences. For example, states in which a monotheistic religion is dominant are more likely than those with polytheistic religions to demand religious conformity.

MORAL CAREER　　In *Stigma* (1963b), Erving **Goffman** used the term to refer to the changes in character imputed to those who were stigmatised. It is a feature of some labelling processes that those doing the labelling (and the labellee in some circumstances) do not stop at diagnosing the person's current condition but also retrospectively re-construct the entire biography to find signs of incipient deviance.

MORAL CRUSADE　　This term was popularised by Joseph Gusfield's study of temperance crusades in the USA at the end of the 19th and start of the 20th century. It has since been used of campaigns to mobilise popular sentiment (and usually legislation) against a variety of putative social ills: pornography, abortion, divorce, homosexuality and recreational drug use are all examples. The term is accurate in that such campaigns are always driven by strongly held moral views but it is worth noting that most such campaigns attempt to win the support of people who do not share the religious or moral sentiments of the core by adding other arguments (such as those of human rights or social benefit). Particularly in the USA, where the Supreme Court has maintained a preference for the defence of individual liberties, groups that believe homosexuality to be sinful, for example, have been forced to campaign on the grounds that it is socially harmful.

On the not-entirely-sound grounds that the sociological observer does not think such campaigns will achieve their stated aims, the apparent goal-orientation of members is often treated as a cover for something less honourable. For example, recruitment to such movements has often been explained in terms of some need or deficiency in those who become involved. Gusfield, for example, argued that the temperance crusade was really a form of **status** defence. Those involved were re-directing what was really a concern for the loss of status of the small-town Protestant middle class onto one particular aspect of the behaviour of those they resented: that is, the cultural conflict was actually a surrogate for an underlying contest for social power.

See **status inconsistency**.

MORAL ENTREPRENEURS　　Howard S. **Becker** used this term to describe those people and agencies that made the rules, the infraction of which constituted deviance, and which label deviants. The phrase is a telling one because it reminds us that crime and deviance are not of themselves characteristics of actions (as wetness is a feature of water) but are social definitions placed on certain actions. Hence, if we are to have a rounded understanding of crime and deviance we need to study and explain not only the actions of the criminals and the deviants but also those of the agents who create and maintain the definitional framework. Although some definitions require little work to be sustained (for example, in almost all times and places an unprovoked violent assault is a crime), many regularly shift and 'entrepreneurism' neatly expresses the innovative work that is done in shifting those definitions. An example of recent entrepreneurship is the feminist success in having domestic violence re-classified from a private matter to a serious crime.

MORAL PANIC British sociologist Stanley Cohen (1972) used this phrase in his *Folk Devils and Moral Panics* to describe an exaggerated mass media-led social reaction to what were initially minor acts of social deviance: in this case gangs of youths (identified by style as either Mods or Rockers) staging minor scuffles at seaside resorts. Far from ending the disturbances, the over-reaction in **labelling** had the effect of attracting greater numbers.

Given that an appropriate response is never described as a 'panic', the phrase conveys that the societal reaction is unwarranted by the scale of the problem. It further suggests that the real explanation of the negative response lies in other interests (conscious or unconscious) of those construing the moral panic. Those interests could be a desire to heighten social solidarity (as in Durkheim's functionalist explanation of **deviance**) or, in the radical version, to distract attention from some problem which the government, the mass media, or the ruling class does not wish to address.

While it is patently useful, the idea of moral panic needs to be applied cautiously. What looks like over-reaction to a distant observer may seem perfectly appropriate to those involved in labelling and hence their actions may need no further explanation.

MORAL STATISTICS One of the precursors of sociology as an academic discipline was the collection of data on social problems

such as illegitimacy, suicide, crime, alcohol consumption and divorce. In 19th-century France such data collection was called 'moral statistics'.

MORBIDITY RATE This is the incidence of a certain disease or disorder in a population, generally expressed as the rate per 100,000 population in one year.

MORES Now rather old-fashioned, this is a useful term for shared rules of behaviour that a society, community or social group strongly supports. In his *Folkways* (1906), William G. Sumner distinguished between mores and folkways. The latter were less fundamental and more specific and offending against them was not a serious matter. Mores might now be called ethical principles and folkways would be conventions.

MORPHOGENESIS Another term borrowed from the biological sciences, morphogenesis is the process though which living things and their component parts develop organised structures. It is the process through which a zebra hide grows its stripes or through which a foetus develops into a child. It is a complex and as yet rather poorly developed aspect of biology although an issue of unquestionable importance. This term is used by **Deleuze** and Guatarri as a way of distinguishing between futures that are open and ones that, even if they appear open, are pre-determined. Morphogenesis appeals to them as a term because, however complex the process that leads from an egg to a chick, it is in some sense pre-given.

Ironically the term is also used by the British sociologist Margaret Archer for an almost opposite purpose. Archer, a **realist** social theorist, is keen to reassert the importance of practical engagement with the world as a key aspect of socialisation and social development. She adopts the term morphogenesis to refer to social action that leads to transformation and not just to the reproduction of social patterns. Just as biological morphogenesis transforms the egg into a chick so certain forms of social action have transformative power.

MORTIFICATION OF THE SELF   This term is used by Erving **Goffman** in his account of **total institutions** such as boarding schools, monasteries, psychiatric hospitals, prisons and army training camps that isolate their members from the wider society. Most total institutions are total because they have the specific aim of bringing about a fundamental change in the personalities of inmates. In the case of prisons, the isolation is punishment but in monasteries, for example, it is intended to make it easier to eradicate the old self and create a new one. That process often begins with what Goffman called 'mortifications of the self'. As a preliminary to learning the new self, the old self is undermined through such rituals as shaving of the head, the removal and destruction of old clothes, showering with disinfectant, the removal of all possessions and even the removal of the former name.

MOSCA, GAETANO (1858–1941)   Along with Robert **Michels** and Vilfredo **Pareto**, this Italian political scientist is regarded as one of the founders of **elite theory**. He believed that all societies consisted of two classes: the rulers and the ruled, which might seem like stating the obvious, except that he meant that it would always be so. Mosca regarded many of the justifications that were offered in various political systems as merely rationalisations for the exercise of power. He was not blind to the distinction between regimes based on some form of elected leadership and autocracies but he did argue that real democracy in the sense of government by the people or majority rule was impossible. Because he is now little read, Mosca is often presented as an advocate of autocracy. He

might be better described as preferring the realistic prospect of government by representative elites to unrealisable hopes of participatory or primitive democracy.

MULTICULTURALISM   In the 1960s the progressive attitude to immigrants was that they should be given every opportunity to become like everybody else: to become fully integrated and absorbed into the society they wished to join. Since the time of Napoleon, the French, for example, have tried to create an homogenous people with a single unified culture; racism is bad because, on the grounds of skin colour or origins, it denied some people the right to be properly French. Although the USA, where the vast majority of citizens are descended from recent immigrants, has generally been more tolerant of a degree of leisure diversity, diversity was generally still seen as a symptom of a problem. Nathan Glazer and Daniel P. Moynihan's (1963) classic *Beyond the Melting Pot* and Glazer's (1975) subsequent *Affirmative Discrimination* assumed that every ethnic group started in some sort of enclave or **ghetto** and then moved upwards and outwards. Provided legally sanctioned discrimination in housing and employment was ended then the ghetto would disappear. Diverse peoples would blend into a single if somewhat lumpy substance.

Since the 1980s, there has been a steady shift in progressive thinking, driven largely by spokespersons for ethnic and racial minorities, so that assimilation is now seen not as fair but as oppressive. Encouraging minorities to lose what is distinctive in order to merge with the dominant culture is now regarded as an infringement of human rights. People also noted the irony that white communities generally never assimilated where they went. Multiculturalism means both the acknowledgement of cultural pluralism and the promotion of a political climate in which the maintenance of diversity is encouraged.

Forty years after *Melting Pot*, Glazer (1998) published *We're All Multiculturalists*

Now in which he accepted multiculturalism as the necessary price the USA had to pay for its inability or unwillingness to incorporate African-Americans into its society in the 'same way and to the same degree it has incorporated so many groups'.

MULTIVARIATE ANALYSIS   In the simplest forms of statistical analysis we might look at just a single variable (e.g. how many people like cabbage?) or at two variables (e.g. what is the relationship between age and alcohol consumption?). Social reality is often complex, however, and most interesting problems require us to look at a number of variables at once. The term 'multivariate analysis' refers to a variety of techniques available for this purpose.

One reason for using multiple variables is simply to reflect reality; if we tried to analyse voting behaviour using information on religion and gender but not income and education, for example, our study would be incomplete. Furthermore it is often the case that certain characteristics are associated with each other in the cases we are studying, and if we leave out one (e.g. income) it could distort the apparent effect of the other (e.g. gender).

Variables may be related to each other in complicated ways. To invent an example, it could be that both independent variables 'income' and 'working for the public sector' are correlated with the dependent variable 'voting for the left' so that poorer people and those who work for the state are more likely to vote left than rich people and people who work in private companies. But income may have an indirect and complex effect so that, as it increases, it influences public and private sector workers in opposite directions. Better paid public sector workers may be more likely to vote for the left (because their increased security makes them more generous) while better paid private sector workers are reinforced in their free-market philosophy. There are a variety of statistical techniques which explore such interaction effects.

MYTH   The common use of myth to mean a story which is untrue makes an essence out of what for scholars is an accidental feature. Myths are not by definition untrue. Rather, they are religious or sacred folktales which explain the origins of the world, a people, a God or some social practice (such as a way of hunting). Because we have often been interested in the social functions that myths perform (and because we know that a God coupling with a swan cannot produce a human) we tend not to take the content of myths at face-value; this rather tends to imply that those people who appear to believe in them cannot be entirely serious. It is worth stressing that shared beliefs can only have **latent functions** if they are actually believed. Hence we cannot expect those whose ritual actions support certain myths to be as sceptical about them as is the observer.

Social scientific interest in myths has concentrated on what they can tell us about the central values of the peoples who hold them; about the perennial psychological and social tensions they express; and about the underlying structure of the human mind that might be discerned through their analysis. The general problem with the interpretation of myths is the same as that for dreams: there is no limit to the competing interpretations that can be generated and no way of knowing which of the diverse alternatives is correct. Hence we can do literary criticism with myths but it is hard to see how we do social science.

See **Lévi-Strauss, structuralism**.

NARCISSISM Narcissus was a figure in Greek mythology who fell in love with his own image in a pool and was punished by falling in and drowning. Narcissism is thus self-love, self-regard or self-absorption to an extent that is self-destructive. The term is used in various forms of psychoanalysis, and in child psychology where it describes an early stage in human development. In *The Culture of Narcissism*, Christopher Lasch (1991) argued that features of modern societies make it difficult for people to develop beyond the stage of alternating between exaggerated self-regard and self-loathing. More generally, the pronounced contemporary interest in fitness, health and bodily appearance has been taken as a sign of widespread narcissism.

NATION, NATION-STATE A nation is commonly described as a 'community of sentiment' (Max **Weber**'s phrase) or as an 'imagined community', as Benedict Anderson put it. The basis for that community is one or more of the following: **race, ethnicity, language,** customs, **religion** and political memory. The nation is 'imagined' in the sense that no member can ever have real relationships with all or even many of the other members (especially not with the previous generations, a vital part of the nation). Nationalists (that is, people who either assert the fact of a nation or advance its interests) see the nation as an objective reality with a long history and clear identity; their job is merely to unearth what

may be hidden. In contrast, social scientists stress the modern and socially constructed nature of the nation. Ernest Gellner argued that nationalists do not discover the nation so much as create it in response to social needs that arise at a particular stage in social development. While not disagreeing with Gellner's key point, scholars such as Anthony Smith qualify it by arguing that although pre-existing (or 'primordial') characteristics are not by themselves sufficient to create a nation (we can, for example, think of racial, ethnic, linguistic or religious communities that have failed to construe themselves as nations) they are often relevant. Major racial, ethnic, linguistic and religious divisions do not entirely prevent the development of national identity (Switzerland, for example, is internally divided by language and religion) but they make the nation harder to construct.

It is possible for nations to retain a sense of identity without a **state** (modern examples would be the Scots or the Kurds: the former enveloped within the British state, the latter divided between Turkey, Iraq and Iran). But the idea that a population which defines itself as a nation deserves to be ruled by its own people is a basic assumption of modern politics and the right to national self-determination is enshrined in the charter of the United Nations.

Social scientists commonly distinguish between ethnic and civic nations. The ethnic nation is what most people have in mind when they use the term: it is a population that claims descent from common ancestors, which shares a common culture, and which expects newcomers to assimilate to that culture. The alternative civic model regards as a nation all people (irrespective of their culture or origins) who inhabit a land mass and show common allegiance to a political unit: what is required is loyalty, not similarity. Although **nativism** is periodically expressed in movement which assert an ethnic core to the USA and wish to give pride of place to the culture of white Anglo-Saxon Protestants (hence 'WASP'), the USA offers a remarkably resilient example of a civic nation.

With religion (and the two often go together) the nation represents the major failure of 20th-century sociology. For different reasons, sociologists of the left and of the right expected that the nation, claiming allegiance to a romantic idea, would decline in significance as the real interests of social class challenged the nation from within and increasing international co-operation (what we would now call **globalisation**) weakened it from the outside. Instead, one of the main carriers of internationalism – communism – collapsed and the Soviet Union was replaced by a large number of putative ethnic nations. A simple measure of the resilience of the nation is the composition of the United Nations. At its foundation in 1945 it had 51 members. In 2004 it had 191.

NATIONAL SOCIALISM, NAZISM This is the body of doctrines associated with the National Socialist German Workers' Party, the political vehicle for the rise to power of Adolf Hitler in the 1930s. 'Socialist' is misleading; although he was a **populist**, Hitler was firmly opposed to class-based politics and to communism. He was, however, a nationalist who believed that true Germans shared a biological racial superiority.

NATIONALISM This denotes both the political programme of nationalists and the dynamic behind the modern formation of nations. There are good evolutionary reasons why modernisation is closely associated with the creation of nations. An economy built on commercial manufacture requires a large market, enforceable laws, an effect medium of exchange, a common language and a reasonably common culture. The old feudal village was far too small for a commercial economy; the multi-ethnic kingdom or empire too large and diverse to attract sentimental attachment. Hence as the commercial economy and the accompanying government structures developed, so too did a sense of common identity within the most advanced territories. There was also a reactive element to the process; peripheral populations which felt themselves left behind could generate nationalisms of grievance.

The West exported nationalism in three senses. First, that the West was organised in nations was taken by others as a model to be emulated. Second, in dealing with foreign peoples, representatives of western powers often assumed that they too formed nations. Where the imperial powers found that there was nothing resembling a nation already in place, they tended to create them by drawing lines on a map. Third, when colonised peoples began to organise either to improve the terms of their incorporation in empires or to win their freedom, they constructed their claims around the rights of nations to independence. In Africa and Asia, 20th-century anti-colonial movements often presented themselves as movements for 'national' liberation even when (for example, in Angola or India) the people patently lacked the cultural cohesion required by nationalist myths or the economic coherence that gave 18th-century European nation-formation its impetus.

NATIVISM This denotes a political sentiment that opposes immigration on the grounds that it threatens the identity and virtues of the current majority population (which sees itself as **indigenous**). In the USA in the 1850s the American party elected over 100 congressmen on a platform to restrict or prevent further immigration, especially from southern European Catholic countries and to curb the power of Catholics and other recent immigrants. An interesting feature of nativism is that it frequently regroups so that a one-time target population can later become part of the nativist block trying to obstruct the next wave of immigrants. A century after they were the target, many Catholics in the USA actively opposed Asian immigration. Although the term is mainly used for US politics, similar processes can be charted for other countries such as Australia and New Zealand.

NATURAL SELECTION   The modern scientific view is that **evolution** occurs through natural selection. Genetic variations are produced by chance and genetic dispositions that confer an advantage in survival and reproduction are naturally perpetuated by being passed on to the next generation. In this way, advantageous attributes are selected and 'blind' nature can seem to introduce design and purpose into the evolution of living creatures. Natural selection is contrasted with human selection, the latter referring to the process by which breeds of dog or horse or rice have been developed by human breeders who deliberately cross individuals with the desired characteristics in the hope of producing more specialised domestic animals or food crops, and so on. In contemporary human societies the impact of natural selection is extremely limited since we use technologies, medicines and care-giving to save individuals from selectional pressure. For example, without glasses and the eye-care industry most academics would be reduced to hopeless non-productivity by early middle age. Nonetheless the idea of natural selection is commonly used in a metaphorical way in the social sciences. For instance, we may say that governments encourage small businesses to set up and the successful ones are judged by 'natural selection' in the market.

NATURE   Social scientists have struggled with the idea of nature because there is something paradoxical about it. Humans are clearly natural. We arose through natural selection and we have natural needs: for oxygen to breathe and water to drink. On the other hand, humans invented the concept of nature and have often used it to distinguish between things in their wild state and things associated with civilization. Humans are both inside and outside of nature.

Precisely because of this paradoxical quality, there is no single definition of nature; it is an **essentially contested concept**. Nonetheless, in western cultures, nature is typically understood as meaning the way the world would be without human interference. Thus nature reserves are areas set aside and shielded from modern development, where only traditional land-management practices are typically allowed. Some highly prized natural environments do appear extremely natural in this sense. The Grand Canyon, for example, was formed before humans had much power to alter the landscape. But other valued landscapes, such as the Douro valley in Portugal, have arisen from intensive human management; in the Douro case for the cultivation of grapes for Port production. In such instances, traditional social practices become classified as part of the natural.

Recently, many commentators have begun to speak of the 'end of nature' suggesting thereby that there is nowhere left on earth that is unaffected by the effects of industrial society. Even the Antarctic ice contains the residue of factory emissions, and global warming is slowly changing ecosystems the world over. With the potential for medical scientists to manipulate human genetic transmission, the characteristics of new-born babies may soon no longer be the result of natural chance. In a sense, humans may soon have ended nature as a separate realm.

The close relationship between humans and their natural environment has meant that the natural world has commonly be seen as rich in meaning. Anthropologists, most famously the British social anthropologist Mary Douglas, have made extensive studies of the role of natural symbols. Contemporary environmental concerns even in industrial societies still retain a strong symbolic component.

See **geneticisation, human nature.**

NATURE–NURTURE DEBATE To what extent human behaviour is a result of inherited and innate influences (nature) or a consequence of our environment and learning (nurture) remains a live argument, made difficult to resolve finally in many particular cases by our inability to examine either force in isolation. Humans are part of the natural world by virtue of having bodies and yet they also inhabit a cultural world constructed by language. We can try quasi-experiments such as comparing the lives of identical twins (who share the same genetic make-up) separated at a young age, but even this does not settle the debate because most models of genetic causation suppose that biology supplies only an enhanced potential and that differences in environment will affect how that potential is realised. For example, it may well be that the psychological illness of depression has a major genetic component and that people naturally differ in their innate potential to become clinically depressed; nevertheless differences in life circumstances will explain why that potential is realised in some cases but remains dormant in others.

The resolution of the nature–nurture debate is also hindered by the political interests at stake. Conservatives tend to seize on evidence for innate variations to demonstrate that inequality in society is natural and unavoidable, while those on the left emphasise any studies that show strong environmental influences. Tussles between right and left are sadly often conducted without reference to the advances in the understanding of **heredity**.

NAZISM See **National Socialism**.

NEEDS Needs are often invoked to explain human behaviour but there is little agreement on what needs we have beyond the purely physiological ones of food, sleep and shelter. Move to anything more complex (such as sexual gratification or a desire for achievement) and we find considerable cultural variation in how such putative needs are expressed and met. A recurrent theme of **critical sociology** is the claim that capitalism creates 'false' needs, the satisfaction of which distracts people from what, in the eyes of the analysts, they should be doing. The difficulty with this is that all needs beyond the basic physiological ones seem to be stimulated by agents and systems designed to meet the desires created. For example, we can describe religion as meeting basic spiritual needs but it is equally plausible to regard such needs as a function of religious socialisation. If almost all needs are socially created there seems no objective ground for dismissing some as false.

The idea of needs is also central to **functionalism** where the biological metaphor is applied to societies. Talcott **Parsons** believed that social systems had four basic needs or functional imperatives, which had to be met if they were to survive. These mapped on to the four sub-systems: economic, political, motivational and integrative.

NEGOTIATED ORDER Sociological work on such elements of the social world as organisations and institutions is intended to draw attention to the fluidity and uncertainty of social arrangements and to the fact that even in the most oppressive organisations, order is only sustained by constant negotiation between the parties involved. The orderliness of the organisation is produced through the interactions of its members. It is important to note that nothing in the phrase implies that all parties to the negotiations are equally powerful. That is, appreciating the negotiated nature of social orders does not preclude recognising differences between genders, classes, ethnic groups or individuals in the resources they bring to negotiations.

NEGRI, ANTONIO (1933–)   The publication of *Empire* (Hardt and Negri, 2000) brought Negri worldwide recognition as a postmodern Marxist political theorist. A professor of social theory at the University of Padua in the early 1960s, Negri departed from communist orthodoxy in criticising not just alienated labour but Marx's high notion of the virtue of labour; he argued that workers needed to liberate themselves from work itself. He was active in a variety of Italian extreme left-wing organisations, an involvement that led to his arrest in 1979. He was charged with 'armed insurrection against the powers of the state'. When elected to parliament for the Radical party in 1983 he was released from prison; after his immunity was revoked, he fled to France where he became part of an intellectual circle that included **Foucault, Deleuze** and **Guattari.** He returned to Italy in 1997 where he served a number of years in a very open prison and worked on *Empire*; he was released in 2003.

Empire, an obscure and rambling work, is extremely difficult to summarise but 'postmodern Marxism' is not far from the mark, though it shares Frederic **Jameson**'s critical attitude to the more extreme claims of postmodernism. It argues that capitalism is producing a new form of 'immaterial' labour that transcends the old binary divide of labour and capital and creates an opportunity for a new form of 'spontaneous and elementary communism'. Productivity no longer comes from the regulation of the 'multitude' (the new word for masses) but from the 'productive synergy of the multitude'. Globalisation reconfigures sovereignty: the nation-state is doomed. The empire of the title is not an American imperium but a de-territorialised entity – the status of which is anything but clear. What is clear is that Negri and Hardt believe that the new economic order is vulnerable to a counter-empire: a multitude composed of all those who do not benefit from economic globalisation. Thus the old roll call of **new social movements** (environmentalists, antiglobalisation campaigners, feminists) is read and augmented with workers from the First and Third Worlds.

Empire is not social science: it is prophecy and polemic made impressive only by the obscurity of its prose. If specific propositions are closely interrogated their vacuity is obvious. For example, there is a marvellous-sounding claim that 'The cities of the earth will become at once great deposits of co-operating humanity and locomotives for circulation, temporary residences and networks of the mass distribution of living humanity – an end to borders and nations'. But there is no evidence at all that either nationalism as a sentiment or borders as political realities are weakening.

Finally it is worth noting that Negri has not given up his fondness (in rhetoric at least) for political violence. The victory of the 'the new barbarians' of the multitude will be brought about by 'affirmative violence'.

NEO-COLONIALISM   During the 20th century the western imperial powers gave up their overseas possessions because they were threatened by local liberation movements, because the costs of maintaining control were too high and because the racism inherent in according democratic rights to their home people while denying them to those they controlled in other lands became politically unacceptable. However, in many cases the former colonial powers retained considerable economic influence over their former possessions. This indirect control is one of the social forces described as neo-colonialism. The term is also used to describe the global economic power of trans-national corporations. Additionally, it is also used to describe the global power of the USA, which has often tried to exercise remote control over vital interests abroad.

NEO-EVOLUTIONISM   In the 20th century several sociologists tried to improve on older ideas of societal **evolution** by making use of Darwinian theories from biology. The older approach tended to see the evolution of society as the simple unfolding of an inevitable development plan. Neo-evolutionists tried to improve on this by using Darwinian ideas about adaptation, selection and competition. For example, in his theory of **evolutionary universals**, Talcott **Parsons** tried to suggest how societal differentiation could be seen as a process of evolutionary adaptation. More recently the British social theorist W.G. Runciman has argued for an **evolutionary sociology** based on the adaptation and survival of what he calls 'practices'. Neo- evolutionism is not a school of sociology; rather it is a common strategy taken up in slightly differing ways in many locations.

NEPOTISM   See **kinship**.

NETWORK   The term refers to the patterns in which individuals (and sometimes social roles) are connected by kinship and friendship bonds or by more specialised ties. The tracing of networks was a crucial part of **sociometry**. In the 1960s the analysis of social networks was heavily influenced by the mathematical sociology of Harrison

White and became sufficiently specialised to support its own journal: *Social Networks*.

There are three main types of network analysis. Egocentric network analysis concentrates on the network as seen from the position of one individual. Systemic networks are constructed from all the participants in a network and concentrate on the network itself; an example is Mark **Granovetter**'s work on job-finding. Then there are studies of **diffusion,** which concentrate on the flow of new ideas, illnesses, and information through networks.

Since the invention of the Internet, 'network' has frequently became the preferred metaphor for new forms of social organisations that are expected to supersede institutions (such as the nation-state) rooted in a particular place.

NETWORK SOCIETY   See **information society.**

NEUTRALISATION   People who behave in ways which they know to be unacceptable often attempt to neutralise the expected condemnation of their actions. While some career criminals will admit to not caring what others think of them, many rule-breakers feel obliged to pre-empt criticism (either from others or from their own internalised version of the dominant values). Among the commonest ways of neutralising are denying responsibility (it wasn't me that attacked that child: it was the drink); denying the injury (the insurance company will pay him back); blaming the victim (she was asking for it); and condemning those who would judge (he's no better than me; I bet he fiddles his taxes).

NEW AGE MOVEMENT   In the last two decades of the 20th century there was considerable interest in the West in a wide variety of spiritual exercises, therapies, revelations and forms of 'alternative' scientific and medical ideas. Much of the borrowing of eastern ideas was shallow and trivial. For example, the

Chinese form of necromancy ('the manipulation of the dead') Feng Sui was so bastardised that it was reduced to a minimalist interior decorating style. Central to New Age spirituality are a relativistic **epistemology** (if something works for you then it is true) and a therapeutic ethos (becoming happier, healthier and wealthier are no longer accidental by-products of correctly worshipping God; they are the main point). The movement (a term that suggests a misleading degree of cohesion and organisation) is called 'New Age' because, although many of its core adherents share a romantic critique of some aspects of industrial capitalism, there is also a profound optimism that comes from the astrological claim that the world is now entering an 'Age of Aquarius': a time when people will be able to access and harness positive cosmic energy for the good of mankind.

In many senses the New Age is well suited to the modern world. Despite its language of community, it is thoroughly individualistic; there is no authority higher than the individual. It is organised as a form of consumerism: instead of becoming loyal followers of a religion, people pay for services, revelations, products and ideas and thus determine their own levels of involvement. And its relativism fits well with cultural diversity: there is no need to argue. However, the New Age has not filled the role of replacing the declining Christian churches that some analysts gave it. Although the ideas most concerned with well-being have become widely diffused, it has attracted relatively little serious support for its more spiritual elements and it is drawn from a narrow social base: primarily university-educated middle-class white women.

divided examples according to their basic attitude to the prevailing culture. World-rejecting movements (such as Hare Krishna, the Divine Light Mission and the Moonies or Unification Church) are puritanical and ascetic. Members are expected to give up a great deal for their beliefs, which focus on preparation for the next life. Very different are world-affirming movements (such as Scientology and a variety of quasi-religious psychotherapies such as est) which offer therapies and revelations intended to make people more successful in the world.

The fate of NRMs in the West is important for testing some versions of the claim that people are essentially or inherently religious. There is an argument that the simple fact that we are mortal and intelligent causes us to ask such as questions as 'what is the meaning of life?' and 'what happens after death?' If humans are naturally predisposed to be religious then **secularisation** is not possible. It should be the case that, as the mainstream Christian churches have declined in the West, something else should arise to fill the gap. This may yet happen but none of the NRMs of the 1960s made serious inroads into the very large number of people in modern societies who are not actively involved in mainstream religion. Exotic NRMs attract a great deal of media interest (largely because they are suspected by some of brainwashing recruits) but they are numerically trivial. In Britain in the 1980s the entire membership of all the major NRMs was less than the members who left the Church of England in a week.

See **conversion.**

NEW RELIGIOUS MOVEMENT (NRM)   The passage of time eventually makes any 'new' label inaccurate but this term for a variety of cults and sects founded (or taking off) in the late 1960s has stuck. Following Max Weber's comparative approach to religions, Roy Wallis

NEW RIGHT   This term is used for a variety of right-wing thinkers and organisations of the late 20th century that rejected aspects of the conservatism that dominated most modern polities from the 1950s to the 1980s. The New Right argues that the welfare state, far from aiding the poorest sections of the population, actually creates an **underclass** of people who are perpetually dependent on state welfare. New Rightists are economic liberals (they want to reduce state interference in the economy) and social conservatives (they also want the state to more aggressively enforce such conservative social and moral positions as banning abortion and homosexuality.

NEW SOCIAL MOVEMENT (NSM) The term was developed by French sociologist Alain **Touraine** in 1975 and Italian sociologist Alberto **Melucci** in 1980. What is 'new' about movements to promote gay rights, women's rights and human rights and campaigns to protect the environment or constrain globalisation is that, unlike the key actors in the politics of the first two-thirds of the 20th century, they are not primarily constructed around social class or concerned with economic redistribution. Nor are they interest groups, in that they generally have quite broad agendas and act outside the political mainstream. Although he did not use the term, Herbert **Marcuse** was one of the first Marxists to admit that the working class was not going to lead the revolution and hence that the potential for revolutionary change had to be found elsewhere. This role is now given to a variety of loose and shifting campaigns.

The radical expectation (expressed for example by Antonio **Negri**) is misplaced. The most stable and influential elements of new social movements generally use the conventional methods of interest group politics. Most supporters are middle class and are concerned with reformist change of some small part of the world. The radical element, like that of the 1960s student movement, is tiny and involvement is short-lived.

NGOs This acronym for 'non-governmental organisations' describes groups such as Oxfam, PETA (People for the Ethical Treatment of Animals), the Sierra Club and Greenpeace, which now perform a variety of important national and sometimes international civil society functions. Poverty relief agencies may, for example, try to influence governments, lobby politicians, inform and mobilise public opinion and work in the field. One important value of NGOs is that they may be able to operate in countries or regions where political sensitivies would prevent donor governments assisting directly.

NIETZSCHE, FRIEDRICH (1843–1900) An iconoclastic German philosopher who famously announced that God is dead, Nietzsche was concerned with the possibility of purpose and ethical integrity once humans admit to themselves that they are alone in the world and that they bear sole responsibility for morality and meaning. Unlike most of his predecessors (including **Kant**) who had tried to spell out a human-centred ethical theory, Nietzsche did not accept that there must be a universal morality which is applicable to everyone. He argued that strong noble leaders should not be judged according to the same standards as 'everyman'. Such a view led him to be suspicious of democracy. He was concerned that the democratic privileging of the average would grant power to a creature with desire and reason but no heroic vision to rise above the satisfaction of ordinary wants. Nietzsche's critique of the universalistic assumptions of Enlightenment thought has been influential on Michel **Foucault** and on **postmodern** authors generally.

NOMADS This term describes any people with no fixed residence who move from place to place in search of food, water or pasture for their animals; the Bedouin of North Africa are an example. It in also used in some postmodern analysis of the contemporary condition to depict the rootlessness that is thought to result from globalisation.

NOMENKLATURA   Originally this described those people whose names (hence 'nomen') were on lists of acceptable candidates for office in the communist parties and related organs of communist states in Eastern Europe. It came to mean more generally those people in communist states who exercised considerable power and enjoyed a privileged life because of their positions in the state bureaucracies; that is, it denoted the ruling class of supposedly class-less communist societies. When communism collapsed in the late 1980s many members of the nomenklatura were able to use their political positions to acquire privatised state assets at knock-down prices and thus became the capitalists of the new economic system.

NOMOTHETIC See **idiographic**.

NON-PARAMETRIC STATISTICS   Many of the statistical tests used in the social sciences assume a basic orderliness to the data being analysed. Observations that follow a **normal distribution** (such as the weights of 200 randomly selected adults) are parametric in that they can be encompassed by general statistical assertions. In this case knowing the mean and the deviation will (like knowing the centre of a circle and its radius) fix all the observations. However, much social science data is not parametric (for example, it may be categorical, as in a listing of political parties voted for) and it is important that appropriate statistical tests (such as the Mann–Whitney U test of **significance**) be used for non-parametric data.

See **measurement, levels of.**

NON-RESPONSE   This describes the fact that in any form of social investigation some of our target population will choose not to be studied or be unavailable (because they have died or moved). Some people will decline to be interviewed on the phone or refuse to complete and return the postal questionnaire. Non-response rates vary with the nature of the target population, the research instrument, the research topic and the effort that is required to respond. There are no hard rules but a non-response rate of more than 25 per cent must raise questions about how representative the responses will be. When the nature or cause of non-response is clear, the data that has been collected can be manipulated to compensate to some degree. For example, if we know that most of the non-responders to a survey are young people, we can multiply the responses we do get from young people to bring them up to the appropriate proportion (even though we may worry that there is some important difference between those young people who answered and those who refused). A small amount of such weighting is common in large surveys; too much of it calls into question the value of analysis.

Social scientists are becoming increasingly concerned that modern societies have an **underclass** of people whose mobility and inability or unwillingness to engage with government agencies means that they are overlooked in much social research. Among techniques being developed to try to solve this problem is physical area sampling, where researchers take a block of a town or city and engage the attention of all the people they find in it.

NORMAL DISTRIBUTION   In statistics, the term 'normal' is the adjective from 'norm' and means the most common. The normal distribution provides a hypothetical benchmark which serves to tell us, by contrast, when something unusual or interesting is going on. If we construct a graph for the height of 100 women, where the X axis shows height and the Y axis the number of cases, we will find the data shows a fairly smooth curve with most people bunched in the middle and the numbers falling away to either side. Such a curve looks approximately like a bell, hence the expression 'bell curve'.

NORMAL SCIENCE   This term was introduced by the historian and philosopher of science Thomas **Kuhn** to emphasise that the majority of scientific activity is not expected to make enormous breakthroughs or to overthrow established ways of thinking. On the contrary, most scientific research, even by leading scientists, is conducted within an established framework. For example, after the atomic theory was introduced into chemistry around the end of the 18th century, leading scientists were engaged in discovering new elements. They did not question the overall theory; they were working to create innovative findings within it. This, says Kuhn, is the normal state of affairs. Scientists work within a framework (which he terms a '**paradigm**') often using the exemplary achievements of earlier scientists as a rough template for their activities. Findings that fail to fit the paradigm are explained away or set aside as anomalies to be investigated later on. Occasionally a whole new way of viewing phenomena is introduced and normal science is overthrown in a scientific revolution before the new paradigm settles down and normal science – this time within the newer paradigm – commences once again.

NORMALIZATION   Because most probability statistics start by assuming a normal distribution of the data and identify the extent of deviation from it, statisticians sometimes have to massage data that is not normally distributed. For example, it is inappropriate to use most common statistical tests in studying the effects of urbanisation (say, on churchgoing) in England because London is so much larger than other English cities. If we are not to leave London out altogether then some normalising technique is required before the analysis can begin. One common way of making data sets more amenable to analysis is to use the logarithms of values rather than the values themselves.

NORMATIVE ORDER   This denotes any system of rules and shared expectations governing a particular social situation or institution. It can be as small and as limited as the interaction orders studied by Erving **Goffman**; an example would be the implicit rules about spacing and eye-contact that govern sharing a crowded lift or elevator. It can be as large, complex and far-reaching as the normative order that Talcott **Parsons** takes to be central to the maintenance of society.

NORMATIVE THEORY   Most sociologists regard their task as description and explanation, not moral evaluation. For example, we try to explain the rise of nationalism. We do not also campaign for or against nationalism. Or, to be more precise, we may do so as citizens but not in our roles as sociologists. Normative theory is that sort of social science that explicitly pronounces on what is good, just and desirable. That is, it is prescriptive and proscriptive: it passes value judgements. Most sociologists avoid normative theory, not because we are moral cowards but because there are no factual tests of moral pronouncements. Sociology does not provide any methods for settling arguments about how people should live.

There are two school of thought on the margins of sociology that reject this value agnosticism. One is Marxism, which claims to be both scientific and normative. The other is postmodernism which denies the **fact–value distinction** but it does so to quite the opposite effect of Marxism. It denies that value-neutral social science is possible; hence all we have are alternative moralities.

Although the core of the discipline avoids explicit normative judgements, we should recognise that implicit judgements may appear at every level; from the initial framing of research problems to the interpretation of results.

See **objectivity, value-freedom**.

NORMS   These are the rules that govern social behaviour and are enforced by positive or negative sanctions (i.e. rewards and punishments). They are the embodiment of **values**.

NUCLEAR FAMILY See **family**.

NULL HYPOTHESIS   This is a fancy term for the clear statement of 'nothing is going on' that is often used in formal research to provide a bench mark against which we identify interesting correlations. For example, in embarking on analysis of earnings and ethnicity data we might begin by stating the null hypothesis that 'There is no significant correlation between earnings and ethnic identity' and then present the results in terms of whether that hypothesis is sustained or refuted. In statistics the null hypothesis will include an element of leeway for random sampling error; only if the correlation is greater than that expected once due allowance is made for background 'noise' will the results be described as significant and the null hypothesis explicitly rejected.

0

OBJECTIVITY   This is the characteristic of being 'objective'. We start with an 'object': something (such as the brick on which I trip) that exists independently of our perceptions. This gives us two related senses of 'objective': the characteristic of brickness and our perception of brickness. The brick is objective; it exists whether we like it or not. And we are being objective when we see things accurately, without our perception being distorted by our preferences, biases and prejudices. Hence objectivity comes to mean an attitude to knowledge that is free from bias.

Many contemporary philosophers argue that true objectivity is impossible because our view of reality is inevitably filtered through our fallible senses, our equally fallible reasoning powers, and prevailing theories and concepts, which shape the way we see the world. The precise way our brains have evolved may also influence the kinds of knowledge we develop. We cannot see the world as it truly is but only as creatures like us see it. That we cannot have transcendental objectivity is taken by some as justification for relativism: if pure objectivity is not possible than all descriptions and explanations are equally valid. This view is unreasonably fatalistic and is not followed by most of us in normal life. Perfectly anti-septic conditions are impossible to achieve but we would rather be operated on in a modern hospital than a sewer. That there are obstacles to objectivity need not prevent us trying

to achieve it nor stop us preferring the less to the more distorted perception.

Of course, there is a corresponding danger in rushing too quickly to claim objectivity for our contemporary knowledge. Only 300 years ago most authoritative figures in Europe would have accepted that witches objectively existed. They felt as sure about that as we do about the objectivity of x-rays and radiowaves. A feeling that something is certain can be rather shaky grounds for claiming objectivity.

One weakness of the **postmodern** critique of the search for objectivity is that it fails to distinguish different sorts of knowledge. Whether my son is handsome is subjective (or, if there are widely-shared standards of beauty in my society, inter-subjective). Whether he is taller than average can be assessed objectively. Whether the typical American woman is happier than her grandmother may well involve questions of taste that are hard to transcend, but whether the income of the typical American woman in full-time employment outside the home is closer to that of a comparable man than was the case 50 years ago seems quite amenable to objective measurement and analysis. It is often quite easy in sociological work to separate topic selection, data collection, data analysis, interpretation, conclusions and policy recommendations. The relativist critique would be more persuasive if it recognised that the problem of attaining objectivity in these exercises is not the same.

A complication for social scientists is that we are often seeking to be objective about subjective entities. While some of our raw material (longevity, for example) may have brick-like object-ness, much of it exists only in the heads of other people (religiosity, for example). This may make our task more difficult (for example we may need to accommodate the technical problem that religiosity is expressed in different ways in different cultures) but it neither makes it impossible nor justifies abandoning the pursuit of objectivity.

OBSERVER EFFECT　　In nearly all branches of the natural sciences it is possible to observe and measure a phenomenon without changing what is observed; an agronomist can gauge the wetness of barley without significantly altering it. In much social science studying something may well change it. Asking people their opinions may well encourage them to think about something of which they had previously been unaware. **Participant observation** may well distort the dynamics of the small group being observed. The **Hawthorne** researchers concluded that knowing they were being studied increased the productivity of the Western Electric Company workers. This is an ineradicable problem in the social sciences and one that researchers just have to learn to live with and guard against. Sociologists may draw some comfort from the fact that even in some of the most specialised areas of natural science (particle physics, for example) measuring a phenomenon also inevitably involves interfering with it. In this case it is not because sub-atomic particles are self-aware but because they are so minute and sensitive that any interaction with them will change their state in subtle but unavoidable ways.

See **unobtrusive measures**.

OCCUPATIONAL MOBILITY　　See **social mobility**.

OCCUPATIONAL SCALES　　These measures of the prestige, status and social class of occupations are fundamental to research on social mobility and social stratification. Before we can talk about the ease with which people may move up or down the social scale, for example, we must construct some scale. All scales start with the assumption that occupations can be ranked sensibly in a continuous pattern. There are four broad methods. Researchers can simply make inferences from local knowledge; they can use the assumption that people generally mix with others of like status and take patterns of relations as their guide; they can amalgamate a variety of measurable job characteristics (such as income and educational entry qualifications); or they can systematically assess how a representative sample of the population rank a variety of jobs and use those rankings as the basis for a scale.

There are a variety of difficulties that the designers of scales must manage. Important components of income, an obvious mark of market situation and social prestige, may be hidden: cash payments may be augmented by share options, pension contributions, health benefits, cars, subsidised housing loans, tied housing and a host of other subsidiary benefits. Employment sectors may differ in prestige so that those who work in the health sector are more positively valued than people doing similar jobs in manufacturing industry. Occupations that have associations with fundamental social values (such as religion and education) may be ranked higher than their typical income would suggest. Although length of training has a regular relationship with income and prestige, jobs which require abstract university-based education are often ranked higher than jobs which have similar periods of industrial apprenticeship.

Occupational scales frequently have to be revised to take account of changes in the nature of jobs and in public perceptions of those jobs.

This adds a further layer of complexity because we need to adjust our scales to accommodate the changes they are intended to describe; this creates the danger of **tautology.**

In practice most sociologists do not concern themselves with the details of how scales have been constructed (though perhaps they should) because most major survey data sets code respondents according to one of a few major scales.

ODDS RATIO   A weakness of many ways of presenting comparisons statistically is that they focus only on the likelihood of a particular event occurring. But, in many cases, the chance of something happening changes because of alterations in the context, not because of changes in the underlying mechanism. For example, we may be very impressed by the fact that, since the 1950s, many children of working-class families have risen up the social scale and become middle class, and not appreciate that this may represent less a change in the openness of the class structure and more a change in the size of the various class boxes. If the nature of work has changed so that there are more middle-class jobs, than there will be more upward mobility in 1980 than in 1960 even if the openness of the class system has remained the same. There can be more middle-class jobs, and more people from lowly backgrounds in those jobs without any change in the relative disadvantage suffered by people from the manual-working classes. In technical terms, the odds ratio is a statistic designed to measure association in circumstances where the 'column marginals' of the distribution table have altered. It works by calculating the odds of two related patterns of events occurring and comparing them. In our example, it compares the odds that someone from a middle-class background will get a middle-class job with the odds that someone from a working-class background will get

one. The statistic will equal one when the odds are the same, that is when class factors appear irrelevant to the kind of job one ends up with.

This may seem like a matter of interest only to expert statisticians but it does relate to a crucial issue for understanding certain sorts of social change. Though each is important, changes in patterns within an unchanging structure and changes in patterns that result from the structure itself altering shape have different causes and consequences and often need to be distinguished.

OLIGARCHY   See **iron law of oligarchy**.

ONTOLOGY   This is the branch of philosophy concerned with the fundamental nature of things. Any intellectual enterprise must make assumptions about what kinds of entities can or do exist in the world that it aims to understand. Most sociologists adopt and refine the everyday ontology of the modern world: people, institutions, languages, technologies and so on exist and can impact on each other. Accordingly ontological concerns rarely trouble sociologists. There are two areas where they have become explicitly discussed however. First, some **Marxist** authors have tried to use philosophical arguments to demonstrate that 'classes' exist; they argue not just that people can be categorised into classes and that people may think of themselves as having a class identity but that classes actually exist. Such arguments, briefly popular in the 1970s and 1980s, and associated with a certain style of **realist** argument are no longer popular. Second, the programme of **ethnomethodology** can be understood as an exploration of the ontologies adopted in everyday life. Ethnomethodologists are not interested in assessing whether such ontologies are philosophically correct or not; their concern is to document the assumptions that underlie ordinary people's everyday way of acting.

OPEN AND CLOSED MIND   Although now little attended to, the 1960s work of US social psychologist Milton Rokeach was an important contribution to the tradition started by the **Authoritarian Personality** studies. Rokeach believed that patterns of child-rearing created personality types (polarised as open-minded and closed-minded) that were systematically related to being attracted to liberal and conservative, or tolerant and dogmatic, ideologies, belief-systems and movements.

OPEN SOCIETY   Karl Popper's philosophy of science gave central place to the idea of **falsification.** What distinguished science from other intellectual systems was that its propositions were subjected to repeated attempts to show them false. So long as they withstood such tests they remained current; when they were falsified they were replaced by better ideas. Popper recognised that scientists, being only human, would be less than keen to demolish their own work. Hence falsification as a method could not depend on the personalities or values of individual scientists. But it was served by competition between scientists. Personal ambition would drive the advance of science provided there was the right environment: one in which all ideas could be subjected to critical scrutiny and competition was encouraged.

Popper's model also meant that all knowledge was provisional. The Platonic, **Hegelian** and **Marxist** idea that the fundamental laws of human history could be discovered was held to be not just bad science but also dangerous politics: an encouragement to totalitarianism. Those who were certain they had the truth were likely to treat those who disagreed with them as disloyal or treacherous and were thus likely to feel justified in imposing their will on others. Thus Popper moved from a narrow interest in the philosophy of science to comparative studies of the merits of open and closed societies. Popper's notion of the open society emphasised the virtues of competition at the level of ideas. However, the stress placed on competition has made his position attractive to advocates of **liberalism** pressing for competition in the market for goods and services and for limitations on the role of the state.

OPERATIONALISATION   In order to test any social scientific proposition its terms must be defined in ways that can serve as the basis for data collection and analysis. To make any headway with the claim that modern societies are less religious than traditional societies, we need to specify what will count as modernity and what will count as marks of being religious. That is, we must 'operationalise' our concepts. Something is always lost in translating big ideas into operational terms: is church attendance a reliable and valid mark of religiosity? And there is a constant danger that thoughtful analysis will be displaced by technical questions of data collection. As Herbert **Blumer** warned, instead of looking for the dollar where we dropped it, we look where the light is brightest. For example, it is common in the USA for church-attendance data to be collected by asking people in telephone surveys (cheap and easy to organise) if they went to church. Only in the 1990s did social scientists raise the obvious problem that people may well exaggerate since church attendance may be seen as a 'good thing'. The best social research always remembers that compromises have been made between original ideas and operational concepts.

OPINION LEADER   The term was coined by Elihu Katz, Robert K. **Merton** and Paul **Lazarsfeld** in 1950s research on the effects of mass media to describe a person who is particularly influential in passing on ideas and opinion from the mass media to others. In a variety of studies of the diffusion of fashion, technical innovations and political opinions they found that most people did not respond immediately to impersonal mass media communication; they were influenced by a small number of opinion leaders who added or denied authority (and hence persuasiveness) to the communication. Exactly who these opinion leaders were varied with the topic or issue; specific opinion leaders were not the leaders about everything.

See **two-step flow of communication**.

OPIUM OF THE MASSES   Although Karl **Marx** was well aware of **religion**'s radical potential, he also coined this well-known summary depiction of its anaesthetising effects. Religion both distracts people from the real material causes of their problems (it is my sinfulness, not exploitation by my feudal lord, that explains my misery) and provides a solution (pray more and do not oppose God's divine providence) that defuses revolutionary potential.

OPPORTUNITY COST   One useful way of expressing the cost of an activity is in terms of the opportunities that we forego in doing one thing rather than another. The cost of my new car could be expressed in its monetary price but it could also be described by its opportunity cost: the liposuction I could have had instead. Policy-makers often claim that members of society fail to take into account the opportunity costs of the things they appear to demand. After a rail crash, for instance, there is often a demand for better train safety without much exploration of how many more lives could be saved by spending the same amount of money on improvements to roads or on the prevention of motorists' speeding.

OPPORTUNITY STRUCTURE   The phrase was originally used in 1960 by Richard A. Cloward and Lloyd B. Ohlin in their attempt

to extend Robert Merton's work on **anomie** and deviance. Merton argued that the uneven distribution of the legitimate means to get on in life was a major cause of people engaging in illegal innovation. Cloward and Ohlin added that opportunities to engage in criminal innovation were also unevenly distributed; not everyone had access to the skills, motivational rhetorics, and contacts necessary for a life of crime or deviance. Since then, the phrase has been widely used to convey the sense that opportunities in every sense tend to be socially structured (or 'differentially distributed') so that, unless people are unusually determined, talented or just plain lucky (or the converse), most lives will be patterned by race, class and gender.

ORDINAL DATA   See **measurement, levels of.**

ORGANIC SOLIDARITY   See **mechanical solidarity.**

ORGANISATION   This can denote either an entity or a way of acting. In the first sense, an organisation is a collectivity established for a particular purpose, governed by rules, with clear authority relations, a division of labour and firm boundaries. Schools, hospitals, churches and sports clubs are all examples of formal organisations. In the second sense, organisation is a characteristic way of doing something; people's personal lives may show differing degrees of organisation.

Although the **bureaucracy** is so much the modern standard for organisation that we tend to design all new agencies and associations in that way, not all organisations are based on legal-rational **authority**. Many religious organisations, for example, are built on charismatic leadership and only become bureaucratic after the death of the charismatic founder. Organisations dedicated to artistic and other creative enterprises also usually seek to limit the role of formal principles since the members wish to allow room for individual talent, innovation and free expression.

ORGANISATIONAL CRIME See **corporate crime**.

ORIENTAL DESPOTISM See **Asiatic mode of production**.

ORIENTALISM In the 19th century this meant simply an interest in the history and culture of the East. Scholars of Islam or Buddhism or Chinese languages would proudly identify themselves as orientalists. Following Edward Said's (1978) popular *Orientalism* the term acquired an entirely negative meaning. It came to mean a general organising vision of the Muslim world that has some or all of the following defects. It takes Christianity as normal or paradigmatic and regards Islam as deviant. It treats the history and evolution of the West as normative and regards the East simply as a series of absences or failings. It exaggerates the homogeneity of Christianity and Islam (overlooking significant differences of language, region, regime, sect and class). It also exaggerates the differences between them, often taking Islam to be a truncated and incomplete version of Christianity. It imputes contrasting character types to the inhabitants of West and East: the rational Westerner versus the unpredictable Oriental, the gentle white versus the cruel yellow man. Finally, orientalism's apparent objectivity conceals a clear commitment to the notion that the West is superior.

Although there is value in being reminded of both the distorting effect of **ethnocentrism** and the need for attention to detail, orientalism has been used too loosely as an omnibus insult to be helpful as a term of analysis. For example, giving too much weight to religion as a source of political action in the Middle East and giving it too little weight have both been derided as orientalist failings. The term does too little to distinguish between those who have an argument with Islam (Christian apologists, for example) and those who are just poor scholars. It is also unhelpfully used to dismiss the work of some scholars by imputing to them unpleasant attitudes rather than arguing with the supposedly faulty parts of their work.

ORIENTATIONS TO WORK This generally denotes both the attitudes and motives that groups of workers bring to the work experience and the overall subjective experience of work. The idea became popular in the late 1960s as a qualification to the previously-dominant assumption that workers shared a common desire for community and for intrinsic job satisfaction. The **Affluent Worker** studies suggested that workers brought a variety of orientations to the work setting. For example, many car assembly workers actively sought out and were happy with dull repetitive work because it was highly paid and allowed them to satisfy domestic and private desires. That is, their orientation to work was instrumental.

See **alienation, de-skilling**.

OTHER-DIRECTEDNESS In *The Lonely Crowd*, of which he was the principal author, David Riesman (1950) contrasted three personality types. The tradition-oriented follows the ancient rules; not a type common in modern societies. The inner-directed person is governed by internalised standards and conscience. The other-directed person is heavily reliant for a sense of identity on the approval of others. This contrast was built into a depiction of modern society. Riesman argued that the consumerism of the USA was encouraging other-directedness and anxiety-driven conformity.

OTHERING, OTHERNESS A variety of theorists (including Simone **de Beauvoir**, Sigmund

Freud and Jacques **Lacan**) make great use of otherness: the far end of such binary divides as us–them, self–other, ego–alter, and masculine–feminine. In her work *The Second Sex*, de Beauvoir (1949) adopted the existentialist terminology of 'the other' to express the nature of women's subordination. In mainstream western culture women are defined as 'the other' in contrast to men. Ideas about what women are like have been developed by men as part of men's self-understanding: where men are rational, women are emotional and so on. Women are thus the second sex because their identity has been devised by men in the course of men's development of their own male identities. They are what men are not. In general 'the other' is understood not in terms of what it is, but in relation to what 'we' are not or do not wish to be.

'Othering' is the action of making some group into a clear contrast to 'us'. Although not essential to the idea, it is usually implied that this way of regarding some thing, person or collectivity as 'other' involves factual distortion of what they are truly like. For example, in **orientalism**, western scholars are guilty of misrepresenting the East. Without the implication of distortion, the idea has little explanatory value. If the binary divide male/female merely identifies real differences, calling this 'othering' would not carry the important claim that differences are exaggerated in order to serve some (usually not very honourable) purpose on the part of the person or agency doing the othering.

See **social construction of reality**.

OVER-DETERMINATION   Fortunately fallen into disuse with the decline in popularity of **Althusser**'s structural Marxism, this term was used to mean 'modify' or 'qualify'. Although Althusser wished to maintain that the **contradiction** between capital and labour was still the basic fact of capitalist society, he accepted that other contradictions (for example, urban versus rural) could modify or qualify that between capital and labour: the contradictions and conflicts observed in any particular society would thus be 'over-determined'.

The term is also used in Sigmund **Freud**'s psychoanalysis and in the philosophy of science to refer to situations where an event or occurrence appears to be caused by more than one factor and where the causal pattern cannot be sorted out. For example, given the many interpretations which Freud was able to place on dreams, any particular unconscious image might be attributable to multiple sources. Such images would thus be over-determined.

OVER-SOCIALISED CONCEPTION OF MAN Particularly associated with the 1960s US sociologist Dennis Wrong, this phrase was coined to make the point that functionalist sociology (especially in the work of Talcott **Parsons**) over-stated the extent to which people were socialised into a dominant value system and the extent, therefore, to which their actions simply flowed from these dominant values.

P

PANOPTICON   See **Foucault**.

PARADIGM   Since it was popularised by Thomas **Kuhn** in the 1960s, this term has come to mean any integrated set of ideas that shapes our scientific work by influencing perceptions, setting research agendas, determining what will count as evidence and setting the basic frame for explanation. A paradigm is more general than a theory but narrower and more focused than a worldview. The **secularisation** account of religious change is a paradigm.

PARAMETRIC STATISTICS   See **non-parametric statistics**.

PARETO, VILFREDO (1848–1923)   An Italian engineer and economist, late in life Pareto turned to sociology because he recognised the limits of economistic models of human behaviour. Economics dealt with the logical; sociology with the non-logical. Most of social life was non-logical. It was based on sentiment rather than methodical observation. He divided sentiments into residues (the basic universal sentiments) and derivations (the variable elements). Of six types of residue, he thought two particularly important: the tendency of people to make connections even when they have no evidence and the tendency to preserve those connections.

Pareto is now best known for his views on the circulation of elites. He rejected progressive and evolutionary models of changes in power structures in favour of the view that elites endlessly circulated, with two types alternating. The Lions were best suited to govern under stable conditions; the Foxes were innovative and better suited to periods of change and dislocation. He can be credited with encouraging Talcott **Parsons** to think of societies as self-equilibrating systems and with a contribution to **elite theory** but, like much economics, his work consists of elegant classificatory systems, which are illustrated with useful examples, but not in any strong sense tested. Hence once his pessimistic conservative vision went out of fashion, his work was forgotten.

PARK, ROBERT E. (1864–1944)   For 20 years from 1914 Park was professor of sociology at the University of Chicago. He was a major force behind the **Chicago School**'s concentration on urban sociology, community and race relations. From his previous career as a journalist he brought the emphasis on detailed ethnography and participant observation which formed the basis for his studies in what he termed 'human ecology'. He trained a whole generation of sociologists at Chicago; he also influenced the direction of the discipline throughout the Anglophone world through the textbook *Introduction to* the *Science of Sociology* (co-written with Ernest Burgess), which was first published in 1921 and was still being reprinted in the early 1960s.

PAROLE   See **langue and parole**.

PARSONS, TALCOTT (1902–79)   Arguably the most influential US sociologist of the 20th century, Parsons was significant for introducing Americans to European thought (for example, he translated Max **Weber**'s [1904] *The Protestant Ethic and the Spirit of Capitalism*) but he is best known for creating **structural-functionalism**.

His (1937) *The Structure of Social Action* was an attempt to synthesise the work of Weber, Pareto and Durkheim (he ignored Marx) into a solution to the **Hobbesian** problem of how social order was possible. It was cast in an explicitly voluntaristic frame. Social action could not be understood as an automatic response to stimuli or by some simple principle such as coercion. Rather it was shaped by shared norms and values. The voluntarism gradually disappeared as Parsons recast his ideas in terms of **systems theory** and functions. The final stage of his development was the embrace of an evolutionary perspective in *Societies: Evolutionary and Comparative Perspectives* (1966).

Until the 1960s Parsons dominated US sociology; thereafter he was largely ignored. His leaden prose, endless classificatory systems, **over-socialised conception of man**, the **tautology** inherent in much of this theorizing and the generally conservative tone of his work all contributed to his neglect, which is unfortunate because, alongside theoretical tomes, Parsons produced a number of useful studies of substantive topics. Although some of his work on the family has not worn well, he made insightful observations on the identity crisis of women, and his writings on the **sick role** education, race relations and the

appeal of authoritarian politics still repay reading.

See **evolutionary universals, functionalism, Mills, Merton, pattern variables, systems theory**.

PARTICIPANT OBSERVATION   This signifies a type of social research in which the researcher (either openly or covertly) joins in some naturally-occurring activity in order to study it. One advantage of participant observation (especially in covert mode) is that it avoids the **Hawthorne effect** of inducing people to change their behaviour because of their awareness of being studied. Another it is that it adds an additional source of data for constructing the motives and feelings of those we study: our own experience of the same things. Because we are in the field for research purposes, we withhold something from the activity and we have additional interests. Nonetheless, living as a believing member of, say, the Moonies will give the researcher far greater insight than watching from afar.

There are major drawbacks. It is time-consuming and has a very short reach. It often presents the researcher with numerous ethical problems. It always creates emotional problems: even short periods of involvement can create strong friendships and loyalties, encourage **going native**, and make ending the research painful.

See **covert research, ethics of research**.

PARTICULARISM   This is the opposite of universalism and it means an orientation in which values are confined to the group to which one belongs. Particularistic people act in very different ways towards different sets of people. The tax system of the Ottoman empire was particularistic in that strikingly different principles were applied to

Muslims and non-Muslims. There is a general evolutionary principle. Traditional non-industrial societies are more often particularistic; modern industrial societies are more often universalistic. A good example of the change can be seen in the notion of human rights. In many traditional societies there is a very clear difference between what you can do to your own people and what you can do to outsiders (enslave them, for example). Almost all modern societies claim to apply universally a range of basic human rights though it is not clear that many of them live up to the claim.

PAST-MODERNISM　　This ghastly term was coined by Rob Stones in the 1990s to denote a supposed middle-way between 'complacent' modernism and relativistic postmodernism.

PASTICHE　　This mixing of styles and genres (for example, in a building which adds Greek columns to an otherwise brutally modernist structure) is held by some scholars to be particularly characteristic of **postmodern** cultures in combining 'showing off' the depths of our knowledge with the absence of any real aesthetic commitment.

PASTORALISM　　From the same root as 'pasture' for grass field, this denotes an economy based on the regular movement of flocks of sheep, cattle and other domesticated animals around feeding grounds. Remaining pastoral societies often come into conflict with settlement-based ways of living since pastoralists seldom develop precise codes about land ownership and they may find that others have taken advantage of their periodic absence to lay claim to their customary pastures.

PATERNALISM　　This signifies a style of government or management in which subjects or employees are treated as if they were young children. The governors justify their rule with the claim that the ruled are too immature to govern themselves. In **patriarchal** societies, men treat women as if they were children; in colonial societies, imperialists maintain the same attitude to their subjects.

Paternalism is now a term of criticism but in some contexts it signified a marked improvement on the alternatives. In the early industrial period, for example, the factory owner who built a chapel for his workers and a school for their children, and who employed a home visitor to check on their domestic hygiene and a temperance lecturer to hector them about drinking alcohol, generally paid better than average wages and ensured a higher standard of living for his workers, even if he did meddle in their private lives. It is now common to stress the control dimension of this form of paternalism but in a society where the common people had few rights, paternalism was better than neglect.

PATH ANALYSIS　　This form of statistical analysis uses the basic idea of **regression** but employs it in an attempt to model the supposed interaction of a set of variables. The analyst interested in, say, social class, will guess how certain variables (father's **O**ccupation, **E**ducation and class **D**estination of the respondent: the classic O–E–D triangle) interact and construct a diagrammatic model in which a temporal sequence is assumed and regression coefficients are calculated for each 'path'. In the O–E–D example, the father's class is assumed to come before the respondent's class and affect it directly. The father's class also comes before and affects the respondent's education; in turn the education precedes and affects the respondent's destination. The relative weight of each path leading to the destination can then be compared. So we can ask if the direct link O–D (father's class – respondent's class) is stronger than the link mediated by education. If we have enough respondents with a wide enough age spread, we can divide them into two age cohorts and see if the path coefficients differ over time. In this example, we might expect that the society has become increasingly meritocratic and that the importance of education for social class (the E–D path coefficient) has increased relative to the importance of class of origin (the O–D path coefficient).

It must remembered that, as in all statistical modelling, the value of path analysis depends on the plausibility of the initially constructed model. That the observed data are compatible with the model is confirmation that we are thinking along the right lines but it cannot prove the causal connections assumed.

PATIENT ROLE   See **sick role**

PATRIARCHY   From the Latin for one who rules because he is the father, this denotes the domination of women by men. Thus we can have the patriarchal family, patriarchal societies or a work setting which is run in a patriarchal manner. Until the late 1960s the term was used simply for describing societies characterised by marked male domination; now it carries a clear stigma. Patriarchal rule is oppressive. It is clearly the case that modern industrial societies remain patriarchal to varying degrees. But, though authors may agree that this is the case, it is harder to work out exactly why patriarchy is so persistent since men hardly act as a 'class' to exclude women. The reproduction of patriarchy seems to take place without it being consciously willed. This leads to a potential problem for users of the term since, if one argues that patriarchy is nearly universal (and that case is made by some feminists), it begins to look as though its roots are natural and even biological: the case that feminists reject.

PATRILINEAL DESCENT   Sometimes called agnatic, this describes a system in which

possessions, identity or whatever else is valued is passed from father to son: that is, through the male line.

PATRIMONIALISM   In general usage this means a right or estate inherited from one's father or ancestors. In narrower use in historical sociology and in evolutionary models of power structures, it signifies a form of political domination by a royal household, which is based on an unusual combination of personal and bureaucratic power. The power is formally arbitrary (there are no legal, traditional or customary restraints) and it is administered by the ruler through intermediaries (such as court retainers, eunuchs or mercenaries) who have no power base of their own (that is, they are not members of the landed gentry or aristocracy). Max **Weber** viewed patrimonial systems as inherently unstable: there are always rivals who seek to usurp the patrimony. He also thought they retarded progress. Lacking crucial elements that could encourage modernisation (such as a system where particular non-royal individuals have rights or where power is based on some form of social contract), patrimonial systems are often displaced but almost always by another similar regime.

PATRON–CLIENT RELATIONS   This denotes any enduring relationship in which a powerful person or agency provides rewards and services to a humbler person or agency in return for loyalty and support. Such relationships can be found between states. The links between the Soviet Union and Bulgaria in the 1960s can usefully be described as patron–client. But the term is more often used for personal relationships that tend to be common in simple agrarian societies (the 'enduring' element being harder to sustain in highly mobile urban societies). In feudalism, the relationship is formalised and precisely what is owed by feudal superior to subordinate and vice-versa is often specified in law. Though it may be every bit as oppressive, the non-feudal patron–client relationship is less formal and is often presented in terms of favours and emotional bonds. The Mafia boss looks after his people in return for love and respect. 'Patron' has the same roots as 'father'; hence the similarity with **paternalism**.

In some agrarian societies with democratic polities, the patron–client relationship has been extended to create bought electorates that can be big enough to rival the influence of political parties. Politicians promise and give favours in return for secure votes. Here we see the limits of scale. Sustaining hundreds of personal relationships is very difficult; maintaining a client base of thousands is impossible. Even when the delivery of favours is bureaucratised (as it was in infamously corrupt Democratic party politics of the north-eastern cities of the USA in the early 20th century), politics based on aggregating thousands of diverse individual interests tends to be trumped by politics based on appeals to shared characteristics (such as class or ethnicity).

PATTERN MAINTENANCE   See **subsystems model**.

PATTERN VARIABLES   In his theory of social action, Talcott **Parsons** proposed five (later cut to four) choices of value orientations for individuals and for cultures. Although the grand theory behind this classification is now ignored, the classification itself (and some of the comparative observations with which Parsons illustrated it) remain highly pertinent.

The first was affective involvement versus neutrality. In any action we can either feel strongly about it or be relatively indifferent. This is an extremely useful distinction; for example, we can neatly describe the tension inherent in some jobs by noting that the client or customer wishes the person to be affectively involved (we would like our

doctors to care about us) while the ability of the person to do the job requires affective neutrality (most doctors do not have the emotional capacity to care about all of the patients they have to see and may even do a better job if they are in some sense detached). The second pair is ascription/achievement (sometimes called quality/performance). Ascription involves judging people (or things) according to their membership of some group or putative possession of some enduring quality. By contrast, to value achievement is to judge people or things by universal criteria related to performance. Gender and ethnicity are ascribed; sporting success is achieved. A class structure in which all positions are inherited is based on ascription; a **meritocracy** is based on achievement. The third choice is **particularism** versus **universalism**: do we treat some person uniquely or in accordance with some general norms? A teacher's relationship with her husband is supposed to be particularistic. Her relations with her students should be based on universalism; treating them all alike except in the award of grades and those should be based on universal criteria applied even-handedly. The fourth pair is diffuseness versus specificity. The relationship between mother and child is diffuse: it covers a very wide of activities. The taxi driver's relations with customers are specific: in return for a fee she drives them from one place to another.

Originally there was a fifth pair (collectivity-orientation versus self-orientation) but this was dropped on the grounds that it was of markedly different nature to the others.

The status of the pattern variables is not clear. Parsons presented them as an essential summary of contrasts made by earlier sociologists (such as Toennies's comparisons of **community** and society) and as having been formally derived from his theory. While few sociologist would now be impressed by the theoretical justification, each of the pattern variables provides a convenient way of describing major considerations in individual action and major differences between traditional and modern societies and the terms are in frequent use.

PEARSON'S *r*   See **correlation**.

PEASANT   From the French for country-dweller, this denotes small farmers who, with limited machinery and the labour power of their families, produce mostly for their own consumption and to meet their obligations to political and economic masters. The peasantry usually has historical roots in the area farmed. Modernisers, both in capitalist and state socialist societies, have typically looked on peasants as conservatively inclined and taken them as obstacles to the modernisation of the countryside. Convinced that the most entrenched peasants were obstacles to the advance of history, Stalin dealt with them with exceptional brutality.

PEER GROUP   This signified a group of people of equal status. The term is most often used in describing the experience of children and adolescents, for whom relations with their peers are so very different from the hierarchical relations with parents, teachers and siblings.

PERCEPTION   This denotes the reception and interpretation of such stimuli as sounds and sights. It involves both sense organs and cognitive appraisal. It is now recognised that perception is not just a question of the processing of current stimuli; instead it is strongly influenced by prior experience, by our emotions and by our expectations.

PERFORMATIVE   This term first rose to prominence through the work of British philosopher J.L. Austin who was concerned with **speech acts**, actions undertaken through speech alone. Austin's early examples of speech acts were so-called 'performatives', where people explicitly performed an act through the use of a standardised term, such as 'I accuse you' or 'we promise him'. More recently, the term has come to be used much more broadly to emphasise the extent to which the regularities of social life are performed, rather than simply pre-existing. For example, many commentators had noted that the way we dress has a symbolic quality. It was argued that dress can be 'read' as a system of **signs**. However, subsequent authors have claimed that this approach is too static and they have tried to focus on dressing as an activity, as a performance. This use of the word performative is associated with, for instance, Judith **Butler**.

PERFORMATIVITY   Jean-Francois **Lyotard** in (1979) *The Postmodern Condition: a Report on Knowledge* argued that science was becoming increasingly an elite activity in which access to proof and disproof was limited to those who had the means to acquire the most advanced apparatus and technology. At the same time, emerging technical difficulties in science (for example, to do with the unpredictability of **chaotic** effects) mean that the traditional idea of proof itself begins to look a little suspect. Under these circumstances, it appears that science might become reduced to being just another opaque language game since no one outside of the scientific elite would be able to question the word of scientists who could – in effect – say whatever they wished. Lyotard claims that, in this context, scientific research becomes judged not in terms of 'truth' or 'proof' but in terms of the commercial benefits it delivers, which he calls its performativity. This claim has two specific weaknesses. First, Lyotard lumps together too many aspects of research under the term performativity. The success of technological innovations is a complex issue which depends on many factors. Suggesting that these factors are all one thing (performativity) does not help. Second, by separating the market benefits of scientific research from its claims to truthfulness, Lyotard appears to beg the question of why research delivers market benefits in the first place. Most scientists would argue that commercially successful science is successful precisely because (among other things) it is based on a correct understanding of the world. Thus truth and performativity are not so unconnected after all.

PERIODISATION   This is the division of the past into periods such as 'the Middle Ages' and 'early modern'. If we want to assert that something has changed (e.g. community has declined) we have to specify, however roughly, when we thought the extent of change was such that one sort of society gave way to another. All periodisation is vague because not every part of a society changes or changes at the same time but this is not a reason to abandon periodisation. Despite church-going remaining popular in the Scottish Western Isles for a further 30 years, Britain since the 1960s has been a secular society; the marginal exception does not invalidate the general description.

Some **postmodernists** argue that there is no legitimate scientific basis to broad brush characterisations but it is difficult to see how even the most elementary description can avoid implicitly dividing the past into periods. After all, postmodernists do this in distinguishing between the modern and postmodern.

PERIPHERY   See **centre and periphery**.

PERSONALITY   This denotes any individual's characteristic ways of behaving. The personality is inferred from behaviour, which it is held to cause. Psychologists have attempted to devise questionnaire tests that are intended to reveal underlying personality traits and,

whatever their scientific justification, these are increasingly used in recruitment and job selection procedures.

PETITE (OR PETTY) BOURGEOISIE   This is the class of small businessmen that Marx expected to disappear. He took the logic of capitalism to require ever greater concentrations of capital. As with most of his specific predictions, he was wrong. Despite the very high failure rates of small businesses, the small business sector remains alive and well 150 years after he predicted its demise.

The petty bourgeoisie is of particular interest to political sociologists because it tends to possess a clear political identity: individualistic, opposed to large organisations, morally conservative, and suspicious of both organised labour and the traditional ruling elite (commercial or landed). This class was particularly likely to support fascist and authoritarian movements in Europe in the 1920s and 1930s, McCarthyism in the USA in the 1950s and Poujadism in France in the early 1960s.

In the 1970s Nikos **Poulantzas** applied the term to non-manual or white-collar workers, who did not own capital (and hence could not in Marx's terms be bourgeois) but who are certainly not proletarian because they administer capitalism on behalf of the bourgeoisie.

PHENOMENOLOGICAL SOCIOLOGY   The main aim of Alfred Schutz's phenomenology was the description and analysis of everyday life (the life-world) and its associated states of consciousness. Central is the claim that all knowledge (and not just ideology or false consciousness) is **socially constructed** and oriented towards the solution of practical problems. From an undifferentiated stream of consciousness we create the objects and the knowledge of the objects that we take for granted in our everyday lives. The basic act of consciousness Schutz called first-order typifications: grouping together typical and enduring elements in the flow of experience, building models of things and people, and insofar as these are shared, creating a social world. For Schutz the job of the sociologist is to construct second-order typifications: a rational model of the world based on the first-order typifications that actors offer as explanation for their actions.

Phenomenology was briefly popular in the late 1960s but was extensively criticised for its concentration on the trivial and its lack of interest in such weighty matters as inequality and power. It lives on now only in **ethnomethodology** but aspects of it did enter the sociological mainstream through Peter L. Berger and Thomas Luckmann's (1967) immensely popular *The Social Construction of Reality*. This used phenomenological terms and ideas to produce a general social theory that combined social action and social structure. Following Schutz, they argued that the social world is constructed through typifications. The more enduring ones acquire an objective quality which confronts the groups that produce them. Subsequent generations are socialised into these typifications. Although reality is socially constructed, it cannot be 'thought away' because it confronts every new member as the culture into which he or she is socialised.

Social Construction was influential not so much for any specific proposition but for the general idea that any adequate solution to the apparently endless action versus system (or agency versus structure) debate lies in recognising the paradoxical nature of human life: society is created by people but people are also created by society. Anthony **Giddens**'s more recent **structuration** theory is similar.

PHENOMENOLOGY   A philosophical method of enquiry devised by German philosopher Edmund Husserl, phenomenology is an attempt to get at the phenomenon of pure consciousness. Husserl claimed that we must set aside (or bracket off) how consciousness or individual personhood appears at any

particular historical time, since that appearance is likely to be contaminated by cultural factors that are historically variable: this bracketing off he referred to as **epoché**. This approach to philosophy appeared highly individualistic but it worked its unlikely impact on sociology through the publications of a student of Husserl, Alfred **Schutz**. Schutz developed the argument for a phenomenological sociology claiming that phenomenology alerted the sociologist to the way in which, from an undifferentiated stream of consciousness, we create the objects and the knowledge of the objects that we take for granted in our everyday lives. For Schutz this was the foundation of social life. In contemporary sociology, it is really only **ethnomethodology** that persists with the suggestion that we can find the foundations for social analysis in all the taken-for-granted cultural assumptions that make life regular and dependable.

PHENOTYPE   See **genotype**.

PHYLOGENETIC SCALE   This is the ranking of all animal life from the simplest, which merely react to external stimuli, to the most complex, which have specific and sophisticated sensory systems, the ability to learn from the past and the ability to reflect on their own experiences. The concept usually appears in sociology in the context of comparing the closed worlds of lesser animals with the world-openness of the human. It should be noted, however, that the phylogenetic scale does not equate to a way of mapping **evolution**. Evolutionary adaptation drives organisms to be better fitted to survive in their environment. Being smarter and more reflective may have adaptive advantages but it may also have drawbacks or impose additional biological 'costs'; evolution can sometimes lead creatures to become simpler.

PIE CHART   This a graph in which a circle is divided into sectors in proportion to the distribution of some property. For example, the proportions of the adult population that voted for various parties in an election could readily be presented in a pie chart.

PILLARISATION   This is a translation of the Dutch *verzuiling* and it describes the vertically divided nature of Dutch society. For most of the 20th century the Netherlands was divided into three quite distinct groups: Catholics, Protestants and Secular. Each pillar had its political parties, trade unions, mass media, schooling and welfare agencies. Patterns of friendship, marriage and job recruitment all reflected those divisions. The Secular block was divided in two by class: the working-class part of the non-religious population was mainly Socialists; their middle-class counterparts were Liberals. However the two religious blocks were cross-class.

In the 1960s the pillars began to fragment. With **secularisation** the size and zeal of the Catholic and Protestant blocks began to decline and their parties merged to form a Christian Democrat party. New lines of social division superseded those based on the religious and political struggles of the late 19th century: the presence of a large number of Muslim immigrants, for example, has given rise to new arguments in which Christian and secular populations are on the same side.

PILOT STUDY   A small boat which guides a large one into harbour is a pilot boat. A pilot study performs the same function for a major study (such as a large sample survey). It gives an opportunity to try out the logic or design of the planned study before the main expenditure is incurred and it is too late to change. It is routine to 'pilot' questionnaires with a small number of respondents who are encouraged to explain any difficulties they have in interpreting or answering specific questions.

PLATONIC   After the Greek philosopher Plato (428–348 BC), in sociology this term usually describes an extreme form of **idealism**. Plato wondered how it was we recognised 'horseness' from the huge variety of large and small, thin and broad creatures, which we described as horses. His solution was that there existed a realm of pure 'ideas' – the horse, the triangle, the dog – which we knew intuitively rather than by empirical research or observation. Sadly for Plato his 'solution' threw up as many problems as it resolved since it was unclear where this realm of ideas might be; there was also the considerable problem of working out how people all recognised the similarity between the Platonic ideal chair and all the different actual chairs they encounter in everyday life. Today, the word Platonic is usually used to refer critically to extreme positions aligned with **idealism** or to an idealised image – often an exaggeratedly ideal one – such as the ideal of **economic man**.

PLURALISM   Plural means more than one. Pluralism describes some situation in which we might expect one but find more than one. So 'cultural pluralism' describes a society with a variety of cultures; religious pluralism a society with a number of religions and so on. Used on its own, it normally refers to the political science idea of a variety of power centres within a polity: a contrast with the concentrated unitary state.

See **plural society**.

PLURAL SOCIETY   Initially this term was used to denote those societies which were so firmly divided into distinct racial, ethnic, religious or linguistic groups, with little contact between them, that they were really not single societies: Burma is an example. It would also describe Switzerland with its cantons and the Netherlands at the time of its **pillarisation**.

POLISH PEASANT IN EUROPE AND AMERICA,
THE   Originally published in five volumes
between 1918 and 1920, W.I. **Thomas** and
Florian Znaniecki's masterpiece was for a
long time held as an exemplar of **qualitative**
research and then largely forgotten. One of
their purposes in studying both ends of the
migration process was to clarify the nature of
social theory. For them, it was a combination
of sociology as the study of social organisation
(which was the totality of social institutions,
which in turn were 'the rules of behaviour')
and social psychology as 'all the attitudes …
more or less generally found among the
members of a social group'. Attitudes were
the subjective component of behaviour;
values the objective part. What was novel
about *The Polish Peasant* was the insistence
that understanding social action required a
method that captured the actor's interpretation of the objective conditions with which
he had to deal; here the study of 'human documents' was essential.

Those documents included 764 letters
to or from emigrants. There is also a 312
page autobiography commissioned from one
Polish peasant migrant by Thomas and
Znaniecki and followed by their gloss on his
life-history. Also included were newspaper
reports, records of Polish parish churches and
Polish-American societies in the USA,
records of social work agencies and court
records. These last two were used to show
the extent of social disorganisation within
the immigrant community in the USA.

As the guardian of the spirit of the
Chicago School sociology, Herbert **Blumer**
was sympathetic to the *Polish Peasant*'s stress
on actors' interpretations but his (1939)
Critiques of Research in the Social Sciences …
the Polish Peasant remains a source of salu-
tary warnings. He concludes that letters and
life-histories can be useful sources of data
but need to be interpreted with due regard
for the circumstances in which they were
produced and the purposes (other than

self-understanding) which they were intended
to serve. Moreover, although it is no worse
than in quantitative research, there is an
issue of representativeness: to the extent that
the authors of the letters and reports used
are insightful, they are probably unusual.
There is also a question of adequacy: can
human documents adequately inform us
about the subjective factors in social action?
Reliability is an issue: are these (or any)
human documents trustworthy? Finally
Blumer raises the issue of testability: if, as
seems to be the case, most of the human documents are capable of supporting various
interpretations, how can we regard them as
testing competing explanations? And if we
cannot, then how can we claim that the data
support the interpretation which Thomas
and Znaniecki place on them?

In fairness it should be said that *The Polish*
Peasant does a better job of demonstrating
the subjective responses of actors to situations than, for example, Max **Weber**'s
Protestant Ethic thesis, which relies on a few
illustrative fragments and Weber's own
guesses about how Calvinists felt.

POLITICAL CULTURE   This denotes the
complex of attitudes, beliefs and rules that
shape a political system. The point is that a
formal description of political institutions
leaves out much that is important for understanding a society's politics. For example, formally similar two-party systems can be
entirely different in reality if, in one case,
there is a widely-shared assumption that the
opposition party has a right to oppose and
that opposition improves government and if,
in the other, opposition is viewed as disloy-
alty to the state. Hence we need to be interested in the general political values into
which people are socialised, the institutions
of civil society, the role of the mass media
and the nature of public education as well as
in constitutional arrangements.

POLITICAL ECONOMY This term has acquired two meanings. Originally, political economy was a product of the various Enlightenments of the 18th century, notably in England, France and Scotland. Political economists were concerned with understanding how wealth was generated in societies that were moving away from an earlier dependence on agriculture. The legacy of political economy divided, with those parts of its study that involved power and social relations evolving into modern sociology and the more individualistic and technical elements (the elaborate system of theorems developed from the proposition that the key to human behaviour was the desire to maximise) becoming modern economics. The other, more modern meaning, derives from the 1960s and the reaction to the **functionalist** orthodoxy in Anglophone sociology. Authors who used the term political economy were asserting their intent to analyse social phenomena in the context of political power and of capitalistic market relations. This laudable intent was often let down by a Marxist-style approach that reduced all sociology to supposed class antagonisms. Thus a political economy of science might assert that expert knowledge under capitalism is, above all else, knowledge at the disposal of large corporations and their political allies.

POLITICAL PARTICIPATION This usually refers to taking part in those processes that lead to the selection of political leaders and that determine public policy. The unqualified right to political participation is a defining feature of liberal democracies and there is considerable concern over the large numbers in western democracies who fail to exercise that right. Even in presidential elections about half of voting-age Americans do not vote and the proportion in other elections is even higher; three-quarters of Californians did not vote in the 2002 presidential primaries. The UK has had one of the highest turnout rates for its general elections but 2001's 72 per cent was the lowest since 1945. Attempts to identify social correlates of non-voting have failed to produce strong relationships.

Two other developments have prompted new thought in this area. In recent decades there has been a growth in supranational political bodies: for example, the European Union (EU) and the World Trade Organisation. Both of these require nations to surrender some of their sovereignty to a new kind of political entity. There is growing concern that these new entities are less open to participation than national governments and, in the context of the EU, there has been explicit worry about the growing 'democratic deficit' since senior figures are appointed, not elected. At the same time, there has been a conspicuous counter-trend towards increased public participation. Pioneering developments in Denmark and the Netherlands, for example, have seen members of the public consulted directly about new policies, for instance about agricultural biotechnology or about national energy policy. The EU itself has been attracted to such participatory initiatives as a way of addressing the democratic deficit.

POLITICAL PARTY This denotes an association set up with the aim of gaining political power, usually through winning an election. It differs from the **pressure group** in seeking to exercise power directly, for a long time, and over a very wide range of matters. In modern democracies, parties are the most common vehicle for expressing and channelling the will of the people.

An important distinction is between parties of integration (such as fascist and communist parties), which seek to bind their members in an all-encompassing ideological community and parties of representation, which compete for the opportunity to represent people in a system of give-and-take, without pressing for ideological closure. Seymour Martin **Lipset** argued that the latter were essential to the stability of liberal democracy while the former tended to undermine it.

In most modern societies the major party divide is left–right over the economy though whether that is expressed in just two parties (Republican versus Democrat in the USA; Conservative versus Labour in the UK) or in a plethora of small parties depends on the voting system used. First-past-the-post elections permit little room for third parties; proportional representation systems allow them to flourish.

POLITICS   Max **Weber** offered a sensible definition: 'Striving for a share of power or for influence on the distribution of power, whether it be between states or between groups of people within a single state'.

POLITY   From the Greek 'polis' meaning a city, this term now signifies the political institutions that with 'society', 'economy' and 'culture' make up the main macro-level concerns of sociologists.

POLYANDRY   From the Greek for 'many' and 'men', this signifies a marriage system in which one woman has two or more spouses. It is rare in the anthropological record and usually involves a woman marrying two or more brothers. One purpose is to preserve property which would otherwise be diffused among the heirs of the males.

POLYGAMY   Although strictly speaking this term for multiple marriage does not specify the gender of multiple spouses, it is usually used to refer to one man having two or more wives. The more accurate term polygyny is rarely used. It is a mark of the power of **patriarchy** that this arrangement is considerably more common than **polyandry**.

POLYSEMY   This denotes the deliberate introduction into any text (such as a novel or a television programme) of multiple meanings.

POPPER, KARL R. (1902–94)   Principally a philosopher of science, Popper left his native Austria and finally settled in London after the Second World War. He is widely known in sociology for three reasons. First, he devised an innovative position in the philosophy of science known as **falsificationism**. In brief, he argued that truly scientific theories are ones that are open to falsification: that is, one could devise a way of decisively testing the theory through experiment or observation. For Popper this indicated what the scientific method should involve – scientists should set out to try to falsify their theories by subjecting them to rigorous tests – and it allowed him to differentiate between genuine science and pseudo-science. Real science can be falsified; bogus science cannot. For example, astrological predictions are so imprecise and hedged around with qualifications that though they may appear scientific they never face falsification.

Popper believed that this means of demarcating between science and non-science held strong implications for the social sciences since he concluded that leading theoretical positions in social science, notably **Marxism** and **Freudianism**, were pseudo-scientific. Just like astrologists, hard-line Marxists had a barrage of techniques for resisting falsification. For example, if the labouring classes did not behave as Marx anticipated (and by and large they did not) this is because they were suffering from false consciousness and not because the theory is flawed. In *The Open Society and its Enemies* (1945) and *The Poverty of Historicism* (1957) Popper developed this point. He argued that the **Hegelian** and **Marxist** idea that the fundamental laws of human history could be discovered flew in the face of falsificationism. Worse, these were not just bad science but also dangerous politics: an encouragement to totalitarianism. Those who were certain they had the truth were likely to treat those who disagreed with them as disloyal or treacherous and were thus likely to feel justified in imposing their will on others. In this way, Popper moved from a narrow interest in the philosophy of science to comparative studies of the merits of open and closed societies.

Finally, Popper is well known as an advocate of incrementalism in social policy. Given his emphasis on the fallibility of ideas, Popper was a natural opponent of grand schemes for social reform. He felt they often misfired and that their impacts could never be accurately predicted. In their place he favoured gradual, piecemeal social engineering.

POPULAR CULTURE   Generally this serves as a contrast with the high culture of the upper classes (opera, orchestral music, fine art, drama and ballet): it is the culture of the masses and encompasses pop music, television, fashion and film.

Cultural critics of the right and left unite in criticising popular culture for being unchallenging and encouraging passivity. The right-wing critics blame the masses for their lack of taste and discretion; left-wing critics (such as the **Frankfurt School**) blame the upper classes for deliberately using the modern equivalent of the Roman circuses to stultify and thus rob the proletariat of its revolutionary potential.

Much criticism is rather thoughtless. Pop music, for example, is not just a product that is passively consumed. Far more than opera and ballet, it encourages imitation: few opera fans sing in amateur choirs but every Friday and Saturday night thousands of amateur pop, rock and country-and-western bands play in pubs and clubs. People familiar with one musical style frequently suppose another lacking in complexity or skill. Modern electronic dance music is often dismissed as unskilled by those who expect complexity of

melody and thus miss the fact that styles such as 'trance' and 'house' music involve considerable skill by mixing engineers in building shifting layers of bass and drum lines underneath a simple melody.

Fears that the mass media would shrink the available range of cultural products have proved largely unfounded. The increasing costs of film-making and the power of US distributors have shrunk the available range of Anglophone films but in other areas technological advance has permitted unprecedented variety. Because unit costs are so much lower, the number of different records available now is far greater than in the 1960s – and digital technology has made it viable for ordinary people to record and distribute their own music. Furthermore, popular culture has become integrated into many movements for cultural and political change and played an important role in the development of, for example, civil rights awareness and mobilisation in the USA.

POPULISM   This term entered the political vocabulary with the formation in the USA in 1892 of the Populist party. Its supporters were mainly small farmers who felt oppressed by bankers (who charged exorbitant rates of interest and foreclosed on farm mortgages) and by railroad companies (who used their monopoly to charge high prices for haulage). The main planks of its platform were the nationalisation of land and of the railways.

Later the term came to signify political parties and movements outside the main left-right party structure that mobilised individuals with a sense of grievance and hostility to governing elites while denying the salience of class divisions. Populist movements are often led by charismatic political mavericks: Juan Peron in Argentina, George Wallace in the USA in the 1960s, Ross Perot in the USA in the 1980s, William Aberhart in Alberta in the 1930s. They often attract people who have not previously been politically active, and they are notoriously short-lived: the charismatic leadership is often unstable, the novices attracted to politics for the first time become disillusioned when they discover that they are not making rapid progress, and the more popular parts of the programmes are accepted but watered down by the main parties.

POSITIONAL GOODS Swan may have tasted better than other game birds but the main pleasure British monarchs gained from eating it was the reminder of exclusivity: they and they alone were allowed to eat swans. Many goods are desired not for their intrinsic qualities but for their scarcity. They establish the social *position* of the consumer; they are a species of status symbol.

See **conspicuous consumption**.

POSITIVE DISCRIMINATION A synonym for 'affirmative action', this denotes policies intended to favour groups (such as women and ethnic minorities) that have previously suffered such disadvantage that, without a head start, they cannot compete realistically in a contest which is procedurally fair. It has proved highly controversial because, while it may at the group level be just, it necessarily involves discriminating against people who are not personally responsible for the disadvantage of the assisted group. For example, if, as a measure of socially desirably affirmative action, a university decides to admit black students with lower grades than it demands of white students, individual whites who were not responsible for the black disadvantage that the policy intends to remedy will be disadvantaged.

POSITIVISM The various meanings derive from Auguste Comte's 19th-century philosophical system, in which the most valid

knowledge is scientific knowledge. At the time this was intended as a progressive philosophy, liberating people from endless disputes over untestable metaphysical and religious arguments. Comte championed sociology as a positive science for society and the term has come to denote any sociology that operates on the general assumption that the methods of the physical sciences (precise observation, numerical measurement, the search for patterns of causal explanation) should also be used in the social sciences. Given that several of these attributes are actively resisted by many of today's sociologists, who see interpretative understanding as more important than the measurement of variables, positivism has come in recent decades to be a pejorative term.

Routine usage of the term betrays a curious lack of self-knowledge in sociology. Most sociologists who study things other than the writings of other sociologists share some of the positivist outlook in a practical sense. They believe there is a reality external to themselves, which can be described, understood and explained. As they weigh the importance of this over that, they count and they measure and they compare. They infer causal sequences. Although they do it in a woollier fashion, they do science. Yet since the 1960s 'positivist' has become a term of abuse meaning old-fashioned, naive and unintellectual; this has limited thought on what is 'positive' for sociology.

POST-COLONIAL THEORY Not so much a theory as an agenda, this is a loosely-related set of ideas concerned with the social, economic and political conditions of former colonies. One notable theorist was Frantz Fanon (1952, (1961) whose *Black Skin, White Masks* and *The Wretched of the Earth* are still widely read. A psychiatrist, Fanon argued that the harm of imperialism was not confined to economic exploitation; it also created socio-psychological problems for the colonised. They had an alien language and culture imposed upon them by the colonisers. Having very little value in the eyes of the colonisers, the colonised lost confidence in the value of their own culture. Fanon's solution was revolutionary change.

Later writers such as Stuart Hall who are sympathetic to the concerns of post-colonial theory nevertheless question the current value of a simple model of native identity undermined by imperial culture. Population movements and the globalisation of communication have weakened many traditional identities and encouraged hybridity and syncretism.

See **subaltern studies**.

POST-EMOTIONAL THESIS   See **Meštrović, Stjepan**.

POST-FEMINISM   From the early 1990s it became common to talk of having moved beyond the **feminism** of the 1960s. Writers such as Naomi Wolff and Camille Paglia argued that women need no longer construe themselves as being uniformly or always the hapless victims of patriarchal oppression and that to continue to press the cause of women in the old language was counter-productive. In a rather different vein, Judith **Butler** and Ann Brooks use the term to suggest that, though patriarchal oppression remain a force to be confronted, the nature of the feminist response has changed; it is thus 'post' the first phase of feminism, not post-patriarchy.

POST-FORDISM   See **Fordism**.

POST-MATERIALIST VALUES   Robert Inglehart's (1990) *Culture Shift in Advanced Industrial Society* and subsequent analyses of further sweeps of the recurrent World Values Survey have promoted the idea (developed from Abraham Maslow's **hierarchy of needs**) that, as societies become more prosperous, so people's values shift from a focus on material needs to more abstract notions such as self-actualisation. Material well-being and physical security give way to concern with the quality of life. Inglehart claims to find support for this thesis not just in the First World but also in a number of Second and **Third World** societies. There is a universal tendency for stability and prosperity to produce a value shift.

If Inglehart is right (and a very large body of survey data supports his interpretation) there are implications for the social sciences because models of human behaviour, which concentrate on socio-economic class and economic issues, will become of decreasing value.

POSTMODERNITY, POSTMODERNISM   This term was first brought to the attention of sociologists largely through the work of Jean **Baudrillard** and Jean-François **Lyotard**, the main champion of the idea that we have entered a period of postmodernity (*La condition postmoderne*, 1979). The central idea of this 'condition' can be illustrated through the example of artistic representation. From the Renaissance, European artists became increasingly interested in making better representations. But the 20th century saw the overthrow of that ideal. Early in the century the artist Marcel Duchamp introduced the 'ready-made' and displayed, not a still life depicting flowers and jugs on a tablecloth, but an actual, shop-bought urinal and a pot rack. His 'representation' was more life-like than anything else because it was the very thing. He was thus simultaneously the most extreme exponent of the modern ideal of representation and its assassin. Artists in the 20th century had to invent a new aesthetic for painting and sculpture, one that acknowledged the death of the modernist project. Lyotard argues that a similar process infects all modernist culture, including the ideals of scientific and political representation. He also insists that the **meta-narratives** (the big 'stories' of modernist scholarship) have lost their credibility too. This made Lyotard an unusual kind of radical since he was a critic of **Marxism**. Baudrillard is best known for the allied argument that modern societies are so saturated by the mass media that reality loses its meaning. People are no longer participants in their own lives but observers of what the media has turned into 'spectacles'. The language of postmodernity has caught on widely. The fanciful, decorative architecture that has succeeded the regular geometry of the modernist movement is commonly described as postmodern. The vogue for complex and unorthodox films and novels fits the pattern too.

In Lyotard's view this process appears as autonomous development within the realm of culture. Critics such as Frederic **Jameson** argue that postmodernism is in fact the 'cultural logic' of late capitalism. Inverting the usual postmodernist account, critics argue that the postmodern aesthetic in design and architecture and so on is engendered by developments in capitalism.

POSTSTRUCTURALISM   An approach to philosophy, literary theory and social theory that is most often associated with the writings of Jacques **Derrida**, poststructuralism is 'post' **structuralism** in two senses. It marks a rejection of structuralist analysis in French Marxism of the sort associated with Louis **Althusser** and a refusal to accept the rather mechanistic studies of **symbols** and of **semiology** in general that are, for example, associated with the anthropological investigations conducted by Claude **Lévi-Strauss**. Invoking the works of pioneering linguist and semiologist Ferdinand de **Saussure**, poststructuralists emphasised that different languages not only label the world with different signs but structure the way the world can be thought

about. In this way language can be a more or less independent source of meaning. There is therefore a great deal about symbols or texts that can be investigated other than their correspondence to the world. Poststructuralists proposed that the semiological construction of texts should be the topic of analysis since we may delude ourselves about how the world is unless we uncover the assumptions about the world smuggled in by the semiological systems we customarily use. Derrida famously used this approach in his analysis of philosophical texts and his work has been widely taken up in the field of literary studies. His favoured strategy in concentrating critical attention on texts came to be referred to as **deconstruction**. Social theorists were influenced by these claims both in their approach to studying the philosophies of other theorists and by deciding to regard social life as a form of text that could be deconstructed.

POSTULATE OF ADEQUACY   Common to both **phenomenological** sociology and to the sociology of Max **Weber**, this is the assertion that sociological accounts must be understandable to the social actors involved in the social settings being described and explained. The 'adequacy' has two elements; for an explanation to be adequate for our purposes it must also be adequate for those being explained.

The postulate is rejected by many sociologists who offer a variety of reasons why we should not ransom our enterprise to the reflexive understandings of our subjects. First, people's understanding is often incoherent. Second, and this is the Marxist response, many people are suffering from **false consciousness** which systematically blinds them to external sources of their actions. Third, we should not rule out sources of action that have unknown internal causes: the unconscious or sub-conscious, for example. All of these objections are on occasions valid though there seems no reason why they should be taken as justification for routinely ignoring actors' accounts of their actions. The problem for those who reject the postulate of adequacy is that we have little else on which to build and test explanations. Simply observing regularities of connections (even if we could produce correlations more impressive than is usually the case) does not tell us what causes what and it is hard to imagine how we explain any action without recourse to guesses about the intentions and motives of actors. Or to view it from the other end, how do we justify telling people 'You think you're doing X but we know you are really doing Y'.

One way to resolve the argument is to treat sociological explanation as a process of translation that begins with actors' meanings, generalises these and augments them with evidence from other sources (such as statistical descriptions of regularities of behaviour) and then offers the sociological explanation back to the actors for confirmation or further elucidation.

See **methodological individualism**.

POSTULATE OF UNIVERSAL FUNCTIONALISM Robert K. **Merton** coined this phrase to denote the assumption of some anthropological versions of **functionalism** that any institution or enduring pattern of behaviour must be adaptive in some manner or it would not have survived. Emile **Durkheim** was slightly more cautious but thought in a similar manner. Merton challenged this view and illustrated the problems with it in his discussion of social structure, **anomie** and deviance.

POTLATCH This anthropological term describes the ritual exchange of gifts in ceremonies intended to establish social standing and honour. It used to be common among the indigenous peoples of the North West coast of North America. In one extreme form, people destroyed large amounts of valuable goods: the status of participants being established by how much they could afford to destroy. The term is sometimes used, slightly ironically, to describe various forms of **conspicuous consumption** in modern societies.

POULANTZAS, NICOS (1936–79) Greek by birth, Poulantzas made his name in France in the 1970s where, with Louis **Althusser**, he was a leading representative of structuralist Marxism. His (1968) *Power and Social Classes* introduced his best-known idea: the relative autonomy of the capitalist state. Against Marxist orthodoxy, which sees the state as being nothing 'but the committee for managing the common affairs of the whole bourgeoisie', Poulantzas argued that the state acted with a degree of independence which (and this is how he remains a Marxist) in the long run, serves the interests of capital better than would the capitalists themselves. For example, by arranging a degree of social welfare and permitting some political representation to the working class, the state diffuses the potential for revolution and ensures a productive labour force.

POVERTY Poverty – the condition of lacking vital resources – is often qualified as 'relative' and 'absolute'. By absolute poverty we mean lacking the truly basic necessities for subsistence: food, water, clothing and shelter. By relative poverty we mean lacking in those things which most people in a society would regard as the minimum requirements for a normal life. As a society prospers, the yard stick for relative poverty changes. Relative poverty need not be just a measure of inequality (as it would be if, for example, we expressed it as having an income below 50 per cent of the modal income). It can still, for any given society, define a point below which people cannot minimally function as that society would expect. For example, people need clothes to stay warm but they also need clothes of sufficient smartness and suitability to be able to get and retain a job. People may not literally 'need' a phone but unless they can get access to a phone they may not be able to access information about social security provisions, phone in their electricity meter readings or participate in society in numerous other ways.

See **citizenship**.

POWER   This single term is used for a very wide variety of purposes by sociologists. Max **Weber** defined it as the probability that one person in a relationship will be able to carry out his will despite resistance. Talcott **Parsons**, Anthony **Giddens** and others define it as the transformational capacity of people: the ability to intervene in a given state of affairs so as to alter them as desired. Power in Weber's sense is clearly zero-sum: the more chance I have of imposing on you, the less chance you have of imposing on me. Transformational power is clearly not zero-sum. The growth in technology has given all of us more power over our circumstances than we used to have: the total amount of power has grown.

POWER ELITE   C. Wright **Mills** popularised this term by making it the title of his 1956 study of three interlocking groups: leading industrialists, military leaders and leading politicians. He did not use 'ruling class' because only in the first group was the basis of power the ownership or control of capital. What bound this elite together was common social origins, common culture and close personal and family ties.

PRACTICAL REASONING   Ethnomethodology takes the study of practical reasoning (or mundane thought in everyday situations) to

be the real stuff of empirical sociology. One very fruitful line of such work are organisational studies that contrast how a job is supposed to be done with how it is actually done by people trying to get on with it. A good example is Egon Bittner's study of plea-bargaining in the California courts; see **bureaucracy**. Ethnomethodologists argue that it is people's everyday reasoning skills that collaboratively produce the orderliness and comprehensibility of social life. In their view, orthodox sociology usually misrepresents social life by trying to identify abstract 'laws' or regularities while paying no attention to the pervasive role of practical reasoning.

See **ad-hocing**, **et cetera principle**.

PRAGMATISM   This US school of philosophy (associated with William James, C.S. Peirce and John **Dewey**) is an important part of the intellectual background to **symbolic interactionism**. Its big idea is that knowledge is not primarily contemplative but is developed in the course of our activities in the world. The meaning of concepts or propositions lies in their practical effects. For example, to say that something is 'true' is to claim that it the best or most accurate statement that can be made about the topic in hand, nothing more. The practical orientation of pragmatism has made it popular with many sociologists, from empirical analysts in the USA to Jürgen Habermas and other **critical theorists** concerned to promote or defend political engagement.

PRAXIS   In Marxist language, this denotes purposive action intended to alter the material and social worlds. Its point is to assert the possibility and necessity of change in line with Karl Marx's dictum that it was not enough to understand the world: we must also try to improve it. However, it is more than a call to action. It also serves an unusual role in **epistemology**. As the fundamental truth of Marxism is a theory of social change, then whether or not any proposition is true or false can be tested by the extent to which it aids or hinders that change. One can go a little further and say that one can make a proposition 'come true' by changing the circumstances that currently render it false. This 'action epistemology' takes Marxism outside the realm of normal social science because it gives practitioners a trump card. A Marxist criminologist concluded a series of criticisms of Edwin Sutherland's theory of **differential association** by asking 'What has Sutherland ever done for popular struggles?'.

A number of feminists, anti-colonial theorists and others representing particular groups take a similar view: that the crucial test of an explanation is not how well it fits with known evidence but how well it allows members of the groups in question to see themselves in the way wished by the author.

PREJUDICE   In common usage, this refers to preconceived opinions or attitudes that are not justified by the facts. Although one can be positively prejudiced (for example, assuming that all Irish people are cheerful and spontaneous) the term is normally used for unwarranted negative views of some people or thing.

PRESSURE GROUPS   Also called 'interest groups', these are organised associations of people which aim to influence governments or other powerful agencies on some particular matter. Unlike **political parties**, they do not normally seek to form a government or have a wide and enduring agenda. Examples are the Sierra Club in the USA which campaigns on environmental issues or the Confederation of British Industry which tries to influence government policy on the economy and the regulation of industry. The existence of a wide variety of pressure groups is usually seen as an important index of the political health of a state because it shows that autonomous political activity is permitted and because the plurality of such channels of influence prevents power becoming concentrated in too few hands.

PRESTIGE   See **status**.

PRIMARY AND SECONDARY GROUPS Charles Horton **Cooley** distinguished between small and immediate groups such as family, friends and work colleagues which are sustained by face-to-face interaction; these are primary. Secondary groups are large and rarely involve direct contact between all or most members: a denomination, trade union and political party are examples of secondary groups.

PRIMARY DEVIATION   See **labelling theory**.

PRIMARY SECTOR   This is one of a useful trilogy of terms used to describe economic activity. The primary sector is that concerned with the production of food and the extraction of raw materials: farming, fishing, mining, quarrying and logging. The secondary sector is concerned with the manufacture of finished goods. The tertiary sector is concerned with services. The proportion of the labour force engaged in each sector provides a convenient way of comparing levels of economic development.

PRIMITIVE SOCIETY   Although now avoided by many scholars for its derogatory overtones, 'primitive' itself replaced other terms (such as 'savage' and 'simple') which had acquired negative connotations. Subsequent replacements include 'tribal society' and 'non-literate society'. The point is simple: a large number of societal features go together. For example, societies that can generate and store a food surplus develop a military capacity to protect it. Primitive societies normally have only the most elementary technology, are non-literate, give a very elevated place to kinship in social organisation and so on. Although we now know this is not the case, the early social scientists took the primitive societies studied by their contemporaries to be relics of the earliest forms of social organisation and inappropriately used the anthropological record to provide material for the first stages of complex evolutionary models.

PRISONERS' DILEMMA   See **game theory**.

PRIVATE AND PUBLIC SPHERES   In general usage this refers to what many regard as a defining characteristic of modern societies: an increasing division between the public world of the polity and the economy and the private world of the family and the home. The language of Parsonian **pattern variables** can be used to describe the different values that are thought to characterise behaviour in each sphere. In the public sphere we are expected to be universalistic, rational, efficient and instrumental. In the private sphere we can be particularistic, sentimental, pay no regard to efficiency and be more concerned with expressive activity than with instrumental activity.

The public/private distinction also allows us to describe the relationship between social **differentiation** and liberty. As a shorthand we can say that modern societies permit a great deal of liberty in the private sphere but exert considerable control in the public sphere. The US constitution's religion clauses, for example, are now interpreted as permitting any religion in private but barring most forms of specific religious expression in public. The explanation for the public/private divide is complex but one obvious cause is the need

to accommodate diversity. If the culture of the public square must also be the culture of the family, then divergent interests must compete to control the public square.

The public/private divide does not, of course, end conflict because some people refuse to accept it: Christian and Muslim fundamentalists, for example, may insist that God requires the state to impose godly behaviour on everyone. And even if everyone accepts the idea of such a divide, we have to argue about where the line lies. For example, until the 1960s, most states took the view that adult sexual activity was legitimately a matter for legislation. Since there has been a steady shift towards regarding the sexual activities of consenting adults as a private matter but every legislative change has been contested.

Sociologists of gender have a specific interest in the public/private divide because it is usually associated with an inequitable estimation of worth; for example, housework is generally viewed as being of lower status than similar work undertaken outside the home.

PRIVATISATION   Since the 1980s, when it was pioneered in the UK by a Conservative government, this has signified the sale into private hands of state assets: a process repeated in Eastern Europe after the fall of communism. Such sales were justified by the assumption that the state had no particular reason to run, for example, the telephone service and the conviction that entrepreneurial business-people would run such enterprises more effectively than had the state.

The term may also refer to changes in the location and reach of certain beliefs and practices. For example, a crucial element of the **secularisation** paradigm is the observation that in many countries the rise of liberal democracy is correlated with religion becoming less prominent in public affairs and being increasingly confined to the home and the leisure sphere.

It is also used to describe the social change in many societies in the 20th century that saw the family home becoming larger, more comfortable and increasingly the place where people spent a lot of their money and their leisure time. The shift from communal to private lifestyles is a key element of the argument in the **Affluent Worker** studies into the politics and orientations to work of the British working class.

PROBABILITY   In the history of western thought probability has generally had one or other of two meanings that it took analysts a long while to disentangle. If we say 'how likely is it in your opinion that your favourite sports team will win tomorrow?' we are asking something different to how likely it is that a large sample of adults from London will contain 20 per cent or less of people with blond hair. In the latter case we can, in principle, list all the possible samples that could be drawn from Londoners and, assuming the sampling has been random, we can talk about the chance of our sample having the appropriate characteristics. This is different from the probability when no one knows what will happen ('will it rain on my birthday in two years' time?' and so on). This is sometimes called epistemological probability and the other, statistical type is known as aleatory.

Sociologists are faced with both kinds of probability. In statistical studies analysts are usually interested in knowing how likely it is that the findings they have obtained from their study, of (say) miners or of Catholics in the USA, will apply to all miners or all US Catholics. They are keen to determine whether their findings are indicative of the situation in the relevant population as a whole. Particularly if they find something unexpected about their sample of miners, they will want to know how probable it is that this result is representative of miners in general or whether this might be a chance characteristic of the miners who happened to

turn up in their sample. By convention, in statistical analyses the probability (usually termed *p*) is given as a number indicating the likelihood of something occurring that ranges between 0 (for impossible) and 1 (for absolute certainty).

By contrast, sociologists usually think about, and are commonly asked to comment on, the likelihood of things happening in the future: will crime decrease next year or will the environmental movement succeed in its objectives and so on. We may think it is probable that crime will decrease but this is not a statistical form of probability even if journalists and others are accustomed to trying to put figures on these projections; journalists will often say, for instance, that there is a 70 per cent chance that crime will decrease. Here the figure serves only to illustrate their degree of confidence in the prediction.

See **null hypothesis**.

PROBLEMATIC   This notion has much the same role in the thought of French Marxist Louis **Althusser** as **paradigm** has in the work of Thomas **Kuhn** and **episteme** has for Michel **Foucault**: it denotes the system of questions and concepts that make up a particular science. Although rarely heard now, it was common in the late 1970s for those who disagreed with Althusser to be accused of 'incorrectly formulating the problematic'. For added effect, the word may be written in the French manner, as problematique.

PROCESS SOCIOLOGY   This term is preferred as a label for their approach by the practitioners of figurational sociology (see **Elias**) because it clearly draws attention to the concern with social processes rather than with social structures.

PROFANE   See **sacred and profane**.

PROFESSION   Sociological conceptions of the profession as a form of occupation or employment took as their starting point the law, the church and medicine. All claimed high levels of technical and intellectual expertise, served foundational social values (religion, legality, health), had a commitment to public service, and all controlled recruitment to the profession and discipline of members. Until the 1970s sociologists tended to take the professions at their own valuation and to repeat the explanations they gave for their privileges. So the right to police themselves and to be free from external control was explained on the grounds that the matters the professions dealt with were too complex for outsiders to understand: only doctors could decide if doctors had done a good job. In the 1970s, sociologists became distinctly more sceptical and argued that the privileges of the professions were primarily beneficial to professionals, not to society as a whole. It became common to argue that the closure exercised by, say, medicine was not inherently different to the desire of skilled craft manual workers to restrict entry and thus improve their market situation. Somewhat ironically it was Conservative governments in the 1980s that started to weaken the professions by opening them up to increased competition. In Britain, for example, the lucrative business of conveyancing (arranging the legal transfer of deeds on the sale of real estate) has been opened up to para-professional groups and the monopoly of barristers to represent clients in certain types of court case has been weakened.

Although the basis on which professions have claimed high status and rewards has been questioned by analysts, **professionalisation** remains a popular strategy for occupational groups seeking to improve their position.

PROFESSIONALISATION   When describing changes in an occupation, this denotes both an attempt to improve quality and an attempt to gain the privileges enjoyed by **professions** (such as self-control and ability to control entrance). In Britain in the 1990s nurses sought to become more like doctors by changing the nature of nurse education. Nursing colleges were taken over by universities. The craft qualifications were replaced by university degrees and abstract learning was added to (and maybe even partially supplanted) what had previously been acquired 'on the job'. In part this reflected real changes in the complexity of tasks nurses were required to undertake but much of the change was intended simply to change the social class associations of the job from a craft to a profession.

PROGRESS   This may mean simply movement towards some desired goal (as in making progress taming my garden). It also denotes a package of scientific, technical, economic, social and political changes. From the **Enlightenment** thinkers of the 18th century to Talcott **Parsons** in the 1960s, most social theorists have seen the general direction of change as progressive (major wars and depressions notwithstanding). Karl **Marx** was profoundly critical of capitalism but only because it was not yet socialism; he accepted it was an improvement on feudalism. Max **Weber** saw progress in the increased rationalisation of scientific, economic, legal and organisational life. Emile **Durkheim** regarded organic solidarity as offering increased prosperity and greater personal freedom than **mechanical solidarity**. With his **evolutionary universals**, Parsons clearly regarded the increase in adaptive capacity as progressive (being able to do more and better).

There has always been a glum strand to social theory, promoted by both sides of the political divide. On the right, Vilfredo **Pareto** and Robert Michels (with his **iron law of oligarchy**) were pessimistic about political progress. On the left, leading Marxist glums such as Theodor **Adorno** and Herbert

Marcuse promoted a dismal vision through such notions as **mass society** and **mass culture**.

In the world at large there have always been reasons to distrust change: the Luddites smashed the machine looms of the early factory age, the 1940s generation had the Holocaust, the 1960s generation worried about nuclear warfare, the 1990s generation worried about the environment.

Whether or not people like change is a topic for sociology; it does not threaten its foundations. Postmodernists have argued that the connection between sociology and 'the Enlightenment project' is so close that the fall of the latter entails the fall of the former. If we sociologists (or most people or some intellectuals; the charge is not quite clear) cannot honestly describe the large patterns of change as progress, then we cannot continue with social science because it was invented by people who believed it central to human progress. This is unconvincing. First, why the founders of sociology created the enterprise and its intellectual value are quite separate matters. Second, intentions of any sort play little part in sociological explanations of social change. Most major change is a result of unintended consequences.

PROLETERIANISATION　　An increase in class conflict was essential to Karl Marx's evolutionary sociology and that required the disappearance of the intermediate classes to the **bourgeoisie** and the **proletariat**. Marx believed that the inherent logic of capitalism would lead to the petty bourgeoisie being forced into the working class. It did not happen. The 1970s **de-skilling** thesis was an attempt to revive this claim.

PROLETARIAT　　Karl **Marx** used this term to denote the class of propertyless labourers who live by selling their labour power to capitalists.

PROPHET　　Max Weber notes that prophets and priests enjoyed very different bases of legitimacy in the Old Testament. The priests commanded traditional authority; they were ritual functionaries in the tradition. Prophets were usually outsiders and their legitimacy was based on personal charisma.

In his comparative studies of religion, Weber distinguished ethical and exemplary prophecy. The ethical prophet (Christ and Mohammed are examples) proclaimed God's will. The exemplary prophet (Buddha, for example) showed the way to salvation through his personal example. The exemplary type is characteristic of the far east; the ethical of the near east.

PROTEAN　　Proteus was a Greek sea god who was able to alter his form at will. His celebrated inconstancy chimes with **postmodern** views about the disintegration of **metanarratives** and is exemplified in the thesis advanced by US psychologist Robert Jay Lifton (1993) in his book about the changing nature of conceptions of the self: *The Protean Self: Human Resilience in an Age of Fragmentation*. He reassures his readers that they are better to be resilient, flexible and on the move than to be fixed and settled.

PROTESTANT ETHIC THESIS, THE　　The best known part of Max **Weber**'s extensive writings on the social consequences of religious belief systems, 'The Protestant Ethic and the Spirit of Capitalism' was first published as an essay in the *Archiv für Sozialwissenschaft und Sozialpolitik* in 1905. It is now often read as a riposte to Karl **Marx**'s materialist view of economic change but it was probably stimulated more by Werner Sombart's writings on the parts played by Jews in the rise of modern capitalism.

For Weber what needs to be explained is the transcending of **economic traditionalism**. Most pre-modern people had relatively fixed notions of their traditional, customary or expected standard of living and, given the choice, preferred less work to more money. The customary rate of return was accompanied by customary ways of working. Those who did exhibit the desire for great wealth tried to find it in extravagant ways: merchants staked their fortunes on single ships and lords invested in foreign wars. What was missing were precisely those features which Weber thought distinguished modern capitalism: the desire for the calculable and steady rate of return on investment; a rational experimental attitude to improving work methods; and a willingness to work hard.

The distribution of early capitalism – Britain, Holland, the USA and the Protestant parts of Germany – rather than France, Portugal, Spain or Italy suggested a connection with religion. Weber argued that key ideas of the Protestant Reformation of the 16th century had the *unintended* consequence of encouraging new attitudes to work and wealth. Martin Luther rejected the idea of a religious division of labour that allowed religious officials to placate God on behalf of others. All people had to be responsible for their own salvation: 'every man his own monk'. This call for universal piety was made compatible with the continuation of normal life by Luther's new concept of the vocation. He taught that any legitimate occupation, performed in the right spirit, was pleasing to God. The Reformers removed the clergy's power to cleanse sin through confession and penance. Without the ability to wipe the slate clean, people had to be constantly attentive to their spiritual state. John Calvin's distinctive contribution was to the doctrine of pre-destination. If God was all-knowing and all-powerful then he must know which of us was destined for heaven and which for hell, even before we were born. The Puritans believed that nothing would change God's mind but they did want to know. They worked hard to the glory of God and avoided temptation. If they prospered they took this

as a sign of divine blessing. This and other ideological innovations (such as a new emphasis on stewardship) create a new ethos which Weber summarised as *this-worldly* asceticism. The Protestant ethic alone could not create capitalism (appropriate material conditions were required) but it did create a personality and a series of attitudes towards work and expenditure – the 'spirit' of capitalism – that were unusually well-suited to rational capitalism.

The Weber thesis has been subjected to 80 years of detailed scrutiny and examination. Many of the criticisms have been irrelevant because they have missed the subtlety of Weber's thought. That Luther and Calvin did not encourage people to become rich is neither here nor there because Weber's connection is of unintended consequences: religious innovations, as they were put into effect, changed personalities 100 years later. That Scotland had a lot of Calvinists but was slow to show capitalist take-off is presented as refutation but again misses the narrow nature of what Weber asserts. He does not believe that ideas alone are enough to create major change. Without the right material conditions to turn the spirit of capitalism into the social product, what you had were frustrated capitalists and Gordon Marshall's study of Sir John Clerk of Penecuik showed exactly that. The Japan refutation is the obverse: lots of capitalism without any Protestants. But it too misses the point because what Weber was trying to do was explain the origins of capitalism the first time. Once the new attitudes to work and social practices were established in western Europe and proved successful, it was open to any other culture to borrow and adapt them. The Weber thesis does not argue that only Protestants could become either this-worldly ascetics or capitalists.

The greatest weakness is actually the least-often noticed, perhaps because it is a common feature of all grand sociology. In his brief essay (augmented by other later writings) he explains the Reformation innovations, illustrates them with some scant references to the Puritan Divine Richard Baxter and then leaps 200 years to illustrate the spirit of capitalism with Benjamin Franklin. At best the empirical material is illustrative and there is almost no attempt to fill the causal gaps.

Subsequent detailed historical research has offered a lot of support for the Weber thesis and the majority opinion is that it remains plausible. More than that, it formed an important part of the wider comparative studies that linked culture, personality and economic organisation. Those studies remain profoundly influential as scholars try to explain why in the second half of the 20th century some Asian societies developed successful capitalist economies and others did not. Although Weber is often set against Marx, his interest in the cultural conditions for economic activity can be seen as a complement, rather than an alternative, to such materialist approaches as **world-systems theory**.

PSEPHOLOGY   This is the study of voting and voting behaviour and gets its name from the Greek for a pebble; the ancient Greeks voted by writing names on stones or bits of pottery.

PSEUDO-SCIENCE   See **science**.

PSYCHOANALYSIS   See **Freud**.

PUTTING-OUT SYSTEM   See **factory system**.

Q

QUALITATIVE AND QUANTITATIVE RESEARCH METHODS Qualitative styles of research (such as **participant observation**) rely entirely on the skill of the researcher to collect data. Quantitative research (a large survey using a questionnaire, for example) impersonalises the research process by formalising the means of enquiry and analysis. To understand what people do with television we could select two families and spend every evening for a week with each, watching television and chatting. Or we could design a survey questionnaire. Provided the questions were well designed, the latter would generate a large amount of thin data about a large number of people's use of television. The qualitative method would allow us to collect rich data about a very small number of people.

The drawbacks to qualitative work concern reliance on the personality of the researcher, the uniqueness of the research event, and the limits on generalisation.

Some sociologists are insensitive, socially inept and dim; they will not bring back anything worthwhile from the field and no matter how long they spend at it, will never say anything worthwhile about the data they have collected. Even the best can only be in one place at once. In quantitative methods, the skill and expertise of the best researcher is formalised so that it can be applied simultaneously by hundreds of trained colleagues.

Second, all research findings can be challenged and the best defence is to repeat the experiment or re-run the drugs trial; because much qualitative social research is intended to access without distorting a naturally-occurring slice of social life, the study cannot be repeated. We either accept the researcher's conclusions or not. With much quantitative work we cannot repeat the data collection but we can access the same data set and repeat calculations or try new ones. In the 1980s, arguments among social class analysts about the value of competing **occupational scales** were advanced by repeatedly re-analysing data using a variety of different scales.

The first and second points combine in this: with quantitative work we can usually see the 'working out': the cross-tabulations and the path analysis diagrams are there to question. With book length reports and detailed quotations from interviews and field notes we may sometimes see how the researcher comes to his or her interpretation of the event or setting but mostly we have to accept the researcher has come to the right conclusion.

Third, the complexity of what is studied with qualitative methods makes it hard to know how far we can generalise from any set of results. I may discover a great deal about my two television-watching families but unless I discover similar things about a large sample of the population, I cannot know how representative they are. There is always the danger that any large survey sample may be unusual in ways that are not obvious (for example, a recent high-profile murder case could increase the salience of crime for respondents in a sample) but because we use large numbers of respondents we can ensure that they are representative in such characteristics as class, gender, age, ethnicity, education and the like.

The drawbacks to quantitative research methods are as great and as obvious. To generate identical interval level data (see **measurement, levels of**) from a number of research sites requires that the investigation be formalised to such an extent that important areas of social life simply cannot be investigated in this way. Only questions that have simple answers can be asked and we have no way of benefiting from the questioner's observations of how the question is answered. In extended discussion we can note and pursue signs of hesitation, uncertainty, even guilt. All of that is lost in a survey questionnaire. The result is that we often end up with data, the meaning of which is not at all clear. What, for example, are we to make of the fact that 72 per cent of people in England and Wales who completed the 2001 Census ticked the box 'Christian' when only 10 per cent attend church?

Perhaps the greatest danger of quantitative methods is that we forget what lies behind the numbers. We forget that there was art in framing the questions and designing the instrument. Even more art goes into the shaping of the results on their way to final interpretation. In the early 1980s a number of survey analyses suggested that 60 per cent of Americans sympathised with the New Christian Right agenda on abortion and other contentious socio-moral matters. This high figure was produced by a series of contestable choices by the analysts. For each item, respondents were offered a range of answers. If we took the New Christian Right agenda narrowly then on each question only the 'Strongly agree' responses would accord, but analysts decided to count all the responses except 'Strongly disagree' as showing sympathy with NCR positions. Putting the cut-off lines in one place produced an NCR support

rate of just 12 per cent; placing it elsewhere raised the apparent rate to well over half. Because the final numbers have the appearance of certainty we may be inappropriately confident of our conclusions.

At times and among certain schools of sociologists, a preference for qualitative or quantitative methods has been tied to theoretical and explanatory preferences; some feminist sociologists, for example, argue that only qualitative methods are proper for the social sciences and it is hard to imagine statistical work in **ethnomethodology**. But most sociologists accept that both are legitimate and that we should choose our methods according to the type of data sought, not the preferred explanation of it. It is also widely accepted that the two approaches overlap: though they may rarely describe their impressions in numbers, qualitative researchers classify, count and compare the frequency of one event observed with another. On the other side quantitative researchers draw on their own interpretations in the way they frame the questions in the first place and they often conduct qualitative **pilot studies** to test the validity and worth of questions. Sociological texts that oppose qualitative and quantitative traditions do a disservice to sociological research.

QUEER THEORY   More a brand of sexual politics than a social scientific theory, this uses the pejorative 'queer' in a positive way to denote a commitment to non-conformist sexualities (such as pornography and sadomasochism as well as homosexuality). Queer theory asserts that there are no natural sexual identities and that queerness is everywhere; everything is a cultural choice. Queer theory encourages novel readings of literary works and cinema but also of cultural products (such as advertisements) in the light of its assumption that queerness is pervasive.

See **Butler**.

QUESTIONNAIRE This is a form containing a large number of simple questions, normally with pre-set answers from which the respondent selects. We use them to acquire descriptive data on demographic characteristics such as age, gender, social class and the like and to assess attitudes and beliefs. Though some are designed as fishing expeditions, in many cases the questions are designed to provide information that will test a particular theory.

Questionnaire design is skilled work. Even when we have a clear idea of what we want to know, design is difficult. So that answers can be quantified, we have to break complex issues (belief in God, for example) into a series of questions. We might start with 'Do you believe in God?' with a 'Yes/No, Don't know' choice. Only those who answer 'Yes' will be asked the next question: 'Which of the following comes closest to your idea of God?' which can be accompanied by five or six alternatives. But then we might want to assess not just the content of the belief but also its stability. One common version of the God question mixes content and stability by offering options such as 'I sometimes have doubts but I do believe that there is a God'.

Asking open-ended answers does not remove the need to anticipate answers because, for the answers to be turned into numbers on scales, someone has to interpret and code the answers in a limited number of options. Leaving the answers open simply defers the problem and for that reason most large surveys use closed questions.

We can use pilot studies to see if respondents have particular difficulties with some questions but the uncertainty always remains. Cross-national surveys such as the World Values Survey are particularly difficult because ensuring that respondents hear the question we intended is complicated by the need to find reliable translations when cultural differences may be exactly the thing that interests us.

Changing the way a question is asked can materially affect answers. Asking directly 'Did you attend church, chapel or synagogue last weekend?' produces higher rates of reported church attendance than asking 'Which of the following did you do last weekend?' and inserting 'Go to church' in a long list with such items as 'Go to the cinema', 'Work in the garden' and 'Visit relatives'. Question order also makes a difference because one question (and its answer) may set the context for the interpretation of the next.

In designing a questionnaire we are severely constrained in the number of questions we can ask. Even without financial constraints there is a limit to how much time people will be willing to spend on responding. Too long a questionnaire will causes respondents to hurry answers to get it over with and will reduce response rates. If one is conducting a large international questionnaire (for example, with samples in all member states of the European Union) each extra question will add thousands of euros or dollars to overall costs.

Finally (though this is shared with the unstructured interview) there is the problem of the accuracy of answers. For a wide variety of reasons people may exaggerate, dissemble or inadvertently mislead. For example, the church-attendance rate claimed by Americans in surveys is almost twice as high as the figure generated by asking the churches how many people regularly attend.

This list of problems might seem to call into question the very method but the fact that questionnaires are very widely used in sociology suggests that they are successful for some purposes. The method may not allow detailed exploration of complex or sensitive issues but it can identify themes we would want to pursue with other research strategies and it can sometimes provide critical tests of clearly formulated ideas.

R

RACE Used narrowly this signifies the scientifically discredited idea that people are divided into biologically distinct groups with unalterable characteristics (invariably superior ones in the case of the speaker's race and degenerate ones in the case of other races). We know now that humankind's genetic material has been thoroughly mixed by centuries of inter-breeding. Given this genetic mixing, if a group of people display some characteristic feature, it is very unlikely to be wholly genetic and is most likely partly a product of the environment. Although most modern sociologists do not believe in race it remains a topic for us because other people believe in it and act accordingly.

Most popular usage of the term is very loose. For example, 'the Negro race' bases racial identity primarily on skin colour and origins while 'the German race' relates to language and territory. Contemporary genetics suggests that many of the genetic factors that people have used to identify 'races' – chiefly skin colour and facial features – are no guarantee of profound genetic similarity. Given the size and complexity of the human genome and given the relatively small amount of genetic information that is associated with 'racial' characteristics, people of different apparent races can share just as much genetic similarity as people of the same 'race'. This means that even if some genetic basis to intelligence or other such socially significant characteristics were found, there is no reason to suppose that its distribution would follow 'racial' lines. In other words, biological research suggests that there is no guarantee that people of seemingly similar race are overall closer genetically than people from different apparent races.

A final irony is that, in a well-meaning attempt to monitor equality of opportunity, job applicants in industrialised countries are now often asked to state their race, quite separately from their application form, for reasons of equal-opportunities monitoring. Bureaucrats have devised 'racial' categories for these forms which have no genetic basis and have invented a whole new series of unscientific racial classifications, albeit with liberal and praiseworthy intentions. These classifications are now social facts to which people have to adapt.

RACISM This signifies beliefs, ideologies or behaviour that distinguishes people on the basis of their supposed membership of some putative racial group (in practice usually defined by culture or land of origin or skin colour). Any system of social classification can be the basis for structured inequality and prejudicial behaviour, but racism is particularly often associated with vicious treatment (such as the **Nazi** holocaust with its extermination of some six million Jews or the South African apartheid regime) because asserting a biological base to differences allows the dominant group to think of divisions as unalterable and of others as not fully human.

See **institutional racism**.

RATIO LEVEL MEASUREMENT See measurement, levels of.

RATIONAL CHOICE THEORY More a paradigm than a theory, this is the heart of conventional economics. It assumes that social action can be explained by the desire of all actors to achieve the best outcome for themselves. When faced with choices, the actor will select that which gives the best return or 'maximises his utility'. For example, if an identical product can be bought at two outlets for different prices, the actor will buy the cheapest because this produces the same utility as the more expensive option while leaving money over that can be spent on something else. On that simple principle, economics has erected a complex edifice of propositions about human behaviour.

Since the 1980s numerous sociologists have borrowed rational choice theory, applying it with varying degrees of formality. Much of it appeal is that, compared to much sociology, it appears rigorous and scientific. By and large it has not proved successful because much of what interests sociologists does not conform to the utility maximisation principle. An initial problem is that much social action either does not involve choice at all or the choices are not those of the economistic model. Tradition, for example, plays a large part in human behaviour, as does altruism.

Making the rational choice requires that we have appropriate information about costs and rewards. But in the case of choosing between religions, for example, we lack entirely the crucial information about rewards. Until we are dead, and then it is too late, we cannot be sure which of two competing religions will deliver salvation. We also cannot compare costs. The price elements of cost in religious choice are trivial. We can try replacing price by what economists call 'shadow prices' (for example using the amount of time we are expected to spend in services and prayer meetings). But to the

person who believes, a two-hour prayer meeting is a blessing and a reward; to the non-believer it is a large cost. If costs may change into rewards at the point of belief than we cannot use the assessment of cost and reward to explain why someone comes to believe.

It is a matter of observation that ideologues do not make rational choices in the mode of the maximising individual. If a car dealer finds he is not making a profit, he will change franchise to another brand, or even get out of car sales altogether. When liberal Protestant churches find their membership falling, they do not become Catholic or give up religion altogether. More likely (and this is very common with extreme left-wing parties) they will continue in the old ways and persuade themselves that their product is too good for the public. Areas of life that are informed by deeply-held beliefs are generally not open to maximising behaviour because people who are wedded to one view do not see other visions as plausible alternatives. Most lifelong Catholics do not consider evangelical Protestant as an equally valid religion that should be explored to see if it offers better rewards for lower costs; they see it as heresy and falsehood.

Economistic rational choice does work well in certain conditions. If there is widespread demand for a general product (say cars) and brand loyalty is not reinforced by powerful group ties (no one gets ostracised, expelled or executed for changing car brands) and the rewards and costs of the alternatives can be effectively compared, then how people behave may well fit the rational choice model. But much social life is not like that.

This does not mean that most human behaviour is irrational. On the contrary, if social action were not minimally rational (in the sense that we can infer the reasons for other people's conduct) we would not be able to understand it and social life would grind to a halt. Our point is that there are forms of **rationality** other than maximising utility.

See **exchange theory, free rider**.

RATIONALISM This philosophical doctrine is the campaigning arm of **rationality**. It asserts that reason is the sole valid basis for objective knowledge. Claims to other sorts of authority (such as divine revelation) are now so rare that there is little cause to press a rationalist case any more, even if rationalists do face some competition from enthusiasts for the **New Age Movement**. Hence its meaning has narrowed and will usually now signify the ideological background to campaigns against the influence of organised religion. For example, rationalists may campaign for secular funeral services.

RATIONALITY To describe a belief or some act as rational is not to say that it is true or correct but that it is held (or done) on reasoned grounds, that it follows from some accountable logic, and that it has been arrived at in ways consistent with the person's other views. Rationality is more a matter of procedure than content: beliefs should be consistent and not contradictory; they should fit with experience and not be known to be false.

At one level, rationality is a precondition for sociology. If ordinary people could not see the rationality of each other's actions then social life would appear mysterious and society would be chaotic. Rationality is so pervasive that some philosophers take the view that 'justified rational action needs no further explanation'. However the fact that people can disagree while still behaving rationally (you rationally favour vegetarianism while I rationally decide to continue eating meat) indicates that rationality does not closely define what we may or may not believe. In fact, the question of rationality throws up some complex conceptual problems for the social sciences.

There may be some specialised areas of life where rationality is more or less supreme. Many scientists assert that in mathematics and the experimental sciences rationality will ultimately lead us to believe the same things. But that still leaves many important issues where, although we debate them rationally, people may come to differing conclusions. Sociologists face a difficulty in explaining beliefs and behaviour in cases where they find it hard to assess the rationality of the actors. Sociologists may try, for example, to understand why terrorists use violent means to achieve political ends. Advocates of terror will typically argue that the circumstances rationally justified abnormal tactics. Some anti-abortion campaigners believe that abortion is so repugnant that they are justified in attacking or threatening to kill doctors who perform terminations. In such circumstances sociologists have a problem in assessing the rationality of the action. Some sociologists will claim that, given these people's beliefs and value commitments, their actions are rational and that this is enough to explain their actions. Other sociologists (including **critical theorists**) will typically argue that the overall framework in which these actions are performed is not rational; they will suggest that there is some deeper or ulterior consideration at work. The practical problem for the sociologist is to know how rationally defensible an action has to be before it can be taken as not needing further explanation. Sociologists face this problem in a way that chemists (say) do not because molecules do not have reasons for action while people do; (ir)rationality does not come into the behaviour of molecules.

A second and related difficulty is that the idea of rationality raises particularly starkly the problem of cultural **relativism**. Is rationality a universal property or do different cultures have very different standards? It is easy to find examples in the anthropological literature (and all around us) of apparent irrationality. But the difficulty is to know whether alien cultures are irrational or whether we just have not yet found the correct way of understanding their beliefs. It is difficult to see how any culture could be irrational for long. Even the most basic language requires that words refer consistently to the same objects and so on. Given that anthropologists have managed to make sense of all peoples discovered so far, it is hard to know whether this is because logic is a human universal or whether it is because we only count a translation of their culture as adequate once it conforms to our standards of rationality.

These conceptual complications surrounding the ascription of rationality have led **ethnomethodologists** to argue that orthodox social science has got the matter the wrong way round. Ethnomethodologists argue that the rationality of actions is produced after the event, in the way that actors **account** for their past actions. It is a property of accounts not of actions.

RATIONALISATION   In common usage (and in the sociology of Vilfredo **Pareto**) this refers to spurious reasons (a rationale) we give others, and sometimes ourselves, for our actions. To rationalise your action is to make it sound better than it really is.

Sociologists more often use the term in Max **Weber**'s sense of things becoming more rational. Rationalisation is **Weber**'s big idea in characterising modernity. We see it: in economic life with the bureaucratic organisation of factories and the use of systematic accounting procedures to calculate profit; in religion with the rise of monotheism, the decline of magic and the rise of personal spiritual responsibility; in law, ad hoc law-making is replaced by deductive reasoning from universal principles; in politics when traditional and charismatic leaderships gives way to bureaucratic parties; and in society as a whole with the growth of bureaucratic administration and the spread of **universalism**.

REALISM   The realist position is a philosophical stance that maintains that the things disclosed by science, including social science, are among the real constituents and the real mechanisms of the natural world. They are – in the philosophical cliché – the furniture of the universe. Realism of this sort is opposed to **idealism**. Some philosophers have argued that invisible forces that we talk about, such as gravity, need not really exist. They are just conventions, just one way of interpreting the world, that helps us make consistent sense of it. Realists assert to the contrary that science succeeds precisely because the entities it names (atoms and so on) really exist. Of course, we cannot check whether realism is correct by 'going and looking' since we have no access to the ultimate constituents of the universe except through science. Instead realists use transcendental arguments to back up their position: they try to deduce, through thought alone, what the world must be like for science to succeed.

In a sense realism is less important in the social sciences since sociologists do not devise many hypothetical entities whose existence is in doubt. Pretty much everyone agrees that people exist, though the status of such entities as **discourses** is admittedly dubious. In recent years, realist arguments have had the strongest appeal for Marxist social scientists (known as **critical realists**) who have wanted to use philosophical arguments to suggest that theoretical entities such as classes really exist.

In a more informal sense realism is also used to refer to the belief that some things are truly real and independent of the way that humans think about them. This position is opposed to **social constructionism**. For example, a social constructionist might point to the different ways that environmental problems are conceptualised in different cultures; realists would argue that there are real environmental problems (such as ozone depletion) that exist independently of cultural differences and which account for the salience of environmental anxieties.

REDUCTIONISM An explanation is reductionist when it tries to account for a wide range of phenomena with a single determining cause. Classic Marxism is reductionist in the way that it explains almost everything by class. From this a related meaning has developed: reductionism as the denial of individual motivation, either in the form of locating the causes of action somewhere else (you think you have chosen this political party but you are merely obeying the demands of your class position) or replacing the claimed motive with a less honourable one (you think you want to ban alcohol because you believe drink causes social problems but really you just want to lord it over the working class).

REFERENCE GROUP Much of what we are and how we think of ourselves comes from comparing ourselves to others. We will often form a relatively stable association with a particular group, whose members' attitudes, beliefs and behaviour serve for us first as a source of norms and second as a yardstick for comparisons. We do not have to be members of the reference group, though that is common: people may often draw inspiration from, and model themselves on, the group to which they would like to belong.

REFLEXIVE The point of this term would have been clearer if sociologists had chosen 'reflective'. A reflex is an automatic response; something produced without anything intervening between stimulus and response: the lower leg flicking up when the nerve under the knee is tapped is an example of a reflex. 'Reflexive' is intended not to remind us of reflexes but of 'reflection' in the sense of seeing ourselves in a mirror, of ourselves being the object of our thought. Generally its use points to two related human abilities: to think about things (as distinct from responding automatically) and to monitor ourselves. In sociological writing the term reflexive does a variety of jobs. First,

some authors, such as Erving **Goffman**, have been struck by the reflexive nature of everyday conduct. People do not concern themselves only with the task in hand but with how they appear to others while performing that task. Goffman described this aspect of reflexivity as 'impression management'. Second, Harold **Garfinkel** used the term in a subtly different way to refer to the way in which ordinary people's understanding of their social context is itself a part of that context. People do not just occupy social spaces, they partly create those spaces through their practical assumptions about what those spaces mean: jurors make up a jury in part through their ideas about what jurors normally and properly do. For **ethnomethodologists**, all social life is reflexive in this sense. Third, some sociologists have been concerned with the applicability of sociological ideas to sociology itself. For example, exponents of the sociology of knowledge claim that knowledge is in some sense a product of social practices and customs; but this assertion must apply to their own knowledge too. Reflexivity as the application of sociology to itself is a widespread theme in sociological theorising though it often gives rise to endless and unproductive contemplation.

REFLEXIVE MODERNITY According to Ulrich **Beck**, modernisation increases our ability to reflect on and to change the social conditions of our existence. It also forces us to do this because it weakens our ties to family, social class and location. As mainstream sociology had long pointed out, modernisation leads us to break with tradition. But Beck observed that this occurs in ever more innovative and unexpected ways. For example, with advancing knowledge about nutrition and diet we are increasingly called on to reflect on how we feed ourselves and our children. With the growth in understanding of genetics we may soon be expected to reflect on and take responsibility for the genetic inheritance we will pass on to the next generation. To a much greater extent than previous generations we have to fashion our own identities and those of our children.

Beck points out that this drive towards reflection also impacts on expertise in contemporary society. To take the example of diet, if people are expecting to assume responsibility for their diets they currently face a dilemma: do they believe the mainstream health authorities and focus on reducing their fat intake or do they follow new diets that focus on the elimination of carbohydrates. This places new demands on experts to demonstrate publicly the basis for their own recommendations. In turn, there is assertion and counter-assertion among experts and this leads to an undermining of expert authority. Reflexive modernity is thus both an account of how life feels for ordinary citizens in advanced modernity and a diagnosis of the advancing crisis of authority that Beck detects. His diagnosis is in some respects similar to that offered by **postmodernists** though he sees the insatiable demands for reflexive justification as the main dynamic that aggravates the problem whereas they put more stress on the undermining of the philosophical foundations of Enlightenment thinking.

REFLEXIVITY   See **reflexive**.

REFORMISM   This denotes political policies and programmes designed to make significant changes without altering the basis of the political or social structure.

REFUTATION   Unfortunately this term is often used when 'rejection' is meant. To refute is to reject an assertion by producing evidence that the assertion is false. It is closer to 'disprove' than to 'deny'. Its use in the social sciences was popularised by Karl **Popper**'s philosophy of science and in particular the book *Conjectures and Refutations* (1963).

REGRESSION ANALYSIS   Like **correlation**, regression is a matter of association between two or more variables. However, whereas correlation measures the strength of the association, regression measures the effect of one on the other. For example, correlation will tell you to what extent there is a linear relationship between income and happiness, while regression will tell you how much extra income is needed to buy an additional unit of happiness – even if the association is not in fact very strong. Thus in regression analysis it is explicitly assumed that one variable is being influenced by others; correlation involves no assumptions about what (if anything) causes what.

The basic idea behind regression is simple: it amounts to finding the best line to draw through a set of points on a graph. We collect information about a large number of people and plot their years of education on the x-axis and their income on the y-axis. We then draw a regression line (or line of 'best fit') through the scatter of cases. Because the regression line is continuous, we can estimate the value of y (income) from any new figure for x (years of education). More importantly, we can see how much additional income is likely to be produced by each additional year of education. Moreover, we can add further variables like gender or years of experience to the equation, both to make predictions more accurate and to be sure that we are controlling for other relevant influences on income.

Regression analysis properly requires data at the interval or ratio levels of **measurement** but there are techniques that allow ordinal data to be used.

REIFICATION   To reify is to treat an idea or concept (the nation, for example) as if it were a real thing. One might think it an easy matter to distinguish real objects (my house) from concepts (my social class) but even **methodological individualists** accept that abstractions (such as my nationality) can have causal power. As we all on occasions reify, describing something as reification carries the implication that it is improper in this circumstance.

RELATIONS OF PRODUCTION   In Marxist economics the **means of production** (the machines, the raw materials, the skills and the labour power) combine with the pattern of social relations between different groups involved in production (primarily the social classes) to form specific modes of production.

RELATIVE AUTONOMY   See **Poulantzas**.

RELATIVE DEPRIVATION   This phrase is closely linked to Robert K. Merton's **reference group** theory: the idea being that people derive their expectations in large part from comparisons. Hence how deprived people feel will be a matter not just of their circumstances but also of whom they use as a comparison.

Relative deprivation can be used in a way that supposes reasoned estimates of what one deserves. It has also been used in a more roundabout manner to explain recruitment to certain sorts of political and social movements. As with **status inconsistency**, it was argued that relative deprivation causes psychological stress which people resolved by joining causes which (according to the observer) were more an expression of frustration than a rational solution to the causes of that frustration.

RELATIVE POVERTY   See **poverty**.

RELATIVISM   In its mildest form this is trite; in its strong form it is a threat to the sociological enterprise as conventionally conceived. Societies and groups within societies have different tastes, norms, values and beliefs; they even have different ways of discerning the truth. It is thus the case that much of life is 'relative' in the sense that whether marrying your cousin is incestuous or recommended depends on your culture. If applied only to others and to ourselves as 'civilians', relativism is merely the recognition of a sociological truth: different people see things differently.

It is usual to distinguish issues that can only be a matter of taste (Is country-and-western music good?) from those which at least in theory can be determined irrespective of taste (Does smoking cause lung cancer?). It seems that we can happily be relativist about the former but not about the latter. However, this division excludes a large number of tricky cases and so does not help us as much as might at first appear. For example, should one be relativistic about the idea that murder is wrong? At first sight we might think not. But nearly all societies permit deliberate killing in some special circumstances: the special circumstances we tolerate include self-defence, times of war, 'mercy killings' of the elderly and extremely sick (this may be done covertly) and abortion. In modern western culture we believe we have good reasons for all these exceptions – even if people are in doubt about the last three – but other cultures believe they have good reasons for their exemptions too. It is hard to see what the universal, absolute rule is in this instance. There are many cases that sit on this tricky border between the relative and the absolute.

Some scholars turn the mild form of social science relativism into an instrument with which to undermine the sociological enterprise (indeed all science). If how people see the world is a product of their culture or their social position (as in the Marxist idea of **false consciousness**) there can be no justification for asserting that one particular approach to knowledge is more likely to produce the truth than any other. The proposition that the Zande chicken poisoning oracle is, for the Zande, a perfectly good way of discovering the truth turns into the proposition that Zande magic is as good as western science. This is the case made by some **postmodernists**: social science (and natural science for that matter) is merely one narrative among many: no worse but certainly no better than the others.

The customary response to such relativism is to point out that it cannot be consistent: to assert that the merits of different **epistemologies** cannot be compared is itself a factual assertion, the truth of which must be established. A better response is to demonstrate that very few people of any culture decline the opportunity to swap one set of ideas for another when the greater efficacy of the new ones can be established (as it very often readily is). But even if this response allows us to dispense with extreme relativists, there are still occasions on which sociologists rightly adopt a relativistic stance. In recent years sociologists of **science** have focused on scientific controversies to try to find out how the scientific community copes with division and uncertainty. In the midst of a controversy, when both sides have reasonable arguments and respectable scientific credentials, sociological analysts have adopted a stance of 'methodological relativism'. If the scientists themselves do not know who is in the right, sociologists can hardly know either. They thus suspend judgement about the facts under dispute and treat both sides even-handedly. A similar approach is justifiably adopted under circumstances of moral controversy as well (for instance over 'animal rights').

RELIABILITY   Though it needs to be carefully distinguished from accuracy, this is an important virtue in social science. A reliable measure is one that gives the same results when it is applied to the same people or the

same data on separate occasions. If we twice administer, at close intervals, a set of questions about belief in God, church-attendance and self-defined religiosity and find that our compound measure of religiosity produces the same result, then we can be confident that it is reliable. Of itself this does not tell us precisely what we are measuring but consistency is a good place to start.

RELIGION   There is no need for a sociological definition of religion any more than there is for a sociological definition of football. From the myriad instances of what ordinary people call religion, we can define it as a social phenomenon that consists of beliefs, actions and institutions which assume the existence of supernatural entities with powers of action, or impersonal powers or processes possessed of moral purpose.

Some confusion is caused by talk of functionalist 'definitions' of religion when it would be more accurate to talk of 'assertions about the consequences' of religion. Whether religion has the functions attributed to it (mainly creating and maintaining social cohesion) is an empirical assertion to be made with the evidence; it is not something we should fix in advance by defining religion in terms of putative functions.

See **civil religion**, **implicit religion**.

RELIGIOUS ORGANISATIONS   The various terms 'church', 'sect', 'denomination' and 'cult' are used in an unfortunately promiscuous manner; their origins in the history of Christianity makes their application to other religions awkward; the supporters and critics of particular organisations use them in a partisan way; and the confusion is compounded by popular press usage differing markedly from professional sociological usage.

A useful place to start is with the contrast between church and sect. The church is usually very large and aims to encompass an entire society. It claims a unique access to religious truth and tries to order the spiritual, moral, ethical and social life of an entire people. But the price it pays for its scale is that, while it does not tolerate challenges to its authority, it accepts considerable laxity. The church normally promotes a religious division of labour in which the core of church officials worships God on behalf of the people while the common people are expected only to accept the authority of the church, take part in the major rituals, live decently and financially support the church. Central to this structure is the idea that religious merit can be transferred from the pious to the less so. The church is hierarchical. The exemplar of the church form is the Roman Catholic Church.

The sect is a radical challenge to the church and to the wider society. It is small (because it has high membership demands and entry qualifications). People become members voluntarily when they meet those requirements (rather than, as in the church, being born into the organisation). It rejects the religious division of labour and expects all members to live a pious life. In rejecting the division of labour, the sect also rejects hierarchy and regards all members as equal. Hence it either has no professional trained ministry or regards that ministry as a matter of administrative convenience. Unlike the church, the sect does not suppose that its officials have quasi-magical powers that allow them to influence God in a manner that is denied to ordinary members. That is, ministry is not a 'sacrament'. Classic examples of the sect form are the Exclusive Brethren, the Methodists and Baptists, in their first century, and the Seventh-Day Adventists.

Both church and sect claim a unique possession of the salvational truth. The denomination and the cult do not make such a claim but instead suppose there are many ways to God and that, while what they have is valuable, it is not unique. Denominations are tolerant and liberal; although they have a shared body of doctrine, they are far more relaxed than the sect in interpreting it and in enforcing commitment to it. Denominations generally have a hierarchical structure and a professional ministry. The denomination thus stands midway between the church and the sect; and that character reflects their origins. New religions very rarely begin in the denominational mode; almost all denominations were once either sects or churches which changed as they came to terms with the fact that in increasingly liberal and egalitarian societies people were not prepared to accept to the authority claimed by church and sect. The church had to accept it could no longer dominate a society and if it became large and survived more than a few generations the sect acquired many of the characteristics of the church form it rejected. The Methodist Church, the Presbyterian Church of Scotland and the Church of England are examples of denominations. The first evolved from a sect; the other two were churches in the sociological sense that gradually had to scale down their claims as they lost market share to dissenters and lost the active support of the state.

The defining characteristic of the cult is most easily seen in the observation that cults do not have members. Instead of recruiting loyal followers, they offer their revelations, rituals and therapies to consumers, who decide which particular elements they will consume. Cults generally operate within a loose 'cultic milieu' of people who synthesise their preferred mix from a vast range of options. The cultist may attend evening classes on channelling wisdom from the spirit world, have his or her astrological chart drawn, read books by a variety of gurus, buy inspirational tapes, attend a weekend workshop in Tibetan overtone chanting of the significance of ley lines and redecorate his or her rooms on Feng Sui principles. Cults tend to be undemanding, very loosely organised, and extremely tolerant and inclusive. **New Age** spirituality is organised as a cultic milieu.

Roy Wallis argued that the essential sociological differences could be grasped

		External Conception	
		Respectable	Deviant
Internal Conception	Uniquely legitimate	CHURCH	SECT
	Pluralistically legitimate	DENOMINATION	CULT

Figure R.1:   The Wallis Typology of Ideological Organisations

if we recognised that the four main types of organisation could be generated from just two questions (see Figure R.1): How does the organisation see itself and how is it seen by the wider society?

The advantages of this model are that it gets away from the specific history of Christianity; it focuses on the those parts of the ideology that have the greatest impact on such important aspects of organisational life as demands on members and relations between members and the wider society; and it can be used to describe non-religious ideological organisations such as political parties. We can, for example, usefully regard most communist parties as sects and most social democratic parties as denominations.

It is important to appreciate that religious organisations change (as in the common transition from sect to denomination); that organisations can behave differently in different contexts (for example, in Poland the Catholic Church tries to claim the prerogatives of a church but in the USA it behaves like a denomination); and that organisations can contain within themselves elements of more than one form (for example, the full-time officials of Transcendental Meditation think of it in sect terms but they market it to the general public in a cultic form).

REPRESSIVE STATE APPARATUSES   See **ideological state apparatuses**.

RESEARCH ETHICS   See **ethics of research**.

RESERVE ARMY OF LABOUR   Marxists believe that capitalists deliberately keep unemployment rates high so that the unemployed, by acting as a 'reserve army', keep wage levels depressed and limit the ability of those who do have jobs to engage in efforts to improve their conditions. Mainstream economists have their own explanation for why unemployment never falls to zero, largely to do with the constantly changing nature of the skills needed in a dynamic economy, though they too acknowledge that the unemployed tend to depress wages for the low-skilled.

RESIDUES AND DERIVATIONS   See **Pareto**.

RESPONSE RATE   See **non-response**.

RESTRICTED CODES   See **elaborated codes**.

REVOLUTION   In a coup d'état, a group seizes state power and displaces the previous rulers. A revolution differs in that it involves the masses and leads to a radical change in the social and political structure. What happened in France in 1792 and in Russia in 1917 were revolutions; what happened in Greece in 1967 when the Colonels seized power was a coup.

Political revolutions tend to be apparent at the time. The term is also used retrospectively (as in 'industrial revolution' and 'sexual revolution') for far-reaching social changes.

RHIZOME, RHIZOMATIC Gilles **Deleuze** and Felix **Guattari**'s (1976) *Rhizome: an Introduction* over-extended a plant metaphor in a neo-Marxist, postmodern depiction of the contemporary world. A rhizome is a root-like stem of some plants that grows under or along the surface and has the unusual property of producing both roots and shoots. Western thought has been dominated by a style which is like the tree in that it grows vertically, is hierarchical and produces static 'placings'. Deleuze and Guattari want to oppose 'tree culture' by the celebration of non-hierarchical rhizomes. Their work is self-consciously allusive and hard to pin down. However, the rise of the world wide web as a largely non-hierarchical system where people can make new connections and promote growth at almost any point has been seen by some commentators as a vindication of the kind of social organisation they had in mind. The way in which the virtual web community has fought off attempts to impose hierarchical control, for example by US government agencies, has further strengthened the appeal of this imagery. No doubt, the rhizome is a suggestive metaphor though it is unclear whether it is any more than that.

RIESMAN, DAVID (1909–2001) In *The Lonely Crowd* (1950), of which he was the principal author, David Riesman contrasted three personality types. The tradition-oriented follows the ancient rules; not a type common in modern societies. The inner-directed person is governed by internalised standards and conscience. The other-directed person is heavily reliant for a sense of identity on the approval of others. This contrast was built into a depiction of modern society: Riesman argued that the consumerism of the USA was encouraging other-directedness and anxiety-driven conformity. That it hit a nerve is shown by its sales. *The Lonely Crowd* sold 1.4 million copies; more than any other sociology book before or since.

RISK Sociologists and anthropologists have long been interested in how cultures cope with risk and chance. Recently, social theorists including Ulrich **Beck** and Anthony **Giddens** have focused on the risks that characterise advanced technological societies. Citizens face many risks that are technologically mediated, for example, the risks involved in flying (regulated by airport security, air-traffic control and airline maintenance teams) or medical risks (controlled through patterns of inoculation and health screening).

The social scientific study of risk is dominated by the assumptions of economics. Mainstream risk assessment is based on a probabilistic approach to risks that tries to calculate the harms we face. In principle, for each harm one could work out the likelihood of its occurrence and the typical damage that arises. Risk analysts try to produce an objective measure of risk by multiplying these things together. For example, the riskiness of frequent problems that harm relatively few people (bicycle accidents) might be compared to infrequent events that harm many people (accidents to passenger ships). Risk professionals tend to work within a **rational choice** framework and assume that the important thing is the balance between the overall likelihood of harm and the benefits that accrue.

Risk assessment is now well institutionalised internationally but it has drawn a lot of criticism from sociologists who point out that the expert presentation of hazards does not coincide with people's experience of risk. For one thing, the figures on which expert calculations are based are often dubious: there have, luckily, been relatively few large-scale problems with nuclear installations so data about the likely harms from reactor incidents are not dependable or robust in a statistical sense. For another, the benefits may be widely dispersed while the potential harms are concentrated (around an oil terminal, for example). People close to the facility may not accept the terms of the risk assessment calculation. Sociological commentators have been critical of the economistic assumptions that lie behind attempts to express risks objectively and have preferred to talk about the social construction of risks.

See **risk society, social construction of reality**.

RISK SOCIETY   German sociologist Ulrich Beck's (1986) *Risk Society: Towards a New Modernity* provided a sweeping characterisation of the contemporary condition at the end of the 20th century that rivalled **information society** and **McDonaldisation**. *Risk Society* is three books in one. The first element is a fairly conventional review of changes in the nature of industrial society that concludes with the assertion that we live in a condition of **reflexive modernity**. The second element concentrates on the nature and status of scientific expertise. According to Beck, science has also been faced with 'reflexive' challenges. He argues that natural scientists can no longer make grandiose claims to the unrivalled possession of knowledge and that people have become more sceptical of scientific claims to authority. The third part of the book draws attention to a wide variety of ways in which modern life is risky; science and technology have created a raft of major hazards. In earlier times risks stemmed mainly from nature. It could rain during harvest or a new disease could sweep through the community. In risk societies, risks come to a large degree from human interventions in nature. To protect ourselves from the winter cold we need energy so we turned to nuclear power. In the process we created new risks, from power-station failures and from the need to store nuclear waste for thousands of years. To overcome fluctuations in the food supply we developed agricultural chemicals but then faced health problems arising from contaminated food.

There are major faults with this case. First, Beck underplays the benefits of technology; for example, he discusses the perils of modern food processing but neglects the point that modern production has eliminated a number of potent natural toxins so that, overall, food in the West is probably safer than it has ever been. Second, he entirely overlooks voluntarily-engaged-in risks; we are all well aware of the dangers of smoking but that we continue to do it is hardly the fault of science and technology. Third, because it does not fit his evolutionary model, he under-estimates the continuing threat from 'natural' hazards: for example (except in the minds of a few conspiracy theorists) AIDS is not a creation of new technology.

The most contentious part of the case is the attempt to join together increasing individualisation and technological hazard in the single idea of 'reflexive modernisation'. Beck makes a number of acute observations of features of the modern world but he tends to exaggerate them into a misleading depiction of the whole.

RITE OF PASSAGE   This translation of the French 'rite de passage' signifies a ceremony or ritual associated with a significant change of status that occurs as part of the life cycle. It is a way of drawing public attention to changes in status and social identity and of handling the strong emotions that may be involved in such a transition.

RITUAL   Narrow use follows the anthropological practice of signifying formal actions in a set pattern that, through symbol, express a shared meaning. The Catholic Mass is a religious ritual. Sociologists tend to use the term for any regularly repeated pattern of action, with the implication that the doing of it conveys more than the content of what is done.

ROLE   Just as we expect the actor who takes on the lead role in *Julius Caesar* to 'play the part' (that is, follow Shakespeare's script and act in character), so we expect someone who takes on the job of doctor to acquire the appropriate mannerisms and patterns of behaviour. More than that, we expect the incumbent to acquire the beliefs and attitudes that come with the role. Those expectations are usually met and when they are not we have recourse to a variety of sanctions and remedial procedures to try to restore the social order. Roles may be more or less detailed in their scripting and more or less enduring and may be performed with varying degrees of **role-distance**. Though it is the co-ordination of roles that constitutes a social institution, it is often the case that people experience **role-conflict**.

The first systematic use of the idea was in G.H. **Mead**'s work where the idea of 'taking the role of other' was an important part of a theory of learning. The self developed as children imaginatively took the role of mother, father, teacher and the like. Adults used role-taking (as in 'put yourself in my shoes') to work out their own roles.

For symbolic interactionists, each role involves interaction with another or others: they come in pairs. For example, 'teacher' only makes sense in relation to 'pupil'; each is defined by the expectation of the other. In everyday interaction the player of one role tests his or her conception of the other and takes the response of the other either as confirmation of the initial performance or as reason to change. Where a role is considerably modified we might talk of 'role-making'. However, this rather fluid view of roles is not taken to mean that we have complete or even great freedom in how we act; the idea of 'role' still contains social expectations and in many settings most people conform to those expectations or are brought back into conformity by sanctions.

A rather static and prescribed notion of roles is used in **functionalist** sociology to describe how a unified culture arranges social action.

ROLE-CONFLICT   Although the drama metaphor is useful, it simplifies enormously

because an actor normally plays only one part in a single play. In real life, most people occupy a variety of roles and competing expectations may be difficult to reconcile: the phrase 'working mother' is intended precisely to express tension between the demands of the roles of worker and mother. Another source of conflict is the presence of two equally legitimate but conflicting sets of expectations of the same role. An actor is required to follow one agreed script for *Julius Caesar*: a young Muslim woman in New York may find herself torn between what her parents expect of the role 'dutiful daughter' and what her non-Muslim friends expect. An actor may be pulled in different directions by the instructions of the director, the expectations of the rest of the cast, and the expectations of the audience and critics, but these inherent tensions are rarely more than slight. Many social roles contain the potential for considerable internal conflict because they are pivotal; the occupant has to mediate a variety of expectations. A manager, for example, has to reconcile the competing demands of owners and workers. The head of a university department has to reconcile the expectations of senior management, colleagues and students.

ROLE-DISTANCE   Just as an actor can so 'camp up' a performance or play a part with so little enthusiasm that we are reminded that the person and the part being played are not the same, so social roles can be played with varying degrees of detachment. In part this may reflect the preference of the actor but it is also a constitutive feature of the role. We would be a little suspicious of people who totally immersed themselves in the role of road sweeper or school janitor. We would be critical of a woman who failed to immerse herself in the role of mother.

ROUTINISATION   This signifies the process in which repetition of actions allows them to be performed with ever-less conscious deliberation. The virtue of routinisation is that it frees us to devote our energy to the realm of things that really demand our attention or that are especially pleasant to attend to. For example, most of us simplify the start of our day by eating the same sorts of things and dressing in the same sorts of clothes. When large patterns of action performed by many people are so routinised we can talk about institutions.

ROUTINISATION OF CHARISMA Max **Weber** regarded **charismatic** leadership as inherently unstable: in the short term the charismatic leader may change his or her mind; in the long term he or she dies. If it endures for any length of time charismatic leadership is normally 'routinised'. The prophet's utterances are written down, codified and published. The spontaneous personal response of followers is ordered into membership requirements and training procedures. Many sects that were founded by charismatic leadership (the Mormons, Seventh Day Adventists, Christian Science and Scientology are all examples) arranged for the charisma of the founder to be transferred to a bureaucratic organisational leadership. In many cases the movement does better after the founder's death because she or he can no longer confuse with changes of revelation or subvert the creation of an effective organisation.

RULE-FOLLOWING Many sociologists, including the **positivists**, have been struck by the similarity of the social and the natural worlds. Both are orderly and seem to be governed by rules. But other thinkers and philosophers, notably Peter Winch (1958) (in *The Idea of a Social Science*) have argued that this similarity is only skin deep. Social rules are unlike natural laws in that people usually need to interpret them before they can follow them and because people have a choice about whether they should follow rules or defy them. Those who emphasised the differences between social rules and natural laws are widely thought to have won this argument though the excitement of victory has been spoiled a little by the recognition that social life is far from exclusively made up of rule following. Many things are done without reference to rules at all, and the rules that do exist are often not followed, suggesting that the rules are not of great explanatory importance to the orderliness of social life.

See **Wittgenstein**.

RULING CLASS This Marxist term now sounds archaic but it has the virtue of clarity: it denotes the class that exercises political domination. This may be done openly and directly, as in the example of the lords of a feudal society. In modern capitalist societies rule is less overt. Ideology will shape behaviour without its origins or its beneficiaries always being obvious. The state may enjoy **relative autonomy**. But the net result is still domination by the capitalist class.

The term is also used by non-Marxists (Vilfredo **Pareto**, for example) to mean the minority that in any society forms the governing political class.

S

SACKS, HARVEY (1935–75)   The founder of **conversation analysis** (CA), Sacks's work has mostly come to be known through a small number of published papers and through lectures given in California that were taped and typed up and only put into book form after his early death. He pioneered the study of conversational interaction as an aspect of sociology, but his interest in language and interaction was wider than the more technical aspects of CA. Another of his socio-linguistic interests was the way in which categorisations function in interaction and interpretation. For example, newspaper headlines often manage to sum up a whole story by careful use of a categorisation: dead-beat dads, for example. Sacks observed how categorisations influence the way that meanings are interpreted and he emphasised that one use of a category tended to make other, related categorisations relevant. This insight has been developed as 'membership categorisation analysis' (MCA). Though less systematically developed than CA, MCA continues to have its adherents studying both talk and written texts.

SACRED AND PROFANE   Emile **Durkheim** (1912) made much of this distinction in his *Elementary Forms of the Religious Life*. The sacred were those things that were set apart and revered; everything else was profane.

SAMING   An unattractive term that has entered sociology to denote the opposite of othering. While othering is the action of making some group into a clear contrast to 'us', saming is the strategy of claiming another group as related or similar to 'us'. In particular, saming is used to describe cases where a claim is made about our similarity to a group that had previously been treated as distinctly different, as the other.

SAMPLE, SAMPLING   Normally, we would like knowledge about a whole society but we cannot afford to study everyone so we take a sample of the general population that interests us. Probability sampling requires that each person in the population studied has a fixed chance of being selected; probability statistics can then be used to measure the risk of drawing the wrong conclusion from samples of various sizes. Fortunately, providing they reach a certain size, samples do not need to be huge to have a good chance of being representative. A sample of about 2500 has much the same chances of being representative of a population of 100,000 and a population of one million. In the 1980s, national surveys in Britain commonly used samples of 2500. Economic constraints have since forced that figure down and many large surveys (such as the British Social Attitudes survey) use 1000.

There are various ways of constructing a sample. The idea of a random sample is that every member of the parent population should have an equal chance of being selected. Techniques for generating a random sample include taking names from an electoral register at fixed intervals or having a computer program randomly dial telephone numbers. An alternative to the random sample is the quota sample. Instead of using some method such as automated telephone number generation, this involves determining what are the salient social characteristics for the study and selecting an appropriate number of people with each chosen characteristic (such as age, gender, income, region).

SAMPLING ERROR   There are two sorts of sampling error. First, there may be bias in the way the selection was carried out. Second, random error may arise from chance differences between those selected and the general population. The second sort decreases as the size of the sample goes up; the first does not. One of the main sources of systematic bias is the use of an incomplete sampling frame. The electoral register is one of the most complete and readily accessible listings of most populations but some people will not be registered to vote and they will differ systematically from those on the register because they are likely to be living on the margins of society. Sampling those on the register will not amount to exactly the same thing as sampling the overall population.

SAPIR–WHORF HYPOTHESIS   Named after two US researchers who formulated and publicised the idea, this hypothesis challenges our normal assumptions about the connection between language and reality. Edward Sapir (1884–1934) and Benjamin Lee Whorf (1897–1941) used their studies of language differences to point out that language and perception are closely related. For example, among arctic peoples there are complicated vocabularies for describing varieties of snow. In most of Europe people can only recognise ice, snow and sleet. In some arctic cultures, where there are up to a hundred words for kinds of snow, ordinary people

obviously see things that we 'southerners' do not. Taken to the extreme, this view suggests that our language is not just a medium for describing the world. Rather, language itself shapes what we are able to observe and thus to think; this is the Sapir–Whorf hypothesis. In its extreme form the hypothesis is not now widely accepted though it is clear that language influences thought to some degree.

SAUSSURE, FERDINAND DE (1857–1913)
A Swiss linguist, Saussure is celebrated for the clarity he brought to the study of languages and sign systems. He named this study **semiology** and introduced a number of distinctions, which have remained central to linguistic analysis. Thus he separated the system of a language (*la langue*) from actual speech or speech acts made possible by that language (*la parole*). He distinguished between the study of a language as a system and the study of linguistic change: the latter is diachronic analysis, the former **synchronic**. He pointed out that words and other signs have two sorts of interrelationships: they have syntagmatic relationships with the words that precede and follow them and paradigmatic relations with the words that could have stood in their place. In the claim that 'the black cat is mischievous', the word 'black' has a paradigmatic relationship to 'white', 'ginger', 'tabby' and so on, and a syntagmatic relationship to 'cat' and 'mischievous'. He also drew a distinction between 'the signifier' and 'the signified'. The signifier is the spoken or written term while the signified is the concept designated by that term. It should be noted that 'the signified' relates to an idea or concept, not to the real thing that is assumed to underlie the idea. Thus we may use different signifiers – 'a dog' or 'a doggie' or 'un chien', 'un perro', 'um cão' or 'ein Hund' – to designate the idea of a dog. The connection between the signifier and the signified is, in Saussure's terms, arbitrary. But on top of this there is no

guarantee that all cultures classify animals in the same way. Others may think of the connection between dogs and wolves and foxes differently to us. Both the signifier and the signified are cultural products. If followers of Saussure want to talk about the assumed real thing to which the signified applies, they will speak of 'the referent'.

Saussure's influence is important in three ways. First, the vocabulary he developed for the systematic analysis of signs has been widely adopted and extended beyond his original ambitions. Researchers in the sociology of culture, for example, will commonly use the words synchronic or syntagmatic and their opposing partners in the course of their analyses. Second, he moved the study of language away from a study of speakers and their intentions and onto a study of language as a system of signs; this encouraged **structuralist** approaches to social phenomena in general. Third, structuralist analysts and those they influenced (including Roland **Barthes**, Jacques **Lacan** and Claude **Lévi-Strauss**) took over the distinction between the signifier and the signified and applied it to sign systems other than language. For example, Lacan argued that unconscious imagery could be looked at as a kind of language while Barthes aimed to read advertisements and even foods in terms of their signification.

SCALE   There are a wide variety of scales used in social statistics. The Guttman scale is designed to generate a single 'score' for what we believe to be a single underlying factor from a variety of questions. For example, we might try to measure anti-Semitism by devising a series of questions (80 to a 100 is desirable) such as 'I would permit my child to marry a Jew' and 'I would be happy for a Jewish family to move into my street'. We then ask a panel of experts to rate how closely each item represents anti-Semitism. Subsequently, we use the consensus of those judgements to accord each item a score. Once

we have our consensually agreed score for each question, we can administer the questionnaire. By assigning each answer its notional score and adding them up we can gauge to what extent our respondents are anti-Semitic. It is unlikely that any attitude perfectly fits this method and in the use of Guttman scales a 10 per cent margin of error is considered acceptable. That is, only if there are differences of more than 10 per cent between responses from different groups do we think we have evidence of a real difference rather than an accident of measurement.

Likert scales are also designed to tap what are taken to be one-dimensional attitudes but rather than use yes/no questions, they involve a range of reactions to items such as 'The world would be better if we all followed the same leader' and 'People need discipline to be happy'. Respondents are asked to state how much they agree or disagree on a three-five-or seven-point scale which has neutral as the middle point. A five-point scale – strongly agree, agree, neither agree or disagree, disagree, strongly disagree – is most common. The responses are coded so that the strongly positive gets the highest score and a Likert scale is then constructed by taking those items the scores for which correlate most closely with the overall scores. That way, we know we have a scale that has internal consistency.

Of three types of Thurstone scaling, the 'equal-appearing intervals' is the most common. Again, because it is a uni-dimensional scaling method, it begins by clarifying the single concept one is trying to tap. Suppose we are trying to assess how respondents feel about people with AIDS. We begin by generating 80 to 100 statements that describe specific attitudes that people may have towards AIDS sufferers (for example, 'You can get AIDS from heterosexual sex' and 'People with AIDS are bad'). They must all have the same grammatical form. A panel of judges is asked to rate how favourable towards people with AIDS each statement is on a scale of

1 to 11. We then analyse the distribution of the ratings of all the statements (by computing the median and inter-quartile range) and select from the long list a number of statements that the judges agree are most favourable, a bit less favourable, middling and least favourable to people with AIDS. The idea is to be left with a number of statements that will allow all the respondents to the survey to express clearly their attitude. Furthermore, and this is the clever part, if the distribution of the ratings of the initial long list of statements has been properly calculated then we should be able to treat the answers as not just a measure of favourable and unfavourable attitudes (a dichotomy) but as a scale of favourableness with evenly-spaced intervals.

SCAPEGOAT   The ancient Jews had a custom of ritually transferring the sins of the people onto a goat and sending it into the wilderness, taking the blame and the guilt with it. The term became widely used for a person or group that is chosen to bear the brunt of frustration or re-directed aggression. When people are unable to identify the real source of their (for example, economic) problems or, having identified the source, are unable to challenge it, they may turn on some convenient target. Ethnic minorities are often the victims of scapegoating.

SCHUTZ, ALFRED (1899–1959)   The main aim of Alfred Schutz's phenomenology was the description and analysis of everyday life (the life-world) and its associated states of consciousness. Central is the claim that all knowledge (and not just ideology or false consciousness) is **socially constructed** and oriented towards the solution of practical problems. From an undifferentiated stream of consciousness we create the objects and the knowledge of the objects that we take for granted in our everyday lives. The basic act of consciousness Schutz called first-order

typifications: grouping together typical and enduring elements in the flow of experience, building models of things and people, and insofar as these are shared, creating a social world. For Schutz the job of the sociologist is to construct second-order typifications: a rational model of the world based on the first-order typifications that actors offer as explanation for their actions.

Schutz's phenomenology was briefly popular in the late 1960s but was extensively criticised for its concentration on the trivial and its lack of interest in such weighty matters as inequality and power. In contemporary sociology, it is really only **ethnomethodology** that persists with the suggestion that we can find the foundations for social analysis in all the taken-for-granted cultural assumptions that make life regular and dependable. However, aspects of Schutz's work did enter the sociological mainstream through Peter L. Berger and Thomas Luckmann's (1967) immensely popular *The Social Construction of Reality*. This used phenomenological terms and ideas to produce a general social theory that sought to combine social action and social structure.

SCIENCE   Science refers to the systematic investigation and understanding of the world around us. The success of science led many philosophers and commentators to think that there must be some single, decisive feature that renders certain kinds of knowledge scientific and others not. The aim of finding this touchstone has now largely been abandoned even though it is clear that the sciences share many family resemblances. They aim for objectivity, use rigorous techniques of empirical testing and strive for explanations of wide applicability. In other respects physics and geology and meteorology differ greatly. Philosophers of science, including Karl **Popper**, had hoped to identify the defining feature of science in order to be able to exclude pretenders to the status of science, known as pseudo-sciences. In Popper's view these included **Marxism** and aspects of Freudian psychology. With the loss of the touchstone goes the loss of the ready ability to identify pseudo-sciences.

Science is of interest to sociologists for two main reasons. First, the ideal of scientific objectivity and accuracy has often motivated social scientists to reform their work by modelling it on natural science. Second, science itself is a social phenomenon that has been of widespread interest to sociologists.

Beginning with the role of science as an ideal, sociologists have long agonised over whether they could improve sociology by making it more like natural science – for example, by using statistical techniques to investigate the connections between social factors mathematically – or whether sociological understanding inevitably differs from the natural sciences. By the close of the 20th century there was an approximate agreement on the answer to this question, though differences of detail remained. The answer is that the social sciences aim to be objective and accurate in just the same ways that the other sciences do. However, because the social world is partly made up through the beliefs and interpretations of actors themselves, there are limits to the success of approaches that have worked in other sciences. Molecules of oxygen do not know how they behave; they just behave. They don't have theories about their own behaviour. People do and it is no use to sociology for sociologists to act as though people were as predictable and law-like as oxygen molecules.

Sociologists are also interested by science as a social phenomenon. Scientific and technological research is a major source of social change in modern societies and science is a key source of legitimation, for example, in relation to the measurement of safety. Systematic work in the sociology of science is generally said to have begun with Robert K. **Merton** who investigated the norms of the scientific career. Noting that scientists are probably just as wilful and ambitious as people that go into other occupations, he asked how the norms prevailing in the scientific profession could give rise to objective and impartial knowledge. He proposed that specific norms – notably those requiring **universalistic** judgement and a willingness to share information – were well institutionalised in science. By the 1960s these claims were being questioned. Other sociologists pointed out that the norms were not as closely followed as Merton's theory would seem to require. For example, scientists appeared sometimes to share information and sometimes to be secretive; both types of conduct could be justified in terms of the demands of scientific progress. The 1960s also saw the publication of Thomas **Kuhn**'s (1962) *The Structure of Scientific Revolutions* which successfully challenged the idea that changes in scientific beliefs occur smoothly and methodically. Kuhn depicted major theory changes as similar to political contests. This opened up the possibility that there could be sociological studies of the cultural and social factors influencing the development of scientific ideas: a sociology of scientific knowledge (often known as SSK). This was alien to the tradition represented by Merton according to which sociological factors simply created the conditions within which science could develop according to its independent logic.

The last 30 years have witnessed a huge growth in the sociology of science and in allied work referred to as 'science and technology studies' or 'science studies'. It has become common to talk of the social construction of science even if there is still a great deal of uncertainty about the exact meaning of the claim that scientific knowledge is socially constructed. A useful example here is current concern over climate change. Without meteorology, earth sciences and atmospheric physics there would be no reasonable basis for claims about our changing climate. However, it is clear that sociological factors within the field of climate science, and in the relationship between climate scientists and politicians and industrialists, affect the exact predictions and the plausibility of the claims made about the greenhouse effect. In such cases it is clearly legitimate for sociologists to ask questions about the shaping of experts' views of the climate and the causes and rapidity of climate change. But the influence of social factors on the development of climate science does not mean that climate science is nothing but a social construct. Extreme views on this issue briefly rose to prominence in the 1990s during the so-called 'Science Wars' when scientists sought to rebut the more extreme claims of cultural commentators on science. Peace appears to have now resettled on this area.

See **Strong Programme, social construction of reality**.

SCIENCE AND TECHNOLOGY STUDIES (STS), SCIENCE STUDIES   See **science**.

SCIENTIFIC LAW   The term scientific law is used to describe scientific generalisations of wide applicability in which scientists feel a great deal of confidence. For example, Boyle's Law asserts that, under normal conditions, the pressure of a gas and the volume that it occupies are inversely related if the temperature remains constant: as the pressure doubles, the volume halves and so on. This is regarded as a law because it is believed to apply to all gases and because it connects two features of gases (their pressure and their volume) in a rigorous, mathematical fashion. Laws are more than just descriptions of what we know already because we believe that Boyle's Law applies not just on Earth but pretty much everywhere and because it applies to all gases so far tested and to all those yet to be tested. To a very large extent, the success of science stems from the fact (itself difficult to explain) that the complexity of the world is law-like and amenable to understanding in terms of the

mathematics that humans have devised. But the example of Boyle's Law also indicates other key features of scientific laws which are particularly important when considering the possibility that there might be laws of social science too.

First, Boyle's Law depends on a simplified model of gases that does not apply under extreme conditions. Most scientific laws have this character: they are laws with exceptions, and controversy or uncertainty often surrounds the exact nature of those exceptions. Second, the atoms or molecules of the gas in question appear to be governed by the law but not in the way that humans are typically governed by laws. Regularities of human society work through people learning or being socialised into the laws and then, through habit or decision, complying with them. Oxygen molecules do not know the law to which they adhere; people typically do – or at least in principle could – know about the regularities in their behaviour. This gives sociology a **reflexive** character absent from natural science and opens social laws to political and ethical evaluation in a way that is absent from the laws that govern molecules.

See **fact–value distinction**.

SCIENTIFIC MANAGEMENT   See **Taylorism**.

SCOTTISH ENLIGHTENMENT   See **Enlightenment, Scottish**.

SECONDARY GROUP   See **primary group**.

SECOND ORDER CONSTRUCTS   See **phenomenological sociology**.

SECOND WORLD   See **Third World**.

SECT   See **religious organisation**.

SECTARIANISM In the sociology of religion, this term is used in a neutral fashion to denote the qualities of the sect form of **religious organisation**. More commonly it is used to describe patterns of discrimination, dislike and conflict based on religious differences.

SECULARISATION This term has a very long and contested history. The Christian Church has long divided the religious from the secular and following Henry VIII's disbanding of the monasteries in England and Wales, secularisation came to mean the transfer of property from the Church to the secular world.

In sociology, it signifies the process of religious beliefs and institutions losing power and popularity. The USA is an important exception but all other modern societies have seen a considerable decline in the extent to which people are actively involved with religious organisations and activities, the extent to which behaviour is shaped by religious values, and the influence of religious institutions on society at large. In Britain in 1851 between 40 and 60 per cent of the population attended church; in 2000 it was under 10 per cent and in northern European countries it is less than 5 per cent. In the 1950s the majority of Britons claimed to believe in a personal creator God; now it is less than 25 per cent and such believers are slightly outnumbered by atheists and agnostics.

The causes of these changes are complex but central is the decline in community. Religious beliefs are strongest when held in common by everyone, deeply embedded in the life cycle (through the religious celebration of birth, marriage and death), built into the fabric of community life (through seasonal celebrations) and re-affirmed in everyday interaction (as when people say 'God be with you' on parting and mean it). The **structural differentiation** of societies sees religious institutions losing vital social functions to more specialised and hence secular agencies.

Economic growth also creates social differentiation as developing social classes become increasingly distant from each other. One consequence of this in Protestant countries is that a single shared religion tends to become fragmented into competing alternatives.

The internal fragmentation of a tradition is one source of diversity. Movement of people is another, as is the expansion of the state to take in new lands and peoples. It is possible for rulers to ignore diversity and to continue to support the imposition of one religion on an entire society or (as in the case of the Ottoman empire) to accord different levels of citizenship to different religions. But when increasing diversity coincides with an increasingly egalitarian ethos (and economic modernisation encourages that), the state has little choice but to respond to diversity with increasing religious tolerance and eventually by creating a secular public space. In brief there are strong tendencies in modernising societies for religion to be shifted out of the taken-for-granted and public realms and into the private leisure sphere. While this ensures that minorities can enjoy their religion without hindrance, it also weakens the presence and plausibility of religion. It is difficult for the state to treat all religions as if they were equally true without also implying that they are equally false.

Another powerful secularising trend is **rationalisation**. The world of science, technology, industrial work and bureaucratic organisation is one which has its own predictable order and which operates without the need to placate gods. It is not the specific content of science that undermines religion (though late 19th-century discoveries did force major revisions to many Christian themes) so much as the general idea that we can understand and master the natural world by rational investigation. And as technology increased our ability to manage the world around us, it reduced the occasions on which we need have recourse to religion. For example, during the Black Death plague of the 14th century, the Christian churches called weeks of fasting and prayer. In the early 1980s the Christian churches responded to HIV/AIDS by calling for more funding for scientific research.

A third strand of explanation concerns individualism and consumerism. It is a natural extension of both the egalitarian idea at the heart of liberal democracy and of the consumerism at the heart of capitalism that we are free to choose. We choose our cars, we choose our governments; therefore we should choose our gods. And in a world where there are many gods to choose from and none has the weight of community support, it is easy to choose none at all. Even regular church-goers now claim the right to select just which of their church's teachings they will accept.

Sociologists who work within the secularisation paradigm are well aware of alternative forces. Religion continues to thrive in the First World where some of the above changes are absent. For example, immigrant minorities often sustain a vibrant religious culture because they sustain a closed community and find their traditional religion offers a variety of important social functions in adjusting to life in the new world. Religion also thrives when it is closely associated with national identity and the religious institution acts as a guarantor of national or ethnic identity against some external threat. The Catholic Church in Ireland and in Poland retained the loyalty of their people because the Church was one of the few vehicles for resisting, respectively, British and Russian imperialism.

The secularisation paradigm is much misunderstood and is frequently caricatured. It is not mapping a route that all societies must follow. Like Max **Weber**'s **Protestant Ethic thesis,** it is an explanation of the past of western Europe; it is not a prediction. Nonetheless we can make some predictions on the basis of past experience. One is that to the extent that Third World countries achieve stable government and prosperity,

there will be increasing demands for individual liberty and a greater reluctance to support unthinkingly the traditionally dominant religion. Cross-national survey data shows a worldwide correlation between increasing prosperity and declining religiosity. Another is that greater liberty for women will weaken the traditionally dominant religion.

No sociologist believes that secularisation is inevitable but most hold that it is irreversible. Religion is a cultural product; like a language it requires use. As most young people in Europe are now raised with no knowledge of Christianity, it is difficult to see how the stock of religious knowledge can be sustained.

The secularisation paradigm has been challenged from a number of directions. Some scholars question the value of particular measures of religiosity (such as church attendance). However, decline characterises every measure. Some assert that in the long run secularisation is impossible because humans have an in-built need for religion. The difficulty with that claim is that there is no evidence of any of the new religions or new forms of spirituality in the West becoming sufficiently popular to make any dent in the gap left by Christianity. A third objection concerns the apparently stable religiosity of the USA. The USA is certainly different but it is so in ways that further illuminate rather then refute the secularisation paradigm. First, the USA continues to be an immigrant society. In 1991, 10 per cent of adults in the USA were born elsewhere and almost all of those are migrants from relatively unmodernised countries. Second, the federal structure of government and public administration in the USA, its greater size, and the much greater freedom of its mass media allows groups of committedly religious people much greater freedom to build effective subcultures. An evangelical in Virginia can be schooled in Christian schools, attend a Christian university and consume only Christian mass media, and thus remain relatively isolated from alternative cultures. While the USA as a nation-state is more diverse than any European country, Americans are much freer than Europeans to create cultural homogenous worlds in which their religion can continue to be taken-for-granted. Finally, it is worth noting that research in the last decade of the 20th century shows signs of weakening commitment. Although the proportion of Americans who say they attend church regularly has remained fairly stable since the 1960s at around 40 per cent, studies of actual attendance suggest that 20 per cent is nearer the mark.

SEGMENTAL SOCIAL STRUCTURES The meaning can be readily seen if we think of segments of an orange: they are all the same. A segmental social structure (characteristic of those societies that Emile **Durkheim** describes as held together by **mechanical solidarity**) is one composed of similar components (such as clans or districts) each of which is composed of individuals who are similar.

SEGREGATION This signifies the deliberate forcing and keeping apart of peoples defined by race or ethnicity. Class segregation does not normally require legal support or government action; the housing market ensures a large degree of residential separation and price acts as an effective means of social closure. For some rich parents the main appeal of expensive schools is that poor people cannot afford them. Race and ethnicity are a different matter. Although some ethnic groups have good reasons to cluster (Orthodox Jews, for example, need to be within walking distance of a synagogue and have access to a kosher butcher), racial and ethnic boundaries can only be maintained with considerable discriminatory effort. In the southern states of the USA, until the late 1950s, public toilets would have separate drinking fountains for whites and blacks. Public facilities such as schools, buses, beaches and restaurants either existed in two parallel systems or, if mixed, had clearly designated areas.

SELF This signifies the mental construct of a person, by that person. It is a central proposition of sociology that the self is in large part social. In the work of G.H. **Mead** and C.H. **Cooley**, the self develops in interaction with the others, and we learn about the social by responding to the images that we think others have of us and by imaginatively taking the part of others. In more structuralist types of sociology, the self is shaped by the imposition of the social in various ways. Generally, it is supposed that the self has a degree of unity and continuity. A very different view is promoted by various school of postmodern thought that emphasise conflicts within the self. Often drawing inspiration from the claims of Sigmund **Freud** about tensions between aspects of the self, these authors suggest that in late modern or **postmodern** times the lack of unity in the self becomes apparent and the self becomes 'de-centred'. Some authors assert that the main reason why the self is no longer seen as a unified thing is because we have realised the extent to which abstract entities such as the self are made up out of available cultural and symbolic resources. Our selves are more the product of the times than of our inner 'essence'. Others, including Anthony **Giddens**, assert that the distinctive thing is that, in late modern societies, our selves become matters of choice; they are no longer viewed as natural entities. Modern people are enjoined to 'work' on their selves through therapy and counselling and so on, and are held responsible in new ways for the kinds of 'selves' they are.

See **de-centred self, looking-glass self**.

SELF-FULFILLING PROPHECY The term was introduced to sociology in 1948 by Robert

K. **Merton** in an extension of W.I. **Thomas**'s dictum about the **definition of the situation**: when people define situations as real, they become real in their consequences. He regarded it as frequently the case that people begin by mistakenly defining a situation but then, by their own actions, make that false definition become accurate. Merton uses the example of a run on the bank. A perfectly sound bank lends more money than it has on deposit because it knows that most of its savers will not want to withdraw all their money at the same time. People hear a rumour that the bank is insolvent. They all rush to the bank to withdraw their money before they lose it when the bank goes broke. Because so many people withdraw their money, the bank does go bust. The false rumour of insolvency causes the action which makes the bank insolvent.

SEMANTICS　　The science of linguistics is usually said to consist of four main branches, syntax, semantics, phonetics and pragmatics. The study of semantics refers to the analysis of the ways that meaning is produced and recognised. Linguists used to treat language as though its component parts were truly independent. In this way, it was thought that utterances could be syntactically correct but meaningless. Semantics involved the study of how the meanings of words together produced the meaning of sentences and so on. Equally it was possible to talk of the semantics of computer languages to refer to the way that the items in the programming code combined to produce their effects. In the last 30 years linguists have become far clearer that much of the meaning of utterances that occur in social interaction is down to what is known as the pragmatics of speech. To say 'hello' when someone has ignored you is typically not to greet them but, for example, to be impertinent or accusing. Thus, though it is correct to say that semantics is the study of meaning, it has to be recognised that there is

much more to meaning than semantics in the conventional sense.

SEMIOLOGY, SEMIOTICS　　Both these terms refer to the systematic study of signs and to the idea that there could be a science of signs. Semiology is the term associated with Ferdinand de **Saussure** while semiotics was employed by C.S. Peirce, a leading US advocate of **pragmatism**. As Saussure emphasised, the programme for a study of signs depends on distinguishing between 'the signifier' and 'the signified'. The signifier is the spoken or written term while the signified is the concept designated by that term. It should be noted that, in Saussure's and most subsequent work, 'the signified' relates to an idea or concept, not to the real thing that is assumed to underlie the idea. Semiology then becomes the systematic investigation of sign systems: it involves the study of the different kinds of signs (for example, **icons** where the signifier is supposed to resemble the signified). It also involves the study of all the cultural and social realms in which things can function as signs, including the symbolism of clothing and appearance, food, and etiquette as well as explicit images and representations.

SENSITISING CONCEPT　　In his extensive writings on methods and the philosophy of the social sciences, Herbert **Blumer** was intensely critical of the pretensions of positivistic social research. In comparison with the natural sciences, our key ideas (such as social cohesion, authority, class conflict) are so vague that much of what passed for tests of them is no such thing. He attempted to rescue something from the wreckage by suggesting that, although of dubious value when treated as formal scientific definitions, many sociological notions were useful in suggesting where to look: they sensitise the researcher to what is important about social reality.

SERF, SERFDOM   A serf is a unfree **peasant** who holds land in return for rent, either in cash or, more typically, some combination of produce and labour. The serf is also bound to his landlord by non-economic ties. In the feudal systems of medieval Europe, serfs could not move or marry without their lord's consent and might even have to pay a fine if a child married and thus left the lord's labour force. In western Europe serfdom had largely disappeared by the end of the 15th century but it was not abolished in Russia until 1861.

The reasons for the decline of serfdom are complex but include the following: the decline of the population in the 14th century created a scarcity of labour and forced lords to compete to retain a labour force; political action (such as rebellion) by the serfs improved their position and in some cases the monarch sided with the serfs in order to weaken powerful lords; and the emergence of an overseas trade fostered a cash economy which enabled more serfs to buy themselves out of their feudal obligations.

One way of characterising the development from feudalism to capitalism is to say that complex reciprocal obligations and legal ties between the rich and the poor were gradually replaced by simple economic exchange based on cash.

SERVICE CLASS   In the 1950s this denoted either the administrative workers who were the servants of capital or white-collar employees in administrative organisations. From the 1980s it was used by John **Goldthorpe** and colleagues to denote all members of higher professional, technical, administrative and managerial occupations. That usage has become standard among social class and social mobility researchers.

SERVICE SECTOR, TERTIARY SECTOR   It is a useful convention to divide economic activity into three types, the invention of which correspond roughly with important changes in the evolution of human societies. The primary sector is concerned with the extraction of raw materials and farming; the secondary sector with complex commercial manufacture; and the third (or tertiary) with the provision of services. In most western economies, more people (ranging from poorly-paid cleaners through school teachers to architects and lawyers) are employed doing things for people rather than making things.

SEXISM   Created in the 1960s from the model of the term 'racism', this signifies attitudes and actions which discriminate against women (or, very rarely, men) on the grounds of sex or **gender**. What makes the use of the term contentious is that 'discrimination' here means inappropriate discrimination. Saying only women menstruate is clearly not sexist and saying women make poor managers clearly is, but there is a lot of contested ground between those extremes.

SEXUAL DIVISION OF LABOUR   This phrase can signify both that work roles are often allocated by **gender**, so that men and women do different sorts of things, or that when men and women do work in the same sorts of occupations, there are major differences in conditions of service. All societies have a sexual division of labour in the first sense and its universality has often been taken as proof that its basis is biological. There is obviously a biological component in that only women give birth but what societies make of that differs greatly. A sexual division of labour may be universal but its content shows considerable cross-cultural variation as do the accompanying notions of **femininity** and masculinity. Indeed, given the stress they put on culture, it might have been better if sociologists had used the term 'gendered division'.

Within the world of paid work there are major gender divisions. Women are concentrated in the service sector (as distinct from extraction and manufacturing), particularly in the caring professions. When they work in the same industry, women are more likely than men to be part time, in insecure positions, to be of lower status than men and hence to be paid less.

The explanation for this is complex. In part it results from general social expectations of femininity and domesticity; certain jobs are thought (sometimes by women as much as men) to be unsuitable for women or for men. In part it results from the demands of domestic roles: with women taking the major responsibility for childcare, part-time work is often attractive because it can better be fitted around childcare. In part it is a continuation of domestic work: a mother who is looking after her own children may be well placed to earn a living looking after additional children. Such factors are compounded by the actions of employers and of organised labour. Just as skilled male workers have historically tried to protect their market situations from 'dilution' by the introduction of less skilled workers, so unskilled male workers in well-paid jobs have sought to exclude women.

As the proportion of women working outside the home has increased so the gendered division of labour has weakened in many sectors. The decline of heavy industry has removed entire male-only occupations (such as shipbuilding and mining) and women are now commonly found in the old professions of medicine and the law. However, it is worth noting that some occupations are becoming more, not less, unbalanced. Primary school teaching in the UK and USA is now almost entirely a female occupation.

SEXUALITY In common usage this refers to the presumably biologically-based desire in people that finds expression through sexual activity and sexual relationships. As in much else, the distinctive sociological take on sexuality is to challenge its biological basis and to draw attention to the great cultural variety in what counts as legitimate sexual activity. In some societies (ancient Greek and nomadic Arab, for example) homosexuality is commonplace; in others it is repressed. In some societies sexual activity is regarded as a source of pleasure; in others it is treated as a dangerous and destabilising force, to be confined to what is necessary to reproduce the society. As in all such biology-versus-culture arguments, there is a danger of sociology over-reaching itself.

See **queer theory**.

SHAMAN The modern replacement for 'witch-doctor', this signifies the provider of services that combine religion and medicine in simple societies. The shaman often qualifies by his ability to enter trance-like states, which are interpreted as evidence of an ability to make contact with, and harness, supernatural powers. A shaman is distinguished from a priest by the fact that the shaman's position is dependent on his personal powers while the priest derives his power from his place within an institution.

SICK ROLE This concept was developed by Talcott **Parsons** in a discussion of the role of medicine in modern societies. The sick role is a special status and basis for social identity distinct from the illness which gives the occasion for it. It is a socially-accepted form of deviance with the following features: the sick person is exempted from normal responsibilities; cannot be expected to look after himself or herself; is expected to want to return to normal functioning; and is expected to seek competent professional help. The key point is that the status implied in the first and second of these may well be desired by people who are unwilling to fulfil their social responsibilities; hence the need for the other two features, which add up to controls on access to the privileged status.

SIGN   A sign is a mark or symbol that stands for, or refers to, or indicates something else. Human cultures are full of signs, from pictures and written languages to our clothing and the consumer goods we select. Modern economies, because they deal so much in services and cultural products, are even more bound to signs than previous ways of life. For this reason sociologists are now centrally concerned with the analysis of signs and have turned to approaches inspired by linguistics, such as **semiology** and **structuralism**, for systematic approaches to understanding signs and their meanings.

See **Barthes**, **Saussure**, **semiology**.

SIGNIFICANCE, TESTS OF   There are a number of statistical tests of significance, designed for different types of data (especially parametric versus **non-parametric**) but what they all do is assess the likelihood that a result could have occurred by chance. With all, the researcher chooses what degree of probability is an appropriate threshold. For example, we can report that a particular result would only occur by chance less than once in 1000 times (the 0.01 level), less than one in 100 times (0.1 level) or less than one in 20 times (the 0.5 level). Clearly the first of these is a more severe test than the last. Having set the level of significance, we choose from the range available in **SPSS** (or other statistical programmes) a statistical test that will tell us, for the pattern we have discovered in our data, if our result is unlikely enough that we can safely assume it to be non-accidental.

SIGNIFICANT OTHER   See G.H. **Mead**.

SIMMEL, GEORG (1858–1918)   Although in published output, Simmel matched his fellow-countryman Karl **Marx** and even Talcott **Parsons**, he has been far less influential and that is almost certainly the result of him not having a clear, narrow doctrine and hence not founding a school. However, he was a considerable influence, particularly on the **Chicago School**. One of his main themes was the centrality of interaction. An institution such as the family was just the crystallisation of the interactions between its members. Even in his analysis of power he stressed that the powerful could only exercise their power with the minimal compliance of their subordinates. Another theme was the importance of analysing the formal properties of social relations and interactions. No matter who the parties involved are, relations between pairs of people will have many things in common and be different from relationships within larger groups.

In addition to his studies of forms and of social interaction, Simmel wrote on the functions of social conflict, on love, on social development and contributed to economic sociology with his (1900) *The Philosophy of Money* which presented an alternative to the Marxist **labour theory of value**.

SIMPLE SOCIETY   See **primitive society**.

SIMULACRA   This term, meaning representations or semblances, has become almost synonymous with the work of Jean **Baudrillard**, who is best known for the argument that modern societies are so saturated by the mass media that reality loses its meaning. People are no longer participants in their own lives but observers of what the media has turned into 'spectacles'. In our 'age of simulacra' there are only signs and representations. All prospect of access to real things and real experiences has disappeared.

SITUATIONISTS   This signifies an international artistic and political movement of the late 1950s and 1960s that took the view that, in the modern world, art was either revolutionary or reactionary; inspired by Guy **Debord**, situationists favoured revolutionary spectacle. Though prone to splintering, the movement attracted French social theorists and radicals disillusioned with the Communist party. Situationist thinking offered them a new view of political episodes such as the student revolts of May 1968. The movement attracted the attention of Louis **Althusser**, Jean-François **Lyotard** and Jean **Baudrillard**.

SLAVERY This signifies treating one person as the property of another. It is most familiar to us in its most recent manifestation: in the great plantation economies of North America, the Caribbean and Latin America. But the ancient Greeks and Romans used slave labour, as did many pre-modern African kingdoms. In those cases, enslavement was on a small-scale and was often the by-product of military campaigns engaged in for other reasons: using the conquered as slave labour was a recognised spoil of war. The trade in slaves captured in Africa for sale in the West Indies and the Americas was on a different scale: it is estimated that between 1562–1867, 28,000 voyages took around 10 million Africans into slavery.

Just as slave systems differ in how slaves were acquired, they also differ in how they were lost. Most allowed freedom (or manumission) for some reason: on the death of the master, on becoming the master's mistress, on being adopted or in recognition of some exemplary service (such as in war). The manumission rate in the southern US cotton plantations was one of the lowest known.

As a form of production slavery may be regarded as an obstacle to progress. In his *Passages from Antiquity to Feudalism*, Perry Anderson (1974) argued that it inhibited the economic development of the ancient world because a sufficient supply of unpaid labour removed incentives to develop labour-saving technology. Slave labour systems have other disadvantages. To have allowed slaves to form families and thus reproduce themselves would have undermined the slaver's view of his property as sub-human. So slaves were often kept in single-sex barracks. They did not produce the next generation and so new slaves had to be acquired. Second, the constant threat of revolt meant a constant burden of control. Third, that labour was literally forced meant it could never become skilled. For these and other reasons, Max **Weber** believed that slavery was incompatible with, and hence an obstacle to the development of, modern capitalism.

SMITH, ADAM (1723–90) *An Inquiry into the Nature and Causes of the Wealth of Nations* (1776) was one of the most influential products of the Scottish Enlightenment. Written towards the end of Smith's 25-year career as professor of moral philosophy at Glasgow University, it followed a seminal account of the **division of labour** with the then-novel argument that the individual pursuit of self-interest (the 'maximising' of modern economics) and the operation of a free market unhindered by government interference would result in the greatest contribution to the common good. These were, in their day, radical and progressive ideas. Smith was quite aware that an extensive division of labour could have a dehumanising effect on workers and discussed how such effects could be limited or ameliorated but he was pessimistic about the benefits of government interference because he imagined that governments would always act on the basis of very narrow interests.

SOCIABILITY This may signify a personality characteristic: someone who is outgoing and friendly and enjoys the company of others will be described as sociable. In a slightly more technical fashion it is used by sociologists such as Georg **Simmel** to refer to social interaction engaged in for its own sake, as a 'play-form' of interaction.

SOCIAL CAPITAL   This term has been used for a confusingly wide range of phenomena. The 'capital' part is fairly standard: the financial metaphor being used to indicate a stock of something which can be used for other benefits and advantages. The differences of meaning stem from different visions of where the capital is stored.

In some work on deprivation and social exclusion (that of Pierre **Bourdieu**, for example), social capital is made up of the resources, trust, and social networks, access to which empowers some people to acquire well-paid and pleasant jobs and to have nice comfortable lives. The problem of the deprived is how to increase their access to this stock of social capital. Social capital is thus like money in a society's bank and the problem is equality of access to it and to the benefits it can bring for the individual.

The term is used in a slightly different way by theorists who are concerned with social order and with the quality of social life in general. Here social capital is seen as a resource for the entire society, which is created by the behaviour of individuals. Working together, especially in civic activities, is virtuous because it builds trust and reciprocity. How we act generates more or less capital for society's bank. Although we do not directly withdraw that money, the more of it that is created, the nicer the world will be for all of us.

Thus the first version is a re-framing of the classic social problem of inequality. The second version is a modern framing of the equally enduring sociological problem of the decline of community.

Robert Putnam's (2000) *Bowling Alone: the Collapse and Revival of American Community* brilliantly re-states the decline of community problem. To illustrate his claim that the late 20th century had seen a marked decline in the popularity of various forms of public association (a crucial element of **civil society**), Putnam presents evidence on American bowling habits. Although 10-pin bowling remained popular, its organisation

had changed. Previously people had gone bowling in teams and participated in bowling leagues. Now they bowled in pairs or alone. The book is an exemplary drawing together of clear argument and masses of data to examine the decline of social capital.

Putnam distinguishes two sorts of social capital: 'bridging' is inclusive and links many people for the purpose of diffusing information; 'bonding' is exclusive and creates ties of solidarity and reciprocity among small numbers of people.

While the core argument seems well-founded, there is a danger of exaggeration. We can counter that while certain forms of public association and trust-building social activity have declined, new forms have arisen. For example, organisations such as Women's Institutes have declined as more women have entered the labour force but new forms have been invented: business women's clubs, for example. Putnam recognises this but argues that newer forms of social participation are narrower, less bridging, and less focused on collective purposes than the ones they replace.

See **trust**.

SOCIAL CLOSURE   This is the process by which groups seek to preserve some advantage by monopolising resources and restricting access to the group. Skilled manual workers use lengthy apprenticeships and closed-shop agreements to limit the number of people with their special skills and thus ensure their advantages over unskilled workers. Professional associations protect the position of doctors and lawyers. Aristocratic and landed gentry families in 18th-century England followed strict rules of **endogamy** to ensure that their wealth, social standing and hence power were not diluted.

SOCIAL CONSTRUCTION OF REALITY   This particular phrase was popularised by Peter

L. Berger and Thomas Luckmann's (1967) seminal *The Social Construction of Reality* but it expresses a number of principles that can reasonably be regarded as encapsulating the essence of sociology as a discipline.

The first and least contentious claim (at least since the triumph of **Enlightenment** thought in the West) is that the world can be understood without recourse to the divine. Even those of us who continue to believe in a creator God tend to think of him having initiated things and then left people to get on with it. Very few theists would argue that God especially devised the single transferable vote system of proportional representation or reality television. Our view is that culture has been devised by people, although not always deliberately. It is a 'social construct'. The chief remaining alternative to social construction is therefore biological necessity. We do not eat only because we have come to believe that we must; we truly have to, otherwise we will die. At its most thoughtful, sociology takes care not to rule out biological causes of some elements of human behaviour, but it generally regards most social regularities as being the work (deliberate or inadvertent) of people.

A second meaning is that much of what we are and do is the result of social influences. Though we may like to think of our 'selves' as our own independent creations, it is pretty clear that much about us is acquired through our being socialised into a particular language and culture. That I find the idea of reindeer blood ice cream revolting is a consequence of me not having been born in northern Siberia.

The third possible meaning is the most radical. In the first and second it is possible to draw a line between reality and our response to it. The reindeer blood ice cream was obviously socially constructed in the sense that people made it; it was not made by God and it is not naturally occurring. And my reaction is clearly culturally formed. I am socialised into one clutch of tastes and I can learn another

(and would do so if I wished to be accepted by northern Siberian reindeer herders). However, I assume that the ice cream does actually exist and that it possesses its characteristics irrespective of what I or anyone else thinks about them: it has an obdurate reality. The third meaning of 'social construction' challenges that assumption by arguing either that there is no obdurate reality independent of what we think about things or that, even if there is, for most sociological purposes the reality is irrelevant because we make our own.

Most sociologists adopt this principle for some matters and purposes. In other words, W.I. **Thomas**'s famous 'definition of the situation' dictum would often be accepted. That the US political leadership in 2003 believed that most Iraqis would welcome them overthrowing the Saddam Hussein regime explains why the USA led an invasion of Iraq. And it explains it whether or not that belief was correct. However, and this is the point where most sociologists would shift back from a social constructionist view to a **realist** one, that the belief was largely wrong explains why the USA was not greeted as a liberator and why the reconstruction of Iraq proved so difficult. For explaining why people do what they do, how they see the world (their 'social construction of reality') is central. For explaining the consequences of their actions, we must additionally understand what the world is really like.

That last sentence probably represents the sociological mainstream. However, there are scholars who take the social construction of reality as a warrant for far-reaching relativism by applying it to scientific (and hence social scientific) activity as well. They are sceptical of all claims about objective reality and favour a methodological attitude of near-universal **relativism**.

SOCIAL CONTRACT   Political philosophers Thomas **Hobbes**, John **Locke** and Jean-Jacques

Rousseau each used the idea of social contract, though to different ends, in their vision of an ideal basis for the state. Hobbes believed order and security would be best served by each individual giving up power in a contract with a central agent (then a sovereign) who would protect life and property. Locke's version was almost the opposite; in his view the individual should cede little to a constrained government, which could easily be deprived of power and legitimacy. Rousseau's contract was based on complete equality and full democratic participation in government based on the general will. None of these ideas hold much sway with current political theorists, who regard them as rather fanciful. But they all represent an important point in social evolution: the popularising of the idea that the legitimacy of state must rest on the wishes of its citizens. And they have had significant consequences. The Hobbesian contract informs the thinking of many people who believe that their obligation to the state depends on the state fulfilling its functions and the Lockean view of minimal government was profoundly influential on the creation of the federal government of the USA.

SOCIAL DARWINISM   See **Darwinism, Social**.

SOCIAL DIFFERENTIATION   This denotes the division of an institutional activity into more specialised parts. *Structural* differentiation is perhaps a clearer way of expressing this idea because what is at stake is not people but realms of activity. In pre-modern societies, the family has economic as well as reproductive and educational functions. In modern societies most work is conducted outside the home (and according to its own distinct values) and there are specialist institutions for education; the family retains responsibility for reproduction and infant socialisation. The medieval church played an important part in the polity and the economy, as well as providing social control and social welfare. As specialist institutions have grown up, the role of the church has narrowed.

SOCIAL EXCLUSION   This term became popular in the 1980s to extend the notion of poverty to bring in non-economic aspects of the problem. The poor not only suffer material hardship but are separated from political, educational and civic rights and opportunities. On this view, disadvantage in modern societies in not just about wealth but about a variety of forms of exclusion.

SOCIAL FACTS   Emile **Durkheim** took it as a founding principle of his sociology that the discipline should deal with a range of social phenomena that were external to the individual and exercised a coercive effect. Social characteristics were to be explained by social facts, not by the desires, motives and interests of individuals. Thus in his classic treatment of **suicide**, the observable societal phenomenon of the 'suicide rate' is to be explained by social facts such as regulation and integration.

Few sociologists now find this idea persuasive. While most recognise that social forces shape and constrain human behaviour, Durkheim's suggestion that social facts be viewed as things quite separate from individual consciousness is regarded as too clumsy.

SOCIAL INTEGRATION AND SYSTEM INTEGRATION   In the 1960s David Lockwood made an important critical observation about **functionalism** when he argued that its treatment of integration often confused two importantly different things. There is first the social integration of individuals into a society that results from **socialisation** and social interaction. Second there is system integration: the extent of the 'fit' between various social institutions such as the education system and the economy. System integration is to a considerable extent the unintended consequence of economic relations and structures of power. Anthony **Giddens** developed the point by suggesting that social integration rested on face-to-face interaction while system integration depended much more on the 'distant' interaction of groups and the operations of institutions: processes which in effect go on 'behind the backs' of the individuals involved.

SOCIAL INSTITUTION   Any pattern of behaviour which by repetition, traditional sanction and legal reinforcement acquires a degree of coercion could be described as a social institution: marriage would be a good example. Social institutions are forever being modified because they rest on repetition (and hence may change if large numbers of people stop acting in accordance with them or become selective in precisely how they will support them) but they have a degree of solidity that allows us to forget that they are human creations. In many traditional societies social institutions are bolstered by being given supramundane origins: marriage, for example, is often presented as a divine obligation. Modern societies are more likely to admit the human origins of social institutions and justify them by claims for efficiency: in the West marriage is now commonly defended with the claim that it provides the most effective way of meeting a wide variety of personal and social needs.

A very useful way of grouping social institutions is as follows: (a) kinship institutions deal with marriage, the family and primary socialisation; (b) political institutions regulate access to and the use of power; (c) cultural institutions deal with religious, artistic and scientific activities; (d) stratification institutions deal with the distribution of social positions and resources; and (e) economic institutions produce and distribute goods and services.

SOCIAL MOBILITY   This signifies the movement of people between positions in a system of **social stratification**. In modern societies this means the movement of people between social classes is defined by occupational scales. It may occur between generations (as when a girl born into a working-class family achieves a middle-class occupation) or be the ups-and-downs of an individual career. It is widely accepted that systems of stratification based on social class are considerably more open than ones based on ethnicity or religion or, as in the case of feudal societies, on estate, or, as in Hindu India, on caste.

Most sociological research has concentrated on inter-generational mobility across the divide between manual or blue-collar work and non-manual white-collar work. Serious empirical research was only possible from the 1950s onwards when large scale surveys generated reliable standardised information about sufficiently large numbers of people for us to make generalisations.

Seymour Martin Lipset and Reinhard Bendix's (1959) *Social Mobility in Industrial Society* was influential in arguing that levels of upward mobility were similar in a variety of societies, despite differences in culture, educational systems and industrial profile; a finding that contributed to the view of modernisation as a general process with roughly similar consequences.

There are two very different explanations for social mobility. Everyone agrees that high rates of upward social mobility have been seen in Britain since the 1960s. On the one hand, this might represent a greater degree of freedom in the class structure. Alternatively, and more likely, it may be explained by a change in the class structure itself. The decline of manufacturing industry (especially of the sort reliant on a large labour force) and the massive growth in the number of white-collar jobs mean that there was more room at the top. The class structure had change from being a pyramid to being a lozenge: narrow at the top and bottom and wide in the middle. The growth of the non-manual sector meant that the jobs in this sector could not be filled by the children of people already there and had to recruit from below.

In order to measure the competitive aspect of social mobility (that is, to correct for changes in the structure itself), it is necessary to compare upward and downward movement. What this shows is that the **service class** has not lost any of its ability to pass its class position on to its children.

At this point arguments about social mobility start to reflect the political preferences of the researchers. Those who see life-chances in competitive zero-sum terms will stress that children of the service class still enjoy a highly privileged position because, in terms of the relative likelihood of getting on in life, they have lost nothing to the working class. However, those who concentrate on the distribution of benefits, will stress that social mobility, even if it is a by-product of a change in the class structure, is real enough. That the children of 1950s miners are now professionals is a real improvement in their lives that is not diminished by knowing that the children of lawyers were not forced to work down the mines.

A difficulty with social mobility research is that it is highly technical. More than in most fields, how one defines and measures the key variables, and how one uses statistics to explore relationships, determines the results. As a result, important arguments, although generally approached by the experts in a spirit of scholarly openness to refutation, are incomprehensible to many colleagues.

SOCIAL MOVEMENT   Sociologists often make a distinction between routine institutionalised life and collective action, the latter being unusual goal-oriented concerted action by a large number of people. So collective action would include strikes, riots and boycotts; it also includes social movements. We may also distinguish a general social movement (say, the campaign for women's suffrage) from any particular social movement organisation (in this case, the National Union of Women's Suffrage or the Women's Social and Political Union).

The study of social movements has generated a considerable body of ideas about the causes of recruitment to non-institutionalised activity (for example, **relative deprivation**, status defence, **status inconsistency**) and about the dynamics of goal-oriented organisations (e.g. **goal displacement**).

The above is essentially the US sociological treatment of social movements as being defined by the form of activity; it is uninstitutionalised. European usage stresses much more the content of such activity: in particular its radical or oppositional nature. When French and Italian sociologists (such as Alain **Touraine**) talk of social movements they have in mind challenges to the political status quo.

See **new social movement**.

SOCIAL ORGANISATION   This can refer to any reasonably stable social pattern or structure or to the processes which sustain it. It may be used to describe something as small and informal as the interaction around a corner shop or a massive bureaucracy such as the US Congress and is often synonymous with social order and **social structure**.

SOCIAL STRUCTURE   This is used so loosely that it is tempting to say its meaning can only be discerned from every separate instance of its deployment but most usage might fit under the following rubric: enduring patterns of relationships between parts of a society. Just quite what the essential parts are is a subject of some disagreement. Functionalists, for example, take the crucial parts to be **social institutions**.

See **social system**.

SOCIAL STUDIES OF SCIENCE AND SCIENTIFIC KNOWLEDGE   See **science**.

SOCIAL SYSTEM   Talking of a society as a social *system* usually carries four important implications: that its parts are to some degree interlocking, that they interlock for a purpose, that the system has clear boundaries, and that it is in equilibrium (or homeostasis). Underlying most usage is the model either of a complex biological organism or of the complex machine and it is because many sociologists find both metaphors misleading that they avoid the term. For a detailed discussion, see **structural-functionalism**.

SOCIALISM, SOCIALIST SOCIETIES   There were many brands of socialism but most agree that a socialist society would have the following features. The means of production and distribution would be commonly owned. The economy would be run by the state on behalf of the people with the free market playing very little or no part. With no private property there could be no classes and hence the state would administer fairly rather than act on behalf of the ruling class. These structural changes would remove ideology (especially religion), and alienation would be overcome.

Socialists argue that such societies would be better than capitalist ones because they would be fairer, more economically efficient and less wasteful, they would not have colonies (because they do not need an outlet for surplus capital or commodities), they would serve real needs rather than false advertising-created ones, and they would be more democratic (in that decisions would be made collectively).

Socialists may argue that it is inappropriate to assess the claims by examining self-labelled socialist societies because they are really **state capitalist** or in some other way deficient. The states of Africa and Asia that call themselves socialist differ so much in

origins and state of economic development from the theoretical model, it seems reasonable to leave them aside. But the communist states of Eastern Europe seem to have been close enough to the model to be worth considering.

Socialist economies proved woefully inefficient: the command economy was wasteful and the lack of personal investment in any enterprise encouraged wide-scale corruption. Black markets arose to satisfy the desires not met by the state's provision and undermined respect for the rule of law, which was further eroded by party cadres cynically using their political power to evade legal control. Instead of being more democratic, they were considerably less so; the party controlled everything and tolerated no criticism, let alone opposition. Even the expectation that socialist states would have no need for imperialism turned out to be false. Many (the Soviet Union most obviously) sought to make up for their own economic short-comings by forming exploitative relations with Third World clients.

It is possible to blame the failure of socialist states to live up to expectations on the machinations of capitalist states and on capitalist domination of the world economy but even the political leaders of the Soviet Union in its last decade admitted that they had failed to meet the expectations of their people. It is an ironic consequence of human forgetfulness that, as the communist era fades, it becomes easier for people to return to the promise of socialism, unconstrained by knowledge of the reality.

SOCIALISATION   Also known as **enculturation**, this refers to the process through which a person (especially a child) acquires both the knowledge and the personality necessary to become a full member of a society. It is an axiom of sociology that society is not just external to the individual self (in the obvious sense that it provides the environment in which everyone, except the hermit, must live out their lives) but is also internal and that the **self** is shaped by what it acquires in social interaction with parents and other **significant others**. Although much sociological interest in socialisation is concerned with the development of the child, the process is also important, in a minor key, at various points in our lives. For example, as the classic *Boys in White: Student Culture in Medical School*, authored by Howard S. **Becker**, Blanche Geer, Everett C. Hughes and Anselm L. Strauss (1961) showed, becoming a doctor is not just a matter of acquiring technical knowledge; it also involves being socialised into the norms, values, attitudes and behaviour patterns expected of and by the profession.

SOCIETY It may seem a curious discipline that has trouble succinctly defining its core term but this word carries a very wide variety of meanings. Broadest and least useful, it can be the totality of human relationships. More useful, it means any self-reproducing human group that occupies a reasonably bounded territory and has a reasonably distinctive culture and set of social institutions. We commonly refer to nation-states as societies: France or Holland, for example. But we may also use the term for a particular people within a state: the Scots or the Welsh, for example. It is also used for distinctive groups that sustain some sort of collective identity by virtue of culture and social interaction but lack a territory. So we might talk of 'Hispanic society' in the USA or 'Pentecostal society' in Uganda. However, the absence of a territorial element probably means that 'subculture' would be a more useful designation.

SOCIOMETRY Out of fashion since the 1980s, this is a widely used method for describing social attractiveness within groups by something like measurement. Invented by Austrian-born US psychologist Jacob Moreno, it involves asking each member of a group to rank others in terms of attractiveness and unattractiveness (either in general or for some specified task). The results are then plotted as a diagram of lines linking each person. Those who are most highly ranked appear as stars in such a diagram with many lines radiating to and from them. Rejectees appear as isolated boxes with few or no lines connecting them to the rest.

SOLIPSISM This philosophical doctrine maintains that the self is all that can confidently be known and that anything external can only be known as an aspect of the impressions it makes on the self. In the extreme, the solipsist doubts that there are minds other than his or her own. This position is very rarely encountered and the more common term 'solipsistic' is generally just a fancy way of accusing someone of extreme individualism or blinkeredness.

SOMATIC Derived from the Greek, this means corporeal or 'of the body' and was popular with sociologists of the body in the 1990s.

SOVEREIGNTY From 'sovereign' which has for centuries been used as a synonym for monarch or ruler, this is the quality of supreme, unrestricted, unqualified power that an absolute ruler may deploy. In modern societies, that ruler is the state. Although the modern state is heavily constrained by the deliberate dispersal of power, by the need to sustain popular legitimacy and by the existence of extra-state agencies such as the United Nations and the European Union, it still makes sense to talk of the state's sovereignty because these constraints exist only because the state permits them; in theory, they can be dispensed with. The term is most often used in discussions of state competition (as in the arguments between Britain and

Spain over Gibraltar) and of anomalous juris-dictions (as in the current status of Northern Ireland where the British government has relaxed its sovereignty by permitting the Irish Republic an institutionalised voice).

SPEECH ACT   In his elegantly titled study *How to do Things with Words* the British philosopher J.L. Austin (1962) pointed out that most thinkers seem to have viewed language as primarily a tool for describing the world. However, we do a lot of things with language other than describe: we promise, we nominate, we confess and so on. The things that we do through such talk are speech acts: actions undertaken simply through speech. Austin's early examples of speech acts were so-called 'performatives', where people explicitly performed an act through the use of a standardised term, such as 'I accuse you' or 'we promise him'. Austin observed that such utterances were not to be assessed in terms of their truth or falsity but in terms of their appropriateness. The work was subsequently extended to much more indirect and subtle forms of speech act. More recently **conversation analysis** has focused on the empirical investigation of naturally occurring speech and has continued to advance the study of 'doing things with words'.

SPENCER, HERBERT (1820–1903)   See **Darwinism, Social**.

SPONSORED MOBILITY   See **contest and sponsored mobility**.

SPSS   The Statistical Package for the Social Sciences is a very widely used computer software program that will, at the click of a mouse, perform all the common statistical tests and procedures. While extremely efficient and representing an enormous advance on the days when statistics had to be calculated by hand, SPSS does have the danger of allowing researchers to use inappropriate statistics and statistics that are only half-understood.

STANDARD DEVIATION AND STANDARD ERROR   See **measures of dispersion**.

STATE   The modern state is an integrated set of institutions (the legislature that passes laws, central and local administration, judiciary, police and armed forces) that acts as a system of political domination and (this for Max **Weber** was the crucial point) has a monopoly on 'the legitimate use of violence'. In pre-modern societies it is less easy to talk of a state because the legitimate use of violence was defused and contested: in feudal England, the major lords, the sovereign, corporate bodies, such as town guilds, and the church often competed for power.

Sociological treatments of the state can be divided into three. In the Weberian view, the modern state is an independent force that has its own rules of action: the legal-rational rules of bureaucracy. In Marxist views the capitalist state is 'but a committee for managing the common affairs of the whole bourgeoisie'. Even those Marxists such as Nicos **Poulantzas** who suppose the state has some relative autonomy from capital, nonetheless think its main purpose is the preservation of capitalism. A third position lies between these two: it sees the state as a partly independent force that may be influenced by the different interests that are politically represented.

It is the case that most modern states encompass and represent nations; hence the popularity of the term **nation-state**. They are also usually co-terminus with a 'society' so that when we talk about 'Swedish society' we mean that which is governed by the Swedish state. However, because the boundaries of nation, state and society may not coincide, care is required in the use of these terms.

STATE CAPITALISM, STATE SOCIALISM
These terms is one of a vocabulary of designations that featured in now redundant debates about the nature of communist states such as the Soviet Union and its eastern European satellites. Choice of terms served mainly to identify the political persuasion of the writer. 'State capitalist' was normally used by communists who argued that the validity of Marxist social theory could not be judged by the character of extant states which claimed the legitimacy of Marxism-Leninism because the method they had used to end the institution of private property (nationalisation and forced collectivisation) had simply replaced the remote capitalist by the equally remote state. 'State socialism' often made the same point but with some writers it indicated a more understanding view of the failures of the Soviet Union because it was presented as a temporary and necessarily preliminary stage on the road to full socialism.

STATE SOCIALISM   See **state capitalism**.

STATE TERRORISM   Although this term is often used only to show that the writer disapproves of some state action (for example, the 2003 US invasion of Iraq), it can have a valuable analytical use. It was coined in the 1970s to make the point that, while we normally think of terrorism as a form of attack on the state or on hapless civilians in order to put political pressure on a state, states themselves can engage in terrorism in two senses. They can do so externally when, instead of waging open war against another state, they engage in covert activities of the sort banned by international conventions on war or offensive to their own citizens' sense of what is proper. An example is Libya's arranging for the blowing up of a Pan-Am jet over Lockerbie in Scotland and a French jet over Niger in 1989. There can also be internal state terrorism. This derives its meaning from

the expectation that, even if it will not be so proper with foreigners, the state will confine its dealings with its own citizens to the rule of law. In the 1970s many Latin American dictatorships kidnapped and murdered thousands of their own citizens in (ironically) a war on terrorism.

It is a small point but for analytical purposes (morality may not require it) it is worth distinguishing between state terror and pro-state terror. The latter term denotes the activities of vigilante groups that use terror against enemies of the state without state approval or support. The line may not always be easy to draw but there is a clear difference between illegal acts by the state and illegal acts by those who wish to present themselves as defenders of the state (loyalist paramilitaries in Northern Ireland are a good example). We can see the difference in their fates. Loyalist killers in Northern Ireland were captured, tried and punished by the state. State killers in Latin American countries such as Chile were not punished until control of the state changed hands.

STATISTICS, INFERENTIAL AND DESCRIPTIVE   Descriptive statistics are ways of organising numerical data so that the social phenomena they represent can be understood. They include **measures of central tendency** (such as modes and means) and **measures of dispersion** (such as range and standard deviation). They also include measures of the association between variables (such as **correlation** and **regression**). Inferential statistics are designed to allow us to make generalisations about a large population from a sample while providing a running commentary on how reliable such generalisations are likely to be.

STATUS   This can be used in two rather different ways. It may refer simply to some position in a social system which has a particular **role** attached: grandparent and grandchild, for example. It may also refer to a position in a hierarchy and signify social worth or prestige; **status symbol** is an example of such usage.

STATUS INCONSISTENCY   If a society has more than one hierarchy, it is possible for someone to rank high on one scale but low on another and the complexity of modern societies is such that inconsistencies of status are common. Status inconsistency has sometimes been invoked to explain individual socio-psychological problems.

When large groups share the same inconsistency, that has been used to explain non-routine social action in two ways. A direct connection can be made in those cases of collective action designed to change or demolish status hierarchies. Wealthy and well-educated lower caste Hindus suffer status inconsistency in that their high position in terms of social class is inconsistent with their low ranking on the religiously-sanctified caste hierarchy; many have tried to resolve that inconsistency by campaigning against the social institution of caste.

A more complex connection is found in the idea that status inconsistency creates various forms of anxiety. People who are very well paid but ill-educated may feel insecure about their social position. Two sorts of argument can be developed from that observation. Some analysts have used it as the basis for explaining involvement in socio-moral crusades: such people are thought to be especially attracted to campaigns that allow them to demonstrate their commitment to conservative platforms and thus cement their membership of the higher status group. Others have taken the general anxiety that is thought to be a typical consequence of status inconsistency to be the cause of involvement in extremist political movements of all sorts. Here the collective action is not thought to be an attempt to resolve a tension between inconsistent statuses; it is merely an expression of that tension.

Although status inconsistency has a certain intuitive plausibility it has not proved successful in explaining involvement in collective action. A major failing is that studies have never demonstrated that status inconsistents are actually troubled by the discrepancy, which may well be more apparent to the observer than to the supposed victim.

See **moral crusade**.

STATUS SYMBOL   Any commodity or service which is valued more for the favourable evaluations it brings from others than for its own inherent benefits is serving as a symbol of the acquirer's status. Designer label clothes are a good example. When paying twice as much for a pair of jeans that carry the name of a fashionable designer as an identical unbranded version would cost, the purchaser is not just buying jeans; he or she is buying proof of wealth, taste and discretion.

See **positional goods**.

STEREOTYPES   A stereotype is an exaggerated and usually prejudiced view of a group of people that is based on little or no evidence and is resistant to modification by evidence. The term implies an explanation: people hold to stereotypes because they create a sense of in-group solidarity and superiority: they allow a group of people to think improperly well of themselves. Stereotyping is a common feature of social life because it serves a number of attractive purposes. People find it useful to view the world (and hence arrange their responses to it) through a limited number of simple categories. We know from many studies of occupations, for example, that workers tend to simplify their business by dividing their raw material into a small number of categories based on the problems they present. While the doctors in a long-stay psychiatric hospital diagnosed their patients in terms of complex medical categories, the nursing staff talked of them as 'wetters' and 'wanderers'.

Stereotypes are resistant to change because we treat confirming and refuting cases in different ways. Confirming cases are added to the stock-of-knowledge that supports the stereotype but refuting cases are held separately as exceptions. It is quite common for people to continue to entertain racist stereotypes, for example, despite being on good terms with some black people who defy the content of the stereotype. The 'black people I know' are regarded as the exception and the stereotype remains in place. A further obstacle to change is that ordinary people have a limited interest in knowledge: having acquired a theory or perspective that 'works' they have little interest in further researching the topic – and because stereotypes act to shape interpretation so that they produce their own confirming evidence, they can remain effective in circumstances where a distant observer would have expected them to be rejected for lack of evidence.

However, stereotypes are rarely perfectly self-perpetuating. Attitudes do change eventually. Race relations in the USA and in South Africa are considerably more harmonious now than they were in the 1950s. When large numbers of Irish Catholics migrated to Britain at the start of the 20th century, anti-Catholic sentiment was common and social distance could be measured in the rarity of inter-marriage. By the end of the 20th century the descendants of the original migrants were as likely to marry a non-Catholic as a Catholic and anti-Catholicism was so rare that it seemed archaic.

STIGMA   This term has been almost entirely reversed. The original stigmata were the marks that Jesus Christ acquired on his hands and feet as a result of being crucified. Periodically through the Christian era, small

numbers of especially pious people have shown physical marks similar to the original stigmata and these were viewed as a sign of divine blessing and were revered. Now a stigma (it is usually used as a singular noun) is any physical (deformity, for example) or social attribute (such as a criminal record) which devalues a person's social identity. Erving **Goffman**'s (1963) *Stigma* offered a pioneering exploration of the forms of stigma and their consequences.

STRATEGIC INTERACTION   This is yet another idea from the enormously fertile sociological imagination of Erving **Goffman**. In the essays in his (1969) *Strategic Interaction*, he explores a variety of situations in which one party's gain from interaction is the other party's loss: for example one may wish to boast about one's new car but worry that someone in the group has an even more desirable car. Decision-making in such situations can be complex as one actor tries to assess not only the other actor's knowledge but also the other actor's assessment of the first party's knowledge and so on. As with much of Goffman's work, once he had explored such interaction and laid out its governing principles, it seemed very obvious: the creativity lay in the fact that he was the first to do it.

STRATIFICATION   When regularly recognised social differences (of wealth, colour, religion, ethnicity or gender, for example) become ranked in some hierarchical manner, we have strata (the Latin for layers). Members of a stratum normally share a range of common characteristics other than the principle of stratification; for example, members of the **petty bourgeoisie** share values and life-chances that mark them off from the grand bourgeoisie and from the working class. Objective similarities within, and objective differences between, strata are often accompanied by some sense of communal identity; in this example, we see a degree of class consciousness in political preferences.

Although the differences on which they are built vary considerably, systems of stratification seem universal. Stratification on the basis of gender is universal and with few exceptions, ethnic, religious, linguistic and national diversity give rise to structured discrimination. The obvious explanation of stratification is that the group with the greatest power (whatever its origins) practises **social closure** in order to maintain its privileges. However, in discussions of inequality in the 1950s and 1960s, US functionalists developed an alternative explanation. In an influential article in the *American Sociological Review* entitled 'Some principles of stratification' (1945), Kingsley Davis and Wilbert E. Moore argued that in all societies some positions were more important than others and required special skills. Such skills were in short supply because talent is naturally restricted and because training is expensive in time and money. Hence all societies need a reward structure which encourages lots of people to compete for the most important position and encourages **deferred gratification**. Doctors and lawyers get paid far more than unskilled labourers because we needed to encourage the most talented people to aspire to the professions. The same case was also made by Talcott **Parsons**.

This functionalist argument generated considerable debate. Social importance is difficult to identify in any neutral manner; every occupation can make a case for its importance. In practice the identification of functional importance tends to be circular: functionalists take high rewards as a mark of social importance and then explain those high rewards by the importance of the job. Functional importance could be identified by surveying opinion but this was not done: Parsons simply asserted that there was a consensus that matched his evaluations. Also circular was the link between position

occupied and individual talent. There was no independent evidence that most of the people in the higher strata were more talented than average. It was assumed that the various admission criteria (such as entry to good schools and to university) were effective in identifying talent. Finally, the Davis-Moore case was challenged on the grounds that it ignored an equally plausible explanation of stratification: power differentials. In their defence it should be noted that Davis and Moore recognised that the inheritance of wealth and position weakened their case but they saw that as softening rather than fatally undermining the theory.

The criticisms were so convincing that the functional theory of stratification died in the 1960s and most sociologists now see it as a symptom of an unwillingness by Americans to recognise the extent and nature of inequality.

STRONG PROGRAMME　　Devised in the 1970s by Edinburgh-based philosopher and sociologist of science, David Bloor, the Strong Programme set out an innovative and provocative approach to the sociological study of **science**. Bloor argued that all human beliefs are equally in need of explanation, whether we think of those beliefs as true or false. Furthermore, the explanations that we give should all be formulated using the same cognitive resources, from, for example, psychology, human biology, sociology and anthropology. These two principles for the study of knowledge he termed 'impartiality' and 'symmetry' and they form the core commitments of the Strong Programme. Bloor thus argued that there is a sociological component to understanding all beliefs, including mathematical and scientific ideas, and his work was a major spur to studies in the **social construction of reality**.

STRUCTURAL　　DIFFERENTIATION　　See **social differentiation**.

STRUCTURAL-FUNCTIONALISM This is the name usually given to the **functionalist** sociological theory associated with Talcott **Parsons**, probably the leading figure in US sociology from the 1940s to the 1960s. Parsons proposed that society could be viewed as a social system and that all social systems had four fundamental **functional imperatives**: for example, they need ways to adapt to their external environments and they have to have mechanisms for internal co-ordination. In turn, the social processes that address each of these functional prerequisites can be considered as a subsystem in its own right. Thus the economic subsystem deals with society's adaptation needs but the economy itself has a need for internal co-ordination and so on. In this **subsystems model**, society is seen as composed of nested structures each meeting the functional needs of the layer above. Parson's increasingly elaborate theory came to appear inflexible and in danger of circularity. It also fell foul of logical and methodological criticisms levelled at functionalism generally.

The term structural-functionalism is also sometimes applied to the work of functionalists in social anthropology such as Alfred R. Radcliffe-Brown and Bronislaw Malinowski.

STRUCTURALISM This may mean one of two things. In general sociology it refers to the view that social structures are very important and that structures influence individuals more than the other way round. In cultural studies, literary criticism and anthropology, it more likely denotes the belief that there are interpretative or cognitive structures that underlie and generate observable social phenomena. The best-known example is Claude **Lévi-Strauss**'s theory of binary opposites. He believes that there are universal features of the human mind which generate pairs of opposites (sweet and sour; hot and cold; raw and cooked). The evidence for their universality is that he discovers such opposites in myths taken from a very wide variety of cultures. The difficulty with this assertion is that, as it is possible with some ingenuity to find almost anything in a myth or a literary text, it is very resistant to testing. Structuralist analysts and those they influenced (including Roland **Barthes** and Jacques **Lacan**) typically took over Ferdinand de **Saussure**'s distinction between the signifier and the signified and applied it to sign systems other than language. For example, Lacan argued that unconscious imagery could be looked at as a kind of language while Barthes aimed to read advertisements and even foods in terms of their signification.

STRUCTURATION This term was coined by Anthony **Giddens** for his particular resolution to the structure versus agency debate. These two possible sources of action and change (and hence two types of explanation) need not be treated as alternatives in a **zero-sum game**. Social structures should not be seen as obstacles or barriers to individual action. They form part of the conditions in which people frame actions and they provide parts of the resources for actions. Structures are also formed by the consequences (inadvertent as well as deliberate) of social action. Structuration theory was intended to clarify how social structures were continuously reproduced by social action while – at the same time – the possibilities of social action were set by social structures. Scholars agreed that Giddens had expressed the problem with great clarity though opinions varied as to whether he had solved or merely re-stated the central difficulties. Though the term structuration is still relatively frequently seen, it is by no means universally used, not even by Giddens himself in his later writings.

STRUCTURE See **agency and structure**.

SUBALTERN STUDIES 'Subaltern' was originally used in the British army to designate officers below the rank of captain. Italian Marxist Antonio **Gramsci** took it to mean 'junior' or 'of inferior rank' and applied it to all social classes except the ruling class: peasants, workers and others denied access to 'hegemonic power'. The term was popularised in the early 1980s by a group of Marxist-influenced Indian historians (such as Ranajit Guha) who wished to challenge the elitism of an Indian historiography (in imperialist and nationalist variants) that saw the peasantry and working class as secondary to the political and economic projects of the colonial period and marginal to the direction of Indian history. They also wanted to draw attention to the fact that elite and subaltern mobilisation took very different forms. Elite mobilisation was achieved by adapting British parliamentary institutions; subaltern mobilisation relied on kinship, territorial and class associations.

The term was subsequently borrowed by left-wing social historians in a variety of countries.

The concept of the subaltern has been criticised on the same grounds as 'working class': that it treats as a unity a diverse body of people (gender being only the most obvious divide) that has little in common beyond not being the elite.

SUBCULTURE This term is used very loosely to indicate a package of values, attitudes, beliefs, tastes and behaviour patterns that distinguishes a group sufficiently from the mainstream for it to stand out as different but which do not clash enough to cause major conflict. Although the meaning is intuitively clear, it is difficult to be precise about just how much deviation from the mainstream, or how large a group, or how little a threat to the status quo is definitive.

The most obvious subcultures are those that are also sub-societies, in the sense that the population that supports the subculture is relatively isolated from the main society. The Old Order Amish, a communitarian sect in the USA, have their own territory and their clearly deviant culture is sustained by a social group that has hard boundaries between members and outsiders. Polish refugees in England in the 1940s were less cut-off because their religion did not require separation but they were clearly identifiable.

SUBJECT, DEATH OF THE On the face of it, **postmodernism**'s rejection of **grand narratives** about progress or enlightenment seems to promote subjectivity. However, the same authors who have argued against these large-scale narratives have also questioned our assumptions about an enduring **self** or subject. For early modern philosophers, such as René **Descartes**, knowledge of ourselves as thinking subjects was the only sure defence against a general scepticism. By contrast, recent discussion of the self as subject (for example by Jacques **Derrida**) emphasises the fragmented nature of the sense of self and regards the self as a cultural or symbolic construct. The death of the subject refers to the demise of the self as an unquestionable reference point.

SUBSISTENCE, SUBSISTENCE ECONOMY To subsist is to produce enough to live, to get by. Subsistence is a type and a level of production sufficient (but only sufficient) for one's own use. Even in the most primitive agricultural economies people have exchanged surpluses but there is a clear difference between producing for one's own use and producing for either an extensive range of barter relationships or for a commercial market. The production of surpluses brings with it the need to store, protect and distribute them. It requires that labour be freed from production in order to perform those 'management' functions and it requires a considerable degree of social organisation. Hence a subsistence economy differs from a market economy in a number of ways that have considerable social, cultural and political consequences.

SUBSYSTEMS MODEL   Talcott **Parsons** bridged social action and the social system with his four **pattern variables**. Social systems were made up of specific combinations of choices on each of the four variables. But each social system has needs of its own (generated by its relationship with its environment and its own internal workings) which must be met. Four major 'subsystem' needs were identified (and came to be known as AGIL from the initial letters of the key terms): Adaptation – the need of the system to take resources from its environment; Goal attainment – the need to define goals for the system; Integration – the need to maintain internal order; and Latency – the need to generate enough motivation for tasks to be performed.

Taken at its most general this model is unobjectionable (though one might want to add other needs or re-group these). The problem is that at its most general it is also not very useful.

SUFFRAGE, SUFFRAGETTE   This 19th-century term denotes the right to vote in elections. The feminine 'ette' ending was added to denote those women who in the early part of the 20th century campaigned to have voting rights extended to women.

SUICIDE   Self-murder has a place in the sociological lexicon because Emile **Durkheim**'s attempt to explain it is one of the first works of empirical sociology. In *Suicide*, he (1897) refutes a number of alternative explanations (such as mental illness) and then compares the suicide rates and various other social indicators for a variety of countries

to make the case that certain types of suicide are typical of certain social conditions. In particular he shows that a decline in social integration leads to an increase in the suicide rate.

One reason Durkheim chose the topic was that it provided a severe challenge for his vision of sociology. He wanted to show that, despite the decision to take one's own life appearing to be highly personal, suicide as a social phenomenon could be explained by **social facts**. Too much social regulation produced fatalistic suicide; too little, anomic suicide. Too much integration produced altruistic suicide (as in the war hero who sacrifices himself for his country); too little, egoistic.

One of Durkheim's students, Maurice Halbwachs, in *The Causes of Suicide* (1930), reasonably argued that the distinction between regulation (meaning the shaping of an individual by shared norms) and integration (meaning the shaping of an individual by binding relationships with others) was unnecessary as it was largely through being integrated that we learn social norms, are reminded of them, and are rewarded for supporting them (and sanctioned for rejecting them). In this simplified version suicide rates are inversely correlated with social complexity. Simple societies have lower suicide rates than complex ones; rural societies have lower suicide rates than urban ones.

Although *Suicide* is an impressive work, both in what it makes of primitive data analysis and in the development of sociological argument, it is far from convincing.

One problem is that a great deal of ad hoc explanation is required to sustain the model. For example, the claim that social integration is inversely correlated with suicide rates works well for widowers (who as a class have a higher suicide rate than married men) but not for widows (who show no such relationship). Durkheim explains the anomaly by saying that women are emotionally simpler than men, are better satisfied with the company of pets, and hence are less affected by the sudden change in the degree of social integration that results from the death of a spouse. He may well be right but he has no evidence for this or any of the similar adjustments he has to make to keep the model intact.

But the biggest problem with the study is its reliance on official records of suicide rates. Whether a death is murder, accident or suicide is something which someone must decide. Those decisions must be recorded, usually for small areas, and then collated to produce data for regions and countries. It is clear that many decisions will be mistaken. Durkheim anticipates this criticism and presents the touchstone of large scale statistical work: that provided you have enough cases, mistakes will cancel out. A suicide mistakenly recorded as an accident will be balanced by an accident mistakenly judged to be a suicide. The data may not be entirely accurate in how it represents each case but overall it is accurate.

Jack B. Douglas's (1967) *The Social Meanings of Suicide* was a devastating critique of Durkheim's work because it showed that, because defining and recording suicide is a matter of social interpretation, and that interpretation is shaped by shared beliefs, mistakes in the data are unlikely to cancel out. Consider the way Durkheim deals with religion: suicide rates for Protestant societies appeared to be higher than for their Catholic counterparts. He took this as evidence for his claim that too little social integration (like too much) created social problems. Because Protestantism had a large number of competing churches and emphasised the individual while Catholicism was a more communitarian faith, Protestants were generally less well integrated than Catholics. However, there are two alternatives. Contrary to Durkheim's assertion, the Catholic church in the 19th century was much more hostile to suicide than any Protestant sect or denomination. Hence irrespective of degrees of social integration, Protestants may have felt freer to act on suicidal impulses. But there is a second alternative

and this is where Douglas's phenomenological perspective becomes important: the cultural difference may enter the equation, not at the point of the original death-causing action (about which we have to remain agnostic) but at the point of social definition. A Catholic coroner, dealing with a Catholic family in a Catholic country, may consciously or unconsciously feel pressed to interpret an ambiguous death as an accident. As many suicides are ambiguous, suicide rates will tell us as much about the decisions that coroners and others make as about the intentions of the now-deceased. Ironically, it may well be that social integration explains, not suicide, but the willingness of people to see an ambiguous death as a suicide.

SUPEREGO   See **Freud**.

SURVEILLANCE   From 'survey' this has acquired the meaning of organised monitoring and supervision of people and activities, usually by the state, although it is also used for smaller organisations (as when a bank fits cameras for the surveillance of its workers).

In the 1970s it acquired a specialised meaning through the work of Michel **Foucault** who argued that many apparently progressive innovations (such as the improvement of medical knowledge) had the consequence of allowing increased surveillance and control. There are two good reasons to think Foucault's position is not entirely correct. The first is that his work is primarily concerned with the formal statements and intentions of the 'providers' of the new disciplines of surveillance. Had he studied the supposed victims he would have found a much more complex picture. For example, whatever the intentions of the theorists, designers and administrators of prisons, most prisoners are quite adept at evading surveillance, and either deliberately or inadvertently many consumers of modern scientific medicine subvert the enterprise.

The second reason for doubting that surveillance is a constitutive feature of modern societies is that there has also been an undeniable increase in individual liberty that results from two very different sorts of change. There are first the unintended consequences of social change. The decline of community, the growth of the city, the increased separation of residence and workplace has allowed much greater anonymity while the shift of much life from public places to the private home has allowed us far more freedom to act as we wish than was the case for our forebears. There are also the intended consequences of cultural change. The 20th century has seen a considerable expansion of the idea of human rights and although some of this can be dismissed as mere form, we only have to consider the way that law has been used to remove the restrictions on homosexuals to see the value of the modern emphasis on individual liberty.

See **panopticon**.

SYMBOL   This word is used by sociologists in two main senses. First, a symbol can be simply a type of **sign**: one where the connection between the **signifier** and the signified is purely conventional. For example, '+' is the mathematical symbol for addition. Second, symbolic can be used as part of a contrast with material or monetary. For example, some prestigious jobs may be said to offer symbolic benefits in addition to the monetary reward. It in this sense that sociologists talk of **status symbols**.

SYMBOLIC INTERACTIONISM   A school or movement within US sociology dating from the early-middle of the 20th century, symbolic interactionism derives its name from its dual emphases: it is 'symbolic' because such work focuses on the meanings that social situations have for the actors involved

and it is 'interactionist' because meanings are seen to be shaped by interactions between actors. Though the term was coined by Herbert **Blumer**, the practical implications of symbolic interactionism are probably best understood through the **labelling theory** of deviance or the well known studies of Erving **Goffman**, even if Goffman was never formally allied with the symbolic interactionist school.

As a theoretical standpoint, symbolic interactionism came to be criticised for paying too little attention to **social structure** and to the limits of actors' ability to negotiate the meaning of situations. **Ethnomethodology** took up the key insights of symbolic interactionism but developed them into a distinctive outlook that focused on detailing everyday actors' own social skills and interactional abilities.

SYMMETRICAL FAMILY   See **family**.

SYNCHRONIC AND DIACHRONIC   This pair of terms was introduced by the Swiss linguist Ferdinand de **Saussure** to distinguish between the study of a language as a system and the study of linguistic change. Although languages undergo constant change, at any given time they can be treated as though they formed a coherent whole. This idealised language can then be analysed as a structure: this is synchronic analysis. Studies that focus on the way languages change are diachronic. Neither approach is truer than the other; they both study aspects of the same phenomenon. Sociologists and cultural analysts have since realised that other symbolic systems share this property so that one can now read of synchronic analyses of fashion or of cinema and so on.

SYSTACT   This term was devised by the British **evolutionary sociologist** W.G. Runciman to refer to the general property of societies that they are divided, in fact and in the minds of their members, into groups of people having specified roles and giving rise to differing interests. In some societies these groups may amount to classes or class factions, in others to castes, and so on. These are all systacts and societies divided in this way are 'systactic'. For Runciman, the differences of interest between these systacts allow for them to develop competing beliefs, ideas and ideologies which are then subject to a form of evolutionary selection.

SYSTEMS THEORY　　Systems theory is the name for the general approach to studying self-maintaining systems, ranging from biological organisms that look after themselves for periods of many years (even centuries in some cases) to robotic and other automated engineering systems. Many sociologists,

struck by the ways in which social entities (societies or cultures or human languages) maintain or reproduce themselves, have tried to develop sociology as a systems theory. In this sense, Talcott **Parsons** was a systems theorist, as was made clear in his '**subsystems model**'. Recent advances in computing and robotics have boosted the credibility of thinking of society in systems-theory terms though the connections are still primarily metaphorical rather than analytically precise.

Engineering analyses of systems point out that no closed system can maintain itself for ever. As systems age they become more disorderly; expressed another way, their entropy increases. Biological systems combat the growth of entropy by steadily absorbing new energy, usually derived (via the growth of plants) from the sun.

See **Luhmann**.

T

TABOO This Polynesian term means anything – a place, food, activity – that is forbidden. For Emile **Durkheim** taboos function as a source of social solidarity. Sharing a taboo is the mark of group membership. Claude **Lévi-Strauss**'s work on **totemism** treated taboos as symbol systems expressing complex relationships between nature and culture.

TAUTOLOGY This denotes saying the same thing twice. For example 'This triangle has three sides' is tautological because by 'triangle' we mean a three-sided object. The second part of the sentence, though it appears to be adding new information, merely repeats what is known from the first part. This is important because it is as common in sociology as syphilis in a 19th-century army – and as damaging. Scholars often claim to have discovered a causal relationship between two social phenomena when they have accidentally pulled the triangle trick. For example, **functionalist** treatments of religion claim to explain the persistence of religion by showing that it performs the function of enhancing social cohesion. But when we go back and look at what they mean by 'religion', we discover it has been defined as that collective activity which has the function of enhancing social cohesion. What is presented as a statement about causal relationships between two separate things (religion and social cohesion) turns out simply to be the elaboration of a definition.

The dangers of tautology did not pass with the decline of functionalist thinking; nearly all complicated social theory edifices also flirt with circularity.

TAYLORISM At the start of the 20th century, Frederick W. Taylor sought to increase the efficiency of factories by introducing scientific management. He had three main points. First, increase the division of labour so that greater specialisation would allow more efficient work and so that craft jobs, once broken down into their component parts, could be carried out by unskilled workers. Second, establish close managerial control over the shop floor. Third, use systematic time-and-motion study to cost all work activities accurately so that managers could make rational choices between production techniques. The first principle informed Henry Ford's development of moving production lines and Fordism, Taylorism and Scientific Management are sometimes used interchangeably to indicate modern industrial production.

TECHNIQUES OF NEUTRALISATION See **neutralisation**.

TECHNOLOGICAL CONSCIOUSNESS In an important application and extension of Max **Weber**'s thought about the increasing rationalisation of the modern world, Peter L. Berger, Hansfried Kellner and Brigitte

Berger's (1973) *The Homeless Mind* argued that the use of technology pre-supposed a number of subtle principles about the nature of the world which came to inform not just the world of work but social relationships beyond it. Technology generated a particular consciousness. One such theme is componentiality: technological work supposes that all complex objects can be divided into simple components that are infinitely interchangeable. Life can no longer be seen as an ongoing flux of unique events. It also supposes repeatability; any action can be repeated endlessly with the same effects. All workers may think of themselves as unique but they are encouraged to think of others as anonymous functionaries in that the assembly line works perfectly well provided there is a trained person at each position, irrespective of the identity of that person.

Processing people through bureaucratic work follows similar principles and the cognitive style of technological work also spills over into our private lives so that leisure activities take on a similar tone: searching for increased efficiency and productivity. It affects personal relationships: for example, in the idea that one spouse can be replaced by another. It effects our view of ourselves so that instead of taking our bodies as merely what biology or our fate has given us we feel obliged to improve them by exercise, dieting and even plastic surgery.

Drawing on phenomenology and detailed studies of work and bureaucratic organisation, Berger, Berger and Kellner produce a powerful analysis of the modern world that is considerably more nuanced and careful than George Ritzer's **McDonaldisation** thesis, which covers similar territory.

TECHNOLOGICAL DETERMINISM Most popular histories of the Industrial Revolution begin with scientific and technical advances (such as the invention of the steam engine) and suppose that the social, economic and political changes that came in the wake of such technical changes were inevitable. Sociologists generally question such technological determinism on the grounds that it neglects to explain the social conditions necessary for technical innovation and the political dimension to technical change. For example, sociologists who focused on the **labour process** argued that technological change was often tied up with relations between employers and workers. New technologies were sometimes introduced to break the monopoly of skilled workers even if, at least initially, the new technology offered no gains in profitability, quality or reliability. The change was 'determined' not by technology but by industrial relations. Other sociologists have been struck by the ways in which people – customers, workers, enthusiastic amateurs and so on – mould technology to their own purposes: DJs' use of turntables would be an example. Users can exploit an unanticipated aspect of a familiar technology so that it makes little sense to talk of cultural change being determined by new technologies.

TELEOLOGY From the Greek 'telos' meaning 'end', this is the branch of philosophy dealing with final ends. The term appears in sociology as an adjective describing a certain form of explanation. Kingsley Davis and Wilbert Moore's functionalist explanation of social **stratification** is teleological in that it uses serving a societal need (in this case ensuring the best people get the most important jobs) as the explanation for a social institution. The problem with this is that it uses a consequence (what happens after) as a cause: an impossibility of timing. Teleological explanation is quite sensible for the actions of individual people or for well-organised agencies: in these cases the outcome is intended and thus the desire to achieve the outcome can exist before (and explain) the action. In those cases we call it purposive explanation.

See **structural-functionalism, systems theory**.

THEODICY Max **Weber** popularised the term to describe an important role of religion: to explain fate, especially ill fate, and most especially why bad things happen to good people. When the Jews of the Old Testament era were taken into exile in Babylon, they explained their fate as divine punishment for their sins. There are also theodicies of success. The Afrikaner nationalists who came to power in South Africa in 1948, after a century of British domination, explained their success as divine reward for their having the correct religion.

THERAPY As in radiotherapy and hydrotherapy, this denotes a cure or medical programme designed to remedy some fault. In common parlance, it is now an abbreviation for psychotherapy and refers to a variety of ways of identifying hidden psychological or psycho-social problems by talking about them, either one-to-one with a therapist or in some group setting.

It is useful in sociology for identifying one aspect of the individualism and concern for (some would say 'obsession with') improving personal well-being that is thought to be associated with modernisation. For example, Christians traditionally worshipped God because they believed God demanded it and would punish them if they failed to worship him. If God chose to give the faithful Christian a healthy and rewarding life, one should be grateful but therapeutic benefits were secondary, a by-product of activity engaged in for other reasons. In contrast New Agers (and many contemporary Christians) see therapy as the primary purpose of spiritual exercises.

THICK DESCRIPTION Anthropologist Clifford Geertz popularised this term for an intensive, highly detailed description of some very small part of social life.

THIRD WAY Popularly ascribed to Robert B. Reich, Secretary of Labor during Bill Clinton's first spell as US President, this term refers to the pursuit of a new type of policy stance for liberal societies. The third way is designed to steer a political course between state control and the free market, between the need for regulation and the responsiveness of the market. It is exemplified by, for example, reforming the public sector (state-owned schools or hospitals) so that they respond in market-like ways to their users' demands but without being privatised. After the election of Tony Blair as the new leader of the UK in 1997, Anthony **Giddens** began to write on the third way. He authored a powerful defence of third way-ism and followed it up with a book of responses to critics. In the USA, the third way disappeared with the election of George W. Bush in 2000; other third-way political leaders, for example Lionel Jospin in France, lost out in an international move to the right. Blair's Labour government continued in office but it dropped talk of the third way which was no longer fresh and newsworthy. Sociological interest in the topic also declined.

THIRD WORLD The history of economic modernisation provides a useful shorthand for describing the world in three blocks. The First World consists of the states of western Europe and their former white colonies (notably the USA), which led the Industrial Revolution; Japan is usually included too. The Second World consists of the states of eastern Europe and the Soviet Union. The Third World is comprised of a range of countries in Asia, Africa, Latin American, the Pacific and the Caribbean, many of which were former colonies. The term was originally used by Third World leaders to suggest their intention to find their own path to development and not imitate either the capitalism of the First World or the communism of the Second. As many of the countries it encompassed failed to prosper, the term acquired negative connotations and some scholars have argued for synonyms such as '**less developed country**' or 'LCD' but none have displaced Third World in popular usage. Some analysts have suggested a Fourth World to designate those countries (such as North Korea and several African states) that are becoming poorer.

See **underdevelopment**.

THOMAS, WILLIAM ISAAC (1863–1947) A student and later professor in the highly influential University of Chicago sociology department, Thomas is best known for two things. The first is his dictum that 'when people define situations as real then they become real in their consequences'. This is as clear a statement as one can have of an essential sociological idea: that the explanation of purposive social actions lies in the subjectivity of the actor. He (1918) was also co-author, with Florian Znaniecki, of the influential *The Polish Peasant in Europe and America*.

THURSTONE SCALES See **scales**.

TIME Sociologists mean by this the same as everyone else: the continuous passage of existence. It is, of course, an element in all of human life but interesting observations can be made about the way different cultures and different sorts of society think of time. Pre-modern societies tend to have little interest in accurately measuring time because they depend on day-light and the annual cycle of the seasons. People were intensely interested

in measuring the seasons and in finding the longest and shortest days. However, the one early modern activity that did stimulate an interest in measuring time on a small scale was navigation. Accurately calculating the position of a ship in open sea required knowledge of the stars and of time.

Consensus about time is important for co-ordinating activities but until the mid-19th century there was little need for such consensus to stretch beyond the local community or for people to be terribly accurate in time-keeping. It was the coming of the railway that brought entire nations into accurately defined single time zones and the factory, which to work efficiently had to have its workforce present at the same time, that turned ordinary people into wearers of watches and owners of clocks. Marxists sometimes describe the modern attitude to time (measured, calculated, divided) as a function of capitalism but it would be more accurate to say that it is a consequence of technology, social complexity and scale.

Now that we live in a society where time is organised and structured one can also investigate how people treat and handle their own time. In sociological studies of work we can see how workers try to manage their long shifts and to recover some feeling of control over the passing of time. In studies of everyday life, sociologists have examined how people handle their leisure time, for example, to ensure that it is treated differently from the regulated time at the office.

TIME-BUDGETS These are detailed records of how they spend their time that research respondents are asked to keep. Time-budgets can be useful for charting basic trends in work and leisure, for example, but they are severely constrained by their lack of accuracy and their omissions. The world according to time-budgets is without sex and crime.

TIME-SPACE DISTANCIATION Anthony Giddens popularised the phrase to refer to the stretching of social relations made possible by new forms of transport, communication and recording. Given the right infrastructure, you can now stay in touch with friends through email over most of the globe. You can make a music recording even if you are in London and your band is in New York. You can collaborate with your architect who is on another continent. According to Giddens, your sense of your community or of who your colleagues are is now much less tied to proximity than it formerly was.

TÖNNIES, FERDINAND (1855–1936) See **community**.

TOQUEVILLE, ALEXIS DE (1805–59) A member of the French Chamber of Deputies, de Toqueville travelled widely in America in the 1830s. His (1835–40, 1833–7) *Democracy in America* and *Journey to England and Ireland* contain interesting and innovative comparative observation. He believed an increase in equality to be an irresistible feature of modern societies but was concerned that, by undermining all hierarchical structures and removing bodies intermediate between individuals and society, it would lead to tyranny: an early version of the **mass society** fear. Like Friedrich **Nietzsche** later, he was suspicious of the common people. His reading of the French Revolution was that too much individualism and centralisation threatened responsible self-government. His experience of America led him to conclude that such a fate had been avoided there by a combination of the previous history of self-government in the American colonies prior to independence from Britain and a federal constitution that allowed lots of opportunities for individuals to participate in civic life.

Although his ideas on the pre-conditions for successful democracy have long been of interest to political scientists, his work was revived by US sociologists of religion in the 1980s who were taken with his assertions about the relationship between voluntarism and religious vitality. He noted that in France where there was one monopoly church, the religious culture was stagnant and there were low levels of popular participation. In America, where a plurality of churches, denominations and sects competed on equal terms, church-going was popular. As Europe has become ever-more secular, that contrast has again become popular as a way of explaining the different fate of religion in the Old and New Worlds. Within the circle of those influenced by de Toqueville there remains considerable dispute about exactly which features of American religious life are salient: diversity, lack of state support for one church, competition between churches, lack of close association between religion and an unpopular political regime, or the lack of centralisation in US public administration.

An overlooked point about de Toqueville's impressions of America is that they were acquired while travelling. It is certainly the case that the USA as a whole has a great deal of religious diversity but many parts of America are religious monocultures. The explanation of US religiosity may not lie not so much in local diversity (seen as presenting any individual with a lot of choices) but in the loose structure of the US state allowing local communities the social and political space to build viable sub-societies which support sub-cultures.

TOTAL INSTITUTION Erving **Goffman** (1961) popularised this term in *Asylums* to signify organisations such as boarding schools, monasteries, psychiatric hospitals, prisons and army training camps that isolated their members from the wider society. It is a defining characteristic that, in contrast to normal life, where we work, play and reside in at least three separate places, members are required to live out their entire day in a single location with the same limited company and under the umbrella of one set of norms. Most total institutions are total because they have the specific aim of bringing about a fundamental change in the personalities of inmates. In the case of prisons, the isolation is punishment but in monasteries, for example, it is intended to make it easier to eradicate the old self and create a new one. That process often begins with what Goffman called 'mortifications of the self'. As a preliminary to learning the new self, the old self is undermined through such rituals as shaving of the head, the removal and destruction of old clothes, showering with disinfectant, the removal of all possessions, and even the removal of the old name.

A major theme of *Asylums* is the tension between the wishes of the totalising institution and the desire of inmates to preserve some vestiges of individuality (through subtly customising uniforms, improvising cosmetics, hoarding objects and the like) and autonomy (by sustaining an inmate culture).

TOTALITARIANISM   This signifies a particularly modern form of political rule in which power is centralised and applied to the control of every aspect of people's lives. Examples of totalitarianism are Hitler's Germany, Stalin's Russia and Saddam Hussein's Iraq. Four things make it particularly modern. First, there is the reach granted by technology and bureaucratic organisation: only in the 20th century with electrical and electronic communication has it been possible to maintain effective surveillance over a large area and a large number of people. Second, is the interest in ordinary people created by democracy: until the rise of liberal democracy rulers only rarely paid attention to what the masses thought about anything. Third, only in the complex inter-connected societies described by Emile **Durkheim**'s **organic solidarity** need dictatorial rulers fear everyone.

Monarchs of the 17th century did not need to fear the peasants of any one town or any one craft guild; only if revolt was widespread was it a problem for stability. The circle that needed constant supervision was the court and major nobles. Fourth and here we return to the first point about technical possibilities, it is generally only modern nation-states that promote an ideology of an entire people being enthusiastically united in some glorious common project. Hence it is only in such societies that dissent poses a serious threat to the rulers.

The core of what the term signifies is clear enough but its edges are inevitably fuzzy. It is useful to distinguish totalitarian and authoritarian regimes and the usual marks are that authoritarian regimes are not purposefully ideological and do not have an interest in total mobilisation of the efforts of the people. Unlike Stalin, Latin American dictators such as Anastasio Somoza (who ruled Nicaragua from 1936 to 1956) were not engaged in an heroic project and required little from the people other than acquiescence.

TOTEMISM   A totem is a non-human object (usually a plant or an animal) with which a group of people symbolically identify. The classic case of totemism is a tribe claiming an animal as a mythical ancestor.

TOURAINE, ALAIN (1925–)   A celebrated French sociologist strongly associated with the Ecole des Hautes Etudes en Sciences Sociales in Paris, Touraine is best known for his work on **new social movements**. He argues that changes in society to a post-industrial form mean that class is displaced and that social movements take over the historical role of classes. Still, these new social movements nonetheless act rather like Marx's idea of class. In short, they define a group in whose interests they fight, define an enemy which they oppose, and develop an alternative model of modernity. In his work, particularly on the environmental and anti-nuclear movements, Touraine focused on the ideological (rather than organisational) character of social movements and thus stands in strong contrast to the US tradition of **social movement** studies.

TOURISM   Travellers were always expected to bring back stories and novel experiences. Tourism refers to the commercial organisation of travel so that people can be their own travellers. As early as the 1870s Thomas Cook was offering to arrange round-the-world trips from London. Tourism is now a vast business that brings many countries (for example the Dominican Republic and Costa Rica) a large part of their national earnings.

Sociologists are interested in tourism for two main reasons. They are interested in the impact of tourism on tourist sites themselves. In a well-known paradox, tourist development can often destroy the very thing (the unspoilt view, the pristine environment) that attracts tourists in the first place. In poorer countries that happen to be attractive to tourists, the tourist industry can have a very disruptive influence on the local culture and local socio-economic development. For example, in Cuba, tourists mostly survive in a dollar-based economy. Cubans who can sell goods or services into this economy can command much higher wages than those who function exclusively in the domestic (peso) economy, producing perverse incentives that discourage people from working in the public services, the professions or many kinds of manufacture. Second, sociologists of culture are interested in the tourist experience and in the way that this experience is produced for and consumed by tourists. For example, sociologists are interested in the way in which the historical heritage of tourist sites is constructed and marketed to visitors.

TRADE UNION   This is an employee organisation intended to improve the working conditions and rewards of its members. Trade unions are based on the simple observation that while any single worker has almost no power, a combination of the entire workforce can be extremely powerful. They differ importantly from professional associations in that professions normally have much greater control over their work and are able to control entry to the profession. They differ from staff associations in that they are not company specific and are not management-led.

TRADE-UNION CONSCIOUSNESS   Marxists saw the activities of organised groups of workers in combining to promote their own interests as preliminary to, but also as an obstacle to, the development of a proper class consciousness. It could be an obstacle because trade unions might focus only on getting a better deal and thus aim to reform capitalism rather than overthrow it. Worse still, some unions, notably those representing male skilled workers, often agitated to maintain advantages over other groups of workers. Such seeming short-sightedness represented 'trade-union consciousness'. V.I. Lenin, the successful revolutionary at the heart of the Soviet Union, believed that the involvement of intellectuals was necessary to help workers transcend the narrow sectional interests of trade unionism.

TRADITIONAL AUTHORITY   See **authority**.

TRANSFORMATIONAL GRAMMAR   See **Chomsky**.

TRANSFORMATIONAL MODEL OF SOCIAL ACTIVITY   See **critical realism**.

TRANSGRESSION   From the Latin meaning to 'step across', this generally means rule-breaking but it has acquired another meaning through the work of Michael **Foucault**. He used it to mean challenging bodies of knowledge and **discourse** by exposing their origins. He did not believe that transgression exposes falsehood by simply revealing hidden truth because he denied that such an essentialist aim as discovering the real self was viable. He emphasised that, contrary to modern common sense, identities are inevitably to some degree historical. For example, it was only possible to be 'mad' or 'depraved' or 'perverted' in anything like the modern sense once new discourses of mental health and morality were in place. Foucault and his followers emphasise that these identities could only emerge at specific historical junctures; in this sense Foucault is a **Hegelian** thinker. His point is not just the general social constructionist claim that identities are constructed (and could therefore have been constructed in other ways) but the more specific claim that certain identities, certain ways of being human, are only available under particular historical circumstances.

TRIBE   This denotes a small group bound by kinship and a sense of duty to other members, and associated with a particular territory. It normally has something like the political autonomy of a nation. More recently, the term has been taken up in an analogical fashion by French social analyst Michel **Maffesoli**.

TROELTSCH, ERNST (1865–1923)   A contemporary and close friend of Max **Weber**, this German theologian made important contributions to the sociology of religion through his (1911) massive *The Social Teachings of the Christian Churches*. In this he explored the tension between two divergent expressions of Christianity: the church and the sect (see **religious organisations**).

TRUST   Social relations depend on trust but much of this trust is taken for granted; it is not explicit. Ordinarily we assume that the world is as we see it: we trust our eyes and ears, our telephones and televisions, our web browsers and routine technologies such as coin-operated parking meters. Both **ethnomethodologists** and interactionist sociologists such as Erving **Goffman** have detailed the pervasiveness of this trust. Ethnomethodologists exposed the degree of routine, background intersubjective trust by carrying out breaching experiments in which volunteers questioned the routine good faith of people they interacted with. Their interactions soon ground to a halt. Goffman collected accounts that demonstrated how, for example, robbers are able to get away with thefts because someone appropriately dressed carrying furniture out of a store is assumed to have a good reason for doing so. Others who have studied bogus doctors – people who pretend to have medical qualifications and who enter hospitals and carry out procedures – find that such deceptions work because, rather than distrust the doctor, their colleagues and patients initially make excuses for them.

With the growth of automated technological systems this routine trust has come to be extended to gadgets and networks which people do not understand. We now routinely give confidential information on-line with only the sketchiest idea of why an on-line bookstore can be trusted with our credit card details. For Anthony **Giddens** this need to put our trust in systems over which we have no control gives rise to the unease that characterises advanced modernity.

TRUTH   The exact nature of truth is more a problem for philosophers than for sociologists (or indeed natural scientists) who usually take a common-sense based attitude: a claim is true if it is correct or as correct as possible. Within philosophy there are two main schools of thought. **Realists** assert something like the following: the proposition 'the cat sat on the mat' is true only if the cat did indeed sit on the mat. This is known as the correspondence theory of truth and it seems attractively concrete, if a little obvious. However, it gets less obvious when the entities one is talking about are less everyday, if, for example, they are sub-atomic particles whose characteristics are bizarre and not known with great certainty or if it is the Big Bang which (by definition) no one can have witnessed. Realists want to assert that truth means the same for these experimental and hypothetical entities. But, unlike with the cat, one cannot check simply by going to have a look at the mat so it seems that the whole question of 'correspondence' is being begged. Even in the case of the cat, the correspondence theory might be on shaky ground since developments in genetics might in the future lead us to the view that the category 'cat' is a mistake and that there are genetically distinct kinds of creature that should have separate names. For this reason, some philosophers are attracted to a competing idea, the consensus theory of truth which derives from the tradition of philosophical **pragmatism**. They claim that a true proposition is one that is 'warrantably assertable' – that is, the best that could be asserted once all the evidence has been taken into account.

Practising sociologists need not be too bothered about all this. However, one should note that as soon as analysts introduce hypothetical entities into sociology (as **realists** do with classes or followers of Michel **Foucault** do with **discourses**) they run up against some of the problems with the correspondence theory. For his part Jürgen **Habermas** has been attracted to the consensus theory because it resonates with his notion of an **ideal speech situation**.

TURN-TAKING   See **conversation analysis**.

TWO-STEP FLOW OF MASS COMMUNICATION
Best explained and illustrated in Elihu Katz and Paul Lazarsfeld's (1955) *Personal Influence*, this idea was part of an empirical rejoinder to

fears that mass communication would create a **mass society**. Katz and Lazarsfeld found that effective mass communication worked through intermediaries and social networks. **Opinion leaders** passed on information and endorsed messages and they tended to be topic-specific so that people might look to one person for a lead in matters of fashion and to another for political information and advice. Hence mass communication flowed in two steps.

See **diffusion of innovation**.

TYPES OF COMPLIANCE   In his *A Comparative Analysis of Complex Organizations*, Amitai Etzioni (1961) grouped the various ways in which compliance was ensured under three headings: coercive power (the threat or use of force); remunerative power (the selective allocation of resources through salaries and wages); and normative power (the allocation and manipulation of symbolic rewards and deprivations).

TYPES OF SOCIAL ACTION   Max **Weber** identified four ideal types of social action. Instrumental (*zweckrational*) action was the sort of rationality assumed by economists in their claims that people would seek to maximise the benefits they enjoyed. The actor weighs the relative costs and rewards of alternative means to an end, and will evaluate the appeal of the various ends themselves. In value rational (*wertrational*) action, the actor weighs up competing means to an end but does not question the end itself since the end is taken to be an ultimate value. Affectual action is governed by emotions and the fourth type was traditional action, governed by custom and habit.

TYPIFICATION   This term is primarily associated with **phenomenological sociology**.

Phenomenologists were concern with understanding how, from an undifferentiated stream of consciousness, we create the objects and the knowledge of the objects that we take for granted in our everyday lives. The basic acts of consciousness, Alfred **Schutz** called first-order typifications: grouping together typical and enduring elements in the flow of experience, building models of things and people, and insofar as these are shared, creating a social world. For Schutz, the job of the sociologist is to construct second-order typifications: a rational model of the world based on the first-order typifications that actors offer as explanation for their actions. In contemporary sociology, it is really only **ethnomethodology** that persists with the suggestion that we can find the foundations for social analysis in the taken-for-granted cultural assumptions that make life regular and dependable. Ethnomethodologists are interested in elucidating the methods that people routinely use in ordering their experiences; ethnomethodology does not seek to pass judgement on those methods or to improve on them.

TYPOLOGY   This is any classificatory conceptual scheme (such as the four-fold categorisation of **religious organisations**). Typologies are never true or false; they are merely more or less useful. That value lies in how well they perform the dual tasks of succinctly describing and making sense of reality in the terms of whatever theory is being tested or advanced.

U

UNANTICIPATED CONSEQUENCES See **unintended consequences**.

UNCONSCIOUS This denotes that part of the mind that remains outside awareness. It becomes evident to us through dreams and day-dreaming where we have thoughts over which we seem to have no control. While the existence of the unconscious is generally accepted, psychoanalysts stand out by believing the unconscious to be surprisingly influential, so much so that it can overrule the conscious mind. The problem with the theories of the unconscious such as those of Sigmund **Freud** or Jacques **Lacan** is that they are peculiarly resistant to testing precisely because the unconscious is mysterious and beyond rational control. The same case material can be used to generate a wide variety of competing views and, though there can be reasoned debate about the consistency of interpretation, the exercise is often more like literary criticism than natural science. The rate of successful cure is not known with any certainty either. Too often, the reason why any scholar prefers one interpretation over others seems to come down to taste and professional and political interests.

UNDERCLASS The social class model of stratification is based on the ranking of occupations. There is thus the possibility of a population that falls below the lowest class because there are people who do not have jobs and (unlike many of those unemployed at any one time) have no employment history and very little prospect of ever acquiring an occupation. Although the term can be used as plain description, it is contentious because it usually figures in proposed social policy initiatives that arouse strong feelings. For example, some conservative scholars believe that extensive social welfare has the opposite of the desired consequence by making it rational for people who would otherwise be low earners to remain dependent on benefits. In order to break the cycle of dependency that sustains an underclass, many governments try to provide welfare support in forms that do not discourage taking paid work (for example, reducing unemployment benefit but also reducing the tax on the low paid).

UNDERDEVELOPMENT Sometimes this term can be simply descriptive of a society yet to undergo the sorts of economic and social changes associated with **modernisation** but more usually it signifies a particular explanation of countries' continued poverty. In this latter usage, underdevelopment is a condition; an economic malaise. Economically weak countries are not just lacking in development; they are the victims of others' exploitation. Andre Gunder Frank popularised the term in his theory of capitalist distortion of the Third World. Through unfair trading relationships, the capitalist countries of the First World extracted most of the economic surplus from the Third World (some stuck to port areas and to the elites which controlled relations with the West), encouraged Third World countries to concentrate their economic activity on extraction or monoculture production (rather than developing their own processing and manufacturing industries), and exported finished goods to the Third World. Though analysts differ on the details (largely on predictable grounds of left versus right politics) the simple point is that the development of the Third World cannot follow the template of that of the First World because the first time round the lead nations had very little competition. Third World countries are not even starting from scratch since their economies have already been organised into a pattern that suits the commercial interests of the First World.

See **dependency theory, imperialism, uneven development, world-systems theory**.

UNDERSTANDING   See **empathy, hermeneutics, Verstehen**.

UNEVEN DEVELOPMENT   Applied to countries and to regions within countries, this term signifies that capitalist economic development proceeds at different rates and takes different forms. Western Europe displays uneven development, but so too does France internally. This may result from independent local differences (some regions have coal deposits and others do not) but, as in the examples of **internal colonialism** and **dependency**, it may result from the lead country or region having a deliberate or accidentally distorting effect on the others. Though the term is most often used in analysing capitalist development, it is clear that uneven development occurred in **state socialist** and many social democratic societies also.

UNILINEAR   It was common in the 19th century, when scholars were starting to form more or less social scientific assessments of social development (and lacked good comparative data or the benefit of hindsight) for the deviser of each grand scheme to suppose it had universal application: that all societies must change in the same single way at the same rate and with the same consequences. Modern social science has long since abandoned such ambition, though it is common for critics to disparage schemes that they dislike by calling them unilinear.

UNINTENDED CONSEQUENCES   A key element of sociology is perfectly summarised in the Scots poet Robert Burns's phrase 'The best laid plans of mice and men gang aft aglay' or, in English, 'often go wrong'. Motives explain what people do (even if we go back further to find causes of those intentions unknown to the actor). But the consequences of action are often other than anticipated or intended. There are three sorts of explanation for this. First, the **unconscious** or subconscious mind may unknowingly shape our actions. Second, there is an external equivalent of the unconscious mind: ideological forces that blind social actors to their own and other people's interests and motives. Third, even if we have perfect knowledge of ourselves and of others immediately involved, we do not have it of key players who are at some distance from us, or of the future. Our actions often form long causal chains and are shaped in environments that are beyond our knowledge or do not yet exist at the time we form our 'best laid plans'. For example the formation of the Trotskyite Militant Tendency within the British Labour party in the early 1980s was intended to shift British politics to the left. Instead it caused the Labour party to lose three consecutive elections and gave power to a particularly right-wing Conservative government.

It is the power of unintended consequences that causes most sociologists to be suspicious of a 'history of ideas' approach to social evolution. Most big ideas do not emerge from a deliberate and careful plan. For example, it is common for patriotic Americans to trace the religious toleration of their country to the wisdom of its founders. But in order to explain why liberal views triumphed over illiberal alternatives, it is necessary to point out that the religious diversity of the American colonies prevented the bigots who wanted to impose their particular religion getting away with it.

UNIVERSALISM   This is the opposite of particularism and forms one of the Parsonian **pattern variables.** Freed from its place in that contentious model, the contrast pair still provides a very useful way of describing a fundamental choice. For any particular matter (say the allocation of military rank), do we treat all people on the basis of universal criteria of competence (the modern bureaucratic method) or do we promote our family and clients (the patronage model)?

UNOBTRUSIVE MEASURES   This denotes any method of collecting data without the knowledge of the subject or, more precisely, without the subject knowing what is being collected or why. Strictly speaking it includes **covert research** which is, by definition, unobtrusive. However, the term is more often used to refer to situations where the research is conducted indirectly in the hope that this will avoid changing the thing being studied. Generally speaking, this raises fewer problems of research ethics than do covert studies. For example, instead of asking respondents if they care about the environment, we could ask about hobbies and about shopping and see whether they mention conservation activities and the purchase of environment-friendly goods. Instead of asking how workers

feel about some major change in their working conditions, we could analyse patterns of productivity, sick-leave, absenteeism and turnover. For any method, the case has to be made that it generates valid and reliable information about the matter in hand; good indirect and unobtrusive measures demand that sociologists approach the study imaginatively.

See **covert research, ethics of research, Hawthorne effect**.

UPPER CLASS   When asked to define the upper class many people cite the possession of aristocratic titles, large income, and certain highly prestigious occupations; what is missing from that list is property. Social scientists normally define the upper class (and distinguish it from the top end of the **service class**) as those who live on earnings from the ownership, control and exploitation of property such as land, capital, large businesses and share-holdings. It is small because wealth is concentrated. In 2000 about a quarter of Britain's wealth was owned by 1 per cent of the population. In the US the top 1 per cent owned 38 per cent of the wealth.

Of all the classes it is probably the upper class that has the clearest sense of its identity as what Karl **Marx** called a 'class for itself'. It has a high degree of **endogamy**, effectively practises **social closure** by educating its children at expensive private schools and uses family connections to maintain the position of those members who do work. In 1973, almost half the bank directors listed in the UK's *Who's Who* also had fathers listed there. In 1970 three-quarters of the directors of the major British banks had been to private schools; one in three to Eton.

See **power elite**.

URBAN, URBANISM   In 'Urbanism as a way of life' (1938), the Chicago School sociologist

Louis B. Wirth argued that the social effects of living in cities had made a greater contribution to the character of modernity than industrialisation or capitalism. The city differs from the country village in size, in density of population and in the diversity of its population. From this follows the social differences. The **division of labour** is considerably more extensive. Most social interaction is with strangers and acquaintances rather than with kin and friends. Relationships tend to be transitory, superficial and **instrumental**. Above all, as Georg **Simmel** noted, in the city it is possible to be anonymous.

Like the **community**–society contrast which it closely mirrors, the urban–rural divide can be criticised for exaggerating differences. For example, cities may contain neighbourhoods in which some aspects of life resemble the rural village (which is why Herbert Gans called his 1962 book *The Urban Villagers*). Nonetheless, the cultural pluralism and the greater freedom from social constraints granted by anonymity typically found in cities gives city life a sophistication not found in the country: hence the common use of 'urbane' to mean elegant and effortlessly sophisticated.

More recently sociologists have picked up on insights (such as those of Walter **Benjamin**) about the city as a centre for consumption and as the source of cultural innovation. Cities inevitably consume vast amounts of foodstuffs, raw materials and other goods and often pay for these in terms of cultural products. Cities thus tend to take the lead in cultural development and provide the setting for new subcultures and trends as expressed in music, art and dress.

USES AND GRATIFICATIONS The first wave of sociological interest in the mass media was profoundly gloomy. Writers on the right and left agreed that the mass media encourage passivity. This assumption was built into their methodology: there was no attempt to study the responses of the audience. The **two-step flow of communication** was one alternative built on empirical research. 'Uses and gratifications' is another. It is built on the idea that media consumption is an action; even lying prone in front of the television is the result of a choice to do that. Rather than ask what the media do to their audiences, this approach asks what audiences do with the media and the answers include seeking information, being entertained, making social contacts, and developing both individual and social identities.

UTILITARIANISM In philosophy utilitarianism is a theory of ethics. It states that the ethical course of action is the one that brings the greatest happiness to the greatest number. The ethical status of an act is judged in terms of its consequences; thus this position is often known as a consequentialist one. Much modern social policy is based on utilitarian premises: for example, health spending by governments is often intended (or so it is said) to use the health budget to bring the greatest relief from pain and illness to the greatest number. In ethics, utilitarianism is opposed to so-called deontological theories (such as that advanced by Immanuel Kant, see **Kantian**), which seek to establish universal ethical codes. In hypothetical situations these two philosophical positions can be brought into contradiction: a group of people with no food on a desert island could, for utilitarians, under certain circumstances, be justified in killing one of their members so that the others may stay alive. Most deontologists would never accept that as ethical.

There are some evident problems associated with the basic utilitarian position as it was developed in the 18th and 19th centuries. It assumes that everyone's happiness is worth the same whatever makes one happy, whether wrestling or higher education. It assumes that all types of being happy can be rated on the same scale, even if one person is happy because they are out of pain and the other is happy because they received an unusually large glass of beer. Finally, it is unclear about what exactly is so good about 'happiness'. It shares many of these weaknesses with other contemporary work in **political economy**. However, some 20th-century utilitarians have argued that the doctrine has radical implications if one extends it to non-human creatures. For example, depending on how the happiness of cows and sheep was assessed, utilitarian principles if applied across the board would likely support mandatory vegetarianism.

Utilitarianism is of interest to socio-logists in two main ways. First, utilitarian reasoning is at the heart of so much public policy that the logic of the approach is a social phenomenon worthy of study. Second, utilitarianism is itself a theory of human conduct since it assumes that people are motivated by the pursuit of happiness. Both Emile **Durkheim** and Karl **Marx** were rightly critical of this approach as

it circulated in the 19th century, yet it has persisted into the 21st.

See **Bentham**, **Mill**.

UTOPIAN   Sir Thomas More called his 1526 depiction of the perfect society *Utopia*, from the Greek for 'Nowhere'. Utopian is com-monly a pejorative term, meaning that the advocate's scheme is unrealisable, often because it depends on people behaving with-out thought to their own interests and with perfect knowledge. However, utopian ideas have also had progressive consequences. For example, early proposals for the liberation of women would have been seen as utopian and utopian thinking about environmental futures has provided valuable yardsticks for measuring progress towards environmentally-sustainable living. By definition, utopias are unrealistic but they provide a form of thought experi-ment for examining how society would be if we followed proposed rules and values.

V

VALIDITY This denotes a humbler and more pragmatic version of '**truth**' and is usually used in relation to something we measure such as the unemployment rate. We describe some measure as being valid if, as far as we can tell, it truthfully represents what it purports to represent.

VALUE-FREEDOM, VALUE-NEUTRALITY Over the decades these terms have taken on a variety of separate meanings and can now mean any of the following. First, and synonymous with **objectivity**, sociology can be scientific in the sense that the values that influence it are only those necessary for the job (such as truth, honesty and diligence) and not, for example, religion, party political support or patriotism. Second, Max **Weber** used the term to suggest that while academics cannot be entirely prejudice-free in the above sense, they can be explicit about their values (for example, their liberalism) and how these values affect their work. Third, it can signify the limits of the sociological enterprise: while we may hope to describe and explain social reality, most sociologists assert that we cannot from that derive any values, any instruction for how we ought to live. Fourth, it follows from the previous item that sociologists should not pronounce on values, at least not in their professional role as social scientists.

All of these propositions have been questioned. Some scholars deny that natural scientists operate objectively and do not see why social scientists should be any better. Others note that the founders of sociology were all driven by strongly-held values and question why research driven by, say, a strong desire to expose the suffering of women, should be any less valid than that motivated purely by intellectual curiosity. The idea that we should not promote particular values is challenged (by **Howard Becker** in his 1967 address 'Whose side are we on?', for example) on the grounds that, if we are not value-promoting, social science will be dominated by the values of the ruling class as there will be no force to resist ideological definitions of social reality.

The **objectivity** issue we discuss under that heading. The second issue is a red herring. The claim for value-freedom is not that scholars should have no normative grounds for carrying out research; it is that having a strong interest in the outcome of research may well distort observation and reasoning and that unless commitment to the scientific enterprise trumps other values there is no point in social research. The Becker case does not seem very persuasive. It makes the interesting (and rather dated) assumption that sociologists are left wing. Our impression is that sociologists generally represent the full range of value positions available in their cultures. The fact that sociologists disagree about values is itself good evidence that fact and value are not the same and that sociology cannot tell us what is the good life. However we must not be too hard-and-fast about dividing facts from values since recent philosophical analyses indicate that there can be a **fact–value distinction** but no fact–value dichotomy; in other words there is no sharp dividing line even if it is easy to distinguish between highly factual and highly evaluative assertions. **Critical theory** authors have been particularly interested in exploring the limits of the fact-value divide.

For the discipline, the main problem of value-freedom is not that this or that study might be somewhat compromised by the researcher's fundamental value commitments. Far more serious is the problem that large areas of intellectual activity (for example, literary criticism, psychoanalysis and Marxism), that lack the same commitment to empirical research, have borrowed from sociology and in repayment sought to undermine the ideal of value-free social scientific research.

VALUES   These are ethical principles and ideals: statements of what should be, rather than of what is. Generally, values are a little more mundane and specific than moral precepts but sometimes the terms are used interchangeably. 'A vegetarian diet is healthier than meat-eating' is in theory a testable empirical proposition; 'A vegetarian diet makes us better people' is an ethical assertion.

Values have a particular place in sociology because they are an important element of what people learn when they are socialised into the culture of a society and they play an important part in social cohesion (although sociologists differ about just how important). Cultures (and subcultures) differ in the values they hold and these differences account in part for the different 'feel' of alternative cultures. For example, in many Scandinavian cultures excessive talking may be seen as a sign of superficiality whereas in much of Britain small talk is socially prized. Despite our ability to pick up on values, some sociologists – notably **ethnomethodologists** – have been sceptical about the explanatory power of values. Values always have to be interpreted and ethnomethodological studies have concentrated more on the variability of these interpretations than on the consistent nature of the underlying values.

VARIABLE   This is any measurable characteristic that varies. The term is commonly used for an index which we use to represent some social phenomenon that interests us. We construct causal explanations by searching for **correlations** between variables. For example we might suspect that, among the interesting departures from the class associations with voting, there is a split in the middle class; with public sector professionals voting to the left and private sector professionals voting to the right. In this case voting one way rather than another is the dependent variable and social class and sector of employment the interrelated independent variables. The difficulty with variables, as Herbert **Blumer** pointed out in his methodological writings, is that they are always a thin shadow of social reality.

VEBLEN, THORSTEIN (1857–1929)   See **leisure class**.

VERIFICATION   See **falsification**.

VERSTEHEN   This German word for 'understanding' came into sociology via the work of Max **Weber**, where it plays an important part in his view of the distinction between the social and the natural sciences. To understand in this sense is to put oneself in the place of others to see what meaning they attribute to their actions and what are their intentions.

VICTIMOLOGY   This denotes the study of victims of crime, rather than its perpetrators. It was first used in the late 1970s to signify a new area of criminology that was needed for two reasons. First, official crime statistics and the convictions that are the outcome of the criminal justice system obviously represent a very partial picture of crime. A different and arguably more complete picture is gained by starting at the other end and using such methods as general social surveys to discover who has been a victim of crime. Second, victims are not chosen randomly. It is clear that many types of crime are patterned so that some people are much more likely than others to suffer. For example, although old people often fear casual violence; most victims are young working-class men. Identifying and studying victims can throw new light on crime.

VOCABULARIES OF MOTIVE These are the verbalisations of motives and intentions that actors use, not just to describe their actions, but also to justify them to others. C. Wright **Mills** regarded such vocabularies as situational; if not actually delivered to such, they are imagined as presentations to a particular group of people at a particular time. This does not mean that we have to see them as after-the-fact rationalisations that are used cynically. Our ability to construct a particular vocabulary of motives which seems appropriate and reasonable is itself an important part of the cause of our actions. Although vocabularies are situation-specific they must be shared to be effective.

The idea has been developed in two contrasting ways. It can be treated as being of a piece with the work of George H. **Mead** and Charles H. **Cooley** on the internalisation of social values through real and imaginary interaction with others and with Erving **Goffman**'s interest in presentations of self and strategic interaction. Or, as in some forms of ethnomethodology, it can be taken as a warrant for supposing that we cannot make inferences about original motivational states from what people say about their actions. In this view, vocabularies of motive are so much a product of the situation in which they are presented that they can only be used to analyse how people make their actions intelligible to others and how they try to make sense of the motives of others.

See **accounts, neutralisation**.

VOLUNTARISM This term is applied to that type of sociological theory in which the explanation for action lies in the intentions of the actor. That is, actors act 'voluntarily'; their actions are not determined by their biology or the social structure. No sociologist is a complete voluntarist, for if all action was entirely a product of unconstrained free will, there would be no society, social structure or social action. Insofar as people are socialised into shared values, for example, or held (through regular patterns of interaction) to the view that some courses of action are more honourable than others, then their actions are not entirely free. In practice, sociologists disagree about just how voluntaristic social action is.

VOLUNTARY ASSOCIATION This denotes any organisation (such as a political party or sports clubs, for example) where membership is optional. Generally voluntary associations are non-commercial, public (in the sense of being open to all), formally constituted and not established by law. The flourishing of voluntary associations is normally taken as a mark of a strong civil society and as a major element in a stable liberal democracy.

See **social capital, community**.

W

WALLERSTEIN, IMMANUEL (1930–) See world-systems theory.

WEBER, MAX (1864–1920) With Emile **Durkheim**, Max Weber is rightly regarded as the founder of modern sociology. In our opinion he was the superior sociologist: he developed a philosophical basis for the social sciences, a conceptual basis for sociology, and a range of scholarly studies that covered economic history, the sociology of law, a comparative sociology of religion, and a sociology of music.

Durkheim tried to model sociology on the natural sciences. Weber started from a conviction that sociology was concerned with the explanation of human action in its historical context and especially in the light of actors' understandings of their situation. Weber's distinctive approach can be illustrated though his best known work, which deals with the origins of capitalism and the social consequences of religious belief systems. 'The Protestant Ethic and the Spirit of Capitalism' was first published as an essay in the *Archiv für Sozialwissenschaft und Sozialpolitik* in 1905. For Weber what needs to be explained is the transcending of **economic traditionalism**. Most pre-modern people had relatively fixed notions of their expected standard of living and, given the choice, preferred less work to more money. The customary rate of return was accompanied by customary ways of working. Those who did

exhibit the desire for great wealth tried to find it in extravagant ways: merchants staked their fortunes on single ships and lords invested in foreign wars. What was missing were precisely those features which Weber thought distinguished modern capitalism: the desire for the calculable and steady rate of return on investment; a rational experimental attitude to improving work methods; a willingness to work hard.

The distribution of early capitalism – Britain, Holland, the USA and the Protestant parts of Germany rather than France, Portugal, Spain or Italy – suggested a connection with religion. Weber argued that key ideas of the Protestant Reformation of the 16th century had the **unintended consequence** of encouraging new attitudes to work and wealth. Martin Luther rejected the idea of a religious division of labour that allowed religious officials to placate God on behalf of others. All people had to be responsible for their own salvation: 'every man his own monk'. This call for universal piety was made compatible with the continuation of normal life by Luther's new concept of the vocation. He taught that any legitimate occupation, performed in the right spirit, was pleasing to God. The Reformers removed the clergy's power to cleanse sin through confession and penance. Without the ability to wipe the slate clean, people had to be constantly attentive to their spiritual state. John Calvin's distinctive contribution was to the doctrine of pre-destination. If God was all-knowing and all-powerful then he must know which of us was destined for heaven and which for hell, even before we were born. The Puritans believed that nothing would change God's mind but they did want to know. They worked hard to the glory of God and avoided temptation. If they prospered they took this as a sign of divine blessing. This and other ideological innovations created a new ethos which Weber summarised as *this-worldly* asceticism. The Protestant ethic alone could not create capitalism (appropriate material conditions were required) but it did create a personality and a series of attitudes towards work and expenditure – the 'spirit' of capitalism – that were unusually well-suited to rational capitalism.

This study encapsulates the distinctive features of Weber's work. First, it grants methodological primacy to **Verstehen**, the explanatory understanding of people's reasons for acting in their historical context. Second, this study exemplifies Weber's belief that there was no logic to history, at least in the way that Karl **Marx** or Georg **Hegel** supposed. Modern capitalism comes about for rather accidental reasons, as the thoroughly unintended consequence of religious reform. However Weber did believe there was a kind of directionality to history. By and large, rationalisation tended to increase. Once modern capitalism was underway, factory owners and managers were driven to run their plants in ever more rational ways. But other aspects of society and culture are subject to the discipline of rationalisation as well – this is indicated in his famous division of types of authority into the traditional, charismatic and legal-rational. Religious beliefs become codified and subject to rational streamlining. Equally, the work of the state becomes bureaucratised. In his analyses of bureaucracy, Weber demonstrated how to use the **ideal-type** in sociological research. From studies of actual bureaucratic organisations he extracted the ideal-typical features of bureaucracy. He was trying to sum up the quintessence of bureaucratic organisation without implying any moral judgements or claiming that any actual bureaucracy would display all those features in just those idealised forms.

Weber pointed out that all these developments might not be rational in the sense that they were good for promoting overall human well-being; they were intended to be procedurally efficient ways of achieving set goals (termed *zweckrational* or instrumentally rational). Weber was pessimistic about this tendency fearing that the world would become progressively disenchanted with more and more attention paid to achieving goals and less heed paid to the worth of the goals themselves.

This last point highlights another decisive feature of his approach to sociology, spelled out in the posthumously published *The Methodology of the Social Sciences* (1949). Weber argued in favour of value freedom in the social sciences, meaning that though the sociologist had professional values as an academic and was drawn to certain topics because of their importance to his or her values, the analysis had to stand independently of those values. Weber was very concerned about these issues, seeing value freedom as central to the independence required by academic scholars; for him this was integral to the freedom that academia should enjoy from the state. In terms of the politics of his day, Weber was a liberal. He was sceptical about the prospects of socialism not least because he suspected that the centralisation of power and control would lead not to universal freedom but to universal bureaucracy.

In his many other works Weber was chiefly concerned with religion and social change in non-European cultures though he wrote essays on many aspects of economic history and on the development of legal systems as well. His work abounds with historical understanding and with compelling theoretical insights, for example, in the classification of the types of authority outlined above.

WELFARE STATE　The foundation of the welfare state is the idea that the state has an obligation to all its citizens to protect their well-being and this cannot be left to individuals, private organisations or the local community. Welfare states typically use taxation and compulsory insurance schemes to protect against poverty with unemployment benefits, sickness benefits, old age pensions and income support schemes for the very poorly-paid, and to provide free education, medical care and public housing.

The earliest state welfare programme was that provided by Bismarck in Germany in the 1880s. In Britain in 1911, Lloyd George introduced national insurance to fund health care and unemployment benefits. After 1945 most European states introduced a raft of welfare provision and this development of welfare systems was commonly interpreted in the light of theories of the **citizen** and citizenship. The USA tended to stand apart from industrial societies in resisting extensive welfare provisions although the extent of its difference is easily exaggerated. In the 21st century the European states, faced with aging populations and higher than anticipated levels of unemployment, are experiencing difficulties in funding their generous welfare provisions and governments of nearly all political orientations are trying to find ways of economising.

WELTANSCHAUUNG See **worldview**.

WHITE-COLLAR CRIME　Confusingly, this term was used by Edwin H. Sutherland to describe what we would now call **corporate crime**: criminal activities such as false advertising, copyright infringement, tax evasion, fraud and illegal labour practices that were engaged in on behalf of the company. Nowadays white-collar crime is generally used for a sub-set of 'fiddling': crimes carried out at work (such as using the firm's resources for your own purposes) by middle-class people.

WHITE-COLLAR WORKER　Originally a US term that was used in contrast with 'blue-collar' or manual worker, this is usually used now for the lower reaches of the service class: non-manual workers with fairly routine jobs.

WIRTH, LOUIS (1897–1952)　German-born US sociologist Wirth was a key member of the **Chicago School**. His (1928) *The Ghetto* remains an inspirational classic of US urban sociology and he is noted for regarding **urbanism** as a more important component of modernisation than either industrialisation or capitalism.

WITCHCRAFT　Both involve invoking the supernatural for a specific purpose but, unlike sorcery, witchcraft usually carries the additional meaning that the power is used to harm people in ways that the community does not approve of. Sociologists tend to be more interested in the medieval European witchcraft crazes or the witch trials in Puritan New England than in its occurrence in simple societies, probably because in these cases accusing someone of witchcraft seems more obviously at odds with an increasing rational and scientific culture and hence more intriguing as a problem to be explained.

The popularity of witchcraft accusations has been explained as follows: such an accusation made sense of misfortune; it provided a way for pursuing interpersonal conflict in small communities; it gave the community an opportunity to re-affirm shared values; and it allowed men to control women. There is something in all of these but, apart from the first, they do not explain why people (including some who claimed to be witches) believed in witches. They are claims about the secondary or **latent functions** of witchcraft trials.

WITTFOGEL, KARL (1896–1988)　See **Asiatic mode of production**.

WITTGENSTEIN, LUDWIG (1889–1951)

Though born in Austria, Wittgenstein is generally associated with the University of Cambridge where most of his philosophical work was conducted. He famously developed two different philosophical approaches, one around the time of the First World War and the second, which contradicted the first, after he returned to England in 1929. It is his second philosophical approach that is of importance to sociology since it focuses on the properties of everyday language and on the connections between language and thought. Wittgenstein wrote up little of this work and the books we have were published after his death some based on the notes taken by his most dedicated students.

There are two aspects of Wittgenstein's later work that have been most influential in sociology. The first concerns the nature of rules. His early philosophy had been highly formal and concerned to establish rules and principles. But he later became fascinated by the openness of rules. Generally speaking, rules do not carry the instructions for their own interpretation. One needs to know more than the rules in order to obey the rules properly. This insight has been celebrated by **ethnomethodologists** and interactionist sociologists who wished to reject what they saw as formalistic sociology, with its heavy focus on norms and roles, and in its place to examine the methods and techniques by which people make sense of their own and others' behaviour.

The second aspect relates to Wittgenstein's arguments against the possibility of a private language. He claimed that there could not be a private language that was intelligible to one person but not to others; for it to be intelligible to that person it would (in principle) have to be intelligible to others too. This is a tricky and highly technical piece of philosophy which still provokes disagreement. But sociologists have been interested because it indicates the extent to which the things we think of as private and personal are inevitably built on intersubjectively-agreed understandings. We use the resources of our culture to build our most private thoughts. The social contaminates (so to speak) the personal.

Throughout his later philosophy Wittgenstein was interested in how we do things with words. Words do not just describe; they are the tools though which many of our actions are conducted. He used the term 'language game' to refer to the relatively discrete activities we do through language and this term too has caught on in sociology.

WORK ORIENTATION See **orientations to work**.

WORKING CLASS

Classically the working class is defined as that class which sells its labour power; it is Karl **Marx**'s **proletariat**. But as such a definition includes almost all of the middle class of modern societies, it is generally refined by narrowing it to those who sell their physical labour power: that is, manual or blue-collar workers. The working class so defined is often divided further for specific analytical purposes. We may distinguish skilled from unskilled workers. We also distinguish a primary sector of secure, well-paid and often unionised jobs and a secondary sector of low paid, often part-time, insecure jobs that lack statutory protection, insurance benefits and the like.

WORLD-SYSTEMS THEORY

Immanuel Wallerstein's (1974) *The Modern World-System: Capitalist Agriculture and the Origins of the European World-economy in the Sixteenth Century* made a powerful contribution to current thinking about globalisation. He argues that modern capitalism is organised on a global rather than a national scale: that the system consists of core regions and peripheries that are dependent on the cores; and that the cores developed as industrial producers while the peripheries became suppliers of raw materials to the cores. In addition there are semi-peripheries which combine some features of cores and peripheries. Wallerstein believes this system has its origins in the 15th-century development of capitalist agriculture in western Europe. He makes the interesting contrast that premodern empires had a common bureaucratic political structure supervising diverse economic systems. In contrast, the modern world has diverse political systems united by a common interlocking economy. As with Andre Gunder Frank's **dependency theory**, a key implication of this model is that nation-states cannot be understood in isolation because economies are shaped by their place in the world-system.

Later scholars have questioned many aspects of this model. One of the most telling criticisms is that of Roland Robertson who believes that Wallerstein gives too much weight to economy and insufficient attention to the separate world-system of global culture.

WORLDVIEW   This translation of the German *Weltanschauung* signifies the bundle of beliefs that forms the particular outlook of a social group. It differs from ideology in suggesting something broader, less well codified, and more implicit. People discuss their ideology; they take their worldview for granted and may not even notice they have one.

X

XENOPHOBIA From the Greek for 'outside' and 'fear', this signifies a strong dislike for foreigners – typically a dislike rather stronger than the analyst considers is reasonable.

Y

YOUTH CULTURE   Since the Second World War, with increasing prosperity and a widening gap between the end of childhood and the start of adulthood, youth has emerged as a distinct social category with its own culture (in clothes and musical tastes, for example). Youth culture has three distinguishing features. It is based on leisure rather than work (hence consumption rather than production). Social relationships are organised around the peer group rather than kin and individual friends. And it is particularly concerned with style.

It might be more accurate to talk of youth cultures because there are often major divisions based on gender, class and ethnicity. However various youth cultures borrow from each other and that borrowing can be used for the common purpose of offending one's parents and adult authorities more generally. Rebellion (in style at least) is a central feature of youth culture. Middle-class youths often imitate working- class styles. White youths commonly borrow patois, music and dress styles from black youths.

See **adolescence**.

ZEITGEIST Georg **Hegel** believed that philosophies could not transcend the spirit (Geist) of their age (Zeit). The term is now used without the baggage of Hegelian epochs to refer simply to some general cultural qualities of a period: 'the swinging sixties' for example.

ZERO-SUM GAME In some activities, it is possible for competitors to all benefit. For example, although mobile phone companies compete they may all prosper (for some time at least) because the market can be expanded. A football match is a zero-sum game in that, to the extent that one team wins, the other must lose. The idea is an important one because whether a contest is zero-sum or not has considerable implications for the strategies that each contestant can follow and the possibilities of resolution by compromise.

ZNANIECKI, FLORIAN (1882–1958) See *Polish Peasant in Europe and America, The*.

Bibliography

Adorno, Theodor. W., Else Frenkel-Brunswik, Daniel J. Levinson, R. Sanford and R. Nevitt (1994) *The Authoritarian Personality*. New York: W.W. Norton and Co.

Anderson, Benedict (1983) *Imagined Communities: Reflections on the Origins and Spread of Nationalism*. London: Verso.

Anderson, Perry (1974) *Passages from Antiquity to Feudalism*. London: Verso.

Austin, J.L. (1962) *How to do Things with Words*. Cambridge, MA: Harvard University Press.

Bauman, Zygmunt (1989) *Modernity and the Holocaust*. Cambridge: Polity Press.

Beck, Ulrich (1986 [1992]) *Risk Society: Towards a New Modernity*. London: Sage.

Becker, Howard et al. (1961) *Boys in White: Student Culture in Medical School*. Chicago, IL: University of Chicago Press.

Bell, Daniel (1960) *End of Ideology*. Cambridge, MA: Harvard University Press.

Bell, Daniel (1973) *The Coming of Post Industrial Society*. New York: Basic Books.

Bell, Daniel (1976) *The Cultural Contradictions of Capitalism*. New York: Basic Books.

Benjamin, Walter (1992) 'The work of art in the age of mechanical reproduction', pp. 211–24 in his *Illuminations*. Trans. Harry Zohn. London: Fontana.

Benjamin, Walter (1999) *The Arcades Project*. Trans. Howard Eiland and Kevin McLaughlin. Cambridge, MA: Harvard University Press.

Berger, Brigitte and Peter L. Berger (1983) *War Over the Family*. London: Hutchinson.

Berger, Peter L. (1974) *Pyramids of Sacrifice*. New York: Doubleday.

Berger, Peter L. and Thomas Luckmann (1967) *The Social Construction of Reality*. New York: Anchor Books.

Berger, Peter, L., Brigitte Berger and Hansfried Kellner (1973) *The Homeless Mind*. Harmondsworth, Middlesex: Penguin.

Blauner, Robert (1964) *Alienation and Freedom*. Chicago, IL: University of Chicago Press.

Bloch, Marc (1961) *Feudal Society*. London: Routledge.

Blumer, Herbert (1939 [1979]) *Critiques of Research in the Social Sciences ... the Polish Peasant*. Somerset, NJ: Transaction Publishers.

Blumer, Herbert (1969 [1986]) *Symbolic Interactionism: Perspective and Method*. Berkeley, CA: University of California Press.

Bourdieu, Pierre (1984) *Distinction: A Social Critique of the Judgement of Taste*. Trans Richard Nice. Cambridge, MA: Harvard University Press.

Braverman, Harry (1974) *Labor and Monopoly Capital: The Degradation of Work in the Twentieth Century*. Monthly Review Press.

Burnham, James (1943) *The Managerial Revolution*. Westport, CT: Greenwood Press.

Butler, Judith (1990) *Gender Trouble*. New York: Routledge.

Castells, Manuel (1996–98) *The Information Age: Economy, Society and Culture*. Oxford: Blackwell. 3 volumes.

Chodorow, Nancy (1978) *The Reproduction of Mothering*. Berkeley, CA: University of California Press.

Chomsky, Noam (1957) *Syntactic Structures*. The Hague: Mouton.

Chomsky, Noam (1966) *Cartesian Linguistics: A Chapter in the History of Rationalist Thought*. New York: Harper and Row.

Cicourel, Aaron (1964) *Method and Measurement in Sociology*. Glencoe, IL: Free Press.

Cloward, Richard A. and Lloyd B. Ohlin (1960) *Delinquency and Opportunity*. London: Routledge.

Cohen, Stanley (1972) *Folk Devils and Moral Panics*. London: Routledge.

Cressey, Paul G. (1932) *The Taxi Dance Hall: A Sciological Study in Commercialized Recreation and City Life*. Chicago, IL: University of Chicago Press.

Davis, Kingsley and Wilbert E. Moore (1945) 'Some principles of stratification', *American Sociological Review*.

De Beauvoir, Simone (1949 [1997]) *The Second Sex*. London: Vintage.

Deleuze, Giles and Felix Guattari (1984) *Anti-Oedipus: Capitalism and Schizophrenia*. London: Athlone Press.

Deleuze, Giles and Felix Guattari (1988) *A Thousand Plateaus: Capitalism and Schizophrenia*. London: Athlone Press.

Dennis, Norman, Fernando Henriques and Clifford Slaughter (1956) *Coal is Our Life: An Analysis of a Yorkshire Mining Community*. London: Routledge.

Dewey, John (1916 [1966]) *Democracy and Education*. New York: Free Press.

Douglas, Jack B. (1967) *The Social Meanings of Suicide*. Princeton, NJ: Princeton University Press.

Durkheim, Emile (1893 [1933]) *The Division of Labour in Society*. New York: Macmillan.

Durkheim, Emile (1895 [1938]) *The Rules of Sociological Method*. Glencoe, IL: Free Press.

Durkheim, Emile (1897 [1970]) *Suicide*. London: Routledge.

Durkheim, Emile (1912 [1926]) *The Elementary Forms of the Religious Life*. Trans. John Swain. London: George Allen and Unwin.

Elias, Norbert (1939 [1978]) *The Civilising Process*. Oxford: Basil Blackwell.

Elias, Norbert (1969 [1983]) *The Court Society*. Trans. Edmund Jephcott. Oxford: Basil Blackwell.

Elias, Norbert (1970 [1978]) *What is Sociology?* Trans. Stephen Mennell and Grace Morrissey. London: Hutchison.

Elias, Norbert (1985) *The Loneliness of the Dying*. Trans. Edmund Jephcott. Oxford: Basil Blackwell.

Elias, Norbert (1987) *Involvement and Detachment*. Trans. Edmund Jephcott. Oxford: Blackwell.

Engels, Friedrich (1845 [1993]) *The Condition of the Working Class in England*. Oxford: Oxford University Press.

Engels, Friedrich (1902) *The Origin of the Family, Private Property and the States*. Trans. Ernest Untermann. Chicago, IL: C.H. Kerr and Son.

Etzioni, Amitai (1961) *A Comparative Analysis of Complex Organizations*. New York: Free Press.

Fanon, Frantz (1952 [1968]) *Black Skin, White Masks*. Trans. Charles Lam Markmann. London: MacGibbon and Kee.

Fanon, Frantz (1961 [1968]) *The Wretched of the Earth*. Trans. Constance Farrington. New York: Grove Press.

Ferguson, Adam (1767 [1966]) *Essay on the History of Civil Society*. Edinburgh: Edinburgh University Press.

Feyerabend, Paul K. (1975) *Against Method*. London: Verso.

Foucault, Michael (1979a) *Discipline and Punish*. London: Allen Lane.

Foucault, Michael (1979b) *The History of Sexuality*. London: Allen Lane.

Foucault, Michael (1989) *Madness and Civilization*. London: Routledge.

Fromm, Erich (1941 [2001]) *Fear of Freedom*. London: Routledge.

Gadamer, Hans Georg (1960 [1975]) *Truth and Method*. London: Sheed and Ward.

Galbraith, John K. (1958 [1962]) *The Affluent Society*. Harmondsworth, Middlesex: Penguin.

Gans, Herbert J. (1962) *The Urban Villagers: Group and Class in the Life of Italian-Americans*. New York: Free Press of Glencoe.

Garfinkel, Harold (1967), 'Good organizational reasons for "bad" clinic records', pp. 186–207 in his *Studies in Ethnomethodology*. Englewood Cliffs, NJ: Prentice-Hall.

Garfinkel, Harold (1967) *Studies in Ethnomethodology*. Cambridge: Polity Press.

Giddens, Anthony (1984) *The Constitution of Society*. Cambridge: Polity Press.

Glaser, Barney and Anselm Strauss (1968) *The Discovery of Grounded Theory*. London: Wiedenfeld & Nicholson.

Glazer, Nathan (1975) *Affirmative Discrimination: Ethnic Inequality and Public Policy*. Cambridge, MA: Harvard University Press.

Glazer, Nathan (1998), *We're All Multiculturalist Now!* Cambridge, MA: Harvard University Press.

Glazer, Nathan and Daniel P. Moynihan (1963) *Beyond the Melting Pot*. Cambridge, MA: The MIT Press.

Goffman, Erving (1959 [1971]) *The Presentation of Self in Everyday Life*. Harmondsworth, Middlesex: Penguin.

Goffman, Erving (1961) *Asylums*. Garden City, NY: Anchor.

Goffman, Erving (1963a) *Behavior in Public Places*. New York: Free Press.

Goffman, Erving (1963b [1986]) *Stigma*. Englewood Cliffs, NJ: Prentice-Hall.

Goffman, Erving (1970) *Strategic Interaction*. Oxford: Blackwell.

Goffman, Erving (1975) *Frame Analysis*. Harmondsworth, Middlesex: Penguin.

Granovetter, Mark (1973) 'The strength of weak ties', *American Journal of Sociology* 78: 1360–80.

Granovetter, Mark (1974) *Getting a Job*. Chicago, IL: University of Chicago Press.

Habermas, Jürgen (1968) *Knowledge and Human Interests*. Trans. Jeremy J. Shapiro. Cambridge: Polity Press.

Habermas, Jürgen (1975) *Legitimation Crisis*. Trans. Thomas McCarthy. Boston, MA: Beacon.

Halbwachs, Maurice (1930 [1978]) *The Causes of Suicide*. Trans Harold Goldblatt. London: Routledge and Kegan Paul.

Hardt, Michael and Negri, Antonio (2000) *Empire*. Cambridge, MA: Harvard University Press.

Hayek, Friedrich (1944) *The Road to Serfdom*. Chicago, IL: University of Chicago Press.

Hechter, Michael (1975) *Internal Colonialism: The Celtic Fringe in British National Development 1536–1966*. London: Routledge and Kegan Paul.

Hobbes, Thomas (1651 [1904]) *Leviathan*. London: Cambridge University Press.

Hochschild, Arlie Russell (1983) *The Managed Heart: The Commercialization of Human Feeling*. Berkeley, CA: University of California Press.

Hochschild, Arlie Russell (1990) *Second Shift: Working Parents and the Revolution at Home*. London: Piatkus.

Hochschild, Arlie Russell (1997) *The Time Bind: When Work Becomes Home and Home Becomes Work*. New York: Metropolitan Books.

Hochschild, Arlie Russell (2003), *The Commercialization of Intimate Life*. Berkley, CA: University of California Press.

Humphreys , Laud (1970) *Tearoom Trade: Impersonal Sex in Public Places*. London: Duckworth.

Inglehart, Robert (1990) *Culture Shift in Advanced Industrial Society*. Princeton, NJ: Princeton University Press.

Irigaray, Luce (1993) *Ethics of Sexual Difference*. Ithaca, NY: Cornell University Press.

Katz, Elihu and Paul Lazarsfeld (1955) *Personal Influence*. Glencoe, IL: The Free Press.

Kuhn, Thomas (1962) *The Structure of Scientific Revolutions*. Chicago, IL: University of Chicago Press.

Lasch, Christopher (1991) *The Culture of Narcissism*. New York: W. W. Norton & Company.

Lazarsfeld, Paul, Bernard Berelson and Hazel Gaudet (1948) *The People's Choice*. New York: Columbia University Press.

Lazarsfeld, Paul, Bernard Berelson and William N. McPhee (1944) *Voting: A Study of Opinion Formation in a Presidential Campaign*. Chicago, IL: University of Chicago Press.

Lemert, Edwin (1951) *Social Pathology*. New York: McGraw-Hill.

Lévi-Strauss, Claude (1967) *The Savage Mind*. Chicago, IL: University of Chicago Press.

Lifton, Robert Jay (1961) *Thought Reform and the Psychology of Totalism*. London: Gollancz.

Lifton, Robert Jay (1993) *The Protean Self: Human Resilience in an Age of Fragmentation*. New York: Basic Books.

Lipset, Seymour Martin (1950) *Agrarian Socialism*. Berkeley, CA: University of California Press.

Lipset, Seymour Martin (1959) 'Some social requisites of democracy: economic development and political legitimacy', *American Political Science Review* 53: 69–105.

Lipset, Seymour Martin (1960) *Political Man: The Social Bases of Politics*. London: Heinemann.

Lipset, Seymour Martin (1985) *Consensus and Conflict*. Somerset, NJ: Transaction Publishers.

Lipset, Seymour Martin and Reinhard Bendix (1959) *Social Mobility in Industrial Society*. Berkeley, CA: University of California Press.

Lipset, Seymour Martin and Earl Raab (eds) (1970) *The Politics of Unreason: Right-wing Extemism in Ameica, 1790–1970*. New York: Anti-defamation League of B'nai B'rith.

Lopata, Helene Z. (1971) *Occupation: Housework*. New York: Oxford University Press.

Lukács (1923 [1974]) *History and Class Consciousness: Studies in Marxist Dialectics*. Trans. Rodney Livingston. London: Merlin Press.

Lyotard, Jean-François (1979 [1984]) *The Postmodern Condition: A Report on Knowledge*. Trans. Geoff Bennington and Brian Massumi. Manchester: Manchester University Press.

Maffesoli, Michel (1988 [1990]) *The Time of the Tribe*. Trans. Don Smith. London: Sage.

Malthus, Thomas (1798 [1826]) *An Essay on the Principle of Population*. London: Murray.

Marcuse, Herbert (1991) *One Dimensional Man*. Boston, CA: Beacon.

Marshall, Thomas (1963) *Class, Citizenship and Social Development*. Westport, CT: Greenwood Press.

Marx, Karl (1970) *Economic and Philosophic Manuscripts of 1844*. Trans. Martin Milligan. London: Lawrence and Wishart.

Marx, Karl (1886) *Capital: A Critical Analysis of Capitalist Production*. London: Sonnesnschien.

Marx, Karl and Friedrich Engels (1925) *The Holy Family or Critique or Critical Criticism*. Moscow: Progress Publishers.

Marx, Karl and Friedrich, Engels (1954) *Anti-Duhring: Herr Duhring's Evolution in Science*. Moscow: Foreign Language Publishing House.

Marx, Karl and Friedrich Engels (1967) *The Communist Manifesto*. Harmondsworth, Middelsex: Penguin.

Marx, Karl and Friedrich Engels (1974) *The German Ideology*. London: Lawrence and Wishart.

Matza, David (1964) *Delinquency and Drift*. New York: John Wiley & Sons.

Mauss, Marcel (1925 [1954]) *The Gift: the Forms and Functions of Exchange in Archaic Societies*. Trans. Ian Cunnison. London: Coehn and West.

McLennan, John Ferguson (1865 [1970]) *Primitive Marriage*. Chicago, IL: University of Chicago Press.

Mead, Margaret (1928 [1943]) *Coming of Age in Samoa*. Harmondsworth, Middlesex: Penguin.

Melucci, Alberto (1996a) *Challenging Codes: Collective Action in the Information Age*. Cambridge: Cambridge University Press.

Melucci, Alberto (1996b) *The Playing Self: Person and Meaning in the Planetary Society*. Cambridge: Cambridge University Press.

Memmi, Albert (1957 [1991]) *The Colonizer and the Colonized*. Boston, MA: Beacon Press.

Memmi, Albert (1999) *Racism*. Minnesota, MN: University of Minnesota Press.

Merton, Robert K. (1938) 'Social structure and anomie', *American Sociological Review* 3: 672–82.

Merton, Robert K. (1970) *Science, Technology and Society in 17th Century England*. New York: H. Fertig.

Meštrović, Stjepan (1997) *Postemotional Society*. London: Sage.

Michels, Robert (1911 [1959]) *Political Parties: A Sociological Study of the Oligarchical Tendencies of Modern Democracy*. New York: Dover.

Mills, C. Wright (1951) *White Collar*. New York: Oxford University Press.

Mills, C. Wright (1956) *The Power Elite*. New York: Oxford University Press.

Mills, C. Wright (1959) *The Sociological Imagination*. New York: Oxford University Press.

Mills, C. Wright (1962) *The Marxists*. Harmondsworth, Middlesex: Penguin.

von Neumann, John and Oskar Morgenstern (1947) *The Theory of Games and Economic Behavior*. Princeton, NJ: Pricneton University Press.

Nietzsche, Friedrich (1887 [1967]) *On the Genealogy of Morals*. New York: Random House.

Oakley, Ann (1974) *The Sociology of Housework*. London: Robertson.

Olson, Mancur (1965) *The Logic of Collective Action*. Cambridge, MA: Harvard University Press.

Park, Robert E. and Ernest W. Burgess (1921) *Introduction to the Science of Sociology*. Chicago, IL: University of Chicago Press.

Parsons, Talcott (1937) *The Structure of Social Action*. New York: Free Press.

Parsons, Talcott (1966) *Societies: Evolutionary and Comparative Perspectives*. Englewood Cliffs, NJ: Prentice-Hall.

Piore, Michael J. and Charles F. Sabel (1984) *The Second Industrial Divide*. New York: Basic Books.

Popper Karl (1945) *The Open Society and its Enemies*. London: Routledge.

Popper, Karl (1957) *The Poverty of Historicism*. London: Routledge.

Popper, Karl (1959) *The Logic of Scientific Discovery*. London: Hutchison.

Popper, Karl (1963) *Conjectures and Refutations: The Growth of Scientific Knowledge*. London: Routledge and Kegan Paul.

Poulantzas, Nicos (1968) *Power and Social Classes*. London: Verso.

Putnam, Robert D. (2000) *Bowling Alone: the Collapse and Revival of American Community*. New York: Simon & Schuster.

Riesman, David (1950) *The Lonely Crowd*. New Haven: Yale University Press.

Ritzer, George (1993) *The McDonaldization of Society*. London: Sage.

Said, Edward (1978) *Orientalism*. London: Verso.

Schein, Edgar (1961) *Coercive Persuasion*. New York: W.W. Norton & Company.

Shaw, Clifford (1938 [1967]) *The Jack-Roller*. Chicago, IL: University of Chicago Press.

Simmel, Georg (1900 [1978]) *The Philosophy of Money*. Trans. Tom Bottomore and David Frisby. London: Routledge and Kegan Paul.

Smith, Adam (1776 [1910]) *An Inquiry into the Nature and Causes of the Wealth of Nations*. London: Dent.

Sudnow, David (1965) 'Normal crimes', *Social Problems* 12: 255–76.

Sumner, William G. (1906) *Folkways*. New York: Ginn.

Sutherland, Edwin H. and Donald R. Cressey (1934 [1960]) *Principles of Criminology*. Chicago, IL: Lippincott.

Tarde, Gabriel (1962) *The Laws of Imitation*. Gloucester, MS: P. Smith

Taylor, Ian, Paul Walton and Jock Young (1975) *The New Criminology*. London: Routledge.

Thomas, W.I. and Florian Znaniecki ([1818/1996]) *The Polish Peasant in Europe and America*. Urbana and Chicago, IL: University of Illinois Press.

de Toqueville, Alexis (1835–40 [1945]) *Democracy in America*. New York: Alfred A. Knopf.

de Toqueville, Alexis (1833–7 [1979]) *Journeys to England and Ireland*. New York: Arno Press.

Tönnies, Ferdinand (1887 [1955]) *Gemeinschaft und Gesellschaft* [*Community and Association*]. London: Routledge and Kegan Paul.

Troeltsch, Ernst (1911 [1931]) *The Social Teachings of the Christian Churches*. London: George Allen and Unwin.

Turner, Ralph H. and Lewis M. Killian (1960) *Collective Behavior*. Englewood Cliffs, NJ: Prentice-Hall.

Veblen, Thorstein (1899 [1965]) *The Theory of the Leisure Class*. New York: A.M. Kelley.

Van Gennep, Arnold (1960) *The Rites of Passage*. Trans. Monika B. Vizedom and Gabrielle L. Caffee. Chicago, IL: University of Chicago Press.

Wallerstein, Immanuel (1974) *The Modern World-System: Capitalist Agriculture and the Origins of the European World-economy in the Sixteenth Century*. New York: Academic Press.

Weber, Max (1904 [1930]) *The Protestant Ethic and the Spirit of Capitalism*. Trans T. Parsons. London: George Allen and Unwin.

Weber, Max (1904 [1949]) *The Methodology of the Social Sciences*. Trans. Edward A. Shils and Henry A. Finch. Glencoe, IL: Free Press.

Warner, W. Lloyd (1940) *Yankee City*. New Haven: Yale University Press.

Whyte, William H. (1956) *Organization Man*. New York: Simon and Schuster.

Wilmott, Peter and Michael Young (1972) *The Symmetrical Family*. London: Routledge.

Winch, Peter (1958 [1990]) *The Idea of a Social Science and its Relation to Philosophy*. London: Routledge.

Wirth, Louis (1928) *The Ghetto*. Chicago, IL: University of Chicago Press.

Wirth, Louis (1938) 'Urbanism as a way of life', *American Journal of Sociology* 44: 1–24.

Wittfogel, Karl (1957) *Oriental Despotism*. New Haven: Yale University Press.

Zorbaugh, Harvey W. (1929) *The Gold Cast and the Slum: a sociological study of Chicago's Near North Side*. Chicago, IL: University of Chicago.